Valérie Nicolet-Anderson

Constructing the Self

Thinking with Paul
and Michel Foucault

Mohr Siebeck

VALÉRIE NICOLET-ANDERSON, born 1976; from 2006 to 2007 Adjunct Faculty at Candler School of Theology, Emory University, Atlanta; 2010 PhD from Emory University, Atlanta; 2008 to 2011 Assistant Professor at Fuller Northwest and Adjunct Faculty at Seattle University and Pacific Lutheran University; from June 2012 Postdoctoral Fellow at Uppsala University, Sweden.

ISBN 978-3-16-151699-3
ISSN 0340-9570 (Wissenschaftliche Untersuchungen zum Neuen Testament, 2. Reihe)

Die Deutsche Nationalbibliothek lists this publication in the Deutsche Nationalbibliographie; detailed bibliographic data are available on the Internet at *http://dnb.dnb.de*

Preface

This monograph is a minimally revised version of my Ph.D. thesis, which was submitted on April 6, 2010 to the faculty of the Graduate Division of Religion at Emory University. Foucault makes it abundantly clear that thinking does not occur in a vacuum. The process of writing a dissertation has taught me in a concrete manner the need for others, to encourage, critique, shape and allow for my own thinking.

Prof. Dr. Luke T. Johnson has played an invaluable role as my advisor. He has been supportive of this project from the very beginning, probably before even I truly believed in it. He has remained consistently encouraging and has provided gentle yet firm and precise criticism, which in the end, I believe has helped me find my own voice in writing. Many pages of this work were made tremendously better thanks to his careful reading. However, the imprecisions, imperfections and downright mistakes that remain are entirely my own. The members of my committee, Prof. Dr. Michael J. Brown, Prof. Dr. Andreas Dettwiler, Prof. Dr. Thomas R. Flynn and Prof. Dr. Steven J. Kraftchick, have offered a careful reading of my work and many valuable and challenging comments. They have provided great discussion during my defense and have given me ample opportunities to continue thinking about this topic and its implications for my understanding of Paul. I also want to express my gratitude to the editor of this series, Prof. Dr. Jörg Frey, for accepting this thesis for publication, and to Dr. Henning Ziebritzki and his excellent editorial staff, in particular Tanja Idler, for their kind and patient assistance while I was formatting the manuscript for publication.

For great interactions, in the real and in the virtual worlds, I am glad to know my fellow students (and recent graduates) in the Graduate Division of Religion at Emory. They have given wonderful and dedicated support and made this process less dreadful and less solitary. They are definitely the best colleagues for whom one could hope. Amy Robertson and Bea Wallins in particular have provided companionship and support, not only as friends and colleagues but also as fellow mothers. Their friendship has gotten me through many stressful times and has made many celebrations even more special.

For babysitting, childcare and very concrete financial assistance that in fact enabled me to finish this work, I am profoundly indebted to my mother-in-law, Eileen, and her husband, Ron, as well as to my father-in-law, Bruce, and his wife, Patricia.

Even though my parents, Elisabeth and Philippe, and my sisters, Sarah and Virginie, live not only a continent but also an ocean away, I have been lucky to feel that they remained close to me at every step of this process and I can honestly say that I could never have accomplished this without them. Florence, Marie and Patty hopefully also know that they share in the role my family has for me. Thank you does not begin to cover the way I feel about the part all of them play in my life.

More than anyone else, my husband Brent, and my children, Gabriel and Miriam, have experienced the wear and tear associated with this work. My children have reminded me time and again that there were many things more important than this dissertation. Brent has provided for our family during all the time I worked on this book. The sacrifices he accepted in order for me to pursue this endeavor, he made in a discreet and graceful manner, with complete trust in my choices. I could not have dreamed for a better partner when it comes to this project. For allowing me to take my focus away from work, for making me laugh often, for their patience, their perseverance, their trust and their love, I am deeply grateful to the three of them.

Finally, my grand-mother, Susanne, has probably been the most un-reasonable and devoted believer in this project. For me, she embodies the quality of hope which Paul discusses in relationship to Abraham. When it comes to her grand-children and now great-grand-children, she firmly hopes without any trace of fear that the most amazing and unseen things will become true. In gratitude for the unwavering and undeserved faith she has put in me from the very beginning and in fond admiration, I dedicate this monograph to her.

Federal Way, 4 June 2012   Valérie Nicolet-Anderson

Table of Contents

Chapter 1

Constructing the Self

The notion of person, of identity, of self, of man, as it was called before we became more gender-sensitive, leaves behind a long history, traces of our various self-understandings, evidences that the idea of subject is not an absolute concept, but rather an ever-changing form with fluctuating definitions. In proposing a conversation between an ancient Christian composition (the epistle to the Romans) and a 20th century French philosopher (Michel Foucault, 1926–1984), I am interested in seeing first how both writers deploy their understanding of the person and second how they seek to shape, if at all, the identity of their respective addressees. The development of Michel Foucault's thought and the influences which played a role in his career provide an appropriate introduction to the particular topic of construction of the self. It explains the choice of Foucault as a partner in a conversation concerned with the notion of subject or self. It will remain to explain how Paul's letter to the Romans plays a role in the conversation, and how the conversation will actually be implemented.

A. Philosophical Engagement of the Question of the Subject

The figure and thought of Descartes (1596–1650) looms large as marking the beginning of a certain type of reflection on the subject, concerned with the "I," the "ego," what is often called "philosophies of the subject."[1] In the philosophies of the subject, as we encounter them in thinkers like Immanuel Kant (1724–1804), Johann Gotlieb Fichte (1762–1814) and Edmund Husserl (1859–1938), a strong accent is placed on the role the subject plays in the constitution of knowledge. The subject, in its relationship

---

[1] See Paul Ricœur's account of the philosophies of the *ego* in *Soi-même comme un autre* (Paris: Seuil, 1990), 15 (English translation, *Oneself as Another* [trans. K. Blamey; Chicago: Chicago University Press, 1992], 5: "If this ambition of establishing an ultimate foundation has seen itself radicalized from Descartes to Kant, then from Kant to Fichte, and finally to the Husserl of the *Cartesian Meditations*, it nevertheless seems to me that it is enough to focus on its birthplace, in Descartes himself, whose philosophy confirms that the *crisis* of the cogito is contemporaneous with the *positing* of the cogito."

to knowledge, is characterized by a "foundational ambition."[2] In the philosophies of the subject, the subject makes sense of all experiences and creates all knowledge.[3] As Paul Ricœur (1913–2005) indicates, Friedrich Nietzsche (1844–1900) already questioned the validity of a subject that guarantees knowledge and resists the attacks of doubt. For Ricœur, Nietzsche pushes Descartes' doubt beyond its limits and practices an even more hyperbolic doubt, doubting doubt itself.[4] Since nothing is protected against doubt, Nietzsche can play with various hypotheses, among them the idea that there is a multiplicity of subjects fighting against each other. Through this play, Nietzsche challenges the notion that one can establish a single supreme subject. As Ricœur notes, this leads to a humiliation of the subject,[5] a disappearance of "man" as marked by its connection to knowledge.

In direct lineage with Nietzsche, philosophies of the second half of the 20th century (often qualified as postmodern, or structuralist, or deconstructionist) continued the unraveling of the philosophies of the subject. In particular, they questioned the possibility for the subject to exist independently from his or her context.[6] The last – now famous – sentences of Foucault's *The Order of Things* sound an ominous warning concerning the destiny of man[7] in the second half of the 20th century:

---

[2] Ricœur, *Oneself as Another*, 5.

[3] See Michel Foucault, "Sexuality and Solitude," in *Ethics: Subjectivity and Truth: Essential Works of Foucault* (ed. Paul Rabinow; vol. 1 of *Essential Works of Foucault, 1954–1984*, ed. Paul Rabinow; 3 vols.; New York: The New Press, 1997–2000), 175–184, here 176.

[4] Ricœur, *Oneself as Another*, 15: " … Nietzsche says nothing other than simply, *I doubt better than Descartes. The cogito too is doubtful.*"

[5] See Ricœur, *Oneself as Another*, 16.

[6] See Foucault's foreword to the English edition of *The Order of Things*: "If there is one approach that I do reject, however, it is that (one might call it, broadly speaking, the phenomenological approach) which gives absolute priority to the observing subject, which attributes a constituent role to an act, which places its own point of view at the origin of all historicity – which, in short, leads to a transcendental consciousness. It seems to me that the historical analysis of scientific discourse should, in the last resort, be subject, not to a theory of the knowing subject, but rather to a theory of discursive practice." ("Foreword to the English Edition," in *The Order of Things: An Archaeology of the Human Sciences* [unidentified collective translation; New York: Pantheon Books, 1971; repr., New York: Vintage Books, 1973], ix–xiv, here xiv)

[7] Michel Foucault does not use inclusive language in his works. The word *man* in particular refers to a concept inherited from the Enlightenment, marked by the development of the human sciences (see James W. Bernauer, *Michel Foucault's Force of Flight: Towards an Ethics for Thought* [London: Humanities Press, 1990], 194, n. 18: "Following Foucault, the term 'man' will be employed in this study to designate the specifically modern concept of the person, originating philosophically in Descartes and articulated most fully in Kant. The term 'human being' is meant to be a broader notion, transcending

If those arrangements were to disappear as they appeared, if some event of which we can at the moment do no more than sense the possibility – without knowing either what its form will be or what it promises – were to cause them to crumble, as the ground of Classical thought did, at the end of the eighteenth century, then one can certainly wager that man would be erased, like a face drawn in sand at the edge of the sea.[8]

The disappearance of man announced in *The Order of Things* stems from Foucault's reaction to the dominant paradigm at the time of his philosophical education. In answer to a question put to him concerning the intellectual climate during his formative years, Foucault explains that French philosophy at the time was dominated by an interest in the history of philosophy. For Foucault, "the history of philosophy, delimited, on the one hand, by Hegel's theory of systems and, on the other, by the philosophy of the subject, went on in the form of phenomenology and existentialism."[9] For both phenomenology and existentialism, Foucault argues, the subject keeps a fundamental value and is what gives meaning to the world.[10] For Foucault, this reliance on the subject needed to be challenged.[11] In addition, growing up in the shadows of World War II and in the aftermath of a society that had permitted Nazism and followed de Gaulle enthusiastically, Foucault reflects that some in his generation needed something completely different, out of disgust for what had gone on before: "we wanted a world and a society that were not only different but that would be an alternative version of ourselves: we wanted to be completely other in a completely different world."[12] Within that context, Foucault saw the limits of Hegel's model of interpreting history in terms of an "unbroken intelligibility."[13]

---

modernity's image and fabrication of man."). As such, I think it is important to keep the vocabulary Foucault uses, even though it does have the effect of reinforcing a male dominated discourse. In discussing concepts that move beyond that narrow understanding of "man," I will use the more neutral human beings, or individual, subject, self.

[8] Foucault, *The Order of Things*, 387.

[9] Michel Foucault, "Interview with Michel Foucault," in *Power: Essential Works of Foucault* (ed. J. D. Faubion; vol. 3 of Rabinow, *Essential Works of Foucault, 1954–1984*), 239–297, here 246. The interview took place at the end of 1978, and was published in 1980, in the Italian journal *Il Contributo* (See Foucault, "Interview with Michel Foucault," 297, n. 1).

[10] Foucault, "Interview with Michel Foucault," 248: "In a philosophy like that of Sartre, the subject gives meaning to the world. That point was not called back in question. The subject dispenses significations."

[11] Ricœur, *Oneself as Another*, 4, sees a similar need to move away from philosophies of the subject, but does so in a manner completely different from Foucault: "Should it be said of the 'I' of these philosophies, as some have said of the father, that there is always either too much or too little of it?"

[12] Foucault, "Interview with Michel Foucault," 248.

[13] Foucault, "Interview with Michel Foucault," 248.

In contrast to this dominant intellectual landscape, Foucault turned to Nietzsche, George Bataille (1897–1962), and Maurice Blanchot (1907–2003) to search for a different way of understanding the world and humans. On the one side, these authors provided an escape from an explanation of history as continuous and, on the other side, they also powerfully called into question the notion of the subject as an indispensable entity: "… the Nietzschean theme of discontinuity, … the theme of an overman who would be completely different from man, and, in Bataille, the theme of limit-experience through which the subject escapes from itself, had an essential value for us. As far as I was concerned, they afforded a kind of way out between Hegelianism and the philosophical identity of the subject."[14] In relationship to the question of the subject, it mattered to Foucault to question the absolute and fundamental value of the subject, and the concept of limit-experience provided one way to do this: "can't there be experiences in the course of which the subject is no longer posited, in its constitutive relations, as what makes it identical with itself? Might there not be experiences in which the subject might be able to dissociate from itself, sever the relation with itself, lose its identity?"[15]

As Foucault was developing this new reflection on the subject, his name became frequently associated with structuralism, even though Foucault himself rejected the appellation of structuralism for his work.[16] In particular, Foucault was linked to Louis Althusser (1918–1990) and Jacques Lacan (1901–1981). For him, the connection with Lacan and Althusser was related to a certain point of convergence in their research: "It was a certain pressing desire to raise the question of the subject in a different way, to free ourselves of the fundamental postulate that French philosophy had never abandoned since Descartes, that was reinforced, even, by phenomenology."[17] As Foucault explains,[18] Lacan, Althusser and himself all ques-

---

[14] Foucault, "Interview with Michel Foucault," 248.

[15] Foucault, "Interview with Michel Foucault," 248.

[16] See Foucault's Foreword to the English Edition of the *Order of Things*, xiv: "In France, certain half-witted 'commentators' persist in labelling me a 'structuralist.' I have been unable to get it into their tiny minds that I have used none of the methods, concepts, or key terms that characterize structural analysis. I should be grateful if a more serious public would free me from a connection that certainly does me honour, but that I have not deserved. There may well be certain similarities between the works of the structuralists and my own work. It would hardly behove [*sic*] me, of all people, to claim that my discourse is independent of conditions and rules of which I am largely unaware, and which determine other work that is being done today. But it is only too easy to avoid the trouble of analysing such work by giving it an admittedly impressive-sounding, but inaccurate, label." Also, Foucault, "Interview with Michel Foucault," 251: "There is a point in common between all those who, over the last fifteen years, were called 'structuralists' but weren't, except for Lévi-Strauss, of course: Althusser, Jacques Lacan, and myself."

[17] Foucault, "Interview with Michel Foucault," 251.

tioned the supremacy of a philosophy of the subject, but they all did it from a different perspective.

For Lacan, the questioning of the theory of the subject came from an attachment to the theory of the unconscious: "From the perspective of psychoanalysis, Lacan brought up the fact that the theory of the unconscious is not compatible with a theory of the subject (in the Cartesian but also the phenomenological sense of the term)."[19] Instead of abandoning the theory of the unconscious, Lacan decided to call into question the theory of the subject. Althusser came at it from his reflection on Marxism. In his reading of Marx's works, Althusser asked "whether they involved that conception of human nature, of the subject, of alienated man, on which the theoretical formulations of certain Marxists ... were based."[20] He answered in the negative. For Foucault, these reflections all shared a similar "reevaluation of the theory of the subject" that might have been supported by some elements of the structural method.[21] However, for Foucault, the definitive influences were in fact Blanchot and Bataille. Especially important for Foucault was the manner in which Blanchot developed the concept of limit-experience taken from Bataille.

In contrast to philosophies of the subject, Foucault insists that "what we need to do is not to recover our lost identity, or liberate our imprisoned nature, or discover our fundamental truth; rather, it is to move toward something altogether different."[22] He develops this understanding of the subject through an explanation of a phrase by Marx: man produces man.[23] For him, the central concept contained in this declaration is not that one should try to recover man in man's essence or as nature designed him. Rather, "we need to produce something that doesn't exist yet, without being able to know what it will be."[24] In contrast to the Frankfurt school in particular, Foucault argues that the production of man is not about freeing man of everything that could possibly alienate him. Rather, "it's the destruction of what we are as well as the creation of a completely different thing, a total innovation."[25]

---

[18] See Foucault, "Interview with Michel Foucault," 251.

[19] Foucault, "Interview with Michel Foucault," 251.

[20] Foucault, "Interview with Michel Foucault," 251.

[21] Foucault, "Interview with Michel Foucault," 251 and 261: "In the mid-sixties the term 'structuralist' was applied to individuals who had made studies that were completely different from each other but presented one common element: they tried to put an end to, or to circumvent, a form of philosophy, of reflection and analysis, centered essentially on an assertion of the primacy of the subject."

[22] Foucault, "Interview with Michel Foucault," 275.

[23] Foucault, "Interview with Michel Foucault," 275.

[24] Foucault, "Interview with Michel Foucault," 275.

[25] Foucault, "Interview with Michel Foucault," 275.

In light of these reflections, Foucault offers a reinterpretation of the last sentence of *The Order of Things* and of the larger purpose of the book as well. For him, the death of man means "putting an end to everything that would set a rule of production, an essential goal for this production of man by man."[26] In *The Order of Things*, Foucault puts forward aspects of this death of man. He explains that the human sciences did not fulfill their promise to reveal what man is: "If the promise of the human sciences had been to make us discover man, they had certainly not kept that promise; but, as a general cultural experience, it had been more a matter of constituting a new subjectivity through an operation that reduced the human subject to being an object of knowledge."[27] Far from presenting us with a new and complete understanding of human beings, the human sciences contribute to the formation of a subject, through the body of knowledge they produce. Various discursive practices produce new objects of knowledge.[28]

For Foucault, this modifying of the subject through scientific practices is characteristic of knowledge understood as *savoir*: "I see '*savoir*' as a process by which the subject undergoes a modification through the very things that one knows [*connaît*] or, rather, in the course of the work that one does in order to know. It is what enables one both to modify the subject and to construct the object."[29] In the history of madness, for example, the constitution of a knowledge about madness is paired with the constitution of a subject capable of determining what madness is.[30] Thus, Foucault can define his own work as an enterprise concerned with highlighting the manner in which obtaining knowledge about certain objects is always connected with the constitution of a particular type of subject:

Everything I've been concerned with up to now has to do basically with the way men in Western societies have produced these experiences – fundamental ones, no doubt – which consist in engagement in a process of acquiring knowledge of a domain of objects, while

---

[26] Foucault, "Interview with Michel Foucault," 275.

[27] Foucault, "Interview with Michel Foucault," 275–276.

[28] See Foucault, "Interview with Michel Foucault," 272: "So I tried to set out for my own part how my works all turned around a set of problems of the same type, namely, how it was possible to analyze the particular object that is constituted by discursive practices with their internal rules and their conditions of appearance. *The Archaeology of Knowledge* resulted from that."

[29] Foucault, "Interview with Michel Foucault," 256.

[30] See Foucault, "Interview with Michel Foucault," 254: "It was a matter of understanding how, in the Western world, madness had managed to become a precise object of analysis and scientific inquiry only from the eighteenth century, whereas previously one had had medical treatises dealing, in a few short chapters, with 'maladies of the mind.' Here one could show that just as this object, madness, was taking form, the subject capable of understanding madness was also being constructed. Corresponding to the construction of madness as an object, there was that of a rational subject who was cognizant of madness and understood it."

at the same time they are constituting themselves as subjects with a fixed and determinate status. For example, knowing madness while constituting oneself as a rational subject; knowing illness while constituting oneself as a living subject; or the economy, while constituting oneself as a laboring subject; or as an individual knowing oneself in a certain relationship with the law... So there is always this involvement of oneself within one's own *savoir*.[31]

Thus, in addition to the reduction of man to an object of knowledge, man is also constituted as a subject of knowledge that perpetually changes, and constructs himself through the various knowledges he establishes. It is impossible to really find man, or its essence, because man is constituted and changed by different types of knowledges. Each time man constitutes a type of knowledge, man itself is transformed.[32] This is the sense in which Foucault understands the death of man, its perpetual deformation and transformation, in the absence of an essence of man on which one could rely in order to define what man is.

In contrast to this approach, Foucault, inhabiting fully the concept of limit-experience developed from his readings of Bataille, Blanchot and Nietzsche, provokes a reflection on the concept of life as art: "Couldn't everyone's life become a work of art? Why should the lamp or the house be an art object, but not our life?"[33] Foucault uses Charles Baudelaire's (1821–1867) reflection on modernity to develop the concept of life as a work of art. He writes that "modernity for Baudelaire is not simply a form of relationship to the present; it is also a mode of relationship that has to be established with oneself."[34] This relationship is one of perpetual change for Baudelaire. It means "not to accept oneself as one is in the flux of the passing moments; it is to take oneself as object of a complex and difficult elaboration."[35] For Baudelaire, this is what the dandy embodies: "the asceticism of the dandy who makes of his body, his behavior, his feelings and

---

[31] Foucault, "Interview with Michel Foucault," 256–257.

[32] Foucault, "Interview with Michel Foucault," 276.

[33] Michel Foucault, "On the Genealogy of Ethics: An Overview of Work in Progress," in *The Foucault Reader* (ed. Paul Rabinow; New York: Pantheon Books, 1984), 340–372, here 350. Also in Hubert L. Dreyfus and Paul Rabinow, *Michel Foucault: Beyond Structuralism and Hermeneutics* (2d ed.; Chicago: The University of Chicago Press, 1983), 229–252, and in Rabinow, *Ethics: Subjectivity and Truth*, 253–280. I am quoting the version found in *The Foucault Reader*. This was later translated in French and the French translation was reworked by Foucault: "À propos de la généalogie de l'éthique: un aperçu du travail en cours," in *Dits et écrits* (ed. D. Defert and F. Ewald; 4 vols.; Paris: Gallimard, 1994), 4:609–631.

[34] Michel Foucault, "What is Enlightenment?" in Rabinow, *The Foucault Reader*, 32–50, here 41. Also published in Rabinow, *Ethics: Subjectivity and Truth*, 303–319. I am quoting from *The Foucault Reader*. In French: Michel Foucault, "Qu'est-ce que les Lumières?" in *Dits et écrits*, 4:562–578.

[35] Foucault, "What is Enlightenment?" 41.

passions, his very existence, a work of art."[36] This work of art does not consist in finding man's essence, or man's authenticity. It does not free man in his essence. Rather, it forces him to elaborate himself.[37] The dandy "is the man who tries to invent himself."[38] Man thus has the responsibility, as stated earlier, to produce itself, anew, each day.

This sounds somewhat similar to Jean-Paul Sartre's (1905–1980) injunction that the self is responsible for his or her own existence and will be what he or she has planned to be. If existence precedes essence, then there is nothing given to human beings beforehand, and they are responsible for the project they elaborate for themselves.[39] In fact, human beings are nothing else than their acts, than the total sum of their acts.[40] For Foucault, Sartre makes a mistake when he turns to the notion of authenticity to motivate the self's quest for meaning: "I think that from the theoretical point of view, Sartre avoids the idea of the self as something which is given to us, but through the moral notion of authenticity, he turns back to the idea that we have to be ourselves – to be truly our true self."[41] Foucault is convinced that one has to replace the notion of authenticity by the practice of creativity: "from the idea that the self is not given to us, I think that there is only one practical consequence: we have to create ourselves as a work of art."[42] In Foucault, the notion of life as a work of art should not be understood as "aestheticized narcissism."[43] Rather, this aesthetics of existence is founded

---

[36] Foucault, "What is Enlightenment?" 41.

[37] Foucault, "What is Enlightenment?" 42: "This modernity does not 'liberate man in his own being;' it compels him to face the task of producing himself." The French is a little more precise here: Foucault, "Qu'est-ce que les Lumières?" 4:571: "Cette modernité ne libère pas l'homme en son être propre; elle l'astreint à la tâche de s'élaborer lui-même."

[38] Foucault, "What is Enlightenment?" 42.

[39] See Jean-Paul Sartre, *L'existentialisme est un humanisme* (Paris: Nagel, 1946; repr., Paris: Gallimard, 1996), 29–30: "Qu'est-ce que signifie ici que l'existence précède l'essence? Cela signifie que l'homme existe d'abord, se rencontre, surgit dans le monde, et qu'il se définit après. ... L'homme est non seulement tel qu'il se conçoit, mais tel qu'il se veut, et comme il se conçoit après l'existence, comme il se veut après cet élan vers l'existence, l'homme n'est rien d'autre que ce qu'il se fait. ... Mais si vraiment l'existence précède l'essence, l'homme est responsable de ce qu'il est. Ainsi, la première démarche de l'existentialisme est de mettre tout homme en possession de ce qu'il est et de faire reposer sur lui la responsabilité totale de son existence."

[40] See Sartre, *L'existentialisme est un humanisme*, 51: "l'homme n'est rien d'autre que son projet, il n'existe que dans la mesure où il se réalise, il n'est donc rien d'autre que l'ensemble de ses actes, rien d'autre que sa vie."

[41] Foucault, "On the Genealogy of Ethics," 351.

[42] Foucault, "On the Genealogy of Ethics," 351.

[43] See Colin Gordon, Introduction to *Power: Essential Works of Foucault*, xi–xli, here xxxv.

on a moral reflection,[44] and can be seen as an alternative to ethical models based on obedience to a code of law.[45]

In the discussion of the notion of self, Foucault's corpus highlights a central question: "is our self, our identity, given to us?" Foucault answers this question negatively and conversely reflects on how we can define, construct, invent ourselves if our identity is not given to us. If the thought of Paul still claims to have a voice in this contemporary world, it is important to situate him in this debate.

B. Engaging the Self in Paul's Letters

Some concerns need to be addressed before taking up the question of the construction of the self in Paul's letters and in particular in Romans. First, as Krister Stendahl reminds us, it is unfair to expect that Paul will necessarily share our modern concerns: "we should venture to suggest that the West for centuries has wrongly surmised that the biblical writers were grappling with problems which no doubt are ours, but which never entered their consciousness."[46] It might seem, especially after the advent of the new perspective[47] on Paul, that this particular question – the construction of the self – is a modern, perhaps even postmodern, question and has nothing to do with the true intentions of a biblical writer such as Paul.

1. The Individual in Antiquity and in Paul

As Gary Burnett also does in his book on the salvation of the individual,[48] I will take into account the findings of the new perspective, especially concerning the collective aspect of human beings' identity in antiquity. It is my conviction, however, that at least in Romans, we can trace elements related to the question of the construction of the self – even though Paul would probably not write about it in these terms – and use these elements

---

[44] See the two last volumes of *History of Sexuality*: *The History of Sexuality vol. 2: The Use of Pleasure* (trans. R. Hurley; New York: Pantheon Books, 1985), *The History of Sexuality vol. 3: The Care of the Self* (trans. R. Hurley; New York: Pantheon Books, 1986; repr., New York: Vintage Books, 1988).

[45] See Gordon, "Introduction," xxxv.

[46] Krister Stendahl, "Paul and the Introspective Conscience of the West," *HTR* 56 (1963): 199–215; repr. in *Paul Among Jews and Gentiles and Other Essays*, (Philadelphia: Fortress Press, 1976), 78–96, here 95.

[47] As is widely recognized today, it is E. P. Sanders' book, *Paul and Palestinian Judaism: A Comparison of Patterns of Religion* (Philadelphia: Fortress Press, 1977) that ushered in the new perspective on Paul. Central to this movement is the conviction that Paul elaborates his thought in a covenantal framework, inherited from Judaism.

[48] Gary W. Burnett, *Paul and the Salvation of the Individual* (Leiden: Brill, 2001).

to enter into conversation with a contemporary question. Since it has been assumed in recent Pauline scholarship that the emphasis of the 1ˢᵗ century Mediterranean world was on the community, the collective, it is necessary to show that one can legitimately assume that Paul could actually have a concept of the individual.[49]

The new perspective on Paul, as Burnett rightly asserts, focuses on the communal dimension of Paul's thought, especially on the significance of the concept of people of God: "In the New Perspective ... with a thorough-going covenantal framework within which to understand the way in which the New Testament writers are interpreting God's unfolding purposes, what emerges as of vital importance is the question of the identity of the people of God and how this group is to be defined."[50] As a result of this

---

[49] See in particular the work of Bruce J. Malina. For example, *The New Testament World: Insights from Cultural Anthropology* (rev. and enl. ed.; Louisville, Ky.: Westminster John Knox, 1993). For him, the first century person in the Mediterranean world would have had no way of understanding the modern idea of an individual. See especially 51–70. In scholarship on classical and late antiquity, see also Christopher Gill, *Personality in Greek Epic, Tragedy and Philosophy: The Self in Dialogue* (Oxford: Clarendon Press, 1996) who stresses the difference between the modern understanding of self and ancient notions of selfhood. The work of Jean-Pierre Vernant goes against the conclusion that the ancient Greeks did not have a sense of individuality. See *Mortals and Immortals: Collected Essays* (ed. F. I. Zeitlin; Princeton: Princeton University Press, 1991), in particular, in this collection, the article "The Individual Within the City State," 318–333 who takes up, among other things, the emergence of individual culpability and responsibility in the 5ᵗʰ century BCE (325). Vernant also notes that "the Greeks of the archaic and classical periods have, of course, an experience of their ego and their person, just as they have of their bodies, but that experience is organized differently from our own. ... This experience is turned outward, not inward. Individuals seek and find themselves in others, in those mirrors reflecting their image, each of which is an *alter ego* for them – parents, children, friends." (327) In that remark, Vernant insists that introspection is not part of the way the ancient Greeks think about the self (328). Thus, Vernant argues that the ancient Greeks do not think of the "self" so much in terms of the "I," rather they think of it in terms of a "he" (329). For Vernant, the idea of self-consciousness takes form in the 3ʳᵈ and 4ᵗʰ century CE, with Augustine as a privileged witness (331 and 332). Vernant's analysis is interesting because it makes room for the concept of an individual and does not focus unilaterally on the collective, while at the same time recognizing that some of the features modern thinkers traditionally associate with the notion of individual are not fully developed in the classical and Hellenistic world. In addition, Shadi Bartsch, *The Mirror of the Self: Sexuality, Self-Knowledge, and the Gaze in the Early Roman Empire* (Chicago: The University of Chicago Press, 2006), offers an interpretation of personhood for the early Roman Empire. In dialogue with Gill, she indicates that, for Seneca, the concept of the self becomes more self-reflexive and cannot be contained in the models established for the ancient Greek philosophers: "the Senecan mirror of the self shows far greater attention to reflexivity as constitutive of the process of coming to know oneself than does that of the *Alcibiades*."

[50] Burnett, *Paul and the Salvation of the Individual*, 3.

focus and as a consequence of a more thorough use of methods developed by the social sciences, "issues of a more abstract, theological sort to do with the nature of human beings and the potential for an individual to participate within God's purpose have tended to become less important in this current way of viewing the New Testament."[51] In fact, Burnett indicates that scholars sometimes affirm that the ideology of the New Testament period was thoroughly anti-individualistic.[52] The self is best understood as a product, or in foucaultian terms, a subject of society and culture.[53] Burnett sets out to show that engaging the question of the relevance of the Pauline gospel to the individual is still worthwhile.[54]

First, he shows that the individual was indeed a topic in the 1st century world. He begins by challenging the fact that Western social sciences see the individual as being totally constructed and determined by the collective society in which he or she lives.[55] Using mainly the findings of the anthropologist Anthony Cohen,[56] Burnett shows that social sciences need to take into account the fact that individuals are active, creative and thinking selves and that they are able to reflect on their own behavior, and not just follow what is imposed on them by society.[57] It is therefore valid to search

---

[51] Burnett, *Paul and the Salvation of the Individual*, 6.

[52] Burnett, *Paul and the Salvation of the Indidividual*, 7. Burnett refers in particular to the article of Luther H. Martin, "The Anti-Individualistic Ideology of Hellenistic Culture," *Numen* 41 (1994): 117–140 which argues that the Hellenistic period did not value any "individualistic view of the self" (117). Martin also insists on the fact that individualism is a term invented only in the 19th century (119), at the same time that the Hellenistic period was created (119). In the Christian societies, Martin explains that care for others (that is "social claims") mattered more than the needs of the individual (129–130). While this is certainly true – and I agree with Martin's judgment that "for the Greeks and Romans, in any case, any concept approaching that of modern, Western individualism was irrelevant" (134) – it does not necessarily mean that the individual as such did not have any importance. For Martin, collective identity is not challenged in the Greco-Roman world. Rather, "alternative strategies of social inclusion" (130) are offered to the person. However, social inclusion does not necessarily mean the suppression of the self (something that Martin seems willing to admit).

[53] See Burnett, *Paul and the Salvation of the Individual*, 9.

[54] See Burnett, *Paul and the Salvation of the Individual*, 10: "This study seeks, by examining a number of texts in Paul's letter to the Romans, to see how important is the relevance of the gospel to the individual in Paul's thinking."

[55] See Burnett, *Paul and the Salvation of the Individual*, especially 23–29.

[56] Anthony P. Cohen, *Self Consciousness: An Alternative Anthropology of Identity* (London: Routledge, 1994), but also Richard Rorty, *Contingency, Language and Solidarity* (Cambridge: Cambridge University Press, 1989); Ward H. Goodenough, *Culture, Language and Society* (Menlo Park, Calif.: Benjamin Cummings, 1981).

[57] See for example Burnett's conclusion to the first part of his book: "Our review of the anthropological and sociological research with respect to the nature of the individual self suggests that there is good reason to be sceptical of sociological approaches which

for traces of the individual even in ancient societies, which might seem at first more preoccupied with community. Burnett affirms Cohen's distinction between individualism, individuality and selfhood.[58] Cohen defines individualism as "a dogmatic posture which privileges the individual over society."[59] In contrast, individuality is the "perception of an individual's distinctiveness." [60] Finally, selfhood implies "the consciousness of the self."[61] A society can recognize individuality and possess selfhood, without being characterized by individualism.

Thus, Burnett turns to the Hellenistic world and investigates whether the self, the individual, played any role in Ancient Greece. Without downplaying the fact that classical Greek society was much more communal than ours, Burnett finds that "human beings of early and classical Greece, and the inhabitants of the Greco-Roman world of the 1st century CE were human beings fully in the sense in which we understand the modern person – self-aware, conscious of him or herself as a unique person, pro-active in the world, making sense of the culture and the world around, and contributing to the continual change of their era."[62] This does not mean that the 1st century world should not be seen as collective; rather it indicates that even in collective societies, individual behaviors were possible and indeed present.[63]

Finally, Burnett considers the way the individual was seen in the Hebrew Bible and in Hellenistic Judaism.[64] He concludes that there are good reasons "to suppose that Judaism had a rich heritage of emphasis on the individual and his responsibility to God, alongside a fundamental focus on the community."[65] Again, the aim is not to replace one extreme – Judaism was exclusively focused on the community – with another – Judaism was only concerned with the individual. Rather it is to present a view where concern for the individual, as it appears in some Hebrew Bible texts

---

subjugate the self to the determining power of the social, and that a fully reflexively-aware and creative self should be found in all societies, including those that might be considered to be less developed than our own," *Paul and the Salvation of the Individual*, 86.

[58] Cohen, *Self-Consciousness*, 168.
[59] Cohen, *Self-Consciousness*, 168.
[60] Cohen, *Self-Consciousness*, 168
[61] Cohen, *Self-Consciousness*, 168.
[62] Burnett, *Paul and the Salvation of the Individual*, 46. For a review of the evidences and a discussion of classical scholarship (in particular on Homer, Plato, Aristotle, the Stoics), see 30–46.
[63] See Burnett, *Paul and the Salvation of the Individual*, 86.
[64] See Burnett, *Paul and the Salvation of the Individual*, 68–85.
[65] Burnett, *Paul and the Salvation of the Individual*, 87.

(Qoheleth, Jer 31:29–30, Ez 18, Daniel 12), can be integrated in a culture centered on the community.

In his work on the way the ancient Israelites understood death and resurrection, Jon Levenson offers a good example of an analysis concerned with the familial and communal dimension of Judaism while at the same time acknowledging the role of the individual in that dynamic.[66] Levenson quotes the four points of contrast that Robert Di Vito sees between modern understanding of the individual and ancient Israelite thinking:

> The subject (1) is deeply embedded, or engaged, in its social identity, (2) is comparatively decentered and undefined with respect to personal boundaries, (3) is relatively transparent, socialized, and embodied (in other words, is altogether lacking in a sense of "inner depths"), and (4) is "authentic" precisely in its heteronomy, in its obedience to another and dependence upon another.[67]

Levenson is quick to point out that Di Vito's "formulation is overstated and too simple,"[68] especially concerning his second and third points, and indicates that biblical characters such as David for example do present a strong inner sense of self.[69] Levenson then goes on to discuss individual characters' actions and motivations at a personal level (Ruth, Naomi, Jacob, Job). He is therefore not unwilling to see a sense of individual identity in ancient Israelite thinking about the self. Di Vito himself, although he strongly emphasizes the differences between the anthropology found in the Hebrew Bible and the modern understanding of human beings, is unwilling to go so far as to say that there was a lack of a concept of individuality in ancient Israel.[70] However, Levenson also insists that Di Vito's first and last points indicate that ancient Israelites were connected to their immediate and extended family in a much more powerful way than is true in the modern world. In particular, for Levenson's own study, it indicates that the identity of a particular person could survive or reappear in one of his or her descendant.[71] Clearly, then, even if one wants to reaffirm the importance of

---

[66] Jon D. Levenson, *Resurrection and the Restoration of Israel: The Ultimate Victory of the God of Life* (New Haven, Conn.: Yale University Press, 2006).

[67] Robert A. Di Vito, "Old Testament Anthropology and the Construction of Personal Identity," *CBQ* 61 (1999): 217–238, here 221, as quoted in Levenson, *Resurrection and the Restoration of Israel*, 112.

[68] Levenson, *Resurrection and the Restoration of Israel*, 112.

[69] Levenson, *Resurrection and the Restoration of Israel*, 113.

[70] see Di Vito, "Old Testament Anthropology and the Construction of Personal Identity," 237–238.

[71] Levenson, *Resurrection and the Restoration of Israel*, 110: "David is, in one obvious sense, dead and buried (1 Kgs 2:10), and his death is final and irreversible. In another sense, harder for us to grasp, however, his identity survives him and can be manifested again in a descendant who acts as he did … and in whom the promise to David is at long

the individual in ancient Israel and in the early Christian world, it is important to remember that individuals were connected to their family and to their people in a way that might seem foreign to persons living in the 21st century.

2. Burnett's Correction to the Collectivistic Approach

Burnett attempts to correct the dominant collectivistic approach to Paul by analyzing three passages in Romans. First, he reads Romans 1:16–17 since these two verses are almost always considered as offering a summary of the letter, and should therefore already indicate whether Paul thinks about the salvation of the individual.[72] They also offer Burnett an occasion to discuss the concept of δικαιοσύνη θεοῦ and to decide whether this concept revolves around "collective issues about the identity of the people of God"[73] or can also reveal a concern for individual soteriology. Second, he takes up Romans 3:21-26 which provides an opportunity for analyzing how the concept of faith relates to the individual. Finally, he analyzes Romans 7:7–25, a passage which offers the possibility of determining the importance of the individual in "a section of Romans (chs. 5–8) which is often seen as one which deals with the ongoing effects of the gospel in the lives of the believers."[74] Burnett's choice of passages allows him to read pericopes in almost all of the usually recognized sections of the letter and he admits that other passages could also have been chosen.[75]

I differ from Burnett on two counts. First, one of Burnett's main objectives is to show, rightly, that Paul is interested in discussing questions concerning the salvation of the individual. My work is in agreement with Burnett's corrections to the collectivistic approaches and his work allows me to say that the individual is indeed a topic of interest for Paul. What I want to address more specifically is what Paul says about the individual, how he conceives of that individual and how his letters, particularly Romans, have the effect of constructing the character of his addressees.

---

last fulfilled. For David's identity was not restricted to the one man of that name but can reappear to a large measure in kin who share it."

[72] See the summary in Charles K. Barrett, *A Commentary on the Epistle to the Romans* (New York: Harper & Row, 1957), 27: "Most commentators recognize in them the 'text' of the epistle; it is not wrong to see in them a summary of Paul's theology as a whole."

[73] Burnett, *Paul and the Salvation of the Individual*, 16.

[74] Burnett, *Paul and the Salvation of the Individual*, 17.

[75] Burnett, *Paul and the Salvation of the Individual*, 18 writes: "there are more possibilities for doing this in chs. 12 and 13, too, in Paul's discussions on roles within the community, spiritual gifts and ethics. Chapter 14, while dealing with the broad group categories of 'strong' and 'weak,' potentially has room for discussion of the implications of Paul's argument about the principles of conscience for the individual ..."

I would also like to insist on the fact that, in recent scholarly work concerned with the differences between biblical understanding of identity and
modern conceptions of the self,[76] the contrast is often drawn between the
collective understanding of the ancient person and the individualistic modern self, neglecting the fact that the understanding of the modern, or in fact
postmodern, self is changing. These analyses content themselves with using the concept of identity inherited from the Enlightenment and thus focus
on a self that is largely seen as independent from its political, social, economic and cultural contexts.[77] In distinction, I would like to consider recent philosophical discussions about the self, evidenced in the works of
thinkers like Foucault, who distance themselves from the heritage of the
Enlightenment and present a different understanding of the self.

Second, I will analyze a section that Burnett does not address, Romans
12–15. This section concludes the letter's argument,[78] and, as such, allows
taking into account the whole letter. I want to show that, in agreement with
recent approaches to Romans that emphasize its narrative dimension,[79] if
one reads Romans in a continuous manner, one can see a story unfolding in
1:18–8:39 – the story of God's relationship with human beings. I will argue that, once Paul has told this story to his addressees, he needs to show
how this story affects their self-understanding and their actions. As such,
the exhortations of chapters 12–15 are important because they reveal the
expectations Paul has for his addressees now that they have "put on Christ"
(13:14) and are living in the world without belonging to it (13:11–12).

The story that Paul is telling reveals elements of the way Paul understands human beings, not only in a prescriptive, but also in a descriptive

---

[76] See Di Vito's article, "Old Testament Anthropology and the Construction of Personal Identity," Malina's book *The New Testament World*, also in Levenson's *Resurrection and the Restoration of Israel*.

[77] Charles Taylor, *Sources of the Self: The Making of Modern Identity* (Cambridge,
Mass.: Harvard University Press, 1989) is often cited as a source for the notion of modern identity and his presentation is largely focused on the self understood through the
concepts of the Enlightenment.

[78] Chapter 16 offers the epistolary conclusion to the letter, and as such is important to
determine Paul's purpose in writing the letter (see for example Robert Jewett, *Romans: A
Commentary*, [Hermeneia; Minneapolis: Fortress Press, 2007], 1: "The basic idea in the
interpretation of each verse and paragraph is that Paul wishes to gain support for a mission to the barbarians in Spain, which requires that the gospel of impartial, divine righteousness revealed in Christ be clarified to rid it of prejudicial elements that are currently
dividing the congregations in Rome.") but it does not offer any significantly new arguments.

[79] Luke T. Johnson, *Reading Romans: A Literary and Theological Commentary*
(Reading the New Testament; Macon, Ga.: Smyth & Helwys, 2001); A Katherine Grieb,
The Story of Romans: a Narrative Defense of God's Righteousness (Louisville, Ky.:
Westminster John Knox, 2002).

way. One should in particular notice the fact that there is a tremendous change between the way Paul initially describes the abilities and capacities of human beings (Romans 1:18–3:20) and what he thinks they are capable of doing by the end of the letter (Romans 12:1–15:13). This difference suggests that a change occurred in human beings, a change in their condition that modifies their self-understanding and allows them to develop new abilities. If this is true, reading Romans in a continuous manner, paying particular attention to the last chapters of the letter, might allow us to define the story Paul tells in Romans, a story with a beginning, a middle, an end, and might help see what kind of identity Paul is trying to construct for his readers. This reading emphasizes the continuity and coherence of Paul's rhetoric in Romans. Through the narrative dimension, it creates linearity, if only because, as Ricœur indicates, one of the results of storytelling is precisely to create concordance out of discordance, to make all the various elements fit in the plot.[80]

The detailed reading of the letter will show that I am aware of moments when Paul has to return to problems he has created within his earlier narratives (see Rom 7 and Rom 9–11). Yet, in focusing on the narrative dimension of the letter, I impose a coherence which the letter, in some places, resists, thus creating opportunities for argumentation and debate. These places should not be ignored. A narrative should not be smoothing out all of the problems, rather as a rhetorical strategy, it aims to make sense of the problems and integrate them in the story itself.

With this approach, I show how Paul's exhortative material contributes to the construction of the identity of his addressees and indicates what that identity needs to be. A focus on the bodily dimension of that identity is an important dimension of my work, especially to better understand what sort of relationship Paul thinks human beings can have with Christ (see in particular the language in 13:14 "put on Christ" and 14:7–8 "we do not live to ourselves, and we do not die to ourselves. If we live, we live to the Lord, and if we die, we die to the Lord; so then, whether we live or whether we die, we are the Lord's"). The narrative reading is appropriate for reflecting on the theme of the construction of identity. At the same time, it offers an alternative to classical works on Pauline anthropology.

---

[80] See Ricœur, *Temps et récit vol. 1* (3 vols.; Paris: Seuil, 1983–1985), 70: "composer l'intrigue, c'est déjà faire surgir l'intelligible de l'accidentel, l'universel du singulier, le nécessaire ou le vraisemblable de l'épisodique."

Excursus: A Way Not Taken: Rudolf Bultmann

In particular, my narrative approach to Romans is at odds with the work of Rudolf Bultmann,[81] which has been criticized by more collectivistic approaches precisely for applying an inappropriate modern existentialist perspective on Paul's enterprise and not taking into account what Paul is really trying to accomplish. As is well known, Bultmann sees anthropology as the central category of Paul's thought.[82] He recognizes however that anthropology is not presented in a systematic manner in Paul's letters. Rather, it is hidden from view. One has to reconstruct Paul's anthropological presuppositions from the material found in the letters. For the purpose of this analysis, I look at two elements in Bultmann's work: how does he read Paul? And how does he use philosophy? In the *Theology of the New Testament*, these two elements are actually closely entwined, but for my purpose, it is important to try to separate them.

When he reads Paul in order to reconstruct his anthropology, Bultmann's method consists of looking at the occurrence of specific words describing some aspect of human life and analyzing their content. As can be seen also in Kittel's *Theologische Wörterbuch zum Neuen Testament*,[83] the focus is on the theological, philosophical and religious significance of a word, rather than on its semantic, linguistic and historical dimensions. Perhaps the best way to understand Bultmann's method is to look at an example from his *Theology of the New Testament*. His treatment of the concept of flesh illustrates two elements that characterize word approaches to Pauline anthropology: the focus on snippets of text, and the creation of larger theological concepts around a word, concepts that are then again imported in to the passages where the word occurs to explain them.[84]

As Bultmann sets out to analyze the word flesh (*sarx*), he is dependent upon his previous definition of evil as "perverse intent," (232) an attitude

---

[81] Rudolf Bultmann, *Theology of the New Testament* (trans. K. Grobel; 2 vols.; New York: Scribner, 1951–1955; repr., Eugene, Oreg.: Wipf and Stock Publishers, 1997), especially 1:190–269; but also Robert Jewett, *Paul's Anthropological Terms: A Study of their Use in Conflict Settings* (Leiden: Brill, 1971); David Stacey, *The Pauline View of Man in Relation to its Judaic and Hellenistic Background* (London – New York: Macmillan – St. Martin's Press, 1956).

[82] See for example Bultmann, *Theology of the New Testament*, 1:191.

[83] James Barr, *The Semantics of Biblical Language* (London: Oxford University Press, 1961) provides a good analysis of the presuppositions behind the work of Kittel.

[84] Barr, *The Semantics of Biblical Language*, 216 indicates that in the work of Kittel the emphasis lays "on the philosophical, religious, and theological uses of idea-histories. The principle that the history of an idea is of the utmost relevance for the history of semantics of words fairly close to it seems to me entirely right. Nevertheless it is important that some possibility of distinction between the two should be kept in view." The possibility of distinction in Kittel's dictionary and in Bultmann's work is fading away.

of considering life not "as the gift of the Creator but procuring it by one's own power." (232)[85] Bultmann admits that this is not stated explicitly in Paul but "it underlies his discussions of sin, as is apparent in his statements about creation and man … and as investigation of the term 'flesh' will above all make clear." (232–233) From the start, the analysis of flesh is not purely lexical but inserted in a strong theological context. In one page, Bultmann treats what one could call the neutral occurrences of flesh, where flesh can either mean *soma*, man in general, person or the human nature. (233) At the end of this brief review, Bultmann then turns to the way flesh can denote "the nature of the earthly – human in its specific humanness – i.e. in its weakness and transitoriness, which also means in opposition to God and His Spirit." (234)

The analysis now moves towards seeing flesh as a negative concept. To make his point in a clearer manner, Bultmann associates flesh with different words that can be used as synonyms: outward, visible, what can be seen, the literal. (234) He reaches a first theological assertion about flesh when he associates it with the concept of *cosmos*: "'flesh' becomes synonymous with the term 'world' (κόσμος), insofar as *cosmos* denotes the world of created things which is the stage and the life-condition for 'natural' life, the world which is at man's disposal, giving him the possibility to live from it and to be anxious about it." (235) This first theological assertion about the meaning of flesh is taken into account in the next analyses of the expressions "in the flesh" and "κατὰ σάρκα." Thus, Bultmann says about life "in the flesh":

this formula shows that according to Paul a man's nature is not determined by what he may be as to substance (in the way the Old Testament says man is flesh) not by what qualities he may have (as Greek thinking would put it), but that his nature is determined by the sphere within which he moves, the sphere which marks out the horizon or the possibilities of what he does and experiences. (235)

Here Bultmann has moved almost seamlessly from an understanding of flesh as simply meaning human nature to a concept of flesh deeply connected to "the sphere" in which human beings lead their life. Flesh, or living in the flesh, becomes a concept associated with a potentially sinful human attitude towards life. So for example when Bultmann discusses Romans 7:5 and 8:8, he is able to use his previous analysis to give a theological content to the verses: "while flesh in itself only means the human sphere as that of the earthly-natural and of the weak and transitory, nevertheless the use made of the formula 'in the flesh' in Rom. 7:5; 8:8f. indicates that life 'in the flesh' is a spurious life; in fact everywhere the formula expresses an explicit or implicit antithesis to a life 'in the Spirit' …"

---

[85] The pages references in parenthesis are to Bultmann, *Theology of the New Testament*, vol. 1.

(236) Notice also how Bultmann takes single verses out of their context in this quotation and does not try to account for the larger context in which they occur.

Furthermore, life in the flesh is contrasted to life in the spirit, which indicates its potential negative dimension, if it is taken as the ultimate sphere in which human beings can live; as such it is the "sphere of sinning." (236) Life "according to the flesh" (κατὰ σάρκα) is discussed in the same manner as life "in the flesh," with an emphasis on its potential to define existence as sinful, especially when it is used with verbs. (237) Finally, Bultmann uses what he has said about the word flesh and connects it to his analysis of sin. (239–246) The determinant category to understand the concept of flesh becomes the following:

> ... the crucial question is whether "in flesh" only denotes the stage and the possibilities for a man's life or the determinative norm for it – whether a man's life "*in* flesh" is also life "*according* to the flesh" – or, again, whether the sphere of the natural – earthly, which is also that of the transitory and perishable, is the world out of which a man thinks he derives his life and by means of which he thinks he maintains it. (239)

Bultmann's move from the concept of flesh as earthly life to the understanding of flesh as that which determines a person's life allows him to continue his presentation of flesh through a discussion of what sin is and to move into theological categories about sin. In this discussion, he looks at the verbs "to desire," "to care" and particularly "to boast" ("the attitude of sinful self-reliance finds its extreme expression in man's *boasting*" [242]) as examples of the ways sin is manifested in human beings' life. (239–242) From there on, the concept of flesh loses its centrality in favor of the category of sin. In fact, what had started as a lexical study of the word flesh ends in a theological discussion centered on the concept of sin; especially sin understood as boasting. As a result, for Bultmann's presentation of Pauline anthropology, the descriptions of *sarx* as a neutral concept loses its importance and the focus is on the aspects of flesh connected to the notion of sin, understood as human beings' false reliance on themselves instead of reliance on God. The analysis of Bultmann's work on flesh has shown two representative elements of his method: a) the reliance on snippets of sentences as well as the fact that the connection between passages is made through the use of certain words, and not through the meaning of the passages, b) the move from a lexical study to theological assertions then reapplied to the single word. In addition, Bultmann's philosophical presuppositions influence his discussion of theological concepts.

Bultmann's philosophical presuppositions are anchored in existentialist philosophy, something he openly recognizes.[86] Existentialist philosophy

---

[86] He testifies to this influence in several places: see for example: Rudolf Bultmann, "Autobiographical Reflections," in *Existence and Faith* (ed. and trans. S. M. Ogden; New

provides Bultmann with a basic scenario in which to fit Paul's theology. To summarize and simplify, in existentialist philosophy, human beings are trapped in inauthentic existence. They have a responsibility to give meaning to their own lives, through their actions and through the understanding they have of their own existence. Only then can they lead what existentialist philosophers call an authentic life. The responsibility to give meaning to existence can provoke fear and angst, as is clear from the writings of some existentialist novelists, such as Albert Camus. In fact, this quest for meaning can even end in absurdity.[87]

Bultmann's decision to focus his reading of Paul on the question of anthropology has its roots in existentialist philosophy, even though Bultmann would claim that it is in accordance with New Testament theology.[88] Or to put it another way, since Bultmann is mainly interested in human existence and how to give it a meaning, existentialist philosophy presents itself as a logical partner for reading the New Testament. The existentialist categories of inauthentic existence and authentic existence find their parallels in Bultmann's presentations of fallen life (or "man prior to faith") and redeemed life ("man under faith"). In Bultmann's reading of the New Testament, and of Paul in particular, the call to authentic life dear to existentialism is replaced by the saving event of Christ's death and resurrection. Faith in that saving event provides human beings with the means to lead an authentic life.

Obviously, the main difference between Bultmann's explanation of the passage from inauthentic life to authentic life and atheistic existentialism is

---

York: Meridian Books, 1960), 335–341, here 341, but also, "Is Exegesis Without Presuppositions Possible?" in Ogden, *Existence and Faith*, 342–351, especially 348–351; "Le problème de l'herméneutique," in *Foi et compréhension: L'historicité de l'homme et de la révélation* (vol. 1 of *Foi et compréhension*; trans. A. Malet; 2 vols.; Paris: Seuil, 1969–1970), 599–626, especially 616 where Bultmann quotes Heidegger's *Sein und Zeit*, and "L'étrange de la foi chrétienne," in *Foi et compréhension: eschatologie et démythologisation* (vol. 2 of *Foi et compréhension*), 229–246, especially 245–246 where Bultmann explains the notion of "destruction de la métaphysique" in Heidegger. See also John Macquarrie, *An Existentialist Theology: A Comparison of Heidegger and Bultmann* (New York: The MacMillan Company, 1955). Even Stendahl, "Paul and the Introspective Conscience of the West," 88, who is not particularly sympathetic to Bultmann's project, recognizes that Bultmann is open about his hermeneutical presuppositions: "... Bultmann makes, candidly and openly, the statement that man is essentially the same through the ages, and that this continuity in the human self-consciousness is the common denominator between the New Testament and any age of human history. This presupposition is stated with the force of an a priori truth."

[87] See Albert Camus, *La Chute* (Paris: Gallimard, 1956).

[88] See Macquarrie, *An Existentialist Theology*, 12: "Bultmann claims, of course, that in making his theology centre in the question of man's existence, he is simply following the precedent of the New Testament."

their evaluations of human beings' capacity to rediscover the possibility of choice.[89] For atheist philosophers, human beings have it in themselves to recover their authentic possibilities.[90] In Bultmann's reading of Paul, this possibility is utterly lost. Left to themselves, human beings have no means of escaping an inauthentic life – a life of sin. Only God's gracious intervention in Jesus Christ can open the possibility for authentic life – life under faith. Despite this major difference, Bultmann does offer an example of existentialist theology, and he reads Paul in the categories of the philosophical system to which he gives allegiance.

His methodology and his philosophical presuppositions require Bultmann to reconstruct Pauline anthropology in a systematic manner, ignoring the larger contexts in which the concepts are used and especially how they fit within the letters as wholes. Bultmann never follows the logic of a specific letter to see what picture of humanity would emerge if one looked at it that way. Furthermore, Bultmann's analysis describes a generic human being, boiled down to her essence, whereas it is clear that Paul writes to real individuals in real communities, rooted in specific contexts and concrete difficulties. From Paul's letters, Bultmann retrieves a model "I" that corresponds – to some degree – to all human beings. What matters is this "I"'s own personal relationship with God, not its involvement with a specific community which maintains its ties to its cultural past, be it Jewish or Greek.

My approach differs from Bultmann's in several respects. First, I distance myself from a word-theology approach to Paul's anthropology and attempt to see what picture of humanity emerges when one looks at one letter – Romans – in continuity, focusing on the story told in the letter, how it depicts human beings, and what it asks them to do. Second, this focus on story also implies that the end of the letter, chapters 12–15 (chapters to which Bultmann pays practically no attention), has as much importance for reconstructing the way Paul understands human beings as does the beginning. The insistence on fallen humanity as the place where one finds most of Paul's anthropological concepts leads to a negative, mostly static and usually individualistic, presentation of human beings. Focusing on the end gives importance to the fact that Paul's understanding of human beings is dynamic and positive as well. It brings into view an image of human beings involved in a story that needs to continue, and that involves a community – even a people – as fundamental elements for the understanding of human beings.

---

[89] See Macquarrie, *An Existentialist Theology*, 141.
[90] In Heidegger, this happens through the category of conscience; see Macquarrie, *An Existentialist Theology*, 141.

Moreover, for Bultmann, it is unnecessary to talk about the self and its relationship to the community, let alone to a people, since what matters to him is the individual's power of decision to lead an authentic life. The person's interaction with others, its belonging to a community and to a people, are only secondary to who the self truly is. Focusing on chapters 12–15 places individuals within a community and a people. Finally, Bultmann is open in indicating that his project takes place in an existentialist framework. He reads Paul's letters through his philosophical convictions. In contrast, I aim to read Romans in order to engage a philosophical question. My analysis of Romans does not give allegiance to any contemporary philosophical system. In fact, Foucault is rather suspicious of philosophical systems and could almost be qualified as putting into place an anti-system, which does not aim at making disciples. Thus, I attempt to enter into conversation with philosophical considerations about the question of the self, rather than reading Paul through a philosophical system.

C. Paul and Michel Foucault in Conversation

By choosing to put Paul and Foucault in conversation, this dissertation works in an interdisciplinary way within the academic fields of New Testament and philosophy. The question at the center of this work, namely the question of the construction of the self, invites an interaction with philosophy. It is important to see if Paul's thought can be put into conversation with 21st century philosophical currents. This said, I do not argue for reading the New Testament in a philosophical manner. I do argue, however, that one should read past texts with an awareness of the way in which they engage one's present situation. In the present case, then, I think about one problem that matters to me through the reading of past texts. If my engagement with past texts changes my own way of looking at the problem of the construction of the self, then the interpretation has reached its goal.

It also happens that this question is particularly appropriate for collaboration with philosophy. Numerous other questions, relevant for New Testament studies in general and for Pauline studies in particular, do not necessarily raise philosophical questions. For the question of the construction of the self, some interdisciplinary work with philosophy is justified.

1. Setting up the Conversation

Perhaps it is helpful to say from the start that there are three things I would like to avoid, things that are sometimes all too common when scholars engage in conversation with philosophy in general and with Foucault in particular. First, I do not offer an apology for Paul, with the final aim of showing that Paul's position is better than any contemporary take on the question of the subject. I do believe that in some ways Paul's thought is still relevant for debate in contemporary philosophical circles, in much the same way that Plato, Aristotle, Descartes or Kant are, since they have not only changed philosophy profoundly but also because they have influenced the Western world tremendously. In that regard, Paul is worthy of being heard in contemporary philosophical debates, but not with the purpose of defending his position blindly.

Second, I do not co-opt Foucault for Christianity, by arguing that he in fact agreed with the main tenets of Christian faith without knowing it. My aim is not to demonstrate hidden agreements behind Foucault's thought and Christian beliefs as one can reconstruct them from Paul. Furthermore, I do not wish to show that Foucault's philosophical reflections could have been improved upon if only Foucault had agreed with Christian faith. Both Foucault and Paul deserve to have their voice heard as their own, without trying to artificially harmonize their positions, and without the interpreter being the judge of which position is the best. Both thinkers are used to construct the problem of the self.

Third, I do not offer a foucaultian reading of the New Testament, even though my interaction with Foucault clearly influences the way I read texts in general, and thus also Paul's letter to the Romans. Such efforts have sometimes yielded good results for New Testament scholarship. In relationship to Paul, three examples can be reviewed, those of Stephen Moore, Elizabeth Castelli and Halvor Moxnes. The first two emphasize Foucault and use him to critique Paul. Moxnes presents a more dialectic approach, and ends up favoring Paul.

In his book, *Poststructuralism and the New Testament*,[91] Moore uses Foucault's *Discipline and Punish*[92] to offer an analysis of the theme of the cross in the letters of Paul: "I shall be attempting to read a central New Testament theme – the power of the cross – through the lens not of Foucault's explicit statements on Christianity, for the most part, but of his sharpest and strongest book, which is largely silent on Christianity. That book is *Discipline and Punish*, and its natural dialogue partner is Paul ..."[93] In this case, the categories that Foucault puts into place in *Discipline and Punish*, notably the idea that power has as its goal the production of a docile body, through torture but also through discipline, are used to illuminate Paul's text and to show how Paul's use of the cross can be

---

[91] Stephen D. Moore, *Poststructuralism and the New Testament: Derrida and Foucault at the Foot of the Cross* (Minneapolis: Fortress Press, 1994).

[92] Michel Foucault, *Discipline and Punish: The Birth of the Prison* (trans. A. Sheridan Smith; New York: Pantheon Books, 1978; repr., New York: Vintage Books, 1995).

[93] Moore, *Poststructuralism and the New Testament*, 94.

seen as an example of what Foucault defends in *Discipline and Punish*: "…
what if the transformation of the believer were merely a more efficient exercise of power, still exercised on the body but now reaching into the psy-
che as well to fashion acceptable thoughts and attitudes yielding acceptable behavior, of power absolutized to a degree unimaginable even in a situation of extreme physical torture? This, above all, is the question that
Discipline and Punish prompts us to ask."[94] In this case, Foucault's work
is used as a key to read Paul's letters.

The result is an innovative reading of Paul, which does not claim to remain faithful to Paul's original intent, but aims to describe an aspect of
Christian life quite foreign to the context of Paul's letters themselves. As
such, it is more a theological reading *from* Paul's texts than a reading *of*
Paul's texts. The distanciation and application to contemporary issues take
place through the application of Foucault's categories on Paul's texts. In
this case, both thinkers are used to spark the reading of Moore about a topic that is not the one that the two original thinkers had in mind.

Castelli presents another example of a foucaultian reading in *Imitating
Paul*.[95] The influence of Foucault on her reading is found at two levels.
First, Foucault's categories of "'regimes of truth' and 'technologies of power' provide the interpretive lens for the … study."[96] Foucault's analyses
are used to produce a new and challenging reading of Paul. Castelli does
this mainly through the use of Foucault's work on the notion of power, or
more precisely, of relations of power. In particular, Castelli uses the five
categories that Foucault sees as necessary to create and maintain relations
of power and applies them to Paul's use of imitation rhetoric.[97] Here Foucault offers tools to provide a new interpretation of Pauline texts.

In addition, Castelli indicates that her use of Foucault intends a critique
of traditional interpretations of Paul: "Foucault's observations about the
nature of power relations and their relationship to truth claims are helpful
in establishing a general corrective in the readings of Paul's use of the
rhetoric of imitation."[98] In Castelli's book, the preference is given to Foucault, used as a partner to produce a new reading of Paul. In fact, Foucault's analyses allow Castelli to develop a hermeneutic of suspicion behind her reading of Paul, aimed at unveiling the ways in which Paul, and
his interpreters, have put into place relations of power that result in the

---

[94] Moore, *Poststructuralism and the New Testament*, 108.
[95] Elizabeth A. Castelli, *Imitating Paul: A Discourse of Power* (Louisville, Ky.:
Westminster John Knox, 1991).
[96] Castelli, *Imitating Paul*, 15
[97] see in particular Castelli, *Imitating Paul*, 48, and 122–124.
[98] Castelli, *Imitating Paul*, 46.

eradication of difference.[99] Paul is here criticized sharply through the use of foucaultian categories, even though in the process Castelli actually comes to ignore a fundamental dimension of Foucault's work on power – the fact that the subordinate actor is neither seen as having no effect on the relationship of power nor as having no option for action inside this same relation – as she casts Paul as an authoritarian apostle reigning with absolute sovereignty over his community.

A more balanced used of Foucault is seen in the work of Halvor Moxnes. In his article on "Asceticism and Christian Identity," Moxnes does in some ways offer a foucaultian reading of Paul: "one might say that I will attempt a foucaultian reading of Paul, but against the position of Foucault on Christian ethics as a set of rules."[100] However, as is already clear from this quotation, Foucault's position is not an overarching grid that Moxnes will blindly use on Paul's text. Rather, after exposing Foucault's work on asceticism in antiquity and in early Christianity, Moxnes uses Foucault's categories to analyze the ethical dimensions of 1 Cor 6:12–20 and to show that this text is about constructing a Christian identity for male Corinthians.[101] Two elements in his analysis are especially significant for my own work.

First, Moxnes argues that 1 Cor 6:12–20 is "not a text that opens itself up for a reading in terms of codes or moral norms."[102] Rather, using Foucault's methodology, it needs to be read "as a text that deals with self-formation of the male ethical subject."[103] The ethical demands are used by Paul to shape the identity of his readers, in this case, his male readers – since the text is about visiting prostitutes. The second element in Moxnes'

---

[99] See for example Castelli, *Imitating Paul*, 103: "Sameness, unity, and harmony are to be achieved through imitation; they also circumscribe the community which is unified, in contrast to those who are different. By implication, difference is equated with diffusion, disorder, and discord. So, difference is placed outside the community, and literally has no place in the community. Any argument against Paul is then cast in these terms: to oppose Paul does not have the status of a mere difference of opinion. Rather, it sets one in opposition to the community, its gospel and its savior. 'Become imitators of me' is a call to sameness which erases difference and, at the same time, reinforces the authoritative status of the model." In her dissertation, Faith K. Hawkins offers a much more nuanced reading of difference and criticizes Castelli for being "too one-sided." (Faith K. Hawkins, "1 Corinthians 8:1 –11:1: The Making and Meaning of Difference" [Ph.D. Diss., Emory University, 2001], 88.) She argues that Paul "constructs a creative tension between identity among the community members and differences between them" (iv) and does not eradicate difference. Paul calls for "a compromise which allows differences to remain in place." (89)

[100] Halvor Moxnes, "Asceticism and Christian Identity in Antiquity: A Dialogue with Foucault and Paul," *JSNT* 26 (2003): 3–29, here 17.

[101] See Moxnes, "Asceticism and Christian Identity in Antiquity," particularly 19–26.

[102] Moxnes, "Asceticism and Christian Identity in Antiquity," 19.

[103] Moxnes, "Asceticism and Christian Identity in Antiquity," 19.

analysis is his insistence that this identity is centered on the body. It is the body, more specifically the relationships in which the body participates, that shapes the identities of Paul's male Corinthian readers.[104] Thus Paul wants to show that their body's "participation in Christ's body" is the "main determining factor" of the Corinthian men's identity. [105] Moxnes states: "The male body did not have its identity in itself; the bodies of Christian men in Corinth were determined by being 'members of Christ'."[106] For Moxnes, the bodies are formed through asceticism in order to express the believers' new self-understanding in Christ.[107]

In this case, a foucaultian reading is appropriate since Moxnes is using Foucault's researches on asceticism in antiquity and seeing if they can apply to Paul as well. In his conclusion, Moxnes uses this analysis to show the limits of Foucault's own description of ethics in early Christianity as a rigid set of rules: "...Foucault's own view of Christian morality as 'obedience to a system of rules' is simply inadequate."[108] Both thinkers are given a chance to be heard and are fruitfully put into conversation.

These foucaultian readings of Paul offer original and sometimes challenging interpretations of the letters. However, Moore and Castelli in particular are too one-sided. Moxnes is more balanced and like him, I present a real conversation between Paul and Foucault, in which both participants are presented in their own right, where disagreements and incompatibilities are taken into account, and where one might be used to critique the other, but also to highlight strengths and particularities. This creates a collaboration aimed at producing a meaningful interpretation of the problem of the construction of the self.

2. Situating the Conversation in New Testament Studies

It should be clear that my analysis aims to achieve two different things. On the one hand, I set up a conversation between a New Testament author and a philosopher. On the other hand, I also offer a narrative reading of a Pauline letter. On both counts, scholars have preceded me and helped put my own approach into place. In New Testament studies, these antecedents can

---

[104] See Moxnes, "Asceticism and Christian Identity in Antiquity," 23: "Bodily experiences were the basis for this identity: baptism and spiritual gifts expressed the union with Christ."

[105] Moxnes, "Asceticism and Christian Identity in Antiquity," 24.

[106] Moxnes, "Asceticism and Christian Identity in Antiquity," 25.

[107] See Moxnes, "Asceticism and Christian Identity in Antiquity," 26: "... because Christians were conscious of their identity as members of the body of Christ, asceticism was the way to form their bodies to express this identity."

[108] See Moxnes, "Asceticism and Christian Identity in Antiquity," 28.

be seen in two domains: the way Paul and the philosophers have been engaged and the development of literary approaches to the Pauline corpus.

Three types of work can fit under the broad category of "Paul and the Philosophers", even though the books themselves are widely different. I will look at them in turn. First, biblical scholars have been interested in seeing how Paul relates to ancient philosophers. Second, some theologians or New Testament scholars have used the thought of modern philosophers to inform their interpretation of Paul's letters. Third, some modern philosophers have engaged the writings of Paul.

Various authors have compared Paul's writings with the works of Hellenistic philosophers, as well as Hellenistic Jews, in order to show how the letters relate to other older or contemporary sources. These books are characterized by a historical approach, comparing similar texts and drawing conclusions about the type of relationship between Paul and other sources.

Hans-Dieter Betz

The first example of such a historical reconstruction is Hans-Dieter Betz's study, *Der Apostel Paulus und die sokratische Tradition*[109] which can perhaps be seen as one of the ancestors to historical approaches interested in showing Paul's relationship with ancient philosophy.[110] Betz's interest in 2 Cor 10–13 leads him to analyze how the apologetic tradition developed around the figure of Socrates influenced Paul, and how Paul modified and appropriated this tradition.[111] Betz compares various ancient apologies and Paul's discourse in 2 Cor 10–13 in order to find analogies between Paul's apology and socratic traditions. His work of comparison allows him to interpret Paul through the categories of Hellenistic philosophy. In particular, he sees that Paul's argument is made even more powerful through the use of Hellenistic traditions, because it can rely on his christology but also on

---

[109] Hans-Dieter Betz, *Der Apostel Paulus und die sokratische Tradition: Eine exegetische Untersuchung zu seiner "Apologie" 2 Korinther 10–13* (Tübingen: Mohr, 1972).

[110] Before him, others had started to see the importance of Hellenistic philosophy to understand Paul: Johannes Weiss, "Beiträge zur paulinischen Rhetorik," in *Theologische Studien: Herrn Wirkl. Oberkonsistorialrath Professor D. Bernhard Weiss zu seinem 70. Geburtstage dargebracht* (ed. C. R. Gregory et al.; Göttingen: Vandenhoeck & Ruprecht, 1897), 165–247, Rudolf Bultmann, *Der Stil der paulinischen Predigt und die kynisch-stoische Diatribe* (Göttingen: Vandenhoeck & Ruprecht, 1910) and Adolf Friedrich Bonhöffer, *Epiktet und das Neue Testament* (Giessen: Töpelmann, 1911). The influence of the history-of-religion approach played an important role in the willingness to examine the texts of the New Testament in their cultural context.

[111] Betz, *Der Apostel Paulus und die sokratische Tradition*, 18: "Mit seinem Verzicht auf das 'ἀπολογεῖσθαι' nimmt Paulus also eine Tradition auf, die von Sokrates ausgeht und die ihm auf dem Wege über die zeitgenössische Philosophie zugeflossen sein muss. Natürlich hat er sie in sein eigenes Denken integriert."

his use of socratic humanism.[112] These socratic traditions are in particular reworked in Cynic and Stoic philosophy. This relationship with Stoicism and Cynicism opened the door to more analyses of Paul's relationship to Hellenistic philosophy, analyses that were conducted on a larger scale than Betz's reading of 2 Cor 10–13.

Abraham J. Malherbe

Abraham Malherbe's book, *Paul and the Popular Philosophers*, is an attempt to show broader connection between Paul's thought and the Cynics.[113] It aims at describing who the Cynics were and how Paul related to their thought.[114] In his fifth chapter in particular, Malherbe highlights the ways in which Paul was like the Hellenistic philosophers and the aspects in which he differed from them. For Malherbe, Paul can stand his ground as a philosopher, especially if one is careful to understand philosophy as a system aimed at moral change:

> There can no longer be any doubt that Paul was thoroughly familiar with the teaching, methods of operation, and style of argumentation of the philosophers of the period, all of which he adopted and adapted to his own purposes. This is not to argue that he was a technical philosopher; neither were his philosophical contemporaries. The philosophers with whom Paul should be compared were not metaphysicians who specialized in systematizing abstractions, but, like Paul, were preachers and teachers who saw their main goal to be the reformation of the lives of the people they encountered ... The points of similarity between Paul and his philosophic competitors may be stressed to the point that he is viewed as a type of hellenistic philosopher.[115]

Despite this proximity with Hellenistic philosophers, Malherbe insists that Paul adapted Hellenistic philosophy to his own use, and that he was no slave to the Hellenistic positions.[116] Paul's originality is preserved. In particular, he differed from the Cynics on two points. First, if Paul is similar to Hellenistic philosophers in his desire to bring changes in the people to whom he preaches, he differs to them in his eagerness to found communi-

---

[112] Betz, *Der Apostel Paulus und die sokratische Tradition*, 55: "Diese Verteidigung ist für Paulus deshalb so bedeutsam, weil er sich nicht nur durch den Rückgriff auf seine Christologie verteidigt, sondern zugleich auf eine bestimmte Tradition hellenistischer Kultur, die des 'sokratischen Humanismus' zurückgreift, welcher offenbar besonders in der kynisch-stoischen Philosophie weitergegeben wurde."

[113] Abraham J. Malherbe, *Paul and the Popular Philosophers* (Minneapolis: Fortress Press, 1989).

[114] Malherbe, *Paul and the Popular Philosophers*, 5: "My studies in this book share in this attempt to gain greater precision in our understanding of contemporary philosophy and of Paul's relationship to it."

[115] Malherbe, *Paul and the Popular Philosophers*, 68.

[116] Malherbe, *Paul and the Popular Philosophers*, 70: "There are, however, sufficient differences between Paul and the philosophers to preclude our viewing him as a slavish, unreflective follower of current practice."

ties.[117] The communal dimension is central to Paul's thought and mission. Second, Paul is acutely aware of God's power at work in his mission. He insists that his achievements are not his own, but are made possible through God's power, something that remains absent from the Cynics.[118]

Malherbe provides a historical approach, aimed at comparative work between Paul and the Hellenistic philosophers. As such, he indicates some of the concerns that were central for ancient philosophy and helps to understand how the person and its abilities were understood. It also gives precious indications on the role of parenesis, which are helpful for a reading of Romans 12–15. However, as I will explain in more detail below, my aim is very different from Malherbe's and I do not present a historical reconstruction of Paul's engagement with the philosophers of his time.

Walter T. Wilson

Walter Wilson's monograph, *Love without Pretense*, falls into the same category as Malherbe's work on Hellenistic philosophy, but his interests are different.[119] Rather than look at the relationship of Paul with Hellenistic philosophers, Wilson wants to explore the influence of Jewish Hellenistic wisdom traditions on Paul, especially Paul's use of gnomic sayings in his ethical teaching, as represented by Romans 12.[120] Without arguing that Paul was directly dependent upon specific Jewish Hellenistic wisdom texts, Wilson aims to show that there is a significant similarity between chapter 12 of Romans and some wisdom texts, both in thought and in the rhetorical articulation of thought. In order to make his point, Wilson analyzes the gnomic saying in antiquity, with special attention given to its context and its genre. In relationship to Paul, three genres of gnomic wisdom in particular "form the most pertinent background for the analysis of Romans 12; they are gnomic poetry, gnomologia, and wisdom instruction."[121] For Wilson, the best way to explain the relationship between Romans 12 and wisdom literature is "to inspect the chapter side-by-side with specific and rel-

---

[117] Malherbe, *Paul and the Popular Philosophers*, 70 "... Paul differs from the philosophers in his goal to form communities of believers rather than only bring about change in individuals."

[118] Malherbe, *Paul and the Popular Philosophers*, 72: "Here [in 1 Thess 2:2] there is nothing of self-attainment, rather an awareness of God's power."

[119] Walter T. Wilson, *Love without Pretense: Romans 12:9–21 and Hellenistic-Jewish Wisdom Literature* (WUNT 46; Tübingen: Mohr, 1991).

[120] See Wilson, *Love without Pretense*, 6: "... the objective here is to investigate Romans 12 against the background of relevant ancient texts that make use of gnomic wisdom and to explore what implications this has for the interpretation of the literary composition and rhetorical function of the chapter as well as for our understanding of the importance of the gnomic style for Paul's ethics."

[121] Wilson, *Love without Pretense*, 41.

evant comparative sources."[122] Wilson chooses four texts: Proverbs 3:11–
35 (LXX), Ben Sira 6:18–37, Pseudo-Phocylides 70–96 and the Testament
of Naphtali 2:2–3:5. These four texts, as well as Romans 12:1–21, are analyzed in detail, with regard to their literary composition and how this structure informs the content of each passage.[123] Romans 12 is then compared
with these sources.

The results of this comparison allow Wilson to highlight some elements
of Paul's exhortative section in Romans. Wilson insists that the structure
of Romans 12 is similar to the structure of wisdom literature, and thus it
develops coherently in the entire chapter. The instructions are not haphazard; rather they follow a pattern also present in Jewish Hellenistic wisdom
literature. Also, the gnomic wisdom that is present in Romans 12 "occu-
pies an important middle ground, so to speak, between ethics expressed in
theory (e.g. Romans 12:1–2) and explicit recommendations directed towards specific historical situations (e.g. Romans 13–15)."[124] These gnomic
instructions emphasize human beings' rational abilities, and "promote in
the audience constant criticism and self-evaluation, in order to maintain a
high level of ethical awareness and moral responsibility."[125]

As was the case with Malherbe's work, Wilson's purpose in his monograph is very different from my own. However, because he offers a careful
study of Romans 12, his analysis helps me delineate what Paul intends to
do when writing his parenetic section.

Troels Engberg-Pedersen

Engberg-Pedersen's book, *Paul and the Stoics*, is the last work I will review in the category historical analysis of Paul's relationship with ancient
philosophers.[126] Clearly, Engberg-Pedersen's main purpose is historical.
The book aims to "situate Paul's thought firmly within the ancient ethical
tradition as this was inaugurated by Plato's Socrates, developed by Aristotle and given classic shape in Stoicism."[127] His ambition is to show that
Paul's letters are best understood historically in relationship to a model
derived from Stoic thought.

However, to this historical purpose expressed in Engberg-Pedersen's
acceptance of the historico-critical challenge of reading Paul, the author
adds two more elements.[128] His second stage, following upon his recogni-

---

[122] Wilson, *Love without Pretense*, 91.

[123] See Wilson, *Love without Pretense*, 92.

[124] Wilson, *Love without Pretense*, 210.

[125] Wilson, *Love without Pretense*, 210–211.

[126] Troels Engberg-Pedersen, *Paul and the Stoics* (Louisville, Ky.: Westminster John
Knox, 2000).

[127] Engberg-Pedersen, *Paul and the Stoics*, ix.

[128] See Engberg-Pedersen, *Paul and the Stoics*, 22.

tion of the historical distance that separates modernity from Paul, is to accept "the modern approaches with their methodological selectivity and material comprehensiveness."[129] This means that Engberg-Pedersen's reading of Paul will place itself at some distance from Paul's own viewpoint and reflect "the reflectiveness and self-consciousness of the modern world."[130] The purpose of this step is to render Paul intelligible to us and is made clear in the third stage of the reading, the hermeneutical step, which aims to articulate "a set of (almost) genuinely Pauline ways of understanding that have a claim to constituting a real option for us even when we look at them in the cool light of historical criticism."[131] This hermeneutical side of Engberg-Pedersen's work makes his study more than a simple historical comparison of Paul with the Stoics. It also aims to make Paul relevant for present discussion. Two aims can be discerned in Engberg-Pedersen's offering of a Stoic reading of Paul: to develop a better understanding of Paul, and to make Paul an option for us.

Engberg-Pedersen's reading of Paul is dependent upon a model derived from Stoicism. In this regard, Engberg-Pedersen is closely related to approaches that read Paul in relationship with a philosophical model (such as Bultmann's) since he uses Stoic categories to interpret Paul. Because Stoic thought is contemporary to Paul, Engberg-Pedersen argues that his reading has more historical accuracy than Bultmann's.[132] He presents this model in his third chapter. The prominent feature of the model is that it "depicts a change that may occur in the perception of individuals of their own identity and what has value for them."[133] This change happens at the level of a person's self-understanding and the model describes a particular vision of this change: "[t]he vision is that of being *taken over* by something 'outside,' 'over' and 'above' oneself (be it God, Christ or reason), though certainly, … something that also has its counterpart *in* oneself. Correspondingly, the vision is that of *giving up* 'oneself,' the self that is precisely being taken over by the other thing."[134] The orientation of the model is communitarian. It describes a change from an I-perspective to a We-perspective.[135] This model is then applied to Stoic philosophy (chapter four) as well as to

---

[129] Engberg-Pedersen, *Paul and the Stoics*, 23.

[130] Engberg-Pedersen, *Paul and the Stoics*, 23.

[131] Engberg-Pedersen, *Paul and the Stoics*, 24.

[132] Engberg-Pedersen, *Paul and the Stoics*, 29.

[133] Engberg-Pedersen, *Paul and the Stoics*, 34.

[134] Engberg-Pedersen, *Paul and the Stoics*, 40.

[135] Engberg-Pedersen, *Paul and the Stoics*, 34. Engberg-Pedersen symbolizes the model in the following manner: I → X → S, where I is the person oriented towards herself, X the change agent (either God/Christ in the Pauline model or reason in the Stoic model) and S is the person in the new perspective, oriented toward the good of the community.

three Pauline letters (Philippians, Galatians and Romans) to show how helpful it is in resolving issues in Pauline interpretation. Without entering into the details of the analysis, there are three results that can be abstracted from Engberg-Pedersen's approach.

First, in light of the model, Engberg-Pedersen argues that in his letters, through the use of elements of the model, Paul "offer his addressees an understanding of where they themselves belong within the picture drawn in the model."[136] Stoicism provides "a coherent account of a specific form of life."[137] This specific form of life hopes to appeal to those who encountered the model through Stoicism. Since Paul, Engberg-Pedersen affirms, makes use of the same model, it is possible to see the letters as basically parenetic letters, aimed at constructing the various communities they address. The first result is that parenesis plays a central role in Paul's letters and in Engberg-Pedersen's analysis of them.

Second, throughout the analysis, Engberg-Pedersen redefines parenesis in light of the model he is using. He affirms that, in Romans in particular, the imperative elements "are to be understood not as forward-looking commands to bring something new into existence, but rather as backward-looking appeals in the form of reminders of something the addressees are taken to know, see and accept beforehand."[138] With this understanding of the exhortative material, there is "plenty of room for the indicative type of statement, which aims to spell out *what* it is that they already know."[139] For Romans, this means that chapters 12–15 should not be seen as mere addition to the theoretical and theological parts of the letter (1–11), but as being an integral part of the letter and as contributing in a significant manner to its purpose as a parenetic letter. For the understanding of Paul in general, Engberg-Pedersen insists that imperative and indicative statements function together to bring about parenesis.[140] Theology and ethics cannot be separated. Neither one is the consequence of the other, rather they work together. Third, Engberg-Pedersen shows that Paul envisions a change at the level of the self-understanding in his addressees and that he tries to bring this change about through his letters.

In his hermeneutical dimension, Engberg-Pedersen's book comes close to my own purpose in reading Paul. I argue that it is possible and indeed interesting to put Paul in conversation with postmodern philosophy. Thus, I agree with Engberg-Pedersen that one facet of the exegetical work is to make Paul a real option for us. I am also in agreement with Engberg-

---

[136] Engberg-Pedersen, *Paul and the Stoics*, 43.
[137] Engberg-Pedersen, *Paul and the Stoics*, 79.
[138] Engberg-Pedersen, *Paul and the Stoics*, 282.
[139] Engberg-Pedersen, *Paul and the Stoics*, 282.
[140] Engberg-Pedersen, *Paul and the Stoics*, 302.

Pedersen in his definition of parenesis and in his insistence on the fact that the change Paul imagined occurs at the level of self-understanding. Furthermore, his description of the regenerated individual as focused on the community and no longer on herself is helpful in strengthening my own presentation of the self as deeply engaged in its relation with its community and indeed its people. In this regard, my work is closer to Engberg-Pedersen's than to Malherbe's or Wilson's. However, I differ from Engberg-Pedersen on two levels.

On a methodological level, Engberg-Pedersen rejects a narrative approach to Paul's letters. He admits that a narrative approach has the advantage of giving coherence to many various topics, but it remains too close to Paul's own language and as such it cannot help Paul's letters in making direct sense for their modern readers.[141] For Engberg-Pedersen, it is necessary to remove oneself from the metaphorical dimensions of Paul's language and to operate at a more abstract level, almost at a meta-level.[142] His use of the Stoic model achieves precisely that. Although I do not want to diminish the historical distance that separates us from Paul and am aware of the critical work one has to do in order to make sense of some of Paul's concepts, I am not as pessimistic as Engberg-Pedersen concerning our possibility to relate to Paul's metaphorical language. In fact, Paul's various metaphors (for example his language of Christ living in one's person) testify to the richness of his thought and might be a chance to engage readers far removed temporarily through their interpretative power. A narrative reading, when kept in check by an awareness of historical distance, might be the best way of giving these various metaphors a chance to speak to their modern readers.[143] Paul's metaphorical language might in fact be more readily understandable to some readers than Engberg-Pedersen's own abstract model.

At a thematic level, I concentrate on the question of the self, and I describe what the self is about in Paul's letter to the Romans. I stay closer to

---

[141] Engberg-Pedersen, *Paul and the Stoics*, 86.

[142] See Engberg-Pedersen, *Paul and the Stoics*, 87: "the basic difference between the two approaches [the narrative approach and Engberg-Pedersen's] is between imaginatively entering the world-view that Paul is articulating – and watching from the outside." Later, Engberg-Pedersen explains that he is looking for the logical pattern of Paul's thought: "the search was for a kind of logical pattern that would be both sufficiently close to Paul's own level of discourse for it to avoid *reducing* the Pauline text unduly and also *sufficiently removed* from it for it genuinely to *illuminate to us* what is being said and done in the Pauline text." (128)

[143] See Paul Ricœur, *La Métaphore vive* (Paris: Seuil, 1975), for example 11: "la métaphore est le processus rhétorique par lequel le discours libère le pouvoir que certaines fictions comportent de redécrire la réalité."

Paul's text in developing categories to describe how Paul tries to construct the identity of his addressees.

Engberg-Pedersen, although he presents an explicit historical reading of Paul, does so through his use of Stoic philosophy. As such he could also be discussed in the next category, namely, authors who read Paul in conversation with philosophers. Before turning to these works, it seems appropriate to summarize my position towards historical engagements of Paul and the philosophers. I do not offer a historical reconstruction of the way Paul used ancient philosophy or Jewish literature. Nor do I show that Paul was a philosopher. Rather, I explore how Paul's thought can be put into conversation with current debate about the question of the self

My discussion of Bultmann and of foucaultian readings of Paul has already touched upon approaches which could be classified as more theological for lack of a better word. Two more books need to be discussed in relationship to my own work.

John L. Meech

In *Paul in Israel's Story*,[144] Meech's purpose in reading Paul appears remarkably close to my own: "to reconstruct the kind of self presupposed in Paul's letters, I explore the relation between Paul's self-understanding and the story he tells to identify his community."[145] In addition, Meech also engages modern philosophy, since he uses Ricœur as his interlocutor to construct his ontology of the self. But my project, as will become clear in the subsequent discussion of Meech's work, departs from his in three aspects, which I can present now in preliminary fashion. First, my understanding of the story told in Paul's letters and particularly in Romans, is different. Also, my method for reading Paul is at odds with Meech's. Finally, my purpose and my methodology for setting up a conversation with modern philosophy are in disagreement with Meech's.

Meech announces four aims for his work[146] but it seems possible to say that his broad purpose is to show that there is a continuity between us and Paul in our understanding of the self.[147] To show this continuity, Meech

---

[144] John L. Meech, *Paul in Israel's Story: Self and Community at the Cross* (Oxford: Oxford University Press, 2006).

[145] Meech, *Paul in Israel's Story*, 17.

[146] Meech, *Paul in Israel's Story*, 4: "This conversation [with postmodern philosophy and the new perspective on Paul] centers around four major aims: 'to locate our interpretations of Paul in a history of interpretation; to provide contextual theologies that will let our interpretations address the church; to let Paul speak again to the church about its relation to Judaism; and, most important, to embrace Paul in one community as another whose concerns sometimes differ from ours'."

[147] Meech, *Paul in Israel's Story*, 71: "... if Paul is not to disappear as a concrete other, then we must interpret Paul's horizon, interpret our own horizon, and narrate the con-

constructs a correspondence between Paul's communal self as he sees it displayed in Paul's letters and his own ontology of the self based on Bultmann and Ricœur. First, he discusses the story Paul tells in his letters and defines it as the story of Israel.[148] The self in this story is seen as strongly communal. In fact, Meech accepts Bruce Malina's descriptions of first century persons as dyadic persons, needing another to know who they are. For the individual Jew, Meech argues that Torah plays this role of constitutive other.[149] For Meech, in Paul's life, the constitutive other moves from Torah to Christ, but in both cases, the engagement with Torah or Christ is mediated through community.[150]

In an excursus focusing on critical engagement with Bultmann, Meech argues that there is no necessity to demythologize Paul's communal personality.[151] In fact, Meech is seeking to demonstrate "a historical kinship between Paul's sense of self and ours."[152] To affirm Paul's relevance, he needs an understanding of the self closely related to a community. Ricœur, particularly in *Oneself as Another*, offers him the basic foundation for this understanding. Once Ricœur's work has been completed with a role given to community, Meech is able to present an ontology of the self in community which he uses to bridge the historical gap with Paul. It allows Meech to argue for a close proximity, at least in thought, with Paul.[153] At the end of the analysis, even the historical distance with Paul seems to be abolished, through community and through the work of the spirit: "Paul can speak again in our interpretations because we live with him in the community of the living and dead in Christ and because the Spirit of Christ speaks in our conversation."[154]

As I already mentioned, despite Meech's purpose being closely related to my own, I differ from his work on three main points. There are two important methodological differences between Meech's study and mine. First, in my reading of Paul, I focus on one letter in its continuity, aiming to stay

---

tinuity between the two as one historical community through time," also 16: "Ultimately, what is called for is a genealogy of selfhood that narrates the historical shift from Paul's understanding of selfhood to ours."

[148] See Meech, *Paul in Israel's Story*, 17: "Paul's story trades on a common Jewish pattern that N. T. Wright identifies as retelling Adam's story as story about Israel."

[149] Meech, *Paul in Israel's Story*, 18.

[150] See Meech, *Paul in Israel's Story*, 37.

[151] See Meech, *Paul in Israel's Story*, 44 and 45.

[152] See Meech, *Paul in Israel's Story*, 46.

[153] Meech recognizes that there is a distance between us and Paul: " to correlate the ontology of the self in community with Paul's communal self is to affirm what we share with Paul while acknowledging our real distance from him," (*Paul in Israel's Story*, 129) but in his actual analysis, he does not address this distance directly.

[154] Meech, *Paul in Israel's Story*, 129.

close to Paul's way of thinking and to avoid picking passages here and there to craft an abstract and essential compendium of his thought. Meech analyzes three passages in Paul's letters (Rom 3:21–26; Rom 7; Gal 3:10–14) and his orientation in his reading is more philosophical and theological than exegetical. As a result, his treatment of Paul remains somewhat superficial and indirect. My reading of Paul aims to be more precise and thorough.

Second, still at the methodological level, in setting up the conversation with modern philosophy, I am to some extent in agreement with Meech, since I also affirm that it is possible to introduce Paul as a valid conversation partner in modern philosophy. However, in contrast to Meech, I want to at least leave open the possibility that Paul's thought is no longer what is needed to define a modern understanding of the self. At the minimum, the option of disagreement needs to be left open. Furthermore, I do not presuppose a historical continuity with Paul's thought about self-understanding. For a critical and scientific analysis of Paul to be valid, one cannot argue that the historical distance that separates us from Paul can be bridged through the work of the spirit. Rather, one needs to be aware of the doors one closes when choosing a particular understanding of the self. One of the purposes of the conversation with Foucault is to show what is at stake for our understanding of the self when we side with Paul or with Foucault. Differences and incompatibilities need to be affirmed as much as convergences and parallels. If not, one runs the risk of deceiving oneself in thinking that nothing has changed in the history of thought since the first century. Finally, in my use of philosophy, I limit myself to the thought of Foucault and I do not try to complete or ameliorate his thinking. Meech creates an amalgam between Ricœur and Bultmann to meet his own need. I prefer to stay with one philosopher, and use him as conversation partner in my attempt to problematize the question of the self.

Third, I do not understand the story that Paul tells as being exclusively about Israel. Clearly, Israel plays a central role in Paul's thinking and Paul does reengage his own past as a Jew and the past of Israel extensively in his letters. However, I am convinced that the story behind at least Romans is broader and concerns the continuing relationship of God with human beings, Jews and non-Jews alike.

Paul W. Gooch
Gooch comes to Paul as a philosopher; he describes his book[155] as "the product of philosophical activity practiced on a biblical writer."[156] Gooch's

---

[155] Paul W. Gooch, *Partial Knowledge: Philosophical Studies in Paul* (Notre Dame, Ind.: University of Notre Dame Press, 1987)

[156] Gooch, *Partial Knowledge*, vii.

methodological interest, which seeks to establish whether Paul's statements can be characterized as right or wrong, reflects this philosophical dimension. In Gooch's case, "philosophy is used as a tool upon an important biblical text in order to expose facets of its meaning."[157] Through several case studies of passages in 1 Corinthians, Gooch proposes an assessment of Paul's arguments about knowledge and ethics for example. He also proposes an evaluation of the consistency and compatibility of Paul's beliefs with the ongoing conversations in philosophy of religion.

I share Gooch's interest in interpretation and in seeing how Paul fares in modern philosophical conversation. However, I read Paul differently, with a concentration on the narrative structure of his letter to the Romans and I pursue the analysis of another topic. Because of these differences, Gooch's case studies of 1 Corinthians, despite being interesting in their own right, have little bearing on my own work. Gooch's book provides a good transition to the works of philosophers engaging Paul. Gooch's reading of Paul retains a strong historical and exegetical dimension, but it is already directed towards involvement with philosophical discussions.[158] This is even more the case for the works of Alain Badiou and Giorgio Agamben,[159] philosophers who directly read Paul.

Alain Badiou
Born in 1937 in Rabat (Algeria), Alain Badiou (1937–) is as much a philosophical figure in France as a political one. On the political side, he is known as a militant for leftist movements. In the late 1960s he participated in a Maoist and Communist movement,[160] a heritage he still embraces. On

---

[157] Gooch, *Partial Knowledge*, 11.

[158] Because of its title, it seems that William S. Campbell's book, *Paul and the Creation of Christian Identity* (New York: T&T Clark, 2006) should also be reviewed in this category. However, his work is concerned mainly with a historical reconstruction of Paul's responsibility in the construction of a Christian identity, distinct from a Jewish or pagan identity.

[159] In addition to these two names, philosophers interested in Paul and New Testament scholars preoccupied with the sudden interest in Paul displayed by philosophers usually add the names of Slavoj Žižek, *The Puppet and the Dwarf: The Perverse Core of Christianity* (Cambridge, Mass.: The MIT Press, 2003) and Jacob Taubes, *The Political Theology of Paul* (trans. D. Hollander; Stanford: Stanford University Press, 2004). For my limited purpose, it is sufficient to engage Badiou and Agamben's work, even though Žižek's work in particular plays an important role for thinkers discussing the intersection between Paul and Foucault. John D. Caputo and Linda Martín Alcoff just published a collection of articles which engage Paul's destiny among contemporary philosophers. It comprises articles by philosophers (among them Badiou and Žižek) and New Testament scholars. See *Saint Paul among the Philosophers* (Bloomington, Ind.: Indiana University Press, 2009).

[160] UCFML (Union des communistes de France marxistes-léninistes)

the philosophical side, he shows a keen interest for mathematics, which are used to construct his main philosophical concepts.[161]

For Badiou, reading Paul is like reading a classic. In *Saint Paul*,[162] the three first chapters explain why and how an atheist philosopher can read Paul. Badiou is interested in Paul because Paul takes truth away from the communitarian hold.[163] He plays a determining role in the possibility of funding universalism and helps Badiou complete a project that is dear to him: "séparer durement chaque processus de vérité de l'historicité 'culturelle' où l'opinion prétend le dissoudre: telle est l'opération où Paul nous guide."[164] Because of this connection with Paul, Badiou can claim Paul as a contemporary and abrogate the historical distance that separates him from Paul.[165] In this sense Paul is read as a classic, because of the timeless value of his thought. Badiou's reading focuses entirely on the universal dimension of Paul's thought: "ce qu'il revient en propre à Paul d'avoir établi est qu'il n'y a fidélité à un tel événement que dans la résiliation des particularismes communautaires et la détermination d'un sujet-de-vérité qui indistingue l'Un et le 'pour tous'."[166] To put it shortly, Badiou think

---

[161] Among Badiou's work, one should note: *L'être et l'événement* (Paris: Seuil, 1988; in English: *Being and Event* [trans. O. Feltham; London: Continuum, 2005]); *Théorie du Sujet* (Paris: Seuil, 1982); *Manifeste pour la philosophie* (Paris: Seuil, 1989; in English: *Manifesto for Philosophy* [trans. N. Madarasz; Albany, N.Y.: State University of New York Press, 1999]), and more recently, *Logiques des mondes: L'être et l'événement 2* (Paris: Seuil, 2006; in English: *Logics of Worlds: Being and Event 2* [trans. A. Toscano; New York: Continuum, 2009]). Badiou has also published works of literature and drama.

[162] Alain Badiou, *Saint Paul: La fondation de l'universalisme* (Paris: Presses Universitaires de France, 1997; in English: *Saint Paul: The Foundation of Universalism* [trans. R. Brassier; Stanford: Stanford University Press, 2003]).

[163] Badiou, *Saint Paul*, 6: "le geste inouï de Paul est de soustraire la vérité à l'emprise communautaire, qu'il s'agisse d'un peuple, d'une cité, d'un empire, d'un territoire, ou d'une classe sociale. Ce qui est vrai (ou juste, c'est en l'occurrence la même chose) ne se laisse renvoyer à aucun ensemble objectif, ni selon sa cause, ni selon sa destination."

[164] Badiou, *Saint Paul*, 7.

[165] Badiou, *Saint Paul*, 38: "Mais en dépit de tout, quand on lit Paul, on est stupéfait du peu de traces laissées dans sa prose par l'époque, les genres et les circonstances. Il y a là, sous l'impératif de l'événement, quelque chose de dru et d'intemporel, quelque chose qui précisément parce qu'il s'agit de destiner une pensée à l'universel *dans sa singularité surgissante*, mais indépendamment de toute anecdote, nous est intelligible sans avoir à recourir à de lourdes médiations historiques (ce qui est loin d'être le cas pour nombre de passages des Évangiles, sans même parler de l'opaque Apocalypse)." Even though Badiou also suppresses the historical distance that separates him from Paul, I believe he does it in a manner very different from Meech (see above). He considers Paul a contemporary because of their closeness in thought and because of the possibility of still understanding the essence of his thought even two thousand years later. Badiou does not invoke continuity or the work of the spirit to justify his feeling of immediacy concerning Paul. He remains in the world of text and ideas.

[166] Badiou, *Saint Paul*, 116.

his own thought with Paul. He analyzes Paul under the category of universalism because this is what he finds remarkable in Paul. He does not claim that he understands Paul in a historical manner, or in a manner that is applicable to Pauline exegesis but he does affirm that he sees something in Paul that is directly relevant for modern philosophical thought.

In this dimension, I find myself in some proximity to Badiou's own work. What is particularly interesting – and perhaps challenging for New Testament studies – lies in the fact that Badiou simply asserts the pertinence of Paul's thought for our own times, with no historical or critical mediation. At some points in his analysis, Badiou makes use of some results of historico-critical analysis of Paul, for example when he distinguishes between authentic Pauline letters and deutero-Pauline material or when he discusses Paul's position towards women, but for the bulk of his analysis, he works with the assumption that Paul is evidently still relevant for modern and indeed postmodern intellectual discourse.

Clearly my reading of Paul is indebted to the exegetical tradition – in its historical, critical and literary dimensions. Because of this, the historical distance that separates us from Paul plays a role in my analysis, and I am dependent upon historical and critical mediation in a heavier manner than Badiou. This allows me to give more space to Paul's own voice and to avoid using him uniquely to develop my own thoughts. At the same time, Badiou's interest in Paul and willingness to see him as a classic functions as a reminder that Paul's letters need to be read not only as historical documents dependent upon contingent circumstances but as writings that contain sufficient intellectual reflection to spark philosophical interest in them.[167]

Giorgio Agamben

An Italian philosopher born in 1942 in Rome, Agamben (1942–) is principally influenced by Walter Benjamin (1892-1940),[168] Jacob Taubes (1923–1987), Carl Schmitt (1888–1985) and Michel Foucault. He is also a specialist of Karl Marx (1818–1883) and Martin Heidegger (1889–1976). His philosophical work addresses various questions, for example the question

---

[167] The renewed interest in Paul by contemporary continental philosophers, such as Badiou, Agamben and Žižek is generally explained by their political projects. Paul, especially for Badiou and for Žižek, is used to enliven a moribund political left. See Matthew Chrulew, "The Pauline Ellipsis in Foucault's Genealogy of Christianity," *Journal for Cultural and Religious Theory* 11 (Winter 2010): 1–15. Cited 12 April 2012. Online: http://www.jcrt.org/archives/11.1/chrulew.pdf

[168] Agamben is the editor of Benjamin's complete work in Italian.

of language, the nature of human beings and the theology of Paul. He is also interested in political issues.[169]

In his commentary on the first verse of Romans,[170] Agamben puts Paul into conversation with various philosophers, but he also offers an interpretation of Paul through philosophical categories. He uses what some philosophers wrote to interpret the text of Paul. Thus, there is a double movement in Agamben's philosophical commentary: he shows how Paul has influenced some philosophers (in particular Benjamin) and he uses some philosophers to explain concepts in Paul. His philosophical reading of Paul is centered on the messianic dimension of Paul's letters. He states the purpose of the book – born out of seminars given in various schools – in the following manner: "first and foremost, this seminar proposes to restore Paul's Letters to the status of the fundamental messianic text for the Western tradition."[171] Here too a basic relevance of Paul for modern intellectual thought is presumed: "[our seminar] seeks to understand the meaning of the word *christos*, that is 'Messiah.' What does it mean to live in the Messiah, and what is the messianic life? What is the structure of messianic time? These questions, meaning Paul's questions, must also be ours."[172] Agamben discusses these questions through a careful reading of the first verse of the epistle to the Romans, a discussion that leads him to analyze various issues in the letter (the language of Paul, the concept of call, the separation between Jews and pagans). In these analyses, his secondary literature is represented by various philosophers (Weber, Marx, Heidegger, Hegel and Benjamin are used in depth), which allow Agamben to present lines of development from Paul to certain philosophers, even when the influence of Paul might have been unconscious.

---

[169] Agamben's major works include: *Homo sacer: Il potere sovrano e la nuda vita* (Turin: Einaudi, 1995; in English: *Homo Sacer: Sovereign Power and Bare Life* [trans. D. Heller-Roazen; Stanford: Stanford University Press, 1998]); *La comunità che viene*, (Turin: Einaudi, 1990; in English: *The Coming Community* [trans. M. Hardt; Minneapolis: University of Minnesota Press, 1993]) and *Stato di eccezione* (Turin: Bollati Boringhieri, 2003; in English: *State of Exception* [trans. K. Attell; Chicago: University of Chicago Press, 2005]).

[170] Giorgio Agamben, *Il tempo che resta: Un commento alla Lettera ai Romani* (Turin: Bollati Boringhieri, 2000; in English: *The Time that Remains. A Commentary on the Letter to the Romans* [trans. P. Dailey; Stanford: Stanford University Press, 2005]). The commentary in its structure focuses on the first verse of the letter. However, in the discussion of each word of the first verse, Agamben analyzes several concepts that appear only later in Paul's letter. As a result, his work is much more comprehensive than just a discussion of the first verse.

[171] Agamben, *The Time that Remains*, 1.

[172] Agamben, *The Time that Remains*, 18.

A good example is Agamben's analysis of the verb καταργέω and its "posthumous life ... in the philosophical tradition."[173] Agamben indicates that Luther's translation of the verb is *aufheben*, "the very word that harbors the double meaning of abolishing and conserving (*aufbewahren* and *aufhören lassen*) used by Hegel as a foundation for his dialectics."[174] For Agamben, Luther is aware of the verb's double meaning and thus it "means that in all likelihood the term acquires its particular facets through the translation of the Pauline letters, leaving Hegel to pick it up and develop it."[175] Agamben then argues for a strong involvement of Hegel and his successors with messianic themes.[176]

The particular orientation of Agamben's commentary towards dialogue with philosophy produces a creative and dynamic interpretation of Paul, one that is truly a philosophical reading of Paul. Agamben, like Badiou, goes beyond what I do. I do not show that Paul can be found behind Foucault's thought (even if sometimes he might well be) and I do not use Foucault to explain Paul, even though some of the material found in Foucault might work creatively in my reading of Paul. Rather I construct the problem of the construction of the self in dialogue with Paul and Foucault, giving room to the thought of both authors, and seeing how my interaction with them shapes the understanding of the self.

Finally, I need to discuss works that pioneer a narrative approach to Paul.

Richard B. Hays
Richard Hays' book, *The Faith of Jesus Christ*, provides the stepping stone for any analysis interested in finding stories in Paul.[177] *The Faith of Jesus Christ* exposes several elements that help my own work in Romans. First, Hays distinguishes the concept of story from the concept of narrative, an important definition when working with letters that take the form of discourse. Narrative, as a noun, is used exclusively for explicit narrations[178] (for example, in Paul, one could see Rom 7 as such a narrative). Story

---

[173] Agamben, *The Time that Remains*, 99.

[174] Agamben, *The Time that Remains*, 99.

[175] Agamben, *The Time that Remains*, 99.

[176] Agamben, *The Time that Remains*, 100: "if this genealogy of *Aufhebung* that I am putting forth is correct, then not only is Hegelian thought involved in a tightly knit hermeneutical struggle with the messianic – in the sense that all of its determining concepts are more or less conscious interpretations and secularizations of messianic themes – but this also holds for modernity, by which I intend the epoch that is situated under the sign of the dialectical *Aufhebung*."

[177] Richard B. Hays, *The Faith of Jesus Christ: The Narrative Substructure of Galatians 3:1–4:11* (2d ed.; Dearborn, Mich.: Dove Booksellers – Eerdmans, 2002).

[178] Hays, *The Faith of Jesus Christ*, 18.

however does not necessarily refer to an explicitly narrated text. Rather, "it can refer to the ordered series of events which forms the basis for various possible narrations."[179] This means that a story does not necessarily have a narrated form.[180] Because of the specificity of the English language however, the "only adjective available that means 'having the form or character of a story' is the adjective 'narrative'."[181] This is how Hays defines the terms and this is how I employ them as well.

Second, Hays also plays an important role in addressing the obvious methodological difficulty of finding stories in a discursive genre (the letter). According to Hays, in some cases, discourses are governed by a story which is only referenced in allusive ways. In these cases, "the discourse would be unintelligible without the story, because the discourse exists and has meaning only as an unfolding of the meaning of the story."[182] Hays first uses Northrop Frye's understanding of *dianoia* to support this assertion.[183] To put it simply, *dianoia* is the theme of a particular story, and it can be expressed through *mythos*, through a particular plot. The *dianoia* is integral to the narrative form; it cannot be detached from it, since it is first recognized in the narrative form. In the discursive form, the *dianoia* can be explained abstractedly from the particular form of the *mythos*, but the meaning of the *dianoia* is dependent upon the narrative in which it was found.[184] In this way, the *dianoia* governs the way the discourse repeats and critiques it. When discussing the *dianoia* of a particular narrative – even in discursive form – one can never completely abstract oneself from the narrative that supports this particular *dianoia*.[185]

Hays draws three conclusions from this understanding of the relationship between story and discourse. It is worthwhile repeating them:

– There can be an organic relationship between stories and reflective discourse because stories have an inherent configurational dimension (*dianoia*) which not only permits but also demands restatements and interpretation in non-narrative language.

---

[179] Hays, *The Faith of Jesus Christ*, 18.

[180] See Hays, *The Faith of Jesus Christ*, 18.

[181] Hays, *The Faith of Jesus Christ*, 19.

[182] Hays, *The Faith of Jesus Christ*, 22.

[183] Hays, *The Faith of Jesus Christ*, 22–23.

[184] See Hays, *The Faith of Jesus Christ*, 22–23.

[185] Ricœur, although using a different language, shares this account of what happens in the relationship between story and discourse. He distinguishes between an episodic dimension characteristic of narrative and a configurational dimension ("The Narrative Function," *Semeia* 13 (1978): 177–202). Ricœur understands Aristotle's *mythos* as the way the story is organized, the plot of the story. To reflect upon the story is inherent to the story itself. In this way, discourse can be seen as a way to configure or reconfigure elements of a story. According to Hays, following Ricœur, "a Pauline letter could be understood as a 'new speech act' that attempts to rearticulate in discursive language the configurational dimension of the gospel story." (Hays, *The Faith of Jesus-Christ*, 25)

– The reflective statement does not simply repeat the plot (*mythos*) of the story; nonetheless, the story shapes and constrains the reflective process because the *dianoia* can never be entirely abstracted from the story in which it is manifested and apprehended.
– Hence, when we encounter this type of reflective discourse, it is legitimate and possible to inquire about the story in which it is rooted.[186]

Hays' definitions of story and narrative and his careful distinction between story and discourse opened up the Pauline corpus to narrative analysis. My work stands in this current. However, I do not follow Hays in the methodology he chose for his work on Galatians. Hays himself, in the preface to the second edition of *The Faith of Jesus Christ*, distances himself from the methodological apparatus he used in his book and insists that A. J. Greimas's structuralism is "now as thoroughly superseded as disco music, or as my Smith-Corona typewriter."[187] What matters is not the method used but "the message of the text, the story that it tells and interprets."[188] This is close to what I do with Romans. I look for a story that is being told and interpreted in Romans. I also find myself in agreement with Hays when he identifies the power of story to "lead hearers into an experience of identification with the story's protagonist."[189] Through this experience of identification, "stories can function as vehicles for the creation of community."[190] This dimension of story is at the heart of my analysis of the story told in Romans and its effect on the letter's addressees.[191]

Closely related to the work of Hays is the one of N. T. Wright, who still holds onto the structuralist approach in *The New Testament and the People of God*.[192]

N. T. Wright

Wright is one of the earliest defendants of a narrative approach to Paul. He develops elements of it in *The New Testament and the People of God*.

---

[186] Hays, *The Faith of Jesus Christ*, 28.

[187] Hays, *The Faith of Jesus Christ*, xxvii.

[188] Hays, *The Faith of Jesus Christ*, xxvii.

[189] Hays, *The Faith of Jesus Christ*, 214.

[190] Hays, *The Faith of Jesus Christ*, 214.

[191] Hays identified this as one of the possible implications of his study for Pauline interpretation; see *The Faith of Jesus Christ*, 215: "The phenomenon of 'participation' in narrative is a complex one in its own right; this language is usually employed with regard to a kind of momentary exercise of the imagination that projects the reader/hearer into a *fictional* world. In the case of Paul, the 'participation' language clearly envisions a more permanent and 'real' transformation of the hearers' existence on the basis of a story which is solemnly held to be nonfiction. Any thoroughgoing attempt to re-think Paul's soteriology with the aid of the category of story-participation would have to address this issue. That task lies, unfortunately, beyond the scope of this inquiry."

[192] N. T. Wright, *The New Testament and the People of God* (Minneapolis: Fortress Press, 1992).

Wright's work is mentioned here because of the great importance he accords to stories in his reading of the New Testament in general and in his interpretation of Paul in particular. In *The New Testament and the People of God*, Wright's task involves "the discernment and analysis, at one level or another, of first-century stories and their implications."[193] For him, a narrative approach to the New Testament allows to keep together three dimensions implicated in a reading of biblical texts: the theological, the historical and the literary dimension.[194] In relationship to Paul's letters, Wright sees the apostle as developing a variant of the Jewish story: "[w]ithin all his letters, though particularly in Romans and Galatians, we discover a larger implied narrative... [T]his larger narrative is the Jewish story, but with a subversive twist at almost every point."[195] In this story, Jesus plays the role of the agent of change,[196] but the basic structure of the story remains the story of Israel. In a similar manner, Paul's own personal story is but "a deliberate and subversive variant on the Jewish story of the devout Pharisee."[197] Through his analysis of Paul's narrative world, Wright emphasizes continuity with the Jewish world and with Israel's story.

Clearly, even after his encounter with Christ, Paul remained deeply anchored in Jewish traditions and in the stories connected with Israel. This dimension of continuity is worth mentioning.[198] In contrast to Wright, I stay closer to the text of Romans and I do not try to abstract a wider story, which stands behind everything Paul does and writes. Rather, I am interested in what Paul does in Romans with the story he is telling there. In Romans, the story Paul tells is the story of God's relationship with the world. He uses Jewish traditions to tell it but, in Romans at least, Paul does more than subvert the story of Israel, although he certainly also does that. The story told in Romans aims at creating a new self-understanding for its

---

[193] Wright, *The New Testament and the People of God*, 79.

[194] See Wright, *The New Testament and the People of God*, *passim*, but for example, 32: "'Story,' I shall argue, can help us in the first instance to articulate a critical-realist epistemology, and can then be put to wider uses in the study of literature, history and theology," also 121: "the aim of this chapter is to suggest what might be involved in a 'theological' reading that does not bypass the 'literary' and 'historical' readings, but rather enhances them ..."

[195] Wright, *The New Testament and the People of God*, 405. For a presentation of the story, see Wright, *The New Testament and the People of God*, 405–407.

[196] See Wright, *The New Testament and the People of God*, 407: "What had made the difference, clearly, was Jesus; or, more fully, Jesus and the divine spirit."

[197] Wright, *The New Testament and the People of God*, 405.

[198] For a narrative approach that emphasizes the element of discontinuity in Paul's story see: John M. G. Barclay, "Paul's Story: Theology as Testimony," in *Narrative Dynamics in Paul: A Critical Assessment* (ed. B. W. Longenecker; Louisville, Ky.: Westminster John Knox, 2002), 133–156.

addressees. This change is told in some parts through the use of Jewish scripture and tradition.[199]

One could add Witherington's book, *Paul's Narrative Thought World*,[200] to this review of major contributions to narrative reading of Pauline letters. Witherington argues that "Paul's thought, including both theology and ethics, is grounded in a grand narrative and in a story that hat continued to develop out of that narrative."[201] In retrieving this story through his reading of Paul's letters, Witherington is close to what Wright advocates in *The New Testament and the People of God*, even though his understanding of the content of the grand narrative is somewhat different than Wright's.[202] As such, my approach differs from Witherington's in the same manner than it differed from Wright's. I do not abstract a broad story that can then be found behind Paul's entire theology. I look for the story that is told in Romans, and how this story affects the identity of the people who hear it. Witherington's interpretation of the grand narrative behind Paul's epistles is closely related to categories that are traditionally connected to a theology of Paul.[203] I present a reading of Romans rather than a theology of Paul.

Since Hays and Wright, other works have engaged stories in Paul without the help of structuralism. Several commentaries on Romans make an effort to read the epistle in a continuous manner and pay attention to the concept of story within Romans, paving the way for this study.

---

[199] David G. Horrell, "Paul's Narratives or Narrative Substructure: The Significance of 'Paul's Story'," in Longenecker, *Narrative Dynamics in Paul*, 157–171 develops this same question and puts more weight on the continuity in Paul's thought, 162: "Paul may present us with a personal story of radical disjuncture and with the rhetoric of a demolished and reconstituted self, but his frequent references to the scriptures and the language in which he describes his experiences and convictions, the identity of the members of the churches, and so on, suggest that this new self-identity has more continuity with the past than the rhetoric of interruption might suggest."

[200] Ben Witherington III, *Paul's Narrative Thought World: The Tapestry of Tragedy and Triumph* (Louisville, Ky.: Westminster John Knox, 1994).

[201] Witherington, *Paul's Narrative Thought World*, 2.

[202] See Witherington, *Paul's Narrative Thought World*, 7, n. 14. Witherington also abandons the structuralist method.

[203] See for example the parts of the story Witherington identifies: part 1 is the story of the fall (sin), part 2 is concerned with the role of Israel (the law), part 3 looks at Christ crucified (Christology), part 4 continues the discussion about the identity of Christ, part 5 discusses "the end and beyond" (eschatology) and part 6 takes up the story of Christians (ecclesiology).

A. *Katherine Grieb*

If Hays's book helps me clarify certain methodological difficulties related to narrative readings of Paul's letters, Grieb's commentary on Romans[204] functions as an important partner in my interpretation of the letter. In her commentary, Grieb explains Paul's argument about the righteousness of God through Paul's use of a great story including many smaller stories: "It is my claim in this book that Romans is Paul's sustained argument for the righteousness of God and that the best way to untangle Paul's complex argument is to understand it as built on a great story – the story of what God has done in Christ – that includes many other stories."[205] In fact, she argues that "Romans is best read as the continuous story of what God has done in Jesus Christ and what God continues to do in the lives of those who are baptized into Christ Jesus."[206] She then reads the letter in a narrative manner and identifies stories at three levels: 1) the grand story of God's action in Jesus Christ already mentioned, 2) the smaller stories (story of Paul, story of the Roman churches, story of Abraham, Sarah and Isaac, of disobedient Adam, etc.[207]) included in this larger story and 3) the stories of the Hebrew Bible that Paul retells or to which he refers.[208]

Her reading of Paul through these three levels allows her to reflect on how the story of God saving a lost world through Christ connects to the rest of Paul's argument. This takes two dimensions: how does it connect with Paul's concern to show God's righteousness, God's faithfulness to Israel in the process of including the Gentiles?[209] And how is it related to Paul's desire for unity between Jewish Christ believers and Gentile Christ believers in Rome?[210] Grieb argues that Paul takes care of these two questions through his use of stories and she proceeds to show this through a continuous, narrative reading of Romans. For example, she indicates in her third chapter how Abraham's story is used by Paul to establish God's "re-

---

[204] Grieb, *The Story of Romans*.

[205] Grieb, *The Story of Romans*, xii.

[206] Grieb, *The Story of Romans*, 35.

[207] See Grieb, *The Story of Romans*, 17: "The many smaller stories are those of Paul and of the Roman churches (1:1–17 and 15:14–33); of how God saved the lost world (1:18–3:31); of faithful Abraham, Sarah and Isaac (4:1–25); of disobedient Adam (and Eve) retold from Genesis 3 (Rom 5–8, especially 5:12–21 and 7:7–11); of Jesus Christ's obedient death on the cross (throughout, but especially 5:12–21); of the Christian baptized into the death of Jesus (6:1–23 and 8:1–39); of creation and its fulfillment (8:18–30); and of Paul's missionary preaching, Gentile responsiveness, and Israel's unbelief (9–11). And there is the ongoing story of what God is doing in the Roman churches and in Paul's upcoming mission to Spain (12–16, especially 14:1–15:13) and, finally, the story of Paul's present journey to Jerusalem and his hopes to visit Rome (15:14–33)."

[208] See Grieb, *The Story of Romans*, 34.

[209] See Grieb, *The Story of Romans*, 45.

[210] See Grieb, *The Story of Romans*, 45.

liability and trustworthiness."[211] Three observable facts points to this:[212] God keeps God's promises (birth of Isaac); God rescues the poor and the one in need (Isaac); God "makes the story come out right in the end"[213] (God provides a sacrifice instead of Isaac, God vindicates Jesus).

At the same time, she insists that the story that Paul tells in Romans has not yet met its ending. It will near its ending when the churches in Rome accept the implications of what Paul writes to them. Paul aims to show that the story of what God has done in Christ "is related to his own story and to the story of his churches, including the congregation at Rome that he hopes will support his work."[214] The last chapters of Romans (Romans 12–15) invite to imitate Christ in order to bring about unity in the Roman churches. Grieb argues that the story will reach its true ending only when the members of the Roman house churches come together in unity and support Paul's mission to Spain.[215]

Grieb's narrative reading of Paul is articulated around two dimensions of story. First, it pays attention to the descriptive dimension of a story. When she focuses her attention on how the story of God's action in the world through Christ demonstrates God's righteousness, she pays close attention to the descriptive power of the story, to what the story says about God's character. When she pays more attention to the reactions that Paul hopes to elicit in Rome through his use of the story of God's action in the world through Christ, she focuses on the prescriptive potential of a story, on what the story can do to the persons who listen to it. Regarding the problem of unity inside the Roman churches, the story that Paul uses is expected to have an effect on Paul's addressees.

I am interested primarily in that dimension of story. Clearly, the fact that in its descriptive dimension, the story says something about its characters has an effect on its readers: if Paul's addressees are described as being in Christ, this surely must have an effect on how they behave towards each other. But, in contrast to Grieb, I concentrate less on God's character and more on the recipients of the story. My angle of approach differs from Grieb's in that I emphasize the way the letter works on its addressees and their self-understanding. In this dimension, I look for elements that contribute to a construction of the self of the readers, emphasizing the dynamic dimension of Paul's letter.

---

[211] Grieb, *The Story of Romans*, 52.

[212] See Grieb, *The Story of Romans*, 52.

[213] See Grieb, *The Story of Romans*, 52.

[214] See Grieb, *The Story of Romans*, 115.

[215] See Grieb, *The Story of Romans*, 117. I think it is necessary to include one more dimension to the open-ending of the story told in Romans. It concerns the eschatological ending of the story that will only come at the very end.

Luke T. Johnson

Johnson's commentary on Romans,[216] even if it does not label itself as a narrative reading of the letter, does argue for a continuous, literary interpretation of the letter. In particular, Johnson wants to pay close attention to the way Paul's argument unfolds in Romans. His reading focuses on the developing argument and avoids endless discussions of problems that, in the end, cannot be properly solved.[217] As a result, the commentary gives "a single, strong reading of Romans from beginning to end."[218] In this reading, Johnson attempts to fill the position both of implied and ideal readers. As implied readers, "we 'discover' the meaning of the text only as it unfolds."[219] In this position, attention is paid to the text in small units and in its details, particularly the language used, rather than to the text as a whole.[220] But Johnson also aims to be an ideal reader and "*this* reader has worked through the text many times before and has some ideas about where the argument is going."[221] In this case, some information about what comes next, or about how that particular sequence of text fits in the overall argument of the letter, is helpful and indeed necessary. In general, Romans is read "in sequence as a developing argument."[222]

This directing drive behind the reading is reflected in the structure of the commentary. It loosely follows the rhetorical pattern of the letter without however using the heavy methodological apparatus of rhetorical approaches.[223] Johnson divides the text in nine parts: 1) Greeting and thanksgiving (1:1–15), 2) Thesis (1:16–17), 3) Antithesis (1:18–3:20), 4) Thesis restated (3:21–31), 5) Example of Abraham (4), 6), Positive demonstration of thesis (5), 7) Answering objections (7–11), 8) Practical consequences (12–15:13), 9) Paul's plan (15:14–16:27).

Through this rhetorical pattern, Johnson presents a continuous reading that emphasizes the unity of the letter, especially the tight relationship between what is traditionally seen as the theological part of the letter (1–8, sometimes 1–11) and what is often labeled the ethical part of the letter (12–15, sometimes 11–15). Thus, Johnson agrees with approaches that of-

---

[216] Johnson, *Reading Romans*.

[217] See Johnson, *Reading Romans*, ix: "To attempt this sort of synthetic interpretation demands a certain willingness to take risks. It also means that many points that could be debated endlessly must finally be decided one way or another and then let go."

[218] Johnson, *Reading Romans*, ix.

[219] Johnson, *Reading Romans*, 19, see also 2–3.

[220] See Johnson, *Reading Romans*, 19: "We most approximate the implied readers when we hear the text read aloud bit by bit rather than when we apprehend it visually as a whole."

[221] Johnson, *Reading Romans*, 19.

[222] Johnson, *Reading Romans*, 3.

[223] See in contrast Jewett, *Romans*.

fer a corrective to the traditional reading of Romans as purely theological (particularly Stanley K. Stowers).[224] He affirms that Paul can "be read intelligibly as a moral philosopher of the first-century Hellenistic world, whose interest is in creating communities of character."[225]

Even though Johnson fully recognizes the importance of seeing a strong connection between 12–16 and 1–11, he is careful not to completely reject the obvious theological dimension of the letter. The simple fact that Romans is about God makes it a theological letter.[226] Johnson argues that it is also theological because it talks about the relationship humans can have with God, because it reflects on God's purpose in the world, because it tries to explain the consequences of Christ's story for human beings, and because it does all this in the language of critical thought.[227] Despite Johnson's conviction that Romans is aimed at developing the character of the community to which it is addressed, the theological dimension is not absent of his reading.

My own reading of Romans benefits from the close connection established by Johnson and others (Stowers, Engberg-Pedersen) between theology and moral exhortation. It is indicative of a recent movement in Pauline scholarship to accord more attention to the final chapters of Romans in the interpretation of the letter and my work is part of that attempt of retrieving the importance of 12–15 for a reading of Romans. Johnson's interpretation will serve as a partner in my reading of Romans, but I focus on one particular element of Paul's thought – how he constructs the self in Romans – whereas Johnson's purpose is broader. I also take a somewhat different methodological approach in my reading of Romans. Even though I pay attention to the developing argument in Romans, I look at it through Paul's use of story in this argument.

In this chapter, I have presented the manner in which the conversation between Paul and Foucault is put into place and how this conversation relates to various works in the study of Paul. In the following three chapters I turn to the conversation partners. Chapters two and three are devoted to Paul. In chapter two, I present a narrative reading of Romans, which enables me to focus on several passages of the letter that are particularly important to establish the categories which Paul uses to construct the self.

---

[224] See Johnson, *Reading Romans*, 9: "He [Stowers] argues that Romans should be seen primarily as a form of *moral exhortation* specifically directed at Gentile believers. Paul's concern was not 'theology,' but the shaping of a certain kind of community ethos." See Stanley K. Stowers, *A Rereading of Romans: Justice, Jews, and Gentiles* (New Haven, Conn.: Yale University Press, 1994).

[225] Johnson, *Reading Romans*, 9–10. See also Malherbe, *Paul and the Popular Philosophers*.

[226] See Johnson, *Reading Romans*, 10.

[227] See Johnson, *Reading Romans*, 10.

Chapter three offers a synthesis of these categories and, using Ricœur's narrative theory, develops them in philosophical language in order to establish the discussion with Foucault. It serves as a turning point towards problematizing the question of the construction of the self. Chapter four focuses on presenting Foucault's thought and concludes by establishing the categories of the self one can find in the writings of the French philosopher. The final chapter implements the conversation, discussing various concepts present in the work of both thinkers, and concluding by presenting the consequences of the dialogue for my own position and work as an interpreter. Presently, it is necessary to turn to the letter to the Romans.

Chapter 2

A Narrative Reading of Romans

A. Narrative Dimension of Romans

Despite the recent interest in seeing narrative dimensions in the Pauline letters – in the wake of Hays' *The Faith of Jesus Christ* – it is not self-evident to describe Paul's epistles as narrative writings. This is so true that Bruce Longenecker can affirm: "For the most part ... the Pauline corpus has been relatively immune from narrative study for obvious reason: Paul wrote letters, not narratives."[1] Certainly, as do most commentaries on the epistle, it is more appropriate, even if not correct, to describe Romans as a "tractate letter,"[2] as "diatribe,"[3] as a "work of Christian rhetoric,"[4] as Paul's "last will"[5] or, as Melanchthon wrote, "a compendium of Christian doctrine."[6] It seems clear, as Ben Witherington points out, that "on the surface of things, it might seem an exercise in frustration to talk about Paul's narrative thought world. After all, Paul's letters are full of practical advice and theological ideas, not stories."[7] Even if one is willing to call into question the fact that Paul is writing a doctrinal piece – as do most Pauline interpreters today – it remains clear that in Romans Paul is developing an argument and that his letter is fundamentally discursive in character. How can one look for a story in such a letter?

---

[1] Bruce W. Longenecker, "Narrative Interest in the Study of Paul: Retrospective and Prospective," in Longenecker, *Narrative Dynamics in Paul*, 3–16, here 3.

[2] Douglas J. Moo, *The Epistle to the Romans* (NICNT; Grand Rapids, Mich.: Eerdmans, 1996), 14: "Romans, then, is a tractate letter and has at its heart a general theological argument, or series of arguments."

[3] Bultmann, *Der Stil der paulinischen Predigt und die kynisch-stoische Diatribe*.

[4] Brendan Byrne, *Romans* (SP 6; Collegeville, Minn.: Liturgical Press, 1996), 4.

[5] Günther Bornkamm, "The Letter to the Romans as Paul's Last Will and Testament," *ABR* 11 (1963–1964): 2–14; repr. in *The Romans Debate* (ed. K. P. Donfried; rev. and enl. ed.; Peabody, Mass.: Hendrickson, 1991), 16–28.

[6] Philipp Melanchthon, *Loci Communes 1521. Werke in Auswahl 2.1* (ed. R. Stupperich; Gütersloh: Bertelsmann, 1952), 7.

[7] Witherington, *Paul's Narrative Thought World*, 2.

1. Methodology for a Narrative Reading of Paul

Narrative approaches to the letters of Paul, especially the work of Grieb, have shown that it is not necessary to have a complex methodological apparatus to identify narrative elements in the Pauline epistles.[8] Here, to introduce the narrative dimension of Romans, I use two elements that Ricœur derives from Aristotle concerning the definition of a story.

First, a story has a plot. Using Aristotle's *Poetics*, Ricœur affirms that story (*récit*) is precisely what Aristotle defines as *mythos*, the way facts are organized.[9] This organization of the facts is no slavish imitation of reality. On the contrary, it involves creative action. Indeed, through the organization of the facts, *mythos* indicates what Ricœur calls concordance.[10] Concordance means that events do not follow randomly but can be organized through a principle of causality, transforming events from being accidental to being likely. To create a story is to create meaning out of events that are seemingly haphazard.[11] For Ricœur, this is the "emploting" (*mise en intrigue*) of the story.[12] In this "emploting," the story triumphs over the discordance of events through concordance. However, Ricœur insists on the fact that the Aristotelian *mythos* is not purely a model of concordance.[13] It is rather "concordance discordante;" all the time, different occurrences –

---

[8] In fact, one sees that the methodological apparatus that Hays uses in *The Faith of Christ* becomes dated quickly and can thus be criticized as a methodological choice: see R. Barry Matlock, "The Arrow and the Web: Critical Reflections on a Narrative Approach to Paul," in Longenecker, *Narrative Dynamics in Paul*, 44–57, here 48: "It may have made sense – assuming a *theory* of narrative is what is wanted – for Hays, as doctoral student in the late 1970s and early 1980s, to turn to the narrative theory of Greimas. This choice is less obvious, however, twenty years later, for one setting out to select an approach to narrative among currently available options. It is not just that structuralism as a movement is no longer current. Structuralism, narratology, and semiotics themselves have not stood still since the narrative theory of the early Greimas. For that matter, Greimas himself appears to have moved on."

[9] Paul Ricœur, *Temps et récit vol. 1*, 62: "… nous appelons récit très exactement ce qu'Aristote appelle *muthos*, c'est-à-dire l'agencement des faits."

[10] Ricœur, *Temps et récit vol.1*, 65–66: "C'est d'abord la concordance que souligne la définition du *muthos* comme agencement des faits."

[11] See Ricœur, *Temps et récit vol. 1*, 70: "composer l'intrigue, c'est déjà faire surgir l'intelligible de l'accidentel, l'universel du singulier, le nécessaire ou le vraisemblable de l'épisodique."

[12] In his tripartite division of story, this is *mimesis* II. *Mimesis* I functions at a level before the story. In *mimesis* I, Ricœur analyzes the pre-comprehension of the world of action that precedes the readers' engagement with the text. *Mimesis* II designates the domain of the intrigue and plot properly. At this level, Ricœur looks at the processes used to create a story. It analyzes the construction of the *mythos*. *Mimesis* III is concerned with the effects the text has on its readers. For a detailed presentation of the triple *mimesis*, see Ricœur, *Temps et récit vol. 1*, esp. 85–129.

[13] Ricœur, *Temps et récit vol. 1*, 71.

notably frightening and pitiful events – threaten the concordance of the story.[14] Creating a story is a process of organizing different events in a plot. There is the possibility of finding a logic between different events.

Moreover, a plot can be divided in different sections. In his *Poetics*,[15] Aristotle indicates that the plot of a tragedy is articulated around two moments. There is a moment when things are set into motion (complication, tying, δέσις) and there is a moment when things come to an end (denouement, loosing, λύσις). In the middle of the tragedy, one can find an event that will transform things and mark the transition from complication to denouement. Aristotle calls it περιπέτεια, reversal.[16] These three moments structure a story around a beginning (complication), a middle (reversal) and an end (denouement). In relationship to the notion of plot, one can see that the "emploting" of a story occurs around these three moments. With these simple elements in mind, I raise the possibility that the obvious argumentative discourse of Romans works within a powerful and only partially hidden story.[17]

Second, Ricœur also expands the second element that Aristotle uses in his characterization of what a tragedy is, the notion of *ēthos*.[18] For Aristotle, *ēthos* is subordinated to *mythos*[19] and concerns the moral capacities of the characters involved in the plot. Aristotle indicates that these moral capacities can be either good or bad: "the objects of imitation are men in action, and these men must be either of a higher or a lower type (for moral character mainly answers to these divisions, goodness and badness being the distinguishing marks of moral differences)."[20]

It is possible to move further than Aristotle and to have *ēthos* play a role in the way a text affects its readers. Ricœur does precisely this in parts of *Time and Narrative* and more clearly in *Oneself as Another*. In the first volume of *Time and Narrative*, Ricœur establishes his reading hermeneu-

---

[14] Ricœur, *Temps et récit vol. 1*, 71.

[15] Aristotle, *Poetics*, 11.1, 18.1–3.

[16] See Edward Adams, "Paul's Story of God and Creation," in Longenecker, *Narrative Dynamics in Paul*, 19–43, here 23: "Theoretical models of narrative trajectory tend to follow Aristotle's division of plot structure into 'complication' ('tying' δέσις) and 'denouement' ('loosing' λύσις), around a key turning point, a 'reversal' (περιπέτεια);" and Daniel Marguerat, Yvan Bourquin, *La Bible se raconte: initiation à l'analyse narrative* (Paris – Geneva – Montreal: Cerf – Labor et Fides – Novalis, 1998), 54.

[17] See the comments already referred to in the previous chapter on the relationship between reflective discourse and narrative in Hays, *The Faith of Jesus Christ*, especially 21–29.

[18] In the *Poetics*, Aristotle defines six elements at work in a tragedy: plot (*mythos*), character (*ēthos*), thought, diction, song, and spectacle (see *Poetics*, 6).

[19] See Ricœur, *Oneself as Another*, 143: "The correlation between story told and character is simply postulated by Aristotle in the *Poetics*. It appears as such a close correlation there that it takes the form of subordination."

[20] Aristotle, *Poetics*, 2.

tics and, using Aristotle's *Poetics* as a starting point, he defines three steps
in his method: *mimesis* I, *mimesis* II and *mimesis* III.[21] I*Mimesis* III is of
particular interest here, especially in its relationship to the characters of a
story. In *mimesis* III, Ricœur discusses how the world of the text encounters the world of the reader.[22] He writes: "the decisive step in the direction
of a narrative conception of personal identity is taken when one passes
from the action to the character."[23] Such a perspective allows one to highlight the effects a text can have on its readers,[24] something that Ricœur develops in relationship to narrative identity and to characters in *Oneself as
Another*. My reading of the story in Romans will pay close attention to the
dimension of *ēthos*, in particular how the *ēthos* of the members of the Roman community is already described inside the story (that is inside chapters 1:18–8:39). In the next chapter of my analysis, I focus my attention
more particularly on the ways in which Paul (in chapters 12:1–16:27) actually constructs the *ēthos* that he has previously described.

2. Hints for the Presence of a Story in Romans

In various recent narrative readings of Paul, scholars often talk about multiple stories at work in the theology of the apostle. They find different

---

[21] On the concept of *mimesis*, see note 12.

[22] See Ricœur, *Temps et récit vol. 1*, 109: "[Aristote] signifie que c'est bien dans l'auditeur
ou dans le lecteur que s'achève le parcours de la *mimèsis*. Généralisant au-delà d'Aristote, je
dirai que *mimèsis* III marque l'intersection du monde du texte et du monde de l'auditeur ou
du lecteur." This focus on the reader is a way of reading that takes into account the rhetorical
effect of a text on its readers; see also Caroline Vander Stichele and Todd Penner, *Contextualizing Gender in Early Christian Discourse: Thinking Beyond Thecla* (London: T&T Clark,
2009), 192: " … the reader and community that consume these texts are also constructed in
light of them. The mimetic (or imitative) function of textual representation thus needs to be
engaged in order to appreciate how representation transforms individuals and communities,
making them 'like' the discourses produced in and through the text." and 193: " … a narrative
shapes not only the perception of the reader related to the events and characters described, but
it also configures the identity of the reader/community in the process. The *ethos* (or 'character') of the reader is thus constructed by the text, and this feature of literary production provides one of the more significant ways by which the ideology of the text is communicated and
absorbed by the reader. Thus, ideologies present in narrative are reproduced in often subtle
ways."

[23] See Ricœur, *Oneself as Another*, 143.

[24] See Pierre Bühler's interpretation of Ricœur in Introduction to *La narration: quand le
récit devient communication* (ed. P. Bühler and J.-F. Habermacher; Geneva: Labor et Fides,
1988), 5–16, here 11: "une telle perspective permet de mettre en évidence *l'effet* de la narration sur son destinataire, lecteur ou auditeur. En l'invitant non seulement à lire ou à écouter,
mais à prolonger cet acte de lecture ou d'écoute jusqu'à en faire l'acte de se laisser entraîner
dans l'histoire elle-même, le récit ouvre son destinataire à des possibilités nouvelles qui le
touchent au plus profond de lui-même, dans son mode d'existence."

ways of organizing these stories around a directing principle. For Grieb, there is one "great story – the story of what God has done in Christ – that includes many other stories."[25] A few pages later, she lists the many smaller stories included in that great story.[26] Her analysis of Romans does not indicate why that grand story is told and how the smaller stories fit in that grand story. It lacks a strong organizing principle. Witherington speaks of "four interrelated stories comprising one larger drama,"[27] which are at work in Paul's thought in general and presumably also in Romans. The four stories (story of a world gone wrong, story of Israel, story of Christ, story of Christians) create a master Story "out of which all his [Paul's] discourse arises."[28] Because of the nature of Witherington's project, the structure of the individual letters and the way individual letters tell the Story or the stories is not taken into account. The number of stories and the way they are related to each other remain problematic, as James Dunn points out: "Are the stories of creation, of Israel, of Paul, and so on, simply facets or phases in a single story? ... Or should we focus on one of the proposed ... stories and either allow it to absorb all the rest or conform all the rest to it?"[29]

To find an organizing principle for the various narratives found in Romans, it is necessary to see two things happening. First, Paul does tell a story in 1:18–8:39, a story focused on how God intervened for the world through Christ. The story starts with humanity in sin (1:18–3:20). Then Paul indicates how God saved "all who believed through Christ," (3:21–26) all who believed and are uncircumcised through Abraham (4:11), all who believed and are circumcised through Abraham (4:12), "we" through Christ (5:1–21). This is the middle part of the story and goes from 3:21–5:21.[30] Finally, in the ending of the story (6:1–8:39), Paul describes how "we" are given a new self-understanding (Rom 6 and Rom 8) and the consequences of this new self-understanding (for the law [Rom 7], and for Israel [Rom 9–11]).

However, there are hints that something else is going on in the letter. First, this telling of the story does not account for the very beginning (1:1–17) and the end of the letter (12–16). In addition, Paul contrasts the character of the human beings described at the beginning of the letter and the

---

[25] Grieb, *The Story of Romans*, xvii.

[26] See Grieb, *The Story of Romans*, 17 (see also the review of Grieb's work in chapter 1).

[27] Witherington, *Paul's Narrative Thought World*, 5.

[28] Witherington, *Paul's Narrative Thought World*, 4.

[29] James D. G. Dunn, "The Narrative Approach to Paul: Whose Story?" in Longenecker, *Narrative Dynamics in Paul*, 217–230, here 224 and 225.

[30] In that middle section, one can also notice a contrast between Christ and Adam that fits the description that Aristotle makes of human beings as either of a higher or a lower type. In this model, Christ is the higher type and Adam, the lower type.

character of the members of the Roman house churches who are addressed at the end of the letter.[31]

At the beginning of the letter (Rom 1:18–3:20), Paul presents a grim image of humanity. Grieb speaks of "a world gone wrong"[32] and commentators on this passage agree that Paul paints a severe portrayal of humankind, [33] concluding with the composite citation from scripture (Rom 3:10–18). Not much good can come from the human beings described in the first chapters of the letter – "all, both Jews and Greeks, are under the power of sin." (Rom 3:9) Clearly, these human beings are not in control of what they are doing; rather, they are enslaved to the power of sin, which obscures their judging and discerning skills (Rom 1:21) resulting in actions with devastating consequences, both for the individual and for the community (Rom 1:22.23.24.29–32).

These consequences affect the human body, the human mind and the human moral tendencies, expressed by the penchant to judge others. At the beginning of the letter, human bodies are described as degraded and the home of lusts and passions, as Rom 1:24–25 makes clear: "Therefore God gave them up in the lusts of their hearts to impurity, to the degrading of their *bodies* (σώματα) among themselves, because they exchanged the truth about God for a lie and worshiped and served the creature rather than the Creator, who is blessed forever! Amen." In 1:28, Paul presents the human mind as debased: "And since they did not see fit to acknowledge God, God gave them up to a debased *mind* (νοῦν) and to things that should not be done." As a consequence, the human mind cannot discern the will of God. In Rom 2:1–16, Paul launches a severe attack on the person who judges

---

[31] For a similar attention to this contrast see Neil Elliott, *The Rhetoric of Romans: Argumentative Constraint and Strategy and Paul's "Dialogue with Judaism"* (JSNTSup 45; Sheffield: Sheffield Academic Press, 1990), 97–98, quoting extensively from Victor. P. Furnish, *Theology and Ethics in Paul* (Nashville: Abingdon, 1968). See for example 98: "Furnish's observations point to a fundamental antinomy that gives structure to the letter: the contrast between human depravity and immorality pictured in 1:18–32, and reflected as the former existence of Paul's audience in Rom. 6, and the new life of holiness and sobriety for which Paul pleads in 12.1–2 – a new life possible within the sphere of Christ's lordship (Rom. 6)."

[32] Grieb, *The Story of Romans*, 19.

[33] Moo, *Romans*, 91 entitles the section "The Universal Reign of Sin," Joseph A. Fitzmyer, *Romans: A New Translation with Introduction and Commentary* (AB 33; New York: Doubleday, 1993), 269 uses the title: "Without the gospel God's wrath is manifested against all human beings," James D. G. Dunn, *The Theology of Paul the Apostle* (Grand Rapids, Mich.: Eerdmans, 1998), 79 entitles his section on the condemnation of humankind "Humankind under indictment" and speaks of the "dark side of humanity;" Witherington, *Paul's Narrative Thought World*, 9–35 seems to be particularly inspired by these chapters and sets free his literary creativity, speaking about "The Darkened Horizon," (9) "Paradise Lost" (10) and "The Human Malaise," (21) and describing the human story as "red in tooth and claw, an endless struggle for survival, an endless competition for superiority." (13)

another: "… you have no excuse, whoever you are, when you *judge others*; for in passing judgment on another, you condemn yourself, because you, the judge, are doing the very same things." Judging concludes the long list of sins started in 1:18 and highlights once more the fact that human beings' basic sin is one of mistaken understanding of themselves since when judging they usurp God's position as judge.

At the end of the letter (12:1–15:13) however, when Paul addresses the Roman community directly, he trusts that they will be able to follow his exhortations. These exhortations exhibit a new understanding of the human body, the human mind and the human tendency to judge. First, Paul believes that the *bodies* (σώματα) of the members of the Roman house churches can be presented as a "living sacrifice, holy and acceptable to God, which is your spiritual worship." (12:1) The members of the Roman house churches are invited to use their bodies in a positive sense, as instruments of worship, "holy" and "acceptable to God." Paul also insists in the next verse (12:2) that his addressees should not be "conformed to this world" but should "be transformed by the renewing of [their] *minds* (νοὸς),[34] so that [they] may discern what is the will of God – what is good and acceptable and perfect." In 12:2, the discerning power of the members of the Roman churches, through a renewed mind, is used to know the will of God, something that humans were unable to do in 1:28, because of a debased mind. One more example should suffice to highlight the dramatic change that occurs in Paul's view of human capacities between the beginning of the letter and the end. Chapter 14 takes up the theme of judging once more, but this time Paul exhorts the Roman community to avoid judgment: "Let us therefore *no longer pass judgment on one another*, but resolve instead never to put a stumbling block or hindrance in the way of another." (Rom 14:13) Judging is replaced by an attitude of caring towards the neighbor and of deference to the needs of the other.[35]

---

[34] In the Greek text, it is not clear of whose mind Paul is speaking. A textual variant attests the difficulty: several manuscripts, among which ℵ and the minuscule 33, read τῇ ἀνακαινώσει τοῦ νοὸς υμων, making it clear that the mind in question is the one of the addressees. However, the best manuscripts (papyrus 46, A, B and D in its original version) read the text without the υμων. It is the *lectio difficilior* and should be chosen as the correct reading for this passage (see also Jewett, *Romans*, 724). However, for Moo and Fitzmyer, it is clear that Paul is talking about the mind of his addressees (see Moo, *Romans*, 756; Fitzmyer, *Romans*, 641). While I agree that Paul is expecting a change in the mind of his addressees, I find Johnson's suggestion that the mind in which they should be transformed is the mind of Christ (Johnson, *Reading Romans*, 191: "In this context, and from the ways Paul will develop his exhortation, it is clear that the 'new mind' to which believers are to be transformed is precisely the 'mind of Christ'.") insightful. It will play a role in the discussion of the manner in which Paul shapes the *ēthos* of his readers.

[35] The connection between chapter 14 and 2:1 has also been noted by Wayne A. Meeks, "Judgment and the Brother," in *Tradition and Interpretation in the New Testament: Essays in*

Paul's addressees are invited to understand themselves in a way that differs from the description of humanity at the beginning of the letter. Paul
does more in Romans than just tell the story of how God saved a world
gone wrong. He indicates why this story is important for the members of
the Roman house churches, how it shapes them and how it needs to affect
who they are and what they do. Through this story, he aims to construct the
self of his addressees. It is used rhetorically, to transform them and shape
their *ēthos*. Therefore in order to understand why Paul tells the story he
narrates in 1:18–11:36, one needs to take into account the very beginning
and the very end of the letter as well.

Before he launches into the description of lost humanity, we note that
Paul addresses the members of the Roman churches and he describes them
in the following terms. They are "beloved of God," "called to be saints."
(1:7) Their faith is "proclaimed throughout the world." (1:8) Paul's rhetorical exaggeration aims not only at winning the favor of his addressees, it
already indicates to them who they really are through God's gift (χάρις),
despite their possible weaknesses and failings. It is precisely to explain
how they became who they presently are, to explain how their identity of
"beloved of God" came upon them that Paul tells the story already mentioned – the story of God's saving action for the world and its consequences. The identity of the Roman house churches is based on the power of the
gospel (1:16–17), and in his letter, Paul tells his addressees the story of the
gospel, the story which grounds the new self-understanding of the members of the Roman churches.

Similarly, in the final chapters of the letter, Paul invites his addressees
to look forward. The story Paul told in 1:18–11:36 has taken the members
of the Roman house churches to a certain point. Now, in 12:1, they stand at
another turning point of the story. How should they act because of the new
self-understanding given to them through the story of the gospel? The final
chapters of the letter give clues to the members of the Roman churches
about the way in which they now need to lead their lives in view of the story that is told in flashbacks in 1:18–11:36. Through the story Paul told in
1:18–11:36, Paul shows how a new self has been given to the members of
the Roman house churches – a self marked by their union with Christ. The
end of the letter aims at showing that this self is still in need of a specific

Honor of E. Earle Ellis for his 60th Birthday (ed. G. F. Hawthorne and O. Betz; Grand Rapids,
Mich. – Tübingen: Eerdmans – Mohr Siebeck, 1987), 290–300, here 296: "Once we recognize how central and forceful these apostrophes are in this last of Paul's admonitions in Romans, it becomes surprising that commentators, as far as I can see, have paid no attention to
the striking parallel in form, substance, and function with the apostrophe that startles every
reader in the middle of the first argument in the letter, 2:1 ..." Referencing Meeks, Dunn also
recognizes the parallel with 2:1; see James D. G. Dunn, *Romans* (2 vols.; WBC 38A–38B;
Dallas: Word Books, 1988), 2:797.

shape. It needs to be constructed, and Paul aims at that construction through his prescriptive language.[36]

In summary, the story of how God saved the world is contained in 1:18–8:39. It is divided in a beginning (1:18–3:20) which describes humanity in sin, it continues with the middle of the story (3:21–5:21), which tells how God saved all who believed through Christ (3:21–26), all who believed and are uncircumcised through Abraham (4:11), all who believed and are circumcised through Abraham (4:12) and "we" through Christ (5:1–21). It ends (6:1–23 and 8:1–39) with a new self-understanding, which triggers some questions about the role of the law (if a new identity is given to the people of God through Christ, what is the role of the law? Rom 7) and about the distinction between Jews and Gentiles and the fate of Israel (Rom 9–11).

This story is framed by two sections (1:1–15 and 12:1–16:27) which portray a self given and a self constructed. In 1:1–15, Paul describes the members of the Roman house churches as beloved of God, called to be saints, with a faith that is proclaimed everywhere. This identity is perceived as God's gift, understood as God's action in the world. It goes back to the gospel (1:16–17). After this introduction, Paul then launches in the story of the gospel, the story that is behind the identity of the members of the Roman churches. In the section that closes the letter (12:1–16:27), Paul presents what the Romans are now called to do, in view of the story that Paul just told in 1:18–11:36. They are called to unity, to an ethics of love and to welcome and extend the mission of Paul.

This outline of the narrative dimension in Romans has the advantage of taking into account the entire letter. It also organizes the multiple stories according to a general principle that explains why Paul decides to tell this particular story (God saved the world) to the members of the Roman house

---

[36] For a somewhat similar understanding of the structure of the letter, although from a different perspective and with a different methodology, see Elliott, *The Rhetoric of Romans*, 59: "This connection [between the beginning and the end of the letter] suggests that the paraenesis in chs. 12–15 is not only directed to concrete circumstances in Rome, but is also prepared for by a *theological reorientation toward God's mercy* in the earlier chapters of the letter. It is the overall thesis of this study that Paul's argumentation in chapters 1–11 provides just such a reorientation." See also Stowers, *A Rereading of Romans*, 70. This approach emphasizes the connection of the final chapters with the rest of the letter, *contra* a view inaugurated by Martin Dibelius, *From Tradition to Gospel* (trans. B. L. Woolf; New York: Scribners, 1935), in which the parenetic sections have nothing to do with 1–11. See also, for a similar importance given to the entire letter, Meeks, "Judgment and the Brother," 290: "In this essay I will argue that, even in the case of Romans, the bipartite pattern encourages misreading. Paul's advice about behavior in the Christian groups cannot be rightly understood until we see that the great themes of chapters 1–11 here receive the denouement. And we do not grasp the function and therefore the meaning of those theological themes in their epistolary context unless we see how Paul wants them to work out in the everyday life of the Roman house communities."

churches. Finally, it gives a reason for the tension between the universal and the particular that is at work in Romans. The problem often seen in Romans is that Paul presents his gospel in very general terms in 1:18–11:36, seemingly without indicating why he connects the Roman community with humanity in general.[37] Reading the letter in a narrative manner justifies the existence and the importance of the final chapters of the letter, and explains how the story of humanity is related to the existence of that particular community of Christ believers in Rome. The story that has been told in rather general terms in 1:18–11:36 needs to affect the Roman community in a concrete manner. The concrete and particular effects of the universal story of God's saving intervention are stated in Romans 12:1–16:27.

B. Fleshing out the Outline

In this section, I show the way in which the plot develops in broad strokes. I do not spend a great amount of space discussing traditional or debated questions related to the text and themes of Romans. Rather, I focus on the literary movement of Romans and on the way each part of the letter fits in that movement. As I have argued, Romans does not start with human sin. Rather it begins with the story of a church which has been graced by God. To explain how this church came into being, Paul starts a flashback and tells a story to his addressees. In certain ways, this story is the story of the Roman community, but that story makes sense only within God's dealings in the world, including Jews and Gentiles. It is not by chance that Paul tells this particular story to his addressees. It has consequences for them.

1. The Roman Church: A Self Given (1:1–17)

In terms of plot, Paul is able to do three things in the opening verses of his letter. He presents the main characters of the story that he is about to tell (Paul, God, Christ, the members of the Roman house churches, the Gentiles). He shows how all these characters are connected, and finally, he indicates that, because of this interconnectedness, Paul and the Roman churches have some obligations towards each other.

---

[37] See for example the presentation of this problem in Elliott, *The Rhetoric of Romans*, 12–14. Also Karl P. Donfried, Introduction (1977) and introduction (1991) to Donfried, *The Romans Debate*, xli–lxxii. For a reflection on Romans' theological coherence, see James D. G. Dunn, "The Formal and Theological Coherence of Romans," in Donfried, *The Romans Debate*, 245–250.

Concerning the characters, Paul starts by giving some autobiographical information about himself (verses 1.5.6) and, from the very beginning, he weaves his own life with the life of Christ. What he says about himself is well known. He describes himself as a slave of Christ, not an insignificant fact since it is eventually the identity that the members of the Roman community are invited to adopt for themselves (see Rom 6:22).[38] He indicates that his vocation comes from God (he is called to be an apostle and set apart for the gospel) and that his mission is endorsed by Christ and directed towards the entire world, and hence also to the Roman community. In the way he describes his own identity, he already prefigures what he wants to see happening in the members of the Roman house churches: in 14:7–8, he defines the lives of his addressees and himself as belonging to the Lord and in 15:24, he asks the members of the Roman house churches to support his mission to Spain, that is the mission of the gospel.

While giving indications about himself, Paul also summarizes the good news about Christ, the son of God, of Jewish descent (1:2–4). However, Paul is not interested in the life of Christ in itself. The events related to Jesus (his life, death and resurrection) happened in the past. Paul wants to show how these past events affect the now of his own life and of the life of the Roman community.[39] In regard to the present, the gospel about Christ is what makes Paul who he is, but it also gives its existence to his addressees ("including yourselves who are called to belong to Jesus Christ"). Because of Christ, Paul does the work he does, and is able to preach to the Roman community as well (v. 6). Even though Paul and the members of the Roman house churches do not formally know each other, they are in contact through the good news about Christ.[40] The long sentence opening

---

[38] This designation can also be seen as coming from Paul's Jewish heritage. See Dunn, *Romans*, 1:7; Leon Morris, *The Epistle to the Romans* (Grand Rapids, Mich.: Eerdmans, 1988), 36–37, also indicates that this designation would have been surprising for Greek thought. In contrast, Dale B. Martin, *Slavery as Salvation: The Metaphor of Slavery in Pauline Christianity* (New Haven, Conn.: Yale University Press, 1990), xiv–xxiii emphasizes the use of the metaphor of slavery in Greco-Roman context. For a careful and detailed discussion of this verse in relationship with the designation "slave of Christ", see Michael Jospeh Brown, "Paul's Use of Δοῦλος Χριστοῦ Ἰησοῦ in Romans 1:1," *JBL* 120/4 (2001): 723–737.

[39] In the present, the work of the spirit has tremendous importance (see Rom 8). The death and resurrection of Christ are past events, which can have a present effect for human beings through the work of the spirit. For a somewhat similar approach: Moo, *Romans*, 50–51.

[40] See Elliott, *The Rhetoric of Romans*, 70 and 71: "By means of adapting conventional epistolary opening formulae, Paul begins in 1.1–7 to create a rhetorical relationship with his readers by relating himself and them to the call of God. ... Their respective identities – Paul's and the Romans' – are determined by the prior initiative of God, who has already announced the gospel in Israel's sacred scriptures (1.2–3) and has by raising Jesus from the dead established him as 'Son of God in power' whom Paul and the Romans alike are now made to confess as 'our Lord' (1.4,7)."

Romans, which intertwines Paul, Christ and the Roman community, testifies to this. Paul's description of the Roman community adds to this feeling of shared identity in Christ. They are God's beloved, called to be saints, and their faith is proclaimed everywhere (1:7.8)

This shared identity comes with responsibilities, and Paul moves on to presenting them in the next paragraph. For Paul, it means remembering the Roman community in his prayers (1:9) and hoping that he will someday be able to come to them (1:10.11.13.14). For the members of the Roman house churches, it means supporting Paul's mission to the Gentiles, as others have done before them (1:13).[41] In exchange for this support, Paul describes how he is indebted to the Greeks and the barbarians (1:14). A sign of this indebtedness is his eagerness to proclaim the gospel to the Roman community and his desire to continue his mission in Spain – a project that the proclamation of the gospel in Rome will make possible (15:24). His proclamation of the gospel will also make clear why the members of the Roman churches should present their financial support to Paul, a fact confirmed by the conclusion of the letter. At the end of the letter, the support asked for by Paul is part of a section in which Paul describes what actions should accompany the self-understanding given to the members of the Roman house churches through participation in Christ's death and resurrection. This identity is already ascribed to the Roman community at the beginning of the letter. In order to make clear who they are because of the gospel, and what they need to do because of the gospel, Paul wants to proclaim the gospel to them (1:15), so that they will know where they are coming from, who they are now and hence what they should do for Paul.

In 1:16–17, therefore, he introduces his story of the gospel, how it has power for life.[42] One can point out several elements that will be developed

---

[41] I agree with Johnson that the expression "τινὰ καρπὸν" refers to the "collection for the saints in Jerusalem," *Reading Romans*, 25 (Also for a similar reading M. A. Kruger, "Τινὰ καρπὸν, 'Some Fruit,' in Rom 1:13," *WTJ* 49 [1987]: 168–170) but that in a more general sense, it also prepares his addressees "for his later appeal for hospitality and financial support," see also Jewett, *Romans*, 129–130: "It seems less likely that Paul is thinking in terms of a Roman contribution to the Jerusalem offering, also described with the metaphor of 'fruit' in 15:28, because the funds were already on their way by the time the Romans received this letter. ... As 15:24 and 28 go on to detail, Paul hopes to gain logistical and tactical support from Rome for his mission to Spain." For Moo, this is simply a reference to the fruit of evangelization (Moo, *Romans*, 61). See also for that reading Charles E. B. Cranfield, *Romans: A Shorter Commentary* (Grand Rapids, Mich.: Eerdmans, 1985), 15 and Morris, *Romans*, 62.

[42] Verses 16 and 17 in chapter 1 are almost universally recognized as giving the theme of the entire letter. For example: John Murray, *The Epistle to the Romans: The English Text with Introduction, Exposition and Notes* (2 vols.; NIBCNT; Grand Rapids, Mich.: Eerdmans, 1959; repr., Grand Rapids, Mich.: Eerdmans, 1984), 1:26; Anders Nygren, *Commentary on Romans* (trans. C. C. Rasmussen; Philadelphia: Muhlenberg, 1949), 65; Ernst Käsemann, *Commentary on Romans* (trans. G. W. Bromiley; Grand Rapids, Mich.: Eerdmans, 1980), 21;

further in the letter, but are already present here in condensed form. The righteousness of God is a theme that traverses the entire letter; it plays a particularly important role in 9–11, in which Paul establishes that God has not forgotten the promises God made to Israel. In close connection to the affirmation of the righteousness of God, the relationship between Jews and Gentiles is already prefigured in 1:16. Both people are included in salvation, and neither one should think that they can dispense with the other. At the same time, the primary role that the Jews play in the history of salvation should not be ignored. They are first and foremost, a point that Paul will repeat again in 9–11. Finally, salvation is said to occur by faith and needs to be expressed in the believers' life. Salvation cannot remain without practical consequences; it needs to be expressed ethically, in a community that, as Paul will write in 14:1 and 15:1, welcomes the weaker in faith.

Now that he has described who the members of the Roman house churches are, Paul, as in a flashback, tells the story he wants to share with the Roman community. The flashback refers to what happened to humanity. It is not arbitrary or accidental that Paul writes chapters 1:18–3:20 to the Romans. The identity he has just ascribed to the members of the Roman house churches needs an explanation in terms of its provenance (how did the members of the Roman house churches become who they are) and of its concrete contents (what does it mean to be beloved of God). This self-understanding – that came about through the story that Paul is about to tell – also needs to be tied to the manner in which the story affects humanity in general, and Jews and Gentiles in particular.

2. The Beginning of the Story: Humanity in Sin (1:18–3:20)

In the language of narrative analysis, a situation of need (the δέσις or complication of Aristotle) is established at the beginning of the story. Human beings are utterly sinful and in need of being saved. The beginning of the story is about humanity. Until 2:9, there is no clear indication that Paul is talking about Jews or Gentiles.[43] In fact, he remains very general. Obvious-

---

Byrne, *Romans*, 47. In regard to the story Paul starts telling in 1:18, 1:16–17 can still play this role. The gospel is presented as God's powerful intervention in the world, and this has consequences for Jews and Gentiles.

[43] While commentaries recognize the universal indictment of humanity, they usually see these verses (1:18–32) concerned more specifically with Gentiles. See for example Frederick F. Bruce, *The Letter of Paul to the Romans: An Introduction and Commentary* (TNTC; rev. ed.; Grand Rapids, Mich.: Eerdmans, 1985), 77; Murray, *Romans*, 1:34; Barrett, *Romans*, 31; Nygren, *Romans*, 101; Dunn, *Romans*, 1:53; Moo, *Romans*, 93; Fitzmyer, *Romans*, 269; Stowers, *Rereading Romans*, 103. Cranfield, *Romans*, 27–28 indicates that Paul had in mind primarily Gentiles in this section, but he thinks that it would be wrong to limit the reference exclusively to Gentiles (see also Morris, *Romans*, 74; Jewett, *Romans*, 152, 192). Deciding to whom the opening section is addressed does not necessarily resolve the question of the histor-

ly, differences between Gentiles and Jews are recognized (as 2:12–16 and
2:17–3:4 make clear) but, at the beginning of the story, Jews and Gentiles
are addressed as being part of humanity. Paul is aware of special circumstances surrounding the Jews' relationship with God; however, Jews are
part of humanity and, at that point in his letter, that is what interests Paul.
Paul, here, is presenting an anthropological analysis, focused on human
beings' relationship with God. The problem of human beings when it
comes to their relationship with God is summarized in 1:21 and applies to
Jews as well as to Gentiles.[44] Human beings have willfully ignored God.
Even worse, they have refused to give God what is due to God. Instead
they have focused on their own thoughts and their faculty of discernment
has been obscured.[45] Human beings have strayed in their relationship with
God. As a result, they have lost their freedom of will and of action
(1:24.26.28) and their relationship to God and to each other is perverted.

The first pages of the letter divide easily in four parts. As we have seen,
1:18–32 highlights the manner in which human beings have lost their sense
of discernment (1:18–23) and are thus abandoned to their desires (1:24), to
their passions (1:26), to a debased mind and to things that should not be
done (1:28). This passage has been abundantly commented, mainly because of its mention of female and male homosexuality in 1:26–27, and has
become (in)famous in the discussion of homosexuality in Christian circles.[46]

---

ical composition of the audience of the letter. For a classical discussion of the problem, see
Wolfgang Wiefel, "The Jewish Community in Ancient Rome and the Origins of Roman
Christianity," in Donfried, *The Romans Debate*, 85–101; A. J. M. Wedderburn, "The Purpose
and Occasion of Romans again," in Donfried, *The Romans Debate*, 195–202 and Francis
Watson, "The Two Roman Congregations: Romans 14:1–15:13," in Donfried, *The Romans
Debate*, 203–215.

[44] Morna D. Hooker, "Adam in Romans 1," in *From Adam to Christ: Essays on Paul*
(Cambridge: Cambridge University Press, 1990), 73–84 sees Adam behind the description of
humanity in chapter 1, see 77: "… the sequence of events outlined in Rom. 1 reminds us of
the story of Adam as it is told in Gen. 1–3" and 78: "It would appear from this remarkable
parallelism that Paul's account of man's wickedness has been deliberately stated in terms of
the biblical narrative of Adam's fall." See also Dunn, *Romans*, 1:53.

[45] A privileged example of this state of affair in Jewish history is found in the episode of
the golden calf (Ex 32: 1–35). See Grieb, *Romans*, 27 and Jouette M. Bassler, *Divine Impartiality: Paul and a Theological Axiom* (Chico, Calif.: Scholars Press, 1982), 122.

[46] It is in fact one of the passages that creates great difficulties for readings that try to regain the freeing aspect of Paul's thought, such as post-colonial, feminist and queer readings
of Paul. See for example the discussion of that problem in Davina C. Lopez, *Apostle to the
Conquered: Reimagining Paul's Mission* (Paul in Critical Contexts; Minneapolis: Fortress
Press, 2008), 15: "In both cases [for feminist and queer biblical interpretation], Paul has been
considered a major obstacle to true emancipatory re-readings of the New Testament due to his
perceived insurmountable hatred of women and gay people, as well as his overall domineering masculine self-presentation and expectation of his community." Lopez indicates that,

However, if this passage, as I have argued, is essentially about human rebellion against God, then what matters is to reflect on the relationship of homoeroticism with idolatry. Homosexuality is described as one of the comportments that derive from a wrong understanding of the organization of the world and from one's distorted relationship with God. Idolatry is the root of the problem and what matters to Paul primordially in this passage.[47] In fact, the problem of judging, for example, is much more developed by Paul in his discussion and is much more central to the point he seeks to make in Romans (see 2:1–16 and 14:1–15:6).

In 2:1–16, using the style of the diatribe, and still addressing himself to anyone (2:2),[48] Paul takes up the case of the ones who think they can judge others and thus rob God of God's place as true judge. Those who judge others commit two mistakes. First, they are hypocritical (2:1–3). They think that they can condemn others for their mistakes, when, in fact, they act in the very same manner. Condemning a certain type of action is not sufficient to escape the judgment of God. One also has to abstain from doing this type of action. But in addition to that, and more importantly, they make themselves guilty of insolence, haughtiness and boastfulness (1:30) in thinking that they can pass judgment on others and ignore God's claim on final judgment (2:5–11).[49] As Johnson points out, this interpretation

---

while Paul was certainly not a feminist or a gay man, these readings of Paul conflate what is perceived to be in the texts with "prejudices that have been *mapped onto it*" and lack complexity. (15) She aims to re-imagine Paul's radicalness.

[47] This passage, thus, despite the way in which it has been used, is not mainly about homoeroticism. Rather, it is about the way human beings pervert their relationship with God, something that Stephen Moore is careful to mention, even though the focus of his discussion of this passage is homoeroticism. See Stephen D. Moore, *God's Beauty Parlor and Other Queer Spaces in and around the Bible* (Stanford: Stanford University Press, 2001), 150. Thus, it is a misinterpretation to use this passage as an occasion to develop a biblical position about homoeroticism. Clearly, Paul condemns homosexual behavior, but he does so in a stock fashion, and is much more concerned with the general problem of idolatry, of which, for Paul, homosexuality is an example. See for a brief discussion of the problem, Moo, *Romans*, 114–115; Grieb, *Romans*, 28–31. Stowers also insists on the necessity to understand that homosexuality in antiquity cannot simply be equated with contemporary understanding of homosexuality (see Stowers, *A Rereading of Romans*, 94–95).

[48] Commentators usually see this section as addressed to Jews. See Moo, *Romans*, 127; Fitzmyer, *Romans*, 297; Nygren, *Romans*, 113–114; Morris, *Romans*, 107; Cranfield, *Romans*, 41. For me, it limits Paul's rhetorical effect unduly if one restricts the comments as addressed to Jews. See for a similar reading, Dunn, *Romans*, 79; Barrett, *Romans*, 43; Stowers, *A Rereading of Romans*, 127. For a list of positions, see Jewett, *Romans*, 197.

[49] See Johnson, *Reading Romans*, 37: "… judging another (in the sense of condemning them) is itself an act of 'insolence, haughtiness, boastfulness.' (1:30) The one who stands in judgment on the morality of another asserts a superior status and is in effect engaging in a moral one-upmanship or self-aggrandizement." See also Barrett, *Romans*, 44: "Behind all the sins of i, 29ff. lies the sin of idolatry, which reveals man's ambition to put himself in the

works particularly well when one remembers that in Rom 14, Paul takes up the question of judging again and condemns it because "no one is in the position to judge 'the servant of another,' namely God."[50] Viewed in this way, judging is the final (and perhaps most important) sin added to the long list of vices of 1:29–32 – which also explains why it plays such a prominent role in Paul's ethical discussions at the end of the letter.[51]

In response to the inappropriate ways in which human beings judge, 2:4–16 establishes the character of God as the impartial judge of both Jews and Gentiles. God's judgment will rest on people's deeds (2:6) but, as Grieb indicates, it will take into account the differences between Jews and Gentiles.[52] The Jews will be judged according to the law, because they possess the law. The Gentiles will be judged positively if they do what the law requires, even though they do not actually possess the law. The possibility of being righteous before God is left open, but only God will judge whether one is truly righteous (2:16).

The third part (2:17–3:8) deals directly with the particularity of the Jews. Paul insists that the Jews should not think that they can exclude themselves from the indictment of humanity set up in the previous passages. The Jews possess many advantages (2:17–20, 3:1–2) but it does not mean that they can abstain from doing what the law requires from them (2:21–24). Their special status as God's people only serves them if they respect the law (2:25). In fact, Paul goes so far as to say that a non-circumcised person – a non-Jew – can be more of a Jew than a circumcised person, provided she respects the law (2:26–29). This however does not call into question the faithfulness of God (3:3). God remains true to God-self, even if all betray God. God's character remains the same, and human beings cannot call God into question (3:5–8). Finally, in 3:9–20, Paul goes back to the story he began to tell in 1:18–32, and repeats its conclusion:

---

place of God and so to be his own Lord. But this is precisely what the judge does, when he assumes the right to condemn his fellow-creatures." (contra Cranfield, *Romans*, 44 and Murray, *Romans*, 1:57)

[50] See Johnon, *Reading Romans*, 37.

[51] A similar point is made by Meeks, "Judgment and the Brother," 296: "Far from marking a sharp break from the previous chapter, 2:1 requires rather that we read the indictments of that chapter in an inclusive sense and connect them closely with 2:1–11 ..." See also Stowers, *Rereading Romans*, 12 and Stanley K. Stowers, *The Diatribe and Paul's Letter to the Romans* (Chico, Calif.: Scholars Press, 1981), 110. Fitmyer, *Romans*, 298–299 also notices the connection and the importance of giving its full inferential meaning to *dio*.

[52] See Grieb, *The Story of Romans*, 31: "God's impartiality will be demonstrated not only when God repays all according to their deeds (2:6) but also when God judges the world in a way that respects the different moral situations of Jews and Gentiles. Jews who have the law will be judged by its provisions. Gentiles, who by nature do not have the law but who do what the law requires, will be judged favorably." See also Morris, *Romans*, 122–123. Paul is making a point about there being no favorites in God's view. See Jewett, *Romans*, 204.

"all, both Jews and Greeks, are under the power of sin." (3:9) He supports this conclusion by a composite quotation of scripture (3:10–18),[53] which echoes the situation he has described in 1:18–32 and takes up several themes enumerated in the vice list of 1:29–32.[54]

For the understanding of the plot traversing the epistle to the Romans, it is interesting to notice that the basics of the story are put into place in 1:18–32 and confirmed in 3:9–20. In between, because his accusation of humanity is so severe, Paul deals with questions and objections that might have arisen in response to his harsh portrayal of human beings. First, he responds to the persons who think that they can judge the behavior of others (2:1–16). These persons can be Jews or Gentiles; it is not made explicit in the passage. What is clear is that they should not think of themselves as better than most. Their attitude of judging is as sinful as – perhaps even more sinful than – the examples of bad behavior highlighted in 1:18–32. Second, Paul takes up the problem of the Jews who might think that their status as God's chosen people renders them immune to God's judgment (2:17–3:8). Here too, Paul rejects that objection and concludes the beginning of his story by saying that all, Jews and Gentiles alike, are under the power of sin (3:9), accountable to God who will judge in impartiality.

In terms of their *ēthos*, human beings at this point of the story are without nuances. Paul presents them as displaying a misshaping of character. Nothing in their actions or in their perceptions is in the proper place and they are utterly incapable of changing their own moral attitudes because

---

[53] Johnson, *Reading Romans*, 46 indicates that this *catena* of scripture is particularly dense and draws from: "LXX Qoh 7:20 (3:10); Ps 52:3–4 (3:11); Ps 13:1, 3 (3:12); Ps 5:10 (3:13a); Ps 139:4 (3:13b); Ps 9:28 (3:14); Isa 59:7 and Prov 1:16 (3:15–17); Ps 35:2 (3:18)." See also Jewett, *Romans*, 254; Dunn, *Romans*, 157; Fitzmyer, *Romans*, 333–334; Moo, *Romans*, 202.

[54] 3:11 (no one has understanding, no one seeks God) parallels 1:21–25; 3:12 echoes 1:29 (full of wickedness, evil); 3:13–14 alludes to the sins committed with the tongue (1:29–30, they are gossips, slanderers); 3:15–17 (sins of violence) echoes more elements of 1:29–31 (full of murder, strife, heartless, ruthless); finally their absence of fear of God (3:18) reflects 1:32, where human beings purposefully ignore God's decree. For a similar and much more detailed reading of the catena, see Leander E. Keck, "The Function of Rom 3:10–18: Observations and Suggestions," in *God's Christ and his People: Studies in Honour of Nils Alstrup Dahl*, (ed. J. J. Jervell and W. A. Meeks; Oslo: Universitetsforlaget, 1977), 141–157, here 146: "Thus the core of the catena asserts things which are not essential to what links it with its immediate context," but Keck recognizes that the frame of the catena as well as the beginning and the end support the point that Paul is making about universal sin (147) and he asserts, 151: "What Paul means by the serpentine language of Rom 3:13, for instance, apparently rests on an interpretive tradition and the links between the catena and the argument are thematic. In this light, we may read Rom 1:18–3:9, 19 again, and detect certain thematic connections" and 152: "What I am suggesting is that Rom 1:18–3:9, 19 is a sustained theological exposition of the catena, an exposition developed neither as pesher nor midrash, but as a forensic indictment, a statement of God's 'case' against the world."

their understanding of the world is fundamentally flawed. They are in a wrong position. The possible success of some is only evoked briefly in 2:13–16 and 2:26–29 to indicate that circumcision does not automatically protect one from the wrath of God.

Paul's description of the *ēthos* of human beings sounds so harsh[55] that one might wonder if in fact he did believe what he was writing about his characters: are all human beings really so deeply flawed? If one thinks of what Paul is writing in terms of story, this objection loses some of its edge. The aim of the first part of the story, when it establishes the *ēthos* of human beings, is not historical accuracy. Rather it is a rhetorical strategy, aimed at showing that misshaping of character, and the twisted perception of the world that comes with it, threatens everyone. In the beginning of the story, Paul creates a human universe in which all can imagine that their own view of the world might be in need of change. In fact, the story describes the characters in such a manner that even the reaction of protest ("surely not all human beings are like that?") is included in the indictment of humanity (through chapter 2 and chapter 3). The story wants to make its readers question their own character to see if indeed they escape the severe judgment contained in 1:18–3:20. It aims at showing its addressees that they do not or did not in fact escape that judgment. This part of the story establishes beyond the shadow of a doubt that, left to its own devices, the self loses its proper character and is mistaken about its own position in the world. It might think of itself as autonomous, but is in fact at the mercy of its passions and desires.

Finally, the beginning of the story also sets up the *ēthos* of God, demonstrated in the next episode of the story. God's characteristic throughout the letter is faithfulness,[56] and this faithfulness is made even more amazing because of human beings' complete failure at the beginning of the story.

---

[55] It might not have sound so harsh in the Greco-Roman world. In fact it was a current practice in Greco-Roman literature in the first century to start a speech with a vice list: see Abraham J. Malherbe, *Paul and the Thessalonians: The Philosophic Tradition of Pastoral Care* (Philadelphia: Fortress Press, 1987), 24 as quoted in Elliott, *The Rhetoric of Romans*, 109: "philosophical speeches 'frequently began by listing vices, which revealed the true condition of the listeners, before setting about to correct them'." However, it might still have been shocking to Paul's addressees since the letter actually started with high praise of their character. Thus it is surprising that this praise is followed by a description of humanity – and so presumably of Paul's addressees as well – as sinful. Some commentators remark on the exaggerations contained in Paul's description of humanity: see Cranfield, *Romans*, 26; Morris, *Romans*, 1:73, Johnson, *Romans*, 31–32.

[56] See Grieb, *The Story of Romans*, xvii: "It is my claim in this book that Romans is Paul's sustained argument for the righteousness of God ..." and 21: "The most important and primary meaning of God's righteousness is God's covenant faithfulness to Israel." See also Bassler, *Divine Impartiality*, 121 who argues for God's righteousness as an essential theme of the letter; Jewett, *Romans*, 272; Käsemann, *Romans*, 29–30; Barrett, *Romans*, 29.

God's faithfulness is also put into perspective by the fact that God is described as judge. God's judgment is at the center of 2:2–16.[57] God's δικαιοσύνη is understood in terms of God's impartial judgment of human beings' actions. It is exposed here in terms of fairness. Impartiality is necessary in order to be truly fair: "'impartiality' is the fundamental expression of 'righteousness' in the context of judging."[58] God knows human beings completely, not only their deeds (2:6) but also their hearts (2:16), and thus God can be absolutely fair and not be influenced by outside appearances (for example, circumcision). In relationship to the concept of faithfulness, Paul makes the point that God can only demonstrate faithfulness if God is also aware of the thoughts and actions of human beings. God is not being faithful because God is oblivious to the deeds and orientations of human beings. On the contrary, God is faithful because God knows the true reality of human beings, and is able in fact to judge what human beings do and think. It is not a blind faithfulness. God is faithful and judge, and because of God's faithfulness, God demonstrates mercy in God's judgment (2:4).

3. The Middle of the Story: God Saves the World (3:21–5:21)

In narrative terms, this section of the story addresses the περιπέτεια, the reversal. The need described in the beginning of the story is taken into account and given a solution. In this particular plot, the reversal consists in God's action to save human beings. The manner in which God saves is described in 3:21–31. Because God saves both Jews and Gentiles, God's manner of saving creates a question about the status of Abraham as ancestor of Jews and Gentiles which is answered in 4:1–25.[59] Paul then returns to the plot of the story in 5:1–21, explaining the consequences of God's saving action for "us" (5:1–5) and developing God's saving action further (5:6–11), while at the same time showing its connection with what happened with Adam (5:12–21).

---

[57] See Johnson, *Reading Romans*, 37: "The judgment of God is, in any case, the major point that Paul asserts in this section." Contra Fitzmyer, *Romans*, 298.

[58] See Johnon, *Reading Romans*, 39.

[59] Paul moves to Abraham not only because he can use him as an exemplum of faith, but also because, as the ancestor of the Jewish people, Abraham's role for the Gentiles needs to be clarified now that both Jews and Gentiles are part of God's people. See for example, Moo, *Romans*, 257; Fitzmyer, *Romans*, 371; Dunn, *Romans* 1:196–197; Nygren, *Romans*, 168. For Abraham understood as the ancestor of the Jewish nation, see Jewett, *Romans*, 308–309.

The Manner in which God Saves (3:21–31)
The middle of the story begins by showing how God has put human beings aright through the faith of Christ (3:21–22).[60] Justification comes from God and does not happen because of the law, but because of the faith of Christ (3:24). At the center in these particular verses are God's saving action and Christ's faith, not the way human beings receive God's gift.[61]

In 3:25 the faith of Christ is put in relationship with his death,[62] underscoring the dimension of obedience to God central to Christ's character. Christ does not only function as a plot figure, a character that moves the intrigue forward through the events of his life, death and resurrection. Rather, this passage already builds Christ's *ēthos*, marked by obedience (as chapter 5 will also do). The story of Christ, and his obedient death in particular, points to his faith. The faith of Christ cannot be understood independently from the event of his death. His death is a demonstration of his faith. Through his death, Paul is able to indicate what characterizes Christ's faith and what is the content of the faith of Christ. Christ's death exemplifies his obedience, which presents an appropriate human response to God, in contrast to the failures of humanity described in 1:18–3:20. Moreover, Christ's faith also carries an active dimension, something that will be made even clearer in chapter 5. It is God who puts Christ forward

---

[60] I side with a growing number of scholars who, following the insights of Hays, *The Faith of Jesus Christ*, in particular 156–161, translate διὰ πίστεος Χριστοῦ in 3:21 (and elsewhere) as "faith of Christ." See also Luke T. Johnson, "Romans 3:21–26 and the Faith of Jesus," *CBQ* 44 (1982): 77–90, and Grieb, *The Story of Romans*, 36–38. For a contrary position, see R. Barry Matlock, "Detheologizing the ΠΙΣΤΙΣ ΧΡΙΣΤΟΥ Debate: Cautionary Remarks from a Lexical Semantic Perspective," *NovT* 42 (2000): 1–23, also Jewett, *Romans*, 276–279; Fitzmyer, *Romans*, 345; Murray, *Romans*, 1:110–111; Cranfield, *Romans*, 70; Moo, *Romans*, 225; Dunn, *Romans*, 1:166. This does not mean that faith in Christ does not play a role in Romans, and in Paul's thought (for a combination of both, see Morris, *Romans*, 174–175).

[61] See Johnson, *Reading Romans*, 62: "Paul's restatement of his thesis in 3:21–26, therefore, does not place its emphasis on the human reception of God's gift through faith, although that is clearly stated in 3:22 and 3:26. His main emphasis is on the fact that righteousness comes about on God's initiative by means of a gift, and on the character of that gift, namely, the profound human response of Jesus the messiah to God in faith, expressed most perfectly in his obedient death as a means of liberation and reconciliation for others."

[62] Here also I accept that διὰ τῆς πίστεως refers to Christ's faith. See Johnson, *Reading Romans*, 61: "The phrase 'through faith' ... is fitted between 'expiation... in his blood' and is clearly intended to qualify the manner of Jesus' death. ... The placement of the phrase next to Jesus and the act of his death make me think that the two phrases 'through faith' and 'in his blood' form what in Greek is called a hendiadys, that is, two phrases that make a single expression. In this case, the two phrases would be the equivalent to "Jesus' faithful death,' which is exactly what Paul seems to want to get at here." Other commentators interpret faith as the response demanded from human beings: Cranfield, *Romans*, 73; Dunn, *Romans*, 1:172–173; Jewett, *Romans*, 288; Barrett, *Romans*, 78.

as sacrifice (3:25), but Christ carries out the sacrifice in an active response
to God's will (5:6 "Christ died for the ungodly").

Through this first description of Christ's *ēthos*, Paul already establishes
that belonging to Christ (1:6) means sharing in that obedience (see also
Rom 6 and Rom 15:7–13) and being willing to give up one's advantage for
the good of the weaker brother (14:1; 15:1.2).[63] The sacrificial language of
3:25 (ἱλαστήριον) is echoed in the reference to sacrifice in 12:1
(παραστῆσαι τὰ σώματα ὑμῶν θυσίαν ζῶσαν), and in the service language of
15:16 and 15:27 (λειτουργὸν; λειτουργῆσαι) as well as in the reference to
the offering of the Gentiles in 15:16 (προσφορὰ τῶν ἐθνῶν). Even though
the vocabulary used in each case is different, a conceptual connection
seems clear between the sacrifice of Christ in 3:25, the worship sacrifice
requested of Paul's addressees in 12:1 and the service expressed in Paul's
mission to the Gentiles (15:16) and in the qualification of the collection as
offering (15:16) and service to the saints in Jerusalem (15:27). Christ's
sacrifice, which symbolizes his obedient response to God's will, serves as
an example for the attitudes of Paul's addressees – and of Paul himself –
towards each other (12:1) and towards the larger world (15:16.27).

Therefore it is not surprising that the theme of the next section concerns
boasting. In 3:21–26 Paul has highlighted Christ's character as the obedient servant and God's quality of righteousness which enables God to restore human beings in a proper relationship to God. Boasting – a theme
already introduced in 1:30 and then in 2:17, when Paul turns to address the
Jews, and taken up again in 4:2, in regard to Abraham[64] – is therefore excluded (3:27), since Paul has just made it clear that everything rests on
God's saving action through Christ. Justification comes gratuitously and
no one can claim that they earned it or deserved it.[65]

---

[63] This will be presented in more detail by Paul in Rom 5, but the language of sacrifice already implicitly points to that attitude of deference developed more fully in Rom 5.

[64] At this point of the letter, boasting seems to be something principally related to the Jews
(but in 11:18, the warning not to boast is addressed to the Gentiles, and, as Jewett points out,
boasting was widespread in the Greco-Roman world and usually seen positively. See Jewett,
Romans, 295–296: "While the question of Jewish boasting dominates the interpretation of this
passage, which correlates with the previous identity of the interlocutor as a Jewish intellectual, it is ordinarily overlooked that Rome was the boasting champion of the ancient world,
filled with honorific monuments and celebrations of imperial glory."). See Moo, *Romans*,
246; Stowers, *Rereading Romans*, 234 interprets 3:27 as a question of a Jewish teacher, asking what basis is left for boasting if the Gentiles are saved by faith alone.

[65] See Johnson, *Reading Romans*, 62–63: "If humans are established in righteousness by
gift, they certainly cannot boast of it as though it were their possession or accomplishment ... ;" Jewett, *Romans*, 298: "God's granting of righteousness through faith in the crucified Christ counters the seemingly universal tendency to claim honor on the basis of performance or social status. It eliminates the claims of cultural or ethnic superiority." See also
Morris, *Romans*, 185; Stowers, *Rereading Romans*, 234.

Thus, because justification is a gift, boasting is excluded. In fact, 3:29–30 indicates that, since God is one, if God wants to justify both Jews and Gentiles, God can only do it by means of faith,[66] which excludes boasting. But Christ's *ēthos* of faithful obedience also sets up an example which rules out boasting. The type of obedience displayed by Christ in his death cannot be the object of boasting. This obedience receives its quality precisely because it does not have an ulterior motive. It is done in faith, as the appropriate response to God.

The Benefit of Abraham (4:1–25)

Paul turns to Abraham in part because he has just affirmed that God sets both Gentiles and Jews right, through faith, and thus he needs to address the position of Abraham. Traditionally, Abraham is seen as the father of the Jewish people – the people of the covenant. Now that the chosen people includes Jews and Gentiles, Paul needs to argue for Abraham's position as ancestor of both the Jews and the Gentiles (4:18) and establish the new nature of the people of the covenant as a multi-ethnic people.[67] In Abraham, Paul is able to confront the past, and through the past, to re-invent the present. The past is not used in a nostalgic manner; rather it creates something new, in an insurgent manner.[68] In verse 11, Paul affirms that Abraham is the ancestor of the Gentiles as well as Jews. The people of the covenant now include Jews and Gentiles (4:16–17) and Paul indicates that this

---

[66] See Johnson, *Reading Romans*, 63 and 64: "If right relationships with God were possible only on the basis 'of the works of the law,' then most of the world would be excluded from the game. ... But if God is both one and fair, then God must make it possible for all humans to respond to God." See also Dunn, *Romans*, 1:185–187, who insists that Paul does not principally critique "piety which boasts in its own achievement" but rather the claim to be the exclusive people of God; Moo, *Romans*, 251–252.

[67] N. T. Wright, *Paul for Everyone: Romans: Part One: Chapters 1–8* (Louisville, Ky.: Westminster John Knox, 2004), 65–66, proposes a similar reading: "Abraham was the beginning of the covenant family, the family to which believers now belong. 'Justification' is God's declaration that one has been adopted into the family. But what kind of family is it? ... [The chapter] is an exposition of God's intention in establishing the covenant with Abraham in the first place, and hence of the nature of Abraham's family. The climax of the chapter comes in a passage often regarded as something of an aside, in verse 17: the point is that Abraham's family is not composed of a single ethnic nation only, but of 'many nations'." As Käsemann (*Romans*, 121) points out, the theme of the discussion of Abraham is "the universalism of the promise of salvation." Also Dunn, *Romans*, 1:196.

[68] See Homi K. Bhabha, *The Location of Culture* (London: Routledge, 1994; repr., London: Routledge, 2006), 10: "The borderline work of culture demands an encounter with 'newness' that is not part of the continuum of past and present. It creates a sense of the new as an insurgent act of cultural translation. Such art does not merely recall the past as social cause or aesthetic precedent; it renews the past, refiguring it as a contingent 'in-between' space, that innovates and interrupts the performance of the present. The 'past-present' becomes part of the necessity, not the nostalgia, of living."

can only happen because Abraham was made righteous through his faith, before his circumcision (4:3.10.11.13).

At the same time, Abraham provides Paul with a great example of the *ēthos* he has already put into place with Jesus. In 4:12, Paul describes Abraham as an example of faith. His faith is illustrated in 4:18–22 and involves complete trust in God, despite the evidences pointing against the possibility of the realization of the promise. A result of this trust is Abraham's obedience to God, a characteristic central to Paul's presentation of Jesus. In 4:23–25, Paul deploys the full force of Abraham's role as example: the same righteousness that was reckoned to Abraham can be reckoned to "us" because "we" share the same faith in God as Abraham. Abraham, like Christ, shows the proper response to God's action in the world. If Paul's addressees imitate this response, they will also be justified.[69]

In terms of the plot that we are following in Romans, the reference to Abraham redefines the composition of the people of God and also functions as an illustration, much like an allusion to a hero in Greek literature,[70] which confirms the main characteristic of the Christian *ēthos* already established with Christ, and invites the addressees to imitate that response of complete trust in God.

Manner and Meaning of God's Saving Action (5:1–21)

In chapter 5, Paul develops the manner and meaning of God's saving action for the world. Paul discusses three things. First, he clarifies Christ's *ēthos*, which already played an important role in chapter 3, and was paralleled by Abraham's *ēthos*, as examples of proper human responses to God. Chapter 5 builds on the first indications found in 3:21–26 and develops Christ's character, especially in 5:6–11 and in the contrast with Adam (5:12–21). However the contrast with Adam is not just a way for Paul to

---

[69] See Johnson, *Reading Romans*, 79: "The faith that makes righteous is the fundamental response to reality as defined by the creating God, and this response is the same for Abraham, for Jesus, and for all humans, including Christians." In addition, commentators often note the connection of the figure of Abraham with the critique of boasting: Fitzmyer, *Romans*, 370–371; Barrett, *Romans*, 87; Käsemann, *Romans*, 106; Dunn, *Romans*, 1:196.

[70] See Johnson, *Reading Romans*, 67: "The literature of the ancient Mediterranean world makes heavy use of examples from the past, out of the conviction that some things were best learned through the hearing of a story, rather than through maxim or principle. Some examples were adduced simply to illustrate a point, sometimes they were employed as models for people to imitate in their behavior." See also Jewett, *Romans*, 306, 310. For Nygren, *Romans*, 168, Abraham is the "type of *those who through faith are righteous*." See also Murray, *Romans*, 1:127 and Cranfield, *Romans*, 81. Dunn, *Romans*, 1:196 sees Abraham as a test case for Paul's argument that God saves by faith and does not limit his saving action to the circumcised. Moo, *Romans*, 255–256 adopts a position similar to Dunn's. In contrast, Stowers, *Rereading Romans*, 227 argues that Abraham is not an example of faith, but is a model for God's faithfulness realized in the integration of the Gentiles in the people of God.

present a clearer picture of Christ's *ēthos*. Rather – and this is the second thing – it also allows him to develop the depth and meaning of the change that happened through God's action in the world. God's intervention through Christ marks a change of master (5:17) and inaugurates a change of æon. At the same time, at the very beginning of the chapter, Paul seems to get slightly ahead of himself, when he gives content, for the first time, to what it means for human beings to be justified by faith (5:1–11) – the third point. His terms do not yet refer to concrete realities, nor are they addressed to the Roman community in particular. Rather, these verses give a first base on which chapters 6 and 8, and then 12–15, will build. I start my discussion of the passage, then, with the results of justification.

Chapter 5 opens with a triple positive reference to boasting (v.2: "we boast in our hope of sharing the glory of God;" v.3: "but we also boast in our sufferings," v. 11: "we even boast in God"), that comes as a surprise after the severe condemnation of boasting both in 1:30 and 3:27. As a result of justification, human beings are in a relationship with God that permits them to boast, but about things that are usually not the regular object of boasting. The object of boasting has nothing to do with human achievements or human honors. Boasting is made acceptable because it is a sign of an appropriate attitude towards God. As verse 1 indicates, this proper attitude towards God reflects the fact that human beings are at peace with God. The distorted relationship with God, which was described in 1:18–32 and which brought turmoil and despair, has been replaced with peace.

This is made possible first and foremost through Christ (5:2), because Christ's death has put an end to the reign of death (5:17). But this new situation takes effect within human beings through the work of the spirit (5:5). The spirit is the power that effects the transformation in human beings. It is through the spirit that human beings receive the love of God, which enables them to live in a hope that will not disappoint them. The spirit is the *dynamis* that allows human beings, now that they are at peace with God through the death of Christ, to adopt Abraham's attitude of hope towards reality (4:18.20.21), an indication that human beings are showing the marks of a new *ēthos*, characterized by faithful trust in and obedience to God.

This faithful obedience is displayed in Christ. Paul now presents a more complete picture of Christ's character and explains what the content of the faith of Christ is. Christ's obedience to God runs so deep that he accepts dying even on behalf of sinners (5:6). This amazing death underscores Christ's response to God, but also signals the depth of God's love for humanity (5:8). The fact that Christ's obedience to the death is an indicator of God's love reminds Paul's addressees that Christ did not take advantage of his own faithfulness. There is no concealed purpose to Christ's obedience. His faithfulness is presented as being one with God's purpose for the world. This is confirmed by the fact that Christ's obedience also has positive eschatological consequences for human beings (5:9.10). Thanks to Christ's act of obedience, human beings will be saved from God's wrath on the day of judgment. Christ's life and God's purpose for the world are in harmony. Christ's obedience and God's love are connected in their common purpose for "us": God's love is for us and so is Christ's death (5:8). Rom 5:10 indicates how God is able to work towards reconciliation through Christ. The same idea is expressed explicitly in 2 Cor 5:19 (θεὸς ἦν ἐν Χριστῷ κόσμον καταλλάσσων ἑαυτῷ), helping to make sense of Paul's contracted language in Rom 5:10: In Christ's death, God was in Christ reconciling the world to God. A dual causality is at work here. God is doing the work of reconciliation, but so is Christ. The unity of purpose is clear.

Paul presents Christ's life and his *ēthos* as examples of the response human beings can offer to God. Thus Christ also exemplifies the way human beings should behave, something that will be made clear in 12:1–15:13. Christ's *ēthos* is marked by a life lived for others. In particular, Christ's willingness to die for those who were not worthy of his death (5:6.7.8) is an illustration of the attitude that Paul demands of his audience in 14:1 and 15:1–2. The good of the neighbor, even if she is weaker in faith, trumps the right of the one who is strong. Moreover, this also prepares the members of the Romans churches to support Paul's efforts in his mission towards Spain. It is all part of what it means to act in ways that will build up the neighbor, whether in Rome or in Spain. The reconciliation through Christ (chapter 5) prepares human beings to do the sort of actions necessary in order to lead a life pleasing to God and oriented towards the good of the community.

The contrast with chapter 1:18–3:20 could not be stronger. The threat of God's wrath which stood at the beginning of the story is now lifted, through Christ's death. In fact, instead of being subjected to God's wrath, human beings now receive God's love (5:5). A major change has taken place, and, with the introduction of Adam as a figure of contrast to Christ, Paul can explain how Christ does not just fix a problem in the old age, but in fact inaugurates a new age.[71] Adam is named only in 5:14 but it is possible to see him as the figure at the source of the pessimistic anthropology that Paul put into place in 1:18–3:20.[72] Adam inaugurated the age of sin,[73]

---

[71] See Elliott, *The Rhetoric of Romans*, 231–232. See also Nygren, *Romans*, 191, 210; Fitzmyer, *Romans*, 406; Dunn, *Romans*, 1:288; Jewett, *Romans*, 372; contra Käsemann, *Romans*, 142.

[72] See Hooker, "Adam in Romans 1." See also Dunn, *Romans*, 1:53, 288.

which brings death (5:13) and has devastating consequences for all (5:12.15.18), consequences Paul describes at the beginning of the story. The beginning of the story, recalled here through the figure of Adam, does not lead naturally to the situation that Paul is putting into place in 3:21–5:21. A complete change was necessary, a change so deep in fact that it gives the feeling that human beings are now part of a new story, which has nothing to do with the beginning of the old story. [74] The differences between the two stories are first emphasized in the construction οὐχ ὡς in v. 15 and 16. They are also seen in the construction ὡς/ὥσπερ...οὗτος of v. 18.19.21. In verse 21, Paul brings the contrast to a climax. It is not just the reign of death and of life that are opposed. The contrast here is between death and eternal life – a new type of life made possible by the obedience of Christ. This new life is given to human beings,[75] but they are still in need of providing it with a concrete content.

In terms of plot, 3:21–31, as well as 5:1–21, are central to the development of the story. They describe God's saving action through Christ (3:21–25a; 5:6–8), and they bring in the first results of this action (5:1–5.9–11), as well as underscore the depth of the change brought about by Christ's death. They also contribute to the portrayal of Christ as a model of obedience (5:12–21) and of God as a just God (3:25b–26). In terms of *ēthos*, the middle of the story puts into place a sharp contrast with its beginning, in particular at the level of anthropology. Through Christ's obedience and the gift of the spirit, human beings receive the capacity for a new self-understanding that transforms what they are able to accomplish. This identity, as chapters 6 and 8 will develop more fully, is indebted to the relationship human beings have to Christ (Rom 6) and to the work of the spirit in them (Rom 8). The addressees are now invited to adopt a new type of *ēthos* for themselves, the *ēthos* of Jesus and Abraham, an *ēthos* that contrasts sharply with the *ēthos* of Adam.

Paul is now moving towards the end of the story he wants to share with his addressees. The story itself reaches its proper conclusion in the gift of the spirit and in the identity of children of God given to Paul's addressees

---

[73] See Hooker, "Adam in Romans 1," 79: "It is not necessary to discuss here exactly how Paul conceived of the relationship between Adam's fall and the sin of mankind in general; it is clear from Rom. 5.12–21 that he *did* regard them as related, that he believed that sin had entered the world through Adam, and that every manifestation of sin is thus in some sense ultimately connected with the initial sin of Adam."

[74] Verse 15: "But the free gift is not like the trespass;" verse 16: "And the free gift is not like the effect of the one man's sin."

[75] See Johnson, *Reading Romans*, 97: "... Paul focuses on the *gift* given through Christ. This is how God got through all the web of human idolatry and the systemic influence of sin, by giving a gift so powerful that it could disrupt those patterns and restructure them on the basis of a new way of responding to God."

through Christ and the spirit (Rom 8). As such, the end of the story is dependent upon the reconciliation given to human beings through Christ.[76] In
terms of plot, Rom 6 and Rom 8 give an appropriate conclusion to the story Paul started to tell his audience in 1:18. Thus, for a narrative reading of
the letter, it is important to treat chapter 6 and chapter 8 together. Both of
these chapters describe the resolution of the story (λύσις), first through the
metaphor of the change of master in chapter 6 and second, through the introduction of the spirit in chapter 8. In terms of plot, thus, the story reaches
its end in chapter 8. The narrative section of the letter ends there and focuses on the power of the spirit that allows human beings to live in the new
æon.[77] But this is not how the letter ends.

In terms of the logic of his argument, Paul has to attend to three more
things in his letter. Two problems are born from the story itself, and indicate the limits of an approach which emphasizes continuity in the reading
of the letter. First, because Paul has affirmed that human beings are reconciled to God through Christ and through the power of the spirit (Rom 5),
the question of norm becomes unavoidable: by what norm (the law or the
spirit) do human beings live? Second, because Paul has argued that,
through the power of the spirit, his addressees – Jews and Gentiles – are
children of God (8:14), Paul has to take up the question of Israel's status as
the people of God. He has to address the question of particularity. Finally,
moving to exhortative language, Paul will explain what the story means for
the members of the Roman house churches (12–16), a section that is concretely aimed at building the self of his audience.

Concerning the question of the norm, Paul has to explain what the story
of God's saving action through Christ's death and resurrection means for
the status of the law. The law was introduced as a character, along with
sin, in several passages before (3:20.31; 4:15), but Paul merely mentioned
the connection between law and sin, almost in a casual manner. With the
affirmations of chapter 5 (in particular 5:13.20), law seems to take its place

---

[76] See Johnson, *Reading Romans*, 99: "The tone of chapter 5 is entirely positive and cele-
bratory. The gift is real; it has been given and has been received. Now Paul must turn to the
hard questions the gift itself poses (chapter 6–11) and then to the manner of life it demands
(chapter 12–15). But all of that follows and builds on this reality: 'we have peace with God
through our Lord Jesus Christ' (5:1)." See also, Jewett, *Romans*, 389.

[77] Clearly, there are narrative elements in chapters 7 and 9–11, but in term of plot, these
chapters do not belong to the story that Paul has been telling in 1:18–8:39. Rather they take
up problems that the story has created. A narrative reading of the letter insists on the continuity seen in the letter, and can be criticized for not taking into account tensions and discontinui-
ties apparent in the letter. In terms of the construction of the letter, clearly, the narrative line
is not as smooth as the manner in which I can reconstruct it in my narrative reading. The difficulties that are born from the plot indicate the ruptures inside the letter itself, which has to
take up objections created by the story.

in the infernal trio sin-law-death – the three powers that ruled over human beings before God intervened for them through Christ's death. Paul therefore has to address the way he has connected law with sin and death. He will turn to that in chapter 7. In terms of the problem of particularity, he also has to consider how the story affects the condition of Israel and what it means for the relationship between Jews and Gentiles and for the nature of the chosen people. Chapters 9–11 take up the problem that has been dormant throughout the letter and is exacerbated when Paul identifies the Christ believers as sons of God in 8:14[78] and as heirs of God in 8:17.[79]

The logic of the plot requires keeping chapters 6 and 8 together, even though the rhetorical arrangement of the letter is different. They present the full denouement of the story, its effects on human beings.

4. The End of the Story: New Self-Understanding (6:1–23; 8:1–39)

At the end of the story, Paul explains to his audience how their self-understanding is changed through God's action in Christ. He describes that self-understanding in two different ways. In chapter 6 Paul uses the metaphor of slavery to impress on the Christ believers the depth of the change that has occurred: human beings no longer have anything to do with sin, because they now have a new master who changes who they are. In chapter 8, Paul refines the metaphor of slavery and states that because of the power of the spirit, the Christ believers are united to Christ and made sons of God. With the introduction of the spirit, the freedom of the believer is put back into the equation, but it is a freedom that will be used to accomplish the requirement of the law.

Slaves of God (6)

Chapter 5 has already established that Christ's death meant the beginning of a new era. Chapter 6 confirms this and opens by affirming that sin no longer rules over Christ believers (6:2.6.7). Human beings are freed from their previous master, because they share in Christ's death and hence they are dead to sin (6:11). One of the purposes of chapter 6 in relationship to the plot is to explain how sin lost its influence on human beings. First and

---

[78] Despite Paul's usage of "sons" in 8:14, reflecting the ancient patriarchal system, it is possible to understand it in a more inclusive manner (because of the beginning of 8:14 "For all who are led...") and to translate it with "children of God," as the NRSV does. See Johnson, *Reading Romans*, 132; Fitzmyer, *Romans*, 499 accepts the inclusive language, but notes that son "more accurately expresses the relationship because of its legal relation to 'heirs'."

[79] Dunn, *Romans*, 1:450 points out the same connection between chapter 8 and chapter 9: "Hence, of course, the transition from chap. 8 to chap 9: the claims made in chap. 8 in particular seem to have transferred Israel's heritage wholly to those who are 'of Christ;' what then of Israel?"

foremost this happens because human beings participate in Christ's death, through baptism. This participation changes who human beings are. It marks an end for the old self (6:6) and there is no turning back to this old way of understanding oneself.[80] A new self-understanding is given to human beings through baptism, and this identity involves being alive to God (6:11).[81] It is in fact an identity similar to the identity of Christ himself (6:10.11)[82] and thus it needs to reflect Christ's faithful obedience to God. Sin might still exist as a power in the world, but it has lost its hold on those who are united to Christ through baptism. Their way of life is no longer marked by sin, but needs to reflect the fact that they are now living to God.

The plot of the story however also does something else. In terms of intrigue, it is centered on the end of the rule of sin over human beings; but it also establishes the identity of human beings as slaves. In terms of *ēthos*, human beings are marked by a lack of autonomy. Being a slave to one's master involves giving obedience to the master (6:16), but Paul also indicates that the master one is serving decides the identity of the one who is serving the master. As 7:14–23 will make clear, when a person serves sin it is no longer the individual who is responsible for what she does or even who she is, because her master seems to inhabit her (7:17). In this case it is as if the individual is being possessed by an outside power. Both chapter 6 and chapter 7 indicate that slavery is more than mere obedience; it is a matter of identity. The master decides the identity of the slave. This understanding of human beings as serving sin as if they were possessed by it also explains why Paul uses violent language (6:2 "we ... died to sin;" 6:4 "we have been buried with him;" 6:6 "our old self was crucified") to express the way liberation can occur for human beings. If human beings are possessed by a master who decides their identity, only death can free them from this master (see also the point made in 7:1–4). A new self-understanding can be given to them only through a new life, lived under a new master.

Thus a change of master also indicates a change of self-understanding. The Christ believers are no longer under the dominion of sin (6:14) but

---

[80] Chapter 6:1–14 poses the question of the status of the believer, particularly in light of the Lutheran *simul justi et peccatores*. For this interpretation see also, Murray, *Romans*, 1:258; Barrett, *Romans*, 129; Cranfield, *Romans*, 139; Fitzmyer, *Romans*, 446. Jewett, *Romans*, 411 indicates that 6:1–14 establishes that the rule of sin is at an end for the believers. See also, Morris, *Romans*, 259; Moo, *Romans*, 387.

[81] See Johnson, *Reading Romans*, 105: "What changes ... is the entire identity of the person and the entire direction taken by the person's freedom."

[82] See Grieb, *The Story of Romans*, 67: "What is true of Jesus Christ is also true of the people of God of whom he is the representative, the covenant family who are in solidarity with him because they have been baptized into his death." See also Morris, *Romans*, 256.

they are now serving a new master. Paul still describes them as slaves (6:18.19.22) but the master has changed and so have they. In fact, in 6:19, when Paul writes "I am speaking in human terms because of your natural limitations," he might point to the fact that the identity of slave understood in the manner it was when the master was sin might not be completely appropriate to describe the identity of the Christ believers.[83] The metaphor and vocabulary of slavery allow Paul to impress upon his addressees how their allegiance to a new master changes who they are, but this language of slavery might not be representative of the degree to which Paul thought of obedience as free obedience, and not contractual obedience. The fact that verse 23 contrasts the wages (ὀψώνια) of sin with the gifts (χάρισμα) of God is another indication of the different way in which Paul conceived of a master-slave relationship when it involved God versus sin. Chapter 8 will in fact indicate explicitly that the Christ believers are invited to move away from the identity of slave (8:15).

However, the metaphor of slavery is a powerful metaphor to indicate that the change of master not only affects who they are but also what they are supposed to do, now that they are serving a new master.[84] Liberation from sin is not an end in itself; rather it is done so that Paul's addressees can now lead a life marked by obedience to the teaching of the gospel (6:17) and by righteousness (6:18.19). The change in self-understanding has to be followed by a change in the manner of acting. Because they are now of the same nature than Christ (6:5), united with him (6:8), they need to share in his *ēthos* and translate this "'christic' identity" in a new moral orientation, marked by the type of obedience which was demonstrated by

---

[83] It is clear from Rom 1:1 that Paul has no problem with the designation δοῦλος as an appropriate description for the Christ believer. However, in Rom 6, because of the association of slavery with sin, Paul might want to indicate that the type of slavery is not the same when the master is sin or God. See Johnson, *Reading Romans*, 109: "... the metaphor of slavery is not adequate to the relationship of which he speaks, but he needs language sufficiently powerful for them to realize what a fundamental shift has taken place in their condition, and therefore in their allegiance (obedience)." See also Murray, *Romans*, 1:233; Cranfield, *Romans*, 144; Fitzmyer, *Romans*, 450; Dunn, *Romans*, 1:345; Moo, *Romans*, 404. For Morris, *Romans*, 264, Paul has to explain why he used a metaphor involving slavery, since it was considered a degraded state. I think that this is not the problem Paul has with slavery, since he is quite comfortable using the designation in other places.

[84] See J. Albert Harrill, *Slaves in the New Testament: Literary, Social and Moral Dimensions* (Minneapolis: Fortress Press, 2006), 31: "The figure of the slave provides a powerful and compelling idiom through with to articulate Christian community formation and self-definition precisely because early Christians shared with wider 'pagan' society the same set of cultural assumptions, literary tropes, and social stereotyping of the slave. As a metaphor for the transformation of the religious self by baptism 'from death to life' existing within the eschatological tension of the Parousia being not yet present, the experience of enslavement was perfect for an ancient audience."

Christ.[85] This in turn will lead to sanctification (6:22) and ultimately to eternal life (6:23). What is given to them is their unity with Christ; what they need to work on is their *ēthos*, so that their *ēthos* imitates Christ's, as their identity imitates Christ's. The role of the spirit will be to assist human beings in this transformation of their *ēthos*.

In terms of construction of the self, this passage gives important clues to the members of the Roman house churches. It indicates who they need to think they are (see λογίζεσθε in 6:11) and what the major *ēthos* of their life now needs to be. Although Paul is still speaking in fairly general terms, without directly addressing himself to the Roman congregation, his use of the first person plural in 6 includes it powerfully in the story and provides Paul with the ground work on which to build his direct and concrete address in chapters 12–15.

Children of God: The Power of the Spirit (8)

In chapter 8, the plot turns to a new character, the spirit, which plays a role in deploying the full force of the new self-understanding given to Paul's addressees and stretches the metaphor of slavery to its limits. In chapter 6, because Paul was contrasting the two masters that the members of the Roman house churches could serve, his addressees were given an identity of slaves that powerfully expressed the change of self-understanding connected to their change of master. In chapter 8, however, Paul moves away from the metaphor of slavery. In verse 2, he indicates that the "law of the spirit of life in Christ Jesus" has liberated his addressees from the power of sin.[86] The change of master which powerfully changed their self-understanding

---

[85] See Johnson, *Reading Romans*, 105: "If they are in a 'new world,' then their behavior should follow accordingly. But although they share in God's life through the gift of the Holy Spirit, they still inhabit mortal bodies and live within the structures of the world. They need therefore to learn how to translate this new 'christic' identity into a consistent and coherent mode of behavior. Before taking up individual deeds, Paul thinks in terms of overall orientation, which for him is always a matter of *obedience*."

[86] In 8:2, the "you" is a second person singular, translating *se*. Important manuscripts support another reading with *me*. On the basis of external support, it is difficult to decide which reading is best, but, if one takes into account the influence of Rom 7 – which would invite a με in 8:2, making *se* the *lectio difficilior* – and the use of *prosōpopoiia* in 7:7–25, it is legitimate to read σε in this place (see Moo, *Romans*, 470 n. 11; Jewett, *Romans*, 474). For the influence of *prosōpopoiia* to resolve the question, see Stanley K. Stowers, "Romans 7. 7–25 as a Speech-in-Character (*prosōpopoiia*)," in *Paul in his Hellenistic Context* (ed. T. Engberg-Pedersen; Minneapolis: Fortress Press, 1995), 180–202, here 193: "in light of ancient προσωποποιία and the sense of the passage, the 'you' fits well indeed. The character's speech ends when Paul addresses him with words of encouragement."). Because of the style of *prosōpopoiia*, it is then possible to argue that the second person singular can also include Paul's direct addressees, even if only in an implicit manner.

in chapter 6 does not simply mean a return to the same type of slavery that was their plight under the rule of sin.

Rather, they are freed for a new type of obedience, for which Christ is an example as previous chapters have made clear, and which is made possible through the action of the spirit in them,[87] something that 5:5 already indicated and which is at the center of this passage. From 5:5, we remember that the gift made possible by the spirit was God's love.[88] The obedience asked from the Christ believers is in response to the gift of God's love. It needs to reflect this love in the actions performed by the members of the Roman house churches. Because their self-understanding has changed and because of the workings of the spirit in them, Paul's addressees are able to, and need to, fulfill the demands of the law (8:4.5–8). Their change of self-understanding needs to mean something at the level of their actions. It has very concrete consequences. The plot told in the previous chapters is now focused on Paul's addressees. It cannot be separated from their new character. In fact the plot of the story now needs to continue in those who have received the spirit (8:9) and transform their *ēthos* through transforming their self-understanding. Paul is aware that, in the same way human beings could not liberate themselves from the dominion of sin, they are not left alone in this transformation. The role and the importance of the spirit are central to this chapter. It is the spirit dwelling in them that makes them able to please God.

The role of the spirit is fundamental in defining the new self-understanding given to the Roman community. 8:3 and 4 make clear that God is behind the end of the rule of sin over human beings. Putting an end to the rule of sin over human beings is not done without a purpose. Rather, it enables the fulfillment of the requirements of the law. Paul then moves on to explain how it is possible for human beings to now fulfill the law. It is because their entire way of seeing things is changed (8:4 "walk not according to the flesh, but according to the spirit;" 8:5 "those who live according to the spirit set their minds (φρονεύω) on the things of the spirit").

---

[87] See Johnson, *Reading Romans*, 129: "In this compelling statement of God's act of liberation, perhaps the most startling element is the *purpose* for which liberation has taken place. ... The change brought about is one that affects humans in their freedom. They are now empowered to live in a new way." For a somewhat similar point, about the possibility to live in a new way, see Moo, *Romans*, 485; also Morris, *Romans*, 304 and Barrett, *Romans*, 161–162.

[88] This can function both as a subjective genitive (God loves the members of the Roman house churches) or as an objective genitive (the members of the Roman house churches have received the same type of love as God's love). The first interpretation is more likely (see Moo, *Romans*, 304; Jewett, *Romans*, 356; Dunn, *Romans*, 1:252; Fitzmyer, *Romans*, 398), but it is still possible to say that to this act of love by God, Paul's addressees have to reply with their own loving obedience.

The change does not just concern what human beings do, it is a matter of the mind; it is a matter of perspective. Their moral orientation, their *ēthos* is transformed, and this is reflected in their actions.[89]

Human beings are able to relate to God – and to each other – in a new way because the power that dwells in them has changed. In chapter 7, Paul used strong language to indicate that, before God reconciles them to God through Christ's death, sin inhabits (οἰκέω, see 7:17.18.20 "sin that dwells within me," "nothing good dwells within me" and "sin that dwells within me") human beings. In chapter 8, he uses the same verb οἰκέω to talk about the way the spirit lives in human beings after God's intervention on their behalf (8:9.11 "the spirit of God dwells in you" and "the spirit of him who raised Jesus from the dead dwells in you"). The same intimacy is presupposed in the case of sin and in the case of the spirit. If the hold of sin was so powerful as to make human beings desperate, the hold of the spirit over human beings is as powerful and has the potential of giving life (8:11) and hope (8:24) to the ones it inhabits. It will also lead human beings to put an end to a way of life marked by flesh and death (8:12.13) and open up a new way of life. Paul does not present concrete examples of actions leading to death. Rather, by sin, he refers to a general attitude of hostility towards God (8:7). As Johnson points out, this is not just a "matter of 'hostile feelings' toward God, but rather a matter of shaping one's life according to choices that are, in fact, closed and opposed to God's activity in the world."[90] In contrast, life in the spirit means that Christ is united to human beings (8:10) and as a consequence, life – eternal life – will be given to them (8:11).

The new orientation given to human beings' life is also made clear through the new manner in which Paul is able to describe them as a result of the action of the spirit in them. They are sons of God (8:14). In this case, Paul moves even further away from the metaphor of slavery which dominated the discussion in chapters 6 and 7. Paul makes this particularly clear in 8:15: "for you did not receive a spirit of slavery (πνεῦμα δουλείας) to fall back into fear, but you have received a spirit of adoption (πνεῦμα

---

[89] See Johnson, *Reading Romans*, 129: "It is significant that Paul focuses not on a specific act as 'right or wrong' but rather on what might be called an orientation of freedom, a characteristic direction taken by a person toward or away from God." For a somewhat similar reading, Moo, *Romans*, 486–487: " ... [Paul] notes the basic tendencies of both the flesh and the Spirit ..."; Dunn, *Romans*, 1:425 insists that Rom 8:5 does not elaborate a condition but an attitude or an orientation. See also Käsemann, *Romans*, 219.

[90] Johnson, *Reading Romans*, 130. See also Murray, *Romans*, 1:286: "The essence of sin is to be against God; it is the contradiction of God;" Dunn, *Romans*, 1:427; Moo, *Romans*, 488–489; Morris, *Romans*, 306. Jewett, *Romans*, 488 underlines the fact that the ancients would have judged active hostility towards God as folly. In contrast, Cranfield, *Romans*, 180 defines "hostility toward God" as hatred for God.

υἱοθεσίας) in which we cry: 'Abba! Father!'."[91] The Christ believers have left behind their obligation to sin and to the flesh (8:12)[92] and they are now free to live according to the spirit. The self-understanding of slave is contrasted to the self-understanding of sons of God. One can see the limit of the metaphor of slavery of chapters 6 and 7. The freedom given by God means more than just a change of master. Because the new master is God, the Christ believers need no longer to think of themselves as slaves; rather the work of the spirit in them allows them to understand themselves as sons of God, that is, coheirs with Christ (8:17 συγκληρονόμοι δὲ Χριστοῦ) members of a new family. Through the spirit, the Christ believers now share in the identity of Christ as son of God and in the relationship that Christ has with God. Such a self-understanding anticipates what will be demanded of Paul's addressees in 12–15, in particular the request to imitate Christ's behavior (15:7).

This shared identity with Christ leads into the last section of the chapter (8:18–39) and clarifies how Paul's audience can reconcile the conviction of being heirs of God with the reality of their daily life, which does not seem to correspond to this new self-understanding.[93] The work of the spirit is at the center of this section once more, as the power that enables the Christ believers to endure sufferings (8:18.23.26). At the same time, in terms of *ēthos*, the figure of Abraham is present behind the references to hope in 8:24–25. Abraham is the example of someone who, because of his faith, believed in something that was unseen, indeed un-hoped for in human terms. His faith allows him to see reality in a new manner and to allow room for God's action in that reality.[94]

---

[91] Here my translation differs from the NRSV's ("for you did not receive a spirit of slavery to fall back into fear, but you have received a spirit of adoption. When we cry, 'Abba! Father!'..."). I follow the punctuation in NA 27 and take ἐν ᾧ κράζομεν to modify πνεῦμα υἱοθεσιας. See Johnson, *Reading Romans*, 133: "It is 'in' or 'by' this Spirit, says Paul, that 'we cry out, 'Abba! Father'' (8:15)." See also Moo, *Romans*, 496; Fitzmyer, *Romans*, 497; Dunn, *Romans*, 1:452 advocates for "by whom we cry."

[92] See Johnson, *Reading Romans*, 132: "The meaning here, then, is that those living by the Spirit are no longer under any obligation to the flesh." Jewett, *Romans*, 493 notes the importance of understanding ὀφειλέται ἐσμέν correctly, as covering "the entire range of social and religious obligations in the Roman environment." Fitzmyer, *Romans*, 492 indicates that flesh is no longer the norm of the redeemed life. See also Cranfield, *Romans*, 185; Morris, *Romans*, 311.

[93] See Johnson, *Reading Romans*, 135: "Paul deals here with the acute problem presented by the gap between appearances and reality." See also Morris, *Romans*, 318; Moo, *Romans*, 509. Dunn, *Romans*, 1:467 emphasizes the link between this section and 9–11: "Paul clearly intends his readers to understand that the blessings they are inheriting are Israel's. Hence the problem: What then of Israel itself?"

[94] See Johnson, *Reading Romans*, 139: "But his [Abraham's] hope enabled him to perceive a possibility from God that goes beyond human possibility." Commentators usually

Human beings are invited to make this attitude of hope their own in relationship to their sufferings in the present world. In terms of the plot I have been following in the letter, Paul here gives the clearest indication that, as he has already argued in chapter 5 when contrasting Adam and Christ, human beings live in a new æon. But this æon has not entirely established itself in the world. Christ's believers can claim to be "heirs of God" but at the same time, they still live in a creation which is awaiting complete redemption (8:19). In such a condition, hope is a fundamental quality. It is what assures perseverance (see 5:4–5), perceives "possibility in 'what is not seen',"[95] and imagines what is unheard of, thus allowing human beings to remain trustful.

In the manner by which he moves into eschatological language and concludes by affirming the union of believers with God's love through Christ (8:39), Paul reaches a fitting end to his story, both thematically and stylistically. He has described the new self-understanding given to Christ believers in terms of the general consequence for the orientation of their *ēthos* and for their own self-perception. Thus the plot of the story reaches an appropriate ending: human beings had a false perception of themselves which made them slaves of sin (beginning). Through God's intervention in Christ's death (middle), they have been put outside of the rule of sin. A new self-understanding is given to them which frees them from sin and makes them children of God, allowing them through the power of the spirit to fulfill the law (end).

5. Logical Difficulties Born from the Plot

The narrative sequence that I have just presented is interrupted by chapter 7. In the rhetorical arrangement of the letter, it is logical for Paul to address the role of the law only at this point of his letter. The problem surrounding the status of the law emerges because of the beginning and middle of the story Paul has been telling; in particular, because the law is unable to provide a solution to the problem exposed in the beginning of the story.[96] For, if the rule of sin over human beings is terminated, it is not de-

---

discuss whether salvation is already accomplished or still to come and note that Paul simply states the obvious about the nature of hope in 8:24–25 (so Moo, *Romans*, 522; Fitzmyer, *Romans*, 515; Murray, *Romans*, 1:309; Barrett, *Romans*, 167). But if one keeps in mind hope as characterizing Abraham's *ēthos*, then hoping for what is not seen goes beyond the obvious. It means adopting God's perspective on the world, and perhaps even imagining things unhoped for. Jewett, *Romans*, 520 refers to the apocalyptic background of hope (also Dunn, *Romans*, 1:475–476), and argues that this appeal to hope is designed to comfort Paul's addressees.

[95] Johnson, *Reading Romans*, 139.

[96] The problem of the law and of how it was found lacking by Paul has been at the center of the reassessment of Pauline thought by the new perspective. In contrast to a position long

stroyed as one might expect through the revelation of the law, but through participation in Christ's death and resurrection. The law is powerless when confronted by sin in the Pauline sense, that is, as disordered freedom. In fact, in some places, Paul has written almost as if the law is on the side of sin (3:20.31; 4:15; 5:13.20). Furthermore, chapter 8 indicates that the Christ believers can now please God because they live in the spirit. It is the spirit that becomes the norm of an *ēthos* leading to life. After having presented his scenario of what happened, Paul now returns to the fate of a seeming casualty of the story: the law. [97]

What Norm? The Role of the Law (7:1–8:4)

It is somewhat surprising that in chapter 7 Paul returns to the condition of human beings under sin, [98] since he has just established that human beings

---

dominant in Protestant exegesis, and influenced by Luther's theology, which saw Judaism as a legalistic system founded on the merit of good works (see for example Günther Bornkamm, *Paul* [London: Hodder & Stoughton, 1971]; Bultmann, *Theology of the New Testament*, 1:259–269, here for example 264), Sanders, and a growing number of scholars after him, re-assessed Judaism as a religion where God's grace plays an important role and in which the law regulates the covenant relationship with God (see Dunn, *Romans*, 1:lxv). In the new perspective on Paul, the understanding of the law is central. In particular, as a result of their work on Paul, Sanders and Räisänen have both argued that Paul's view of the law is incoherent and contradictory (see Sanders, *Paul and Palestinian Judaism*; Heikki Räisänen, *Paul and the Law* [WUNT 29; Tübingen: Mohr, 1983]). In Romans in particular, the issues are related to the references behind the use of νόμος (mosaic law, principle, law; see in particular 3:27–31; 7:23; 8:2; 9:31) and to the role that the law can still have after human beings are reconciled to God (see 8:2; 13:8–10). For my particular purpose, I do not need to settle the issue, however, I agree with the new perspective that law should be understood as an identity marker for Israel (see Dunn, *Romans*, 1:lxix), which underlines Israel's sense as the chosen nation. Paul's concern then is with the fact that "covenant promise and law had become too inextricably identified with ethnic Israel as such." (Dunn, *Romans*, 1:lxxi) Paul attempts to widen the access to God's promise, through the saving action of God in Christ. As Dunn also notes, once the law is freed from a perspective too narrowly ethnical, it has a role to play in "the obedience of faith." (Dunn, *Romans*, lxxii)

[97] A further indication that Paul considers he has dealt with the question of the law appropriately in chapter 7 is that there are only a few isolated occurrences of νόμος after chapter 7 and chapter 8 (for example 9:31; 10:4; 13:8; 13:10), whereas before the language was very dense (23 occurrences in chapter 7 alone). See also Dunn, *Romans*, 1:301.

[98] As many commentators, following Kümmel (Werner G. Kümmel, *Römer 7 und das Bild des Menschen im Neuen Testament* [Munich: Kaiser, 1974]), recognize today, it is important to see the rhetorical dimension of the 1st person singular used by Paul in this passage. The passage does not necessarily record a personal experience of Paul. Rather the use of the 1st person singular allows Paul to identify himself with all the individuals that might be able to associate themselves with the painful experiences described in chapter 7. The technique of *prosōpopoiia* allows Paul to make his position more convincing by appealing to the emotions of his readers. See Lauri Thurèn, *Derhetorizing Paul: A Dynamic Perspective on Pauline Theology and the Law* (Harrisburg, Pa.: Trinity Press International, 2002), 121 n. 132: "...*ego*

are in fact now free from the rule of the sin (6:2.6.7.11.12.13.14.17.22).[99] In terms of plot, Paul returns to a previous episode of the story, one that was already developed in 1:18–3:20. This apparent problem in the plot happens because Paul in chapter 7 is compelled to answer a question about the role of the Torah. To answer the question about the status of the law, Paul returns to the plight of humanity before God's saving intervention in Christ, to expose that the law is unable to put an end to this plight. In doing so, he explains the plight of humanity in terms that are in accordance with the assertions of chapter 6 about sin being a master of human beings before God's saving action. Thus, chapter 7 provides a good illustration of

---

is here a good literary device: it identifies the apostle with Adam, the addressees and all humanity. It also allows the rhetorical merger with a more personal, emotional affective *ego* at the end of the chapter;" see also Johnson, *Reading Romans*, 115: "The first-person discourse is less a window giving access to Paul's personality than it is a mirror for the reader's reflection and self-examination. ... Such personification enables an author to bring a logical position vibrantly to life, by 'performing it.' The ancient rhetorical designation for such 'speech-in-character' was *prosōpopoiia* ('making a mask'), and it fits what Paul is doing here very well." A similar technique is described as indirect communication by Søren Kierkegaard, *Concluding Unscientific Postscript to Philosophical Fragments* (ed. W. Lowrie; trans. D. F. Swenson; Princeton: Princeton University Press, 1944), 246–247. See Valérie Nicolet-Anderson, "Tools for a Kierkegaardian Reading of Paul: Can Kierkegaard Help Us Understand the Role of the Law in Romans 7:7–12?" in *Reading Romans With Contemporary Philosophers and Theologians* (ed. D. Odell-Scott; New York: T&T Clark, 2007), 247–273, here 260: "Paul does not think of an entire theory of indirect communication when he writes to the Roman community using 'I.' However, he does think of them as 'existential subjects.' This leads him to tell them one of his truths by using an 'I' discourse that gives him the opportunity to include them in what he is telling them. The 'I' of Rom 7:7–12 does not need to represent Paul himself, Adam, or the people of Israel. Paul uses these three sources to express one of his convictions and to bring his readers to live in that truth." On the question of *prosōpopoiia*, see Stowers, "Romans 7:7–25 as Speech-in-Character (*prosōpopoiia*);" also Jean-Baptiste Édart, "De la nécessité d'un sauveur: rhétorique et théologie de Rm 7:7–25," *RB* 105 (1998): 359–396.

[99] This "glitch" in the plot is in fact at the origin of many protestant interpretations of Rom 7 which, following Luther's lead, see Rom 7 as talking about the life of the Christian believer after salvation: see Moo, *Romans*, 444: "The interpretation of vv. 14–25 in terms of 'normal' Christian experience was typical of Lutheran and Reformed theology right in to the twentieth century and is still widespread." See Martin Luther, *Lectures on Romans: Glosses and Scholia*, (vol. 25 of *Luther's Work*; ed. J. Pelikan; trans. J. A. O. Preus; Saint Louis, Mo. : Concordia, 1972), 328–329: "Thus the first expression which proves that these are the words of a spiritual man is this: *But I am carnal* (v. 14). For it is characteristic of a spiritual and wise man to know that he is carnal and displeasing to himself, to hate himself and to approve the law of God because it is spiritual" and 335: "... it is a comfort to hear that such a great apostle was involved in the same sorrows and afflictions as we are when we try to be obedient to God." In the footsteps of Luther, see for example Karl Barth, *L'Épître aux Romains* (trans. P. Jundt; Geneva: Labor et Fides, 1972), 249; Theodor Zahn, *Der Brief des Paulus an die Römer* (Leipzig: Deichert, 1910), Nygren, *Romans*, Murray, *Romans*; Barrett, *Romans*.

what it means to be a slave of sin, even though in terms of the plot, Christ believers are actually no longer slaves of sin.

While Paul affirms the basic value of the law (7:7.12), he also indicates that sin used the law in order to become alive in human beings (7:7.8.9). The basic problem with the law is that it "can *identify* sin, but cannot *prevent* it."[100] The rule of sin over human beings cannot be avoided by the law. In terms of plot, we are right at the beginning again: human beings are slaves of sin (7:14–23). The law has the capacity to describe a new *ēthos* for human beings but it cannot create it. The law is exonerated from this inability in 7:7–25.[101] Paul indicates that the law has fallen victim to the power of sin (7:7–11). Instead of suppressing sin, the law has in fact been seized by sin and sin has been able to use the commandment as an ally in its effort to take hold of human beings.[102] The law was not responsible for that fact (7:13), it was simply powerless to resist sin. The power of sin exculpates the law. Paul also strengthens his apology for the law in 7:14–23, by showing that human beings, even when they are in the dominion of sin, realize that the law should be upheld and respected (7:22–23). Because of

---

[100] Johnson, *Reading Romans*, 118. Dunn, *Romans*, 1:381 indicates that the "giving of the law did not provide a realm (Israel with its cult) where the power of sin was broken; on the contrary, as Gen 3 shows, the giving of the commandment simply provides sin with a more effective leverage on man (the devout Jew not excluded)." While I agree in principle with the idea that one of the difficulties Paul has with the law is its function as identity-marker, I do think that in Rom 7, Paul is more concerned to show how the law is unable to act against sin. Only the intervention of God through Christ could break the power of sin and death. See also Moo, *Romans*, 443. Contra Jewett, *Romans*, 452 who sees the problem of the law in relationship to Paul's personal life, as the deception of "believing that superior performance of the law would earn honor both from fellow humans and from God and that such obedience would ultimately usher in God's kingdom." For Jewett, *Romans*, 444, the problem is "legalistic zealotism."

[101] See Elliott, *The Rhetoric of Romans*, 245: "The passage constitutes an 'apology for the Law,' shaped on the one hand by the rhetorical questions in 7.6 ('Is the Law sin?') and 7.13 ('Did the good [the Law] become death for me?') and on the other by the crescendo of approval of and consent with the Law from 7.12 ('the Law is holy and the commandment is holy just and good') to 7.14 ('we know that the Law is spiritual') to 7.16 ('I agree that the law is good') and 7.22 ('I delight in the law of God in my inmost self')." See also Dunn, *Romans*, 1:376–377. Jewett, *Romans*, 440 notes that it is not quite appropriate to define Rom 7:7–25 as an apology for the law because it really aims "to clarify its [the law's] bearing on the situation of the Roman church."

[102] The story of Adam and Eve (already alluded to in Rom 1) in Gen 3 stands behind these verses and sheds light on the point of the passage, even though one cannot exclude a reference to the gift of the law to Israel as well. For the reference to Adam, see Ulrich Wilckens, *Der Brief an die Römer* (3 vols.; EKKNT 6; Zurich – Neukirchen: Benziger Verlag – Neukirchener Verlag, 1978–1982), 2:79; Käsemann, *Romans*, 196–197; Dunn, *Romans*. For the reference to Israel, see Moo, *Romans*, 428–431. For a conflation of both, see Grieb, *The Story of Romans*, 72–73.

the complete possession of sin over them, however, human beings are unable to act upon the realization that the law is worthy to be respected. Rather, they agree, even involuntarily, to the rule of sin in them. The law cannot be made responsible for its failure to create in human beings an *ēthos* capable of resisting sin. It is exonerated from blame and can still be described as something in which one should delight. The law is described as an ideal but it cannot be enacted by human beings because of the power of sin. Once the power of sin is removed, the law is fine (8:4). The defense of the law also implicitly supports God's *ēthos* in giving the law in the first place. The demands of the law should not be rejected. They become problematic only because of sin's hold on human beings. Thus the solution to the problem of the law comes in the form of God's intervention on behalf of human beings.

The new *ēthos* in human beings can only be created by God's intervention manifested in two ways, as *exemplum* through Christ and as power (δύναμις) through the spirit. God's intervention not only puts an end to the rule of sin, but also creates the ability in human beings to conform themselves to the *ēthos* exemplified by Christ, through the help of the spirit. As a consequence, the law is actually no longer a problem. As the ἄρα νῦν opening chapter 8 indicates, human beings, because they live in a new æon, are now in a new relationship towards the law. In 8:3–4, Paul makes clear that human beings are now in a position to fulfill the law, because of God's action through Christ's death and because of the gift of the spirit. Through human beings' new situation, the law is no longer the ally of death and sin, rather it is something that can now be followed and upheld, in imitation of Christ's obedience and with the help of the spirit. What could not be done in the old æon can now be done through the power of the spirit. This also helps to clarify the role of the law. It was never meant to be abandoned; rather it can now be fulfilled.[103] Thus, indeed, the law is

---

[103] See Johnson, *Reading Romans*, 129: "The freedom given by the Holy Spirit, in other words, leads not to an abandonment of God's will as revealed in the Torah but to the fulfillment of its righteous requirement." See also Elliott, *The Rhetoric of Romans*, 244 who insists that this is also the point of 7:1–6: "Just as the (marriage) law remains valid in constituting the woman's second marriage as legitimate and not as 'adultery,' so, the analogy implies, the sovereign claim established in Torah remains valid (cf. 3.31, νόμον ἱστάνομεν) so as to declare the Christian 'righteous' *within the sphere of Christ's lordship*. So much Paul declares explicitly in 8.1–4: the Law's righteous demand (δικαίωμα) is fulfilled by those who walk by the Spirit (8:4)." Elliott actually sees Romans as an argument against a Hellenistic-Christian understanding of justification by faith as cheap grace, which liberates from the demands of the law. See also, for the continued validity of the claims of the law and the possibility of the Christ believers to respect them, Morris, *Romans*, 304; Dunn, *Romans*, 1:437–438; Jewett, *Romans*, 485–486 who insists on the community aspect of the fulfillment; Cranfield, *Romans*, 178–179 indicates that the fulfillment is a matter of direction: "They fulfill it [the law] in the

holy (7:12). Its commandments, however, can only be fulfilled through the gift of the spirit. The spirit becomes the new norm that enables Christ believers to fulfill the requirements of the law (8:4). Because it transforms the *ēthos* of the ones it inhabits, the spirit has the power to give guidance to Christ believers, accomplishing what the law was unable to do previously. The power of the spirit, however, raises another difficulty for Paul. If the norm is now the spirit, and if, in particular, it is the spirit that establishes human beings in the status of sons of God, giving them a spirit of adoption (υἱοθεσία, 8:14.15) then the privileged status of Israel is called into question.[104]

The Problem of the Particular: The People of God and God's Faithfulness (9–11)
In 9:4, after having emphasized the sorrow that the situation of his own people creates in him (9:1–3), Paul describes the privileged status of Israel and he presents "adoption" (υἱοθεσία) as the first of their belonging.[105] This

---

sense that they do have a real faith in God (which is the law's basic demand), in the sense that their lives are definitely turned in the direction of obedience, that they do sincerely desire to obey and are earnestly striving to advance ever nearer to perfection." Murray, *Romans*, 1:283–284 is similar to Cranfield. Contra Fitzmyer, *Romans*, 487–488 who insists on the passive aspect of the fulfillment; so also Moo, *Romans*, 483.

[104] The vocabulary connection (see Dunn, *Romans*, 2:522) with chapter 8 should make it clear that 9–11 cannot be understood separately from the rest of the letter. These chapters belong to it in a very important manner; in terms of the plot of the story, they answer a problem raised by the plot itself. For the connection with chapter 8, see Elliott, *The Rhetoric of Romans*, 253–270. In recent years, commentaries increasingly recognizes the relationship of these chapters with the rest of the letter (contra the view that it was merely an addition, see for example Charles Dodd, *The Epistle of Paul to the Romans* [MNTC; New York: Harper and Bros., 1932], 149–150 who sees these chapters as an independent sermon inserted in the letter). They usually emphasize the manner in which 9–11 takes up a problem that the previous argumentation has raised: God's faithfulness to Israel and Israel's destiny. See for example Dunn, *Romans*, 2:519–520; Nygren, *Romans*, 357 (who, despite the fact that he accepts that the section discusses issues related to God's promises, refuses to see theodicy involved in the discussion); Cranfield, *Romans*, 214. Fitzmyer, *Romans*, 539 sees these chapters as the climax of the doctrinal section of the letter (following Stendahl, *Paul among Jews and Gentiles*); Käsemann, *Romans*, 256; Murray, *Romans*, 2:xii; Morris, *Romans*, 343–344, without seeing the chapters as the most important part of the epistle, recognizes the strong connection with what Paul has written earlier; see also Moo, *Romans*, 548–549, 551.

[105] Seeing Rom 9–11 as answering questions raised by the plot of the story that Paul has been telling in 1:18–8:39 does not amount to going back to a reading of Romans as a compendium of Christian doctrine, in which these chapters do not fit because they do not correspond to categories of Christian theology (See Grieb's comments on that tradition of reading in *The Story of Romans*, 86: "Since the Protestant Reformation, commentators have had a hard time seeing how these chapters belong to Paul's letter because they don't fit into the standard progression of doctrinal topics: Doctrine of God, Creation and Fall, Sin and Need for Salvation, Justification, Sanctification and Christian Life. ... And if Paul's theological argu-

is precisely the notion he has universalized earlier in the letter (chapter 8). In terms of plot, therefore, chapters 9–11 start with the question of the place of one important character of the story – Israel – among the children of God (see also 9:8).[106] This question however is not discussed for itself at any point of the section. Rather, Paul moves directly to the fact that this difficulty with one of the characters of the plot – Israel as the people of God – has consequences for evaluating the *ēthos* of another character central to the plot – God – and, as will become clear in chapter 11, for the *ēthos* of yet another character, the Gentile believers. In 6a, the affirmation "it is not as though the word of God had failed" shows that what concerns Paul in the question of the composition of the people of God is primarily what it says about God's *ēthos* and secondarily what it means for the future of Israel. Thus, chapters 9–11 are constructed as a triple defense of God's *ēthos*,[107] which also has consequences for the future of Israel and for the *ēthos* of the community.

The first defense of God's *ēthos* is found in 9:6b–29 and consists in an affirmation of God's sovereignty. In 9:30–10:21, Paul, in his second way of defending God's *ēthos*, points out that Israel has encountered a problem; they failed to recognize the messiah. Finally, in 11:1–32, Paul proposes a third manner of defense, which highlights the fact that God will remain faithful in the end. It is only in this third way of defending God, which clearly presents God's faithfulness, that Paul makes the connection with the question about the children of God clear again. In the end, Israel will be joined to the people of God (11:2–7. 23–32), which also indicates that the community will be a mixed community, including both Jews and Gentiles. Thus Paul already gives some instructions in order to promote peaceful cohabitation in this community (11:11–22), instructions that will be made more explicit in chapters 14–15.

---

ment is reduced to the dimensions of a set of topics in systematic theology, then it seems to work without Romans 9–11, especially if it is also argued that Israel's problem is not our problem and Israel's story is not our story.") In terms of plot, these chapters do form a digression, but they are not unconnected to the plot. In fact, because they explain the doings and moral attitudes of two characters of the plot, they are very much related to the main plot. In addition, these chapters also have an important role to play in preparation for Paul's exhortation for harmony inside the community in chapter 15.

[106] As Grieb, *The Story of Romans*, 90 points out, this section of Romans also goes back to answer questions raised at the beginning of chapter 3: "it [Rom 9:1–5] is a flashback to Romans 3:1–6, revisiting the questions raised and answered much too summarily there, and placing those questions on the table here at the proper place in Paul's argument … ." See also Johnson, *Reading Romans*, 149; Nygren, *Romans*, 357; Moo, *Romans*, 549; Fitzmyer, *Romans*, 539; Dunn, *Romans*, 2:519, 531; Stowers, *A Rereading of Romans*, 286.

[107] See Johnson, *Reading Romans*, 151. The fact that God's righteousness is a key theme in this section is recognized by most recent commentaries (see note 104).

First Defense of God's Ēthos: *God's Sovereignty (Rom 9:6b–29)*
In his first attempt to explain that the word of God has not failed, Paul insists on God's absolute freedom in choosing who God's true descendants are. He adduces the examples of the choice of Isaac and of Jacob to support his assertion that God has the freedom of choosing who belongs to God's people (9:6b). Looking at God's action in the past provides Paul with a "pattern of God's action with respect to forming a people for himself."[108] This pattern is based on God's own promise and election, not on a particular birth (Isaac) or on particular moral qualities, since Jacob is chosen over Esau even before their birth (9:11). The story of Jacob and Esau gives Paul an example of God's sovereignty when it comes to choosing descendants.[109]

It also however creates the opportunity for a misinterpretation of the story. It opens the possibility of accusing God of being unjust (9:14 ἀδικία), something that Paul rejects vehemently, as he has already done in 3:5. Paul finds an answer to that misinterpretation in another passage of the Torah (Ex 33:19) and, through the use of that passage, Paul insists on God's mercy in choosing one individual over another (9:16).[110] This dimension of mercy will play a role again in the section, especially at the end of chapter 11, when Paul affirms that God will indeed be merciful to all (11:32) and assures Israel of her final participation in the people of God (11:26.29.31). At the same time, the example of Pharaoh (9:17–18) highlights the fact that God's sovereignty can also express itself in hardening. God's mercy is not dependent upon human pressure and cannot be understood as cheap grace, rather it only responds to God's will.

---

[108] Johnson, *Reading Romans*, 158.

[109] See Elliott, *The Rhetoric of Romans*, 265: "The principle established and maintained throughout this discussion [9:6–29] is divine *sovereignty* ..." See also, Nygren, *Romans*, 362–364, 366; Morris, *Romans*, 351; Moo, *Romans*, 568, 588, 590.

[110] For Grieb, *The Story of Romans*, 92, this is an example of the way Paul is arguing with God in this passage, trying to find answers to questions about Israel that plague him: "Paul is arguing with God like Job; he is praying a lament psalm, begging God to show him why the conclusions he does not want to reach are wrong. When Paul tries to understand what is going on with Israel, terrible thoughts come to him, which he lifts up to God for correction. ... We can see in Paul's argument that every time he gets to one of these terrifying places, God gives him a clue, usually a biblical text, suggesting that there is another way to see it. The text from Malachi that Paul has thought of may not apply to Paul's situation after all. Instead, perhaps the more helpful text is Exodus 33:19. ... Indeed, we can read all of Romans 9–11 as a record of Paul's thought process as he works his way through the painful question of God's justice to Israel in dialogue with God – and also with the churches in Rome whom he allows to overhear the transcript of his prayer journal." While I agree that Paul is wrestling with a hard personal question, I do not think that Rom 9–11 is the candid transcript of Paul's own difficulties. It makes a rhetorical point in the letter, aimed at defending God's righteousness and at establishing a *modus vivendi* for a community composed of Jews and Gentiles.

Human beings, however, are in no position to criticize God's will (9:19.20) because of the absolute difference between creatures and creator (9:20–21). God's purpose is beyond contestation (9:22–23), even if it seems confusing to human spectators. It is precisely because human beings lack the perspective of the creator that they should refrain from criticizing a plan that they can neither see in its entirety nor clearly understand.[111] When Paul reminds his addressees of their position as creature, he also re-calls for them the criticism of arrogance (1:18–32) and boasting (3:27) at the beginning of this letter.[112] Creatures do not have the stature to call into question the plan of God. It remains that God's plan implies including the Gentiles in God's people (9:24.25–26), a fact that Paul establishes through two quotations of Hosea (Hos 2:25; Hos 2:1 LXX). In contrast to the met-aphor of the potter (9:22–23), God does not actually destroy any of the peoples God has chosen. Rather, Paul can affirm that God has expanded God's people beyond Israel by including the Gentiles.[113] For the Israelites, only some of them will be included in the people of God (9:27). Concern-ing the ethnic Israel, the people of God seems to be contracted, at least in the present time.[114] The next section explains how this contraction of Israel to a remnant has happened and how, again, it does not call into question God's faithfulness to Israel.

Second Defense of God's Ēthos: The Problem of Israel (9:30–10:21)
In this section, Paul argues that God has not abandoned Israel. He explains why a part of Israel has actually been unable to recognize God's hand in the giving of the messiah. This section is concerned with explaining what went wrong for Israel, but implicitly it also establishes God's faithfulness. God's messiah was recognized by the Gentiles making them part of the

---

[111] See Johnson, *The Story of Romans*, 162: "The full citation [of Is 29:16] is important here, for it asserts not only the derivation and dependence of the creature on the creator but also the inability of anyone not having 'maker's knowledge' to know the entire plan within which each piece might fit. The creature is not in the position to state of the creator, 'he has no understanding,' because the creature is never in the position of observing the plan whole, much less grasping it." For a careful reading of the tradition behind the quote and the impact it has on Paul's argument, see Jewett, *Romans*, 592–593.

[112] See Jewett, *Romans*, 592.

[113] See Johnson, *The Story of Romans*, 164: "Israel can also be *larger* than the boundaries of Jewish ethnicity … For this conclusion, Paul also finds support in Torah, this time in the words of Hosea the prophet." Moo, *Romans*, 613 notes that Paul interprets Hosea freely when he applies the quotations to the Gentiles. This is not what Hosea had in mind, when he ad-dressed himself to the northern kingdom of Israel. However, Paul uses the Hosea quotes to make a point about the breaking down of ethnic boundaries in the constitution of God's peo-ple.

[114] See Johnson, *The Story of Romans*, 166. Morris, *Romans*, 371 notes the same contrast between the inclusion of the Gentiles and the exclusion of a part of Israel.

people of God; but it was rejected by some in Israel, thus excluding them, at least temporarily, from the people of God.[115] It is not that God turned away from Israel. Rather, it is Israel who could not open herself to the new way in which God was revealing Godself. Paul develops the difficulty that Israel has with the messiah in 9:31–10:13. The reversion to the language of the gospel in 9:30–10:13 – a language which dominated 1:16–17 and 3:21– 4:25 – might be a supplementary indication that the problem of Israel is precisely her relationship to the gospel about Christ.[116] In addition, and this is yet another way in which Paul establishes God's faithfulness towards Israel, Paul also argues in this section that Israel could in fact have recognized the revelation of the messiah in the gospel about Christ because it was announced to her in her scriptures.[117]

In 10:9, Paul affirms that the condition of salvation is to confess that Christ is Lord and that God raised him from the dead. From this verse, it seems that Israel is not saved because she did not recognize Jesus as the messiah. The status of Jesus as messiah is the stumbling stone over which Israel has tripped (9:32–33). This basic error of judgment indicates in what way Israel's zeal was not κατ' ἐπίγνωσιν (10:2). The problem of Israel is that she did not recognize God's action in the world. When faced with the choice between God's paradoxical revelation in a crucified Christ and the writings of Torah, which condemn a crucified messiah, Israel trusted in Torah. Thus she closed herself to God's revelation in Christ, which was God's new way to reveal God's righteousness (10:3). As Paul has already established in 1:18–3:20, a wrong relationship with God comes from an unwillingness to accept God's perspective on the world. For Israel, the unwillingness to recognize God's perspective is translated in her refusal to accept Jesus as messiah. As a consequence, Israel has kept her focus on the law, but her focus is misguided since she does not see that the law is actually pointing to Jesus as the messiah – a fact that will be made clear by Paul in 10:5–21.[118] The problem of Israel is that she has not recognized the

---

[115] This section also emphasizes the importance of human response to God's initiative, especially in 10:14–21. See Dunn, *Romans*, 2:618; Moo, *Romans*, 661; Fitmyer, *Romans*, 576; Morris, *Romans*, 374.

[116] See Moo, *Romans*, 618. Also Dunn, *Romans*, 2:591–592; Jewett, *Romans*, 611–612.

[117] See Moo, *Romans*, 618: "[Paul] shows (1) that Israel's situation is the result of her failure to recognize in the gospel and in the Jesus proclaimed in the gospel the culmination of salvation history (9:30–10:13); and (2) that Israel's failure to recognize this is inexcusable, because the OT itself points to this culmination (10:14–21 especially)." This is against the traditional protestant interpretation which sees the mistake of Israel as being the fact that she sought salvation through works (see Barrett, *Romans*, 193; for a classic formulation, see Bultmann, *Theology of the New Testament*, 1:264).

[118] See Johnson, *Reading Romans*, 170: "[Paul] means that Jesus messiah was what Torah was pointing to all along. ... Not to recognize Jesus as messiah, therefore, means also not to

beginning of a new æon starting with Christ and has not accepted that this new æon implies the participation of the Gentiles in the people of God.[119]

However, Paul, building on what he has established in Rom 7, also argues, in addition, that Israel's attempt to pursue righteousness through the achievement of the law is misguided. It is not that Paul finds the law's demands illegitimate. In fact he is quite comfortable with the idea of doing works and of fulfilling the demands of the law (see 2:13; 6:13.19; 8:4).[120] But Paul has also made clear that, because of sin, the law is unable to defeat sin in human beings (7:7–13). So the problem with the law is not that it cannot be kept. Rather, even when it is respected, it cannot liberate one from the hold of sin, especially when the perspective is from works. In such a perspective, keeping the law becomes a matter of accomplishment (9:32) and a ground for boasting (see 4:2). One loses sight of the fact that keeping the law is essentially "a response in faith to the living God."[121]

God's *ēthos* receded somewhat in the background in 9:30–10:4. In 10:5–21 Paul reaffirms God's righteousness and faithfulness. He argues for what he has boldly affirmed in 10:4, namely that Torah was already pointing to Christ as the mean of salvation for everyone who believes.[122] In the

---

have understood Torah itself!" and Elliott, *The Rhetoric of Romans*, 266: "The *pathos* of the paradox in 9.30–10.4 lies in Israel's dismaying failure to realize the goal of the Law, Israel's peculiar treasure, by recognizing the Messiah as the manifestation of God's righteousness." Also, Moo, *Romans*, 618 and Dunn, *Romans*, 2:577 note that the messiah marks the end of a narrow view of the law.

[119] This view of the problem of Israel according to Paul became prominent following the work of scholars such as E. P. Sanders, *Paul, the Law and the Jewish People* (Philadelphia: Fortress Press, 1983) and Räisänen, *Paul and the Law* and characterizes the approach of the new perspective on Paul. See Dunn, *Romans*, 1:lxiii–lxxii who notes that this is precisely why the law is criticized by Paul. See also James D. G. Dunn, "What Was the Issue Between Paul and 'Those of the Circumcision'?" in *Paulus und das antike Judentum* (ed. M. Hengel and U. Heckel; Tübingen: Mohr Siebeck, 1991), 295–312; repr. in *The New Perspective on Paul* (rev. ed.; Grand Rapids, Mich.: Eerdmans, 2008), 153–171.

[120] See Johnson, *Reading Romans*, 167: "[Paul] does not suggest, we notice, that his fellow Jews could not keep the law. The ability to keep the law is everywhere assumed by this letter." See also Jewett, *Romans*, 624. Dunn, *Romans*, 2:581 makes a similar remark: "The verb [διώκω] simply describes, in terms his fellow Jews would approve (see on 9:30), the committed lifestyle of the devout covenant member ... It is not the 'pursuing' which Paul criticizes but how that was understood ..."

[121] See Johnson, *Reading Romans*, 167. I think Dunn, *Romans*, 2:582–583 is too unilateral here in arguing that the problem of the law is solely at the level of nationalistic claims. This is undoubtedly true, but in this section, Paul does seem to refer back to the problem he has with the law in chapter 7, which is that it cannot fight the power of sin.

[122] In the debate about the meaning of Christ as the law's τέλος, I side with the scholars who understand τέλος as meaning the goal or purpose of the law rather than the termination of the law. See Johnson, *Reading Romans*, 170 (who also accepts that τέλος points to the end of the epoch of the law, see also for this combined meaning Moo, *Romans*, 641; Dunn, *Romans*,

verses that follow, Paul is showing that Christ was announced in Israel's scriptures,[123] and thus that God has not proven unfaithful to Israel in revealing Godself in Christ. Israel had what she needed to see that Jesus was indeed the messiah. Paul uses texts from Deuteronomy (the law) and Isaiah (the prophets) to make his point. As Johnson indicates, in these verses (10:14–21), Paul is not referring to the proclamation of the gospel to Jews by Christ believers,[124] rather he is "collapsing the horizons" between present and past and engaging in a reading of the prophet Isaiah that will yield a "'pre-promising of the good news in the sacred writings through the prophets' (1:2)."[125]

God remains faithful to Israel because the gospel about Christ and about the inclusion of the Gentiles in the people of God was preached to Israel already in the past, through the prophets. God's faithfulness is established through the use of Israel's scripture, in order to prove that the good news about Christ is already contained in Israel's own sacred writings. The same is true of the inclusion of the Gentiles. Here too, God did not catch Israel by surprise. Paul uses several quotations of scripture in 10:19–20 to prove that the inclusion of the Gentiles is announced in Israel's own Torah, once more affirming God's absolute justice and fidelity, which become the main argument of 11.[126]

2:589, For Dunn, the aspect of the law that is terminated is the understanding of the law that strives to preserve Israel's distinctiveness); Grieb, *The Story of Romans*, 98–99; Fitzmyer, *Romans*, 584; Moo, *Romans*, 636; Jewett, *Romans*, 619. Contra Käsemann, *Romans*, 281–283.

[123] See Johnson, *Reading Romans*, 170: "Paul will read Christ back into Torah, and thus show that the good news was 'pre-promised in the sacred writings through the prophets' (1:2) and was 'witnessed to by Law and Prophets' (3:21)." See also Morris, *Romans*, 376; Jewett, *Romans*, 625; Dunn, *Romans*, 2:614; Moo, *Romans*, 653.

[124] See also Dunn, *Romans*, 2:627, but Dunn also sees a clear reference to Paul's mission in 9:14–15 (Dunn, *Romans*, 2:628–629). For a contrary reading, see Grieb, *The Story of Romans*, 100–101: "Romans 9–11 is structured as a lament psalm, which describes (in 9:1–5 and 10:1–4) Paul's anguish about Israel's continued unbelief and here (10:14–21) details Paul's complaint to God that in spite of his and his coworkers' best preaching of the gospel, the Gentiles were coming into the church in great numbers while Israel's people failed to believe that Jesus Christ was the promised savior." For Moo, *Romans*, 663, Paul refers both to the OT and to "the worldwide proclamation of the Gospel" but Moo reads 10:15–28 as referring principally to the proclamation of the gospel by authorized messengers. It is clear that Paul is anguished by the failure of Israel to recognize the gospel about Christ, but his defense involves showing how Israel's own writings pointed to the identity of Jesus as messiah, as well as affirming God's faithfulness to Israel. Paul is not upset with God in this section. He rather is confident that God's plan for the Gentiles and for Israel will eventually succeed.

[125] Johnson, *Reading Romans*, 172.

[126] Isaiah in particular is understood by Paul as announcing the message about Christ (10:17), as made clear in the servant songs of chapters 52 and 53 – a strong influence behind the writing of Romans (see Grieb, *The Story of Romans*, 102 and Johnson, *Reading Romans*,

Third Defense of God's Ēthos: *Israel's Future Salvation (11:1–36)*
Because Israel has failed to recognize the messiah announced by her scriptures, and because the Gentiles are described as being the new recipients of God's revelation (10:20), one can legitimately wonder whether God has abandoned Israel. 11:1 asks exactly that question, challenging not only the status of Israel as the people of the covenant, but also God's *ēthos* as the God who keeps God's promises. Paul's answer to that question centers on God's faithfulness (11:29), displayed in the present choice of a remnant (11:2.5) and in the future salvation of all of Israel (11:12.23.26.32).[127]

Thus, Paul is able to return to the question that opened the discussion about the fidelity of God, namely the status of Israel as children of God (9:4.8) and to affirm that God has not replaced Israel with the Gentile Christ believers. The question of the faithfulness of God and the status of Israel are closely interrelated. God's *ēthos* as faithful and merciful is definitely established (11:32), and, as consequence of God's *ēthos*, so is the future salvation of all of Israel. At the same time, this section does not lose sight of the overall purpose of the letter, which is the transformation of the *ēthos* of the community. This concern is central in 11:13–32; to address it, Paul again bases his argumentation on God's *ēthos* of mercy and faithfulness, putting an end to all claims of presumptuousness (11:25, which already uses the language of φρόνεσις, central in 12:16) and trying to establish a harmonious community.

Paul defends God's *ēthos* by reaffirming the fact that God has not rejected God's people, despite their refusal to recognize the messiah in Jesus. The arguments advanced by Paul emphasize elements of God's *ēthos* already put into place in the previous passages (sovereignty, fidelity and

---

174). Through the use of Isaiah in 10:16, Paul is able to show God's faithfulness in the gift of the words of Isaiah, who announced a suffering servant. Thus Israel should have been able to recognize her messiah in Jesus crucified (See Johnson, *Reading Romans*, 174: "If, then, Paul thinks that Isaiah already proclaimed a 'message about Messiah,' and that this message was about a messiah who, despite being 'counted among the lawless' (Isa 53:12), was actually 'bearing the sins of many and was handed over for their sins' (Isa 53:12), suffering as a righteous person who made others righteous (53:11), then those who read Torah *should* have been able to 'recognize' the messiah in the death of the righteous person Jesus."). In contrast, for Jewett, *Romans*, 642 the reference is here to the preaching of the missionaries, in whom Christ was thought to be spiritually present.

[127] In 11:25–32, it is clear that Paul has in mind the salvation of all of Israel as the final way in which God will deal with God's chosen people. However, until then, as Dunn notes, Israel is divided and only a remnant is saved (see Dunn, *The Theology of Paul the Apostle*, 508). The tension between 9:6–13 and 11:1–32 is noted by Heikki Räisänen, "Römer 9–11: Analyse eines geistigen Ringens," *ANRW* 25.4:2891–2939, here 2893, 2910–2912, 2927–2928, 2930–2935. Dunn, *Romans*, 2:540 insists that it is not a question of the reality of the election of Israel, but rather the character and mode of it.

mercy). First, Paul reminds his addressees of God's sovereignty, displayed in God's choice of a remnant for Godself (11:3–6). In the story of Elijah, used as a scriptural reference for the notion of remnant, God spares some because they have shown their faithfulness to God by not bowing to Baal. Paul in contrast insists that the remnant is selected through grace. The insistence on grace allows him to testify to God's sovereign right to choose (11:3) – a theme that Paul has already established in 9:16.18.[128] God's sovereignty is also the reason behind Israel's failure (11:7). It is God's sovereign right to harden whomever God chooses that stands behind Israel's failure, as the scripture quotation makes painfully clear (11:8–10). God's sovereignty is here expressed in positive terms – through the choice of a remnant by grace – and in negative terms – through the hardening of Israel. However, even this hardening of Israel cannot question God's ultimate faithfulness to God's people. Even in the worst of times, as the reference to Elijah makes clear, God remains faithful to God's people, since God chooses a remnant among this people (11:2).

Moreover, the notion of God's faithfulness is also made clear in 11:11–16, where Paul proceeds to explain the eschatological reason behind Israel's failure. In chapter 10, Paul presented the content of Israel's stumbling. Here, Paul explains how the failure of Israel fits in God's plan for the Gentiles and for Israel.[129] The hardening of Israel – as the hardening of Pharaoh mentioned in 9:17 – is not gratuitous. It allows for the inclusion of the Gentiles in the people of God (11:11). This does not suffice to explain how, even through failure, God remains faithful to Israel and Paul is keen to explain that the story does not end with the inclusion of the Gentiles. Rather, the inclusion of the Gentiles, made possible through Israel's failure, also works towards the final salvation of Israel (11:11.14).[130] In fact, Paul goes so far as to say that the purpose of his own ministry, directed towards the Gentiles, is ultimately to the advantage of the Jews and that

---

[128] See Grieb, *The Story of Romans*, 106: "It is a remnant chosen by grace, insists Paul, mindful of the sovereign freedom of God to elect some and not others that he reviewed in 9:6–29." See also Dunn, *The Theology of Paul the Apostle*, 521 and *Romans*, 2:639; Moo, *Romans*, 677–678.

[129] See Johnson, *Reading Romans*, 178: "God is simply using their mistake to advance God's own purpose. In an instant, Paul sketches his sense of what function is being served by their 'trespass'." Also Murray, *Romans*, 2:76; Cranfield, *Romans*, 274. Paul also gives an answer to the objections that had been raised in 3:3–5 and is able to explain even more fully how Israel's injustice establishes God's righteousness.

[130] In view of what Paul has argued previously in the letter, especially in light of 5:6–11, and because of the eschatological tone of the passage, it seems that the concept of "salvation" for Israel means that Israel will be spared from God's wrath on the day of judgment. Because Israel will be incorporated in God's people again through its belief in Christ, and thus reconciled to God, she will also escape God's wrath and be saved.

Paul works for their salvation as well (11:14). Thus, even when God is working towards the salvation of the Gentiles through the hardening of Israel, God is in fact still reaching out to Israel, and demonstrating God's faithfulness towards God's people. Israel is not forgotten and her zeal for God is recognized as the quality that will in the end allow her to come back to her God (11:14).[131]

Finally, God's faithfulness is manifested in the strongest manner at the end of chapter 11. Having presented Israel's role in the plan of God – and having established Israel's importance in this plan – Paul feels confident that all of Israel will in fact be saved in the end. This conviction comes from the understanding of Israel's role in the inclusion of the Gentiles in the people of God (11:25). Only when all of the Gentiles have come into the people of God will all of Israel be saved. But Paul's conviction is also supported by his belief in God's sovereignty, faithfulness and mercy. Because God is sovereign, God has the capacity to include those who had previously been cut off as an effect of the same sovereignty (11:23). Because God is faithful to God's gifts (χαρίσματα) and to God's election (κλῆσις), God will not reject Israel. In fact, in order to remain true to God's *ēthos*, God cannot reject Israel (11:28–29). Finally, because God is merciful, God will include everyone in the people of God. God's *ēthos* allows Paul to be confident in Israel's role in God's plan for the salvation of the world and in Israel's final salvation, even though presently, she is described as an enemy concerning the gospel since she has not recognized Jesus as the messiah (11:28).[132] In a return movement, Paul's conviction that all of Israel will be saved also confirms God's *ēthos* as a faithful God.

---

[131] See Johnson, *Reading Romans*, 180: "The term *zēlos* can serve both for 'zeal' and for 'jealousy.' To be zealous for God is also in a sense to be jealous for God. So when Paul says that he will 'stir them to jealousy,' he is also saying that he is stirring their zeal. It is not, in other words, out of envy of the Gentiles that the Jews will turn to Christ but out of their zeal and jealous love of the God they regard as their own." For the reading insisting on jealousy, see Cranfield, *Romans*, 276; Moo, *Romans*, 688. 692; Morris, *Romans*, 407; Murray, *Romans*, 2:80. Jewett, *Romans*, 674 indicates that the translation "make jealous" creates several problems (envy as a motivation for salvation; why would Jews be jealous of Gentiles believing in a false doctrine). He, like Johnson, prefers "make zealous" (although he does not explain it in the same manner) and I agree with them.

[132] The addition of "of God" in the NRSV is a misinterpretation. Israel is not qualified as enemy of God, but as enemy when it comes to the gospel. Israel is opposed to the gospel because she has not recognized Jesus as the messiah. She is not the enemy of God. See Grieb, *The Story of Romans*, 111: "With respect to the good news that Paul and his coworkers have been proclaiming about Jesus Christ, Israel stands in opposition. In that sense, the people of God can be described as 'enemies' (of the gospel, of course, not of God, as in the NRSV)." Contra Moo, *Romans*, 730 n. 80; Fitzmyer, *Romans*, 625; Dunn, *Romans*, 2:685; Murray, *Romans*, 2:100.

God's *ēthos* combined with the notion of Israel as the people of God establish the salvation of all of Israel and the faithfulness of the God of Israel.

The role of Israel in God's plan and God's fidelity to the promises made
to Israel also ensure that Paul can drive home a point that will play an important role in chapters 12–15, namely the necessity for the community in
Rome to include Jews and Gentiles harmoniously. The point is made
through the address to the Gentiles in 11:13 not to boast over Israel
(11:17–18). The sin of boasting, which was previously associated mainly
with the Jews (2:17), is now turned against the Gentiles. They have to
guard themselves of thinking that their belonging to the people of God and
their participation in Christ puts them in a position in which they can judge
others, and Jews in particular.[133] Gentiles need to remember that their inclusion in the people of God is dependent upon the promises that God
made in Israel's scriptures and that Israel continues to play an "irreplacea-
ble role"[134] in God's plan, which should also put an end to the logic of
those (expressed in 11:9) which argue that Gentiles have replaced Israel as
God's people. Rather, the Gentiles should beware of their own position.
They have been included in the people of God, only because God did not
spare Israel (11:21). Thus, they still stand under the possibility of God's
wrath.

The use of the verb φείδομαι in 11:21 is reminiscent of the language of
8:32 ("God did not spare [ἐφείσατο] his own son") and might indicate a
connection between the role that the Jewish people play towards the Gentiles and the role that Christ plays towards humanity.[135] If the Jewish people plays a messianic role in relation to the Gentiles, in allowing "the full
number of the Gentiles" to come in (11:25), the Gentiles are not in a position to feel superior over the Jews, especially if one also takes into account
the eschatological role of Israel delineated in 11:12.15. Because of that
role and because God has not rejected Israel, it is clear that the Gentiles are

---

[133] See Johnson, *Reading Romans*, 179: "Now it is arrogance on the part of Gentiles because of their relationship to God and 'possession of the messiah' that must be forestalled.
Paul confesses that his 'glorifying' his mission to the Gentiles (see 1:5) is really in service to
his kinsmen, 'that I might make my fellow Jews jealous, and I might save some of them'
(11:4)." See also Dunn, *Romans*, 2:662 who indicates that Gentiles are warned in the same
manner than Jews were.

[134] See Johnson, *Reading Romans*, 181. Attention to 11:13–24 should make clear that it is
not Paul's intention to replace Israel by the church. See Moo, *Romans*, 550; Dunn, *Romans*,
2:520: "the church is not a separate entity from Israel, but, if anything, a subset of Israel ..."

[135] See Johnson, *Reading Romans*, 182: "Is it too much to suppose that Paul is once more
making a connection between the Jewish people (who had, we remember, the first claim to
'sonship,' 9:4), and the messiah himself? God did not spare them, for the sake of the Gentiles.
As in 11:12, the role assigned to the people is to continue the messianic pattern found in Jesus." See also Richard B. Hays, *Echoes of Scripture in the Letters of Paul* (New Haven,
Conn.: Yale University Press, 1989), 61.

in no position to reject Israel or to think of themselves as superior when it comes to Israel. This close relationship between Israel and Gentiles as well as the necessity of leading a life in accordance with the messianic pattern is at the center of Paul's discussion in 15:1–13. The *ēthos* of conformity to Christ is here demanded already of the Gentiles and is central to Paul's exhortations in 12:1–15:13.

To summarize: in establishing the *ēthos* of God as faithful, merciful and sovereign, Paul is able to affirm the present salvation of a remnant of Israel and the future salvation of all Israel. In arguing for the importance of Israel's role in God's plan, Paul has reaffirmed God's faithfulness to Israel and has also put an end to a possible temptation for Gentiles to feel superior to Israel. Paul's engagement of the question of the status of Israel and more widely of the shape of the relationship between Jews, Gentiles and God is fundamental in order to understand what Paul hopes to accomplish concerning the construction of the *ēthos* of the members of the Roman house churches. Now that he has answered the two logical objections that emerge from the narrative told in 1:18–8:39, he can turn to the exhortative part of the letter, building upon the story he has told.

6. The Roman Church: A Self Constructed (12:1–16:27)

In the section concluding his letter, Paul goes back to the particularities of the Roman church, in order to show what the story which explains who they have become means for who they need to be now. Paul's addressees stand at a turning point. They have heard a story that described for them the gift of a new self-understanding and the reception of a power that can support them in their efforts to lead a righteous life. They now need to see the concrete content of their new existence in Christ. Earlier, Paul has given hints of what the story means for his addressees (particularly in chapters 6, 8 and 9–11) but he has done so in a rather implicit manner, without addressing himself to them directly.[136] Chapter 12 opens up with a direct address using a verb of exhortation (παρακαλῶ οὖν ὑμᾶς, ἀδελφοί) and inaugurates a section in which Paul is connecting the story of humanity told in 1:18–8:39 to the particular situation of the Roman church.[137] In fact, it is

---

[136] In chapters 9–11, there are a couple of direct addresses (10:1 ἀδελφοί; 11:13 ὑμῖν δὲ λέγω τοῖς ἔθνεσιν; 11:25 ἀδελφοί) perhaps already indicating the particular relevance of the Jew-Gentile relationship for the Roman church.

[137] See Grieb, *The Story of Romans*, 115: "Now, in his concluding chapters, [Paul] must show directly and concretely the implications of his argument for the Roman Christians and their life in Christ. He must demonstrate how the story of what God has accomplished in the death and resurrection of Jesus Christ is related to his own story and to the story of his churches, including the congregations at Rome that he hopes will support his work." Dunn, *Romans*, 2:705 also remarks on the connections of 12:1–15:13 with the rest of the letter: " ...

only if Paul can show to his addressees the concrete consequences which the story needs to have for them that he will reach his rhetorical goal, which is to construct the self of the members of the Roman community and create harmony among them. Far from being an afterthought, or random ethical exhortations, this section (Rom 12–15) plays a fundamental role in the letter and allows Paul to encourage the community in living out the identity of children of God that has been given to them.[138] In this final section of the letter, Paul uses the story he has told in the previous chapters in order to move into the final purpose of the letter: shape the self of the members of the community so that they can reflect the *ēthos* of Christ central to the story told previously.

---

chaps 12–15 follow naturally from and constitute a necessary corollary to the overall argument of chaps. 1–11; they should not be regarded as a piece of standard parenesis which has no direct material or thematic connection with what has gone before and could have been discarded or wholly reordered without loss." Contra Fitzmyer, *Romans*, 637–638 and Walter Schmithals, *Der Römerbrief: ein Kommentar* (Gütersloh: Gütersloher Verlaghaus Gerd Mohn, 1988) 417–424 who sees these chapters as a separate letter (Romans B).

[138] For the importance of Rom 12:1–15:13 in the overall letter, see Johnson, *Reading Romans*, 187–188; Grieb, *The Story of Romans*, 117: "Paul's request that the Roman Christians order their lives according to the pattern of Christ is based on everything that has gone before, particularly God's covenant faithfulness to Israel by means of the inclusion of the Gentiles in the covenant promises." Elliott, *The Rhetoric of Romans*, 290–291; Moo, *Romans*, 744: "Romans 12:1–15:13 is therefore integral to the letter and to its purposes. It is not an appendix, a last-minute 'add-on' relatively unrelated to the real – theological – heart of the letter," also Paul S. Minear, *The Obedience of Faith: The Purposes of Paul in the Epistle to the Romans* (Naperville, Ill.: Allenson, 1971), 31–34, esp. 35; for a contrary reading, see Krister Stendahl, *Final Account: Paul's Letter to the Romans* (Minneapolis: Fortress Press, 1995), 45–51, also Dodd, *Romans*, 214–219; Alfred Wikenhauser, *New Testament Introduction* (New York: Herder and Herder, 1958), 407.

Chapter 3

A Self Constructed

The final chapters of Romans (12:1–16:27) show how Paul thought the members of the Roman house churches could concretely embody the *ēthos* created by the story he has told. The story told in 1:18–8:39 is the story of a change of *ēthos*, or rather, the story shows how the members of the Roman house churches became "beloved of God." (1:7) The story opens with a description of humanity's *ēthos* as misshapen, unable to recognize God in the world or pay proper respect to God. Through the reversal that happens in Christ and is energized for the Christ believers through the gift of the spirit, human beings have the possibility of living according to a new *ēthos*. This new *ēthos* allows Paul to speak of his addressees as children of God (8:16), sharing the identity of Christ (8:17) and displaying the same quality of hope as Abraham (8:24–25). In his references to Christ and Abraham, Paul already depicts the type of *ēthos* given to the Christ believers: it displays obedience to God's will as the proper response to God, but it also demonstrates trust in God and God's plan, thus recognizing the role of creatures in relationship to their creator.

In this story of *ēthos* reversal, Paul provides the narrative premise supporting the identity of the Roman Christ believers as "beloved of God" and "saints." (1:7) Now, in 12:1–16:27, he gives concrete content to this identity. It is not that Paul doubts the reality of the gift to the Romans; precisely because Paul believes in the reality of this gift, he is obliged to show that it can be practiced in everyday life through appropriate moral behavior. So, in 12:1–16:27, Paul sets out to achieve two things. First, he tells his addressees in Rome how they can translate their identity of "children of God" into their dealings with each other and with the world (12:1–15:13). Second, he indicates what that *ēthos* means for Paul's dealings with that community and for their own relationship to Paul's work among the Gentiles (15:14–16:27).

A. Constructing the *Ēthos* of the Community (12:1–15:13)

1. How to Embody Christ's Ēthos *in the World (12:1–13:14)*

Chapters 12–13 are united by a common problematic concerned with the fact that even though the Christ believers no longer belong to this world (12:2; 13:14), they are still in fact spending their days in this world. The solution to what could be seen as a problem of double allegiance is given at the very end of the discussion, in 13:14: the Christ believers should clothe themselves in Christ and this will help them not to be defined by mundane concerns. Because of their new self-understanding, Christ believers should be able to embody Christ in their dealings with the world and thus not be conformed to the world. At the same time, the knowledge that the Christ believers are living in a different æon (13:11–13) should help them behave in a manner that reveals the new self-understanding given to them in Christ. The call to remain detached from the world frames the entire discussion (12:1–2 and 13:11–14).[1] In between these two sections, Paul delineates the manner in which members of the Roman community should behave towards each other in the community (12:3–8) and towards the external world (12:9–13:10).

Rom 12:1–2 Call to a Renewed Mind
In 12:1–2, Paul provides his addressees with a basic orientation that should enable them to actualize their new *ēthos* in concrete situations, because it dissociates them from the ways of the world and directs them to the will of God.[2] In the opening verses of chapter 12, Paul presumes certain aptitudes in his readers and insists on his addressees' ability to participate in a "spiritual worship" and to discern the will of God. Thus Paul establishes a strong contrast with his description of humanity in 1:18–32. There, Paul presented human beings as hopelessly bound to the earthly world, defined by their desires and thus unable to properly honor God. In 12:1–2, Paul affirms that his addressees are able to discern the will of God. Their identity of children of God changes their perspective on the world. In contrast to the degradation of the body in 1:24, they are now able to use their bodies

---

[1] See Johnson, *Reading Romans*, 205: "This entire section of moral instruction [12:3–13:9] has been framed on one side by the call to the transformation of consciousness in 12:1–2, and this eschatological reminder in 13:11–14. Both stress a separation from the 'frame of this world' and a change into a new identity."

[2] See Wilson, *Love without Pretense*, 129: "Paul establishes the foundation of his ethical program in 12.1–2. Significantly, he does not merely prescribe a certain type of behavior or a specific set of actions. Instead, he formulates a fundamentally new ethical program as well as a new social medium within which moral responsibilities are to be determined and carried out."

in a manner pleasing to God (12:1). The renewing of their mind enables a transformation at a spiritual, rational and bodily level. It is because they perceive themselves in a new manner that they can now use their bodies and their spiritual and rational abilities in new and creative ways, which allow them to follow the will of God.

Their identity of belonging to God (Rom 6 and 8) opens up new ways of perceiving the world and it is their responsibility to let their minds see these new possibilities of thinking. The transformation of the mind that occurs is not about following new rules; rather it is a new moral orientation that allows for new uses of the body.[3] Four elements give its general orientation to the entire section.

First, the members of the Roman house churches are invited to actualize in worship (λατρεία 12:1) the freedom given to them through the spirit (8:2). The language, as Johnson has noted, is reminiscent of 1:25, where idolaters worshiped (ἐλάτρευσαν) the creature rather than the creator.[4] Such false worship is reversed in 12:1. Λατρεία language is also used by Paul when talking about his own work as an apostle (1:9; 15:16). In 15:16 in particular the worship language is connected to Paul's ministry with the Gentiles and to the offering of the Gentiles. The similarities in the language of these various sections of the letter (12:1; 1:9; 15:16) suggest that the rational or spiritual worship of the Gentiles refers to their moral orientation and their *ēthos*, which finds its origin in the activities of their minds.[5] Their ethical behavior is presented as the proper kind of worship of God.

Second, even though Paul does not make this theme implicit, these two verses, as well as the entire section that follows, put into place a reflection

---

[3] See Johnson, *Reading Romans*, 191. For Johnson, Paul argues that the renewal of the mind needs to reflect Christ's mind. This is an astute reading especially when seen in light of the sacrificial language of 12:2 which can also allude to Jesus' destiny.

[4] See Johnson, *Reading Romans*, 190. Some commentators insist on the contrast with Jewish sacrificial ritual (see Murray, *Romans*, 2:111; Moo, *Romans*, 750, 753–754; Dunn, *Romans*, 2:710). While this is clearly possible, I find Johnson's reading more interesting in the context of Romans.

[5] See Johnson, *Reading Romans*, 190: "Here [Paul] calls his Gentile readers to the sort of 'spiritual worship' through the disposition of their freedom that will enable them to be the 'acceptable sacrifice' that fulfills Paul's priestly work. From beginning to end, however, this is cultic language that is used to express not what is usually regarded as liturgical acts but the disposition of the self through moral behavior in the church and in society." Also Elliott, *The Rhetoric of Romans*, 272: "We have argued above, in part on the basis of an observed syllogistic structure spanning Rom. 1.18–32, 6.1–23, and 12.1–2, and in part by examining 15.14–16, that Romans is written to secure the 'obedience' and 'holiness' of the Romans, including the mutual regard and respect of Jewish and Gentile Christians. Their reception of his exhortations can ensure the spiritual sanctity of the 'offering of the Gentiles' throughout the world. This is the immediate epistolary exigence."

on freedom and the limitations placed on this freedom. In 12:1–2, a certain
amount of freedom is given to the members of the Roman house churches.
They are clearly left with a spirit of initiative. This might explain the partial inadequacy of the language of slavery used in Rom 6 to describe the
relationship Paul's addressees have with God. Slavery language is dependent upon a way of thinking about freedom and submission that is still too
deeply anchored in the ways of this world. As restored creatures, human
beings are invited to use their thinking capacities in an independent manner, in order to accomplish the will of their master, becoming slaves gifted
with freedom.[6] Nonetheless, freedom is never thought of as absolute. In
12:1–2, this freedom is dependent on God's intervention on behalf of human beings.[7] Furthermore, human beings' freedom is only used correctly if
it leads to service of God. This freedom will be further limited in the rest
of the section because of the needs of the weaker member of the community.

Third, in terms of construction of the self, Paul drives home a point that
he has been preparing in the previous chapters of his letter, especially in
chapter 6 and in chapter 8. Becoming a slave of God, presenting one's
members in service of righteousness, adopting the perspective of the spirit,
receiving a spirit of adoption, all these things that are given to human beings through God's saving intervention need to shape the way in which
Paul's addressees make decisions. It needs to change their mind so that
they can look at the world in a way that is enlightened by the knowledge of
God's will.

Fourth, the Christ believers need to adopt the perspective of Christ and
Abraham and make decisions in agreement with that new perspective. The
sacrificial language of 12:1 (παραστῆσαι τὰ σώματα ὑμῶν θυσίαν ζῶσαν)
indicates from the beginning that the attitude of Paul's addressees should

---

[6] The good slave should creatively reflect the will of her or his master. See Harrill,
Slaves in the New Testament, 21: "The Roman notion of mastery defined the ideal slave
not in terms of obedience to individual commands of the master but in terms of having
accepted the master's wishes so fully that the slave's innermost self could anticipate the
master's wishes and take the initiative. Romans did not want automatons for their
slaves"; 23: "Rather than merely following individual orders in mechanical fashion, the
good slave (*servus frugi*) completed and developed what the master had only suggested
or even unconsciously desired – a task that in the practice of Roman slaveholding encouraged the actual slave to develop moral intuition" and 29: "Converts must likewise
accept God's point of view so fully as to anticipate the divine personal will and to make
it effective in the world, even when the Eschaton is not yet present. This theme corresponds to the classical Roman topos of the 'faithful slave,' who acts and dies on behalf of
her or his master (*de fide servorum*)."

[7] See Wilson, *Love without Pretense*, 129: "Hence in these verses Paul articulates a
very careful balance between individual achievement and the divine empowerment upon
which it ultimately depends."

be modeled on Christ's own life of obedience (5:19) and sacrifice (3:25).[8] Just as Christ has offered himself in accordance to God's will, the members of the Roman house churches should in response to God's gift in Christ be willing to offer their entire person, body and mind, in worship to God.[9] The motivation behind their ethical behavior is thus a faithful response to God's gift of Christ, a response made possible by the gift of the spirit and modeled on Christ.[10]

The *ēthos* put into place in 12:1–2 has consequences for the way each individual behaves in the community. The verbs used are in the second person plural, indicating that Paul sees this individual behavior as anchored in the community and as having consequences for the community (see Phil 2:1–4).[11] In fact, it is in these consequences that the *ēthos* of each Christ believer takes on its proper dimension.

Rom 12:3–8: In the Assembly (ἐκκλησία), Be Humble
In 12:3–8, Paul exposes the first consequences of the new moral orientation: behavior inside the assembly. In verse 3, the language of φρονεῖν is predominant, confirming the connection with the rational transformation demanded of Christ believers in 12:2. The transformation effected in Paul's addressees through the renewal of the mind (12:1) needs to be displayed in an attitude of humility (12:3). For Christ believers, the new *ēthos* needs to be concretized in correct judgment of one's own capacities. The

---

[8] A similar attention to sacrificial language is found in Grieb, *The Story of Romans*, 117–119.

[9] The fact that human beings are asked to use their entire person in a manner pleasing to God in answer to God's intervention can help to understand the function of διὰ τῶν οἰκτιρμῶν τοῦ θεοῦ in 12:1. See Johnson, *Reading Romans*, 189: "The phrase 'through the mercies of God,' however, is oddly placed. It can modify either what the Romans are to do or Paul's exhortation. I think it basically functions here as a bridge: given the *mercy* with which God has gifted you (11:22. 31–32), how should they behave?" For a similar idea, Moo, *Romans*, 750.

[10] See Wilson, *Love without Pretense*, 129: "The motives for Christian ethical action are not to be predicated upon popular Hellenistic morality, the Torah, or even the teachings of Jesus, but upon the righteousness of God, revealed in his mercy, which empowers those who are justified to dedicate themselves to him and to do his will in their daily lives. In view of God's act of salvation in Christ, the only appropriate response on the part of the faithful is the self-offering to God of one's life in its entirety." See also Johnson, *Reading Romans*, 191: "In this context, and from the ways Paul will develop his exhortation, it is clear that the 'new mind' to which believers are to be transformed is precisely the 'mind of Christ.' They are to view reality from a perspective shaped by the Holy Spirit, according to the image of Christ."

[11] See Wilson, *Love without Pretense*, 129–130: "We should quickly add, however, that Paul does not propose a merely personal, intellectual, or spiritual program. Indeed, the main thrust of chapter 12, as well as the ensuing exhortation, concerns the practical, social implications of the ethical course chosen by those who have been justified."

members of the Roman house churches need to think εἰς τὸ σωφρονεῖν, that is, towards an attitude of wisdom, what a Greek "would regard as good moral character: reasonableness, self-control, moderation, prudence."[12] Paul emphasizes the dimension of proper self-understanding: not evaluating oneself too highly, but remembering that God has gifted each one in the community in a particular manner (12:3.6) and that one needs to use one's gift while remembering that one is part of a community. As 12:1 had already made clear, the new attitude of conformity to God's will is an attitude of the mind and thus it starts with correct self-perception, devoid of haughtiness and of occasions for boasting.[13] In addition, if one adopts correct thinking about one's own capacity, one is already in a position that discourages judgment of others (14:1–15:7).

The community context of such discernment is established by the image of the body (12:4–5). God has given each different gifts in faith (12:3) and each gift has its function inside the community. Each member of the community has a role to play, as each part of the body plays a role, but the roles are different in each case. However, as the metaphor also makes clear, the various body parts do not call into question the unity of the body and so the various gifts of individuals should not threaten the unity of the community (12:5). In order to preserve the unity of the community, thus, no one should claim that her gift is more valuable than someone else's but should remember that each gift works towards the good of the community. Paul's list of gifts concentrates on the manner in which each gift is to be performed.[14] Moderation and humility (12:3) should apply to the use of the gifts each person has received (12:6–8). This first section provides the members of the Roman churches with the tools necessary to find the appropriate answers to the problems that the community might face and to promote the well-being and the harmony of the community (14:1–15:13). It also gives them a basic orientation to handle difference and diversity. The gifts are different, and their difference should not be suppressed, but these differences do not threaten the good of the community. In the han-

---

[12] Johnson, *Reading Romans*, 192; see also Moo, *Romans*, 760 n. 12: "The word group denoted a cardinal virtue among the Greeks, from whom it found its way into Hellenistic Jewish literature;" Fitzmyer, *Romans*, 645; Wilson, *Love without Pretense*, 140: "By introducing the concept of σωφροσύνη at this point, Paul connects his ethical teaching to the Romans with a distinctively Greek ideal, an ideal which relates both to proper self-understanding and to restraint in moral conduct." See also Jewett, *Romans*, 740–741.

[13] Again, the contrast with 1:30 in particular and with 1:18–3:20 in general is striking, see Johnson, *Reading Romans*, 195.

[14] Johnson, *Romans*, 193: "In contrast to the similar lists in 1 Cor 12:8–10 and Eph 4:11–12, the present one attaches qualifiers to each one, which has the effect of emphasizing the *manner* of using the gifts."

dling of various gifts, Paul already suggests that each member's freedom is limited by the members' interaction with one another.

Because of Christ's death and the work of the spirit, Paul's addressees can choose to work for the construction of a new community, marked precisely by its difference from the description of the *ēthos* of humanity in 1:18–3:20. Remembering what the world left to its own device became, they can together see what non-conformity to the world might mean.

Rom 12:9–13:10: In the World, Practice Love

Paul frames this unit with two references to love, at the beginning (12:9 "Let love be genuine") and at the end (13:10 "Love does no wrong to a neighbor; therefore, love is the fulfilling of the law").[15] These two references encompass a section devoted to love as the attitude which should characterize the behavior of the Christ believers in the world.[16] 12:9a in particular functions as the title of the entire passage.[17] 12:9b–21 form a first subsection which delineates principles for acting towards members of the community (12:10.13a), strangers (12:13b) and enemies (12:14.17.19–21). In a second subsection (13:1–7), Paul gives concrete indications concerning one's relationship to the empire. Finally, in a third subsection, he returns to his general principle of love as the guide for ethical behavior (13:8–10).

Instead of being arrogant or boastful and focusing on their own accomplishments (12:3), the members of the Roman churches are invited to compete against each other in the domain of τιμή (12:10). Honor is made manifest in service of the Lord (12:11) and is characterized by zeal and the possession of the spirit. These are the only things worthy of competition. Thus, if one understands honor as the proper recognition of one's worth by others, as was common in the Greco-Roman world,[18] one's worth was not

---

[15] See Johnson, *Reading Romans*, 203: "Paul began his 'Christian virtue list' in 12:9 with the exhortation 'Let love be sincere,' and he concludes his sketch of Christian social obligations with a fuller and richer affirmation of love (*agapē*) as the central Christian moral principle." Also Moo, *Romans*, 810: "Yet, while joined to vv. 1–7 by means of the notion of obligation, vv. 8–10 are connected by their content to 12:9–21, where Paul expounded the meaning and outworking of 'sincere love.' These verses therefore return to the 'main line' of Paul's exhortation after the somewhat parenthetical advice about government in 13:1–7."

[16] Contra Käsemann, *Romans*, 342: "*Agapē* in v. 9a is not then clearly presented as a heading, as it is in 1 Corinthians 13. It is simply one mode of behavior among others, not the criterion and true modality of all the rest."

[17] See Wilson, *Love without Pretense*, 150: "The initial maxim, ἡ ἀγάπη ἀνυπόκριτος ('Let love be without pretense') fills the role of a thesis statement: everything that follows can be subsumed under this theme."

[18] See Malina, *The New Testament World*, especially 28–62, here 32: "Honor, then, is a claim to worth *and* the social acknowledgement of that worth." For a detailed discus-

defined by one's personal achievements, or one's familial credentials, rather, one's worth was determined by one's willingness to serve the Lord and embody God's will.

The list of 12:10–21 is somewhat haphazard,[19] and, for my purpose, it is more to the point to seek the general orientation Paul demands from his audience than to look for the connection between each individual sentence.[20] In this section, Paul asks for the same attitude towards three different groups of people: the community, strangers, and enemies. In all these cases, the members of the Roman house churches are invited to demonstrate an attitude of gentleness (12:10.14.18), attentiveness to the others' needs (12:13.15.20) and humility (12:16). Humility in particular already played a role in 12:3 and will be central to the exhortations of 14:1–15:7 (14:4.10; 15:1). It is an attitude characterized by deference to the other and is personified by Christ (15:3). It opposes competitiveness and supports the good of the community and its harmony (12:16). If love translates itself in an attitude of humility and concern for the other, it can help solve the tensions discussed in 14:1–15:7 and support the building of a harmonious

---

sion of honor in New Testament culture, see David A. deSilva, *Honor, Patronage, Kinship and Purity: Unlocking New Testament Culture* (Downers Grove, Ill.: Intervarsity Press, 2000). deSilva notes in particular how the early Christian authors redefine the use of honor-shame language in their own communities (*Honor, Patronage, Kinship and Purity*, 43): "These authors [in the New Testament] continue to use the language of honor and shame to articulate the value system of the Christian group, and to build up the church into a court of reputation that will reinforce commitment to those values through honoring those who distinguish themselves in acts of love, service and faithful witness and through censuring those who fail to embody those values."

[19] Contra Grieb, *The Story of Romans*, 121. She argues that the section is more "carefully crafted" than it appears at first, especially through the "pun that Paul employs as a transition between verses 13–14." In her reading, 12:14–16 pairs "recommendations to live imaginatively into the situation of the other ... and to live in harmony" with "injunctions to avoid community-disrupting behaviors." 12:17–21 are set apart by "an *inclusion* on the subject of dealing with evil" and deal "with the active peacemaking behavior that is expected of the community conformed to the mind of Christ." Clearly thematic units can be found, but it is more difficult to delineate them precisely. For example, 12:17–21 is clearly preoccupied with the dealings with one's enemies, but this theme is already introduced in 12:14.

[20] See Johnson, *Reading Romans*, 194: "There is little continuity of thought to be discerned. ... As with any such list, dissection of the individual term is possible, but not necessarily instructive for a sense of the list's function as a whole, which is to provide a certain kind of moral impression." Also Moo, *Romans*, 771. For a defense of a more organized structure, see David A. Black, "The Pauline Love Command: Structure, Style, and Ethics in Romans 12.9–21," *Filología Neotestamentaria* 1 (1989): 3–21. For an analysis of each verse and its parallel in Jewish Wisdom literature, see Wilson, *Love without Pretense*, 149–198. Wilson also proposes a structure for the passage, arguing that the passage, at least 12:14–21, is structured by "a literary device employed regularly in gnomic wisdom, ring composition." (175–176)

community.[21] This attitude of humility is expressed through choosing the good (12:9b.21).

The good (τὸ ἀγαθον) mentioned in 12:9 echoes the language of 12:2, in which the good was described as related to discerning the will of God.[22] It also recalls 8:28, where, for those who love God, all things "work together for good." Good and love are similarly equated in 12:9. In love, the good is displayed in the community. One concrete way for the members of the Roman churches to show their transformation is precisely to act on their ability to discern the good and to choose good over evil, in agreement with their new rational capabilities and in contrast with 1:18–32 and 7:14–23 (7:19 in particular "For I do not do the good I want, but the evil I do not want is what I do.").[23] The connection with 12:1–2 also makes clear that this new ability to demonstrate love in choosing good over evil is made possible through God's transforming power, shown particularly in the gift of the spirit (8:3–4).

Choosing the good, however, is not done in a naïve fashion, or based on the utopian idea that the world is ultimately a good place. Paul has shown that he realizes that the world is filled with dangers for Christ believers (8:18.35) and he is not above wishing vengeance upon his enemies (12:19b.20). However, he insists that this vengeance should not come from the hands of the Christ believers themselves (12:19a). They should strive to live in peace (12:18), thus reflecting in their relationship with the world their inner relationship with God, also marked by peace (see 5:1). This attitude of peace and goodness is to be adopted because Paul knows that ultimately God is lord and God is the one who will deal with enemies. In the end, it is God who will judge the world, and thus Christ believers are not to take God's place in thinking that they can enact God's judgment. Their responsibility is to "overcome evil with good." (12:21)

---

[21] For the centrality of humility in the section, see Johnson, *Reading Romans*, 195: "We see also that in contrast to the arrogance and boasting that were characteristic of life under sin, Paul here stresses a profound spirit of humility."

[22] For the connection between 12:9 and 12:2, see Wilson, *Love without Pretense*, 154.

[23] See Wilson, *Love without Pretense*, 154: "Thus it seems clear that for Paul the potential of love as a human attribute is predicated upon divine mercy and divine enabling. As the argument of the chapter demonstrates, this divine enabling stands behind not only the various charisms which the members of the church enjoy but also the rational ability of its members to determine their ethical responsibilities and to discriminate between what is good and evil." The divine enabling is actually more about the capacity to act over the rational discrimination than over the ability to discriminate between good and evil.

Scholars often consider that the argument of 13:1–7 is introduced in an unexpected manner and has little connection with what comes before.[24] However, the reappearance of ὀργή language (in 13:4) connects it with 12:19.[25] According to this reading, Paul turns to discussing the relationship of his audience with the governing authorities because he has to present one of the possible ways in which the wrath of God will be executed on the enemies of the Christ believers.[26] In Paul's understanding, the empire will act as the agent of God's wrath (3:4) and will punish the evil doer.[27]

13:1–7 cannot and should not be construed as a full-fledged theological reflection on the relationship the Christ believers need to have with the larger political world.[28] At best, it indicates that when it comes to living in the world without belonging to it, Christ believers also come into contact with political authorities. In their dealings with authorities, furthermore,

---

[24] Moo, *Romans*, 790–791: "this argument comes on the scene quite abruptly, with no explicit syntactical connection with what has come before it – and not much evidence of any connection in subject matter either." See also Käsemann, *Romans*, 352. Some scholars, noting the connection between 12:9–21 and 13:8–10, have taken 13:1–7 as a later addition: Schmithals, *Der Römerbrief*, 458–462; John C. O'Neill, *Paul's Letter to the Romans* (PNTC; Harmondsworth: Penguin, 1975), 207–209; James Kallas, "Romans 13:1–7: An Interpolation," *NTS* 11 (1964): 365–374.

[25] See Johnson, *Reading Romans*, 200.

[26] See Johnson, *Reading Romans*, 200: "The question then arises, how is God's wrath to come against those who do the sort of public wrong that cries out for revenge, if Christians are themselves not to retaliate? This question leads Paul to the governing order and the role he sees it playing in God's plans." See also John Howard Yoder, *The Politics of Jesus: Vicit Agnus Noster* (Grand Rapids, Mich.: Eerdmans, 1994), 198, as quoted in Richard B. Hays, *The Moral Vision of the New Testament: Community, Cross, New Creation: A Contemporary Introduction to New Testament Ethics* (San Francisco: HarperSanFrancisco, 1996), 245–246; also, in a somewhat less trenchant manner, Moo, *Romans*, 792 (Moo sees the necessity of counter-acting tendencies towards rebellion against Rome as another reason why Paul includes this section in his letter).

[27] This opinion clearly generates a host of questions, particularly the question of how to act if a government is patently unjust in its dealings with human beings. This question cannot be answered here obviously, but the fact that Paul insists that Christ believers need to live in the world while not belonging to it indicates that he might be open to the option of resisting a state that would display wickedness. Grieb, *The Story of Romans*, 125 (following Neil Elliott, "Romans 13:1–7 in the Context of Imperial Propaganda," in *Paul and Empire: Religion and Power in Roman Imperial Society* [ed. R. A. Horsley; Harrisburg, Pa.: Trinity Press International, 1977], 184–204) sees in the language about being subject and in the positive description of the empire "subtle reminders that the imperial sword is *not* idle: it continues to threaten destruction of the most vulnerable population, namely the Jews around and among the Roman Christians."

[28] As Grieb, *The Story of Romans*, 123 rightly remarks, this is not Paul's doctrine of the state: "It is wiser to read the passage in its historical context than to read it as if it were a timeless source for a Christian doctrine of church and state." See also Johnson, *Reading Romans*, 202.

they have to be aware that these authorities are appointed by God (13:1). Thus, they owe obedience to them, not as if the authorities had a natural right to allegiance; rather, the Christ believers need to be submitted to them on behalf of God's rule, which they are able to know through their renewed mind (13:5 "because of conscience," understood as knowledge of God's will).[29] Love and God's sovereignty are the two factors guiding the behavior of the Christ believers. Paul revisits the overall theme of his ethical instructions in 13:8–10, using a vocabulary connection (13:7 τὰς ὀφειλάς; 13:8 ὀφείλετε).[30]

In 13:8–10, Paul returns to love as foundational for the *ēthos* of the community. 12:9–21 described concrete attitudes that manifested a sincere love towards others. In 13:8–10 Paul connects love to Torah. In 13:8b and 9, Paul repeats the point of 8:3–4. The Christ believers are able to fulfill Torah, because they practice love. Love and Torah are not in opposition; rather law can only be practiced through love. Paul insists that love is directed towards the other (13:8a) and does not do any harm (13:10). Love is the appropriate response to what God has done for the Roman community. The members of the Roman community are God's beloved (ἀγαπητοί 1:7); they have received God's love in their hearts (5:5). In 13:8.10, Paul shows that, because of the gift of God's love, the Christ believers need to act in a way that expresses this love. Who they are – a community created by God's love – needs to be apparent in what they do. They need to practice love towards the neighbor.[31]

---

[29] See Moo, *Romans*, 803. As Johnson, *Reading Romans*, 203 points out, this ultimate sovereignty of God also theoretically leaves the door open to resistance to the state if the state does not respect God's will. Paul, because he is making contingent remarks, however does not engage this question. In this passage, he "sketches the Christian's relation to the larger world in terms of basic accommodation to its structures." (See Johnson, *Reading Romans*, 202) In recent years, there has been a renewed interest in integrating the political in readings of Paul. In particular, postcolonial readings have made efforts to show how Paul (and the New Testament writings in general) can also be seen as resisting the politics of the Roman empire. See: Richard A. Horsley, *In the Shadow of Empire: Reclaiming the Bible as a History of Faithful Resistance* (Louisville, Ky.: Westminster John Knox, 2008), Fernando F. Segovia and R. S. Sugirtharajah, eds., *A Postcolonial Commentary on the New Testament Writings* (Bible and Postcolonialism; London: T&T Clark, 2007), Neil Elliott, *The Arrogance of Nations: Reading Romans in the Shadow of the Empire* (Paul in Critical Contexts; Minneapolis: Fortress Press, 2008), Lopez, *Apostle to the Conquered*, Joseph A. Marchal, *The Politics of Heaven: Women, Gender, and Empire in the Study of Paul* (Paul in Critical Contexts; Minneapolis: Fortress Press, 2008).

[30] This connection is often noted: Grieb, *The Story of Romans*, 125; Johnson, *Reading Romans*, 203; Moo, *Romans*, 810; Käsemann, *Romans*, 360 speaks of a "skillful transition to the summary;" Fitzmyer, *Romans*, 678.

[31] This interpretation is developed in Johnson, *Reading Romans*, 203–204: "If God's *agapē* – his effective and disinterested disposition for their good – has created them as a community, then on the principle of *agens sequitur esse* (acting follows upon being),

Rom 13:11–14: Know the Proper Time

13:11–14 echoes 12:1–2 by stressing separation from this world. Here, however, Paul takes up the theme through eschatological language, indicating that the particular time period in which his addressees live also justifies the ethical exhortations of 12–13. He tells his audience that salvation (ἡ σωτηρία) is near (13:11). Salvation has already been mentioned in 5:9.10 where Paul used the verb σῴζω. In 5:9.10, eschatological elements were present, especially because of the mention of God's wrath. Reconciliation with God has already happened through Christ, but salvation is still a thing of the future. 8:18–24 and 11:11–12 provide indications as to what salvation means for Paul in Romans. In chapter 8, Paul indicates that creation waits for the revelation of the children of God (8:19) and in chapter 11, Paul writes that the stumbling of Israel has meant salvation for the Gentiles (11:11) but that the full inclusion of Israel still has to happen (11:12). In the context of Romans, then, salvation is linked to the revelation of the people of God as being composed of Jews and Gentiles.[32] The identity of the Christ believers is closely related to this "social realization of 'salvation'."[33] (see 15:7–13) This social realization of salvation has already begun inside the community of Christ believers, since it includes Jews and non-Jews.

Because salvation is close at hand (13:11), the behavior of Paul's addressees needs to reflect this particular time (13:12.13) in light of their new self-understanding (13:14). In 13:12.13, the language is reminiscent of 6:13, which emphasizes the same contrast between two ages and uses the same military metaphor (τὰ ὅπλα), and of 8:5, which also contrasts honorable behavior (in 8:5, Paul speaks of doing the "things of the spirit") and inappropriate actions (in 8:5, Paul opposes the "things of the spirit" to the "things of the flesh;" in 8:13, he is more specific in his list of inappropriate behavior, but the thrust of the opposition is similar). What Paul depicted earlier in his grand narrative, he now makes directly relevant to his addressees. The fact that the members of the Roman house churches live in a world not yet fully saved does not mean that they have to behave in the ways of the world. Their identity is now defined by another standard, and this standard needs to be reflected in their ethical orientation. Because of

---

they must be a community characterized above all by the same quality and are indeed 'obliged' to be a community that 'walks in *agapē*.' (14:15)"

[32] For a fuller presentation of this interpretation, see Johnson, *Reading Romans*, 206: "… Paul thinks of *sōteria* as the process of forming the people of God out of Jews and Gentiles." See also Lopez, *Apostle to the Conquered*, 126–163. In her reading, she insists on the concrete implications for Jews and Gentiles in the call to become a Christ believer (in particular, 146–163).

[33] Johnson, *Reading Romans*, 206.

that, Paul invites his addressees "to put on the Lord Jesus Christ." (13:14)[34]

In language that echoes 6:3.4.5 and 8:17, Paul finds a powerful metaphor to express the change of self-understanding experienced by the Christ believers and the consequences this change should have for them. In terms of identity, Paul reminds his addressees that they do not belong to themselves. In their union with Christ, they have received a new purpose and a new manner to fill that purpose. Because they have to fit themselves in Christ (13:14), they receive a new identity, which is not oriented towards the fulfilling of their own needs and desires (13:14b), but which works for another (13:12). They do not have to worry about belonging to the world because they belong to Christ and therefore they need to act in a way that reflects this new self-understanding. Because they have put on Christ, they are liberated from the difficulties they may formerly have had with doing the good (see Rom 7:14–23) and they can now act in a new way. If one wants to translate this in philosophical language – which Paul does not use – one could say that they are liberated from themselves and can move forward. They do not have to worry about who they are or about their tortured inner life (in contrast to Rom 7); rather they can concentrate on concrete ways to deploy the new self-understanding given to them in Christ. It is important to observe that for Paul the question of identity is answered in a practical way.

2. Concrete Examples of Practicing Sincere Love (14:1–15:13)

Inside the community, the Romans are encouraged to actualize their *ēthos* concretely, especially when it comes to the relationships between Jew and Gentile.[35] To summarize the point of the section, one could say that the ex-

---

[34] The language might be a reference to the early practice of baptism among Christ believers, where the putting aside of old clothes and the putting on of new ones was part of the ritual. See Käsemann, *Romans*, 362–363; Johnson, *Reading Romans*, 206–207. Although Moo, *Romans*, 823–825 sees the influence of baptism in the construction of the ethical exhortation, he describes the "imagery of changing clothes" as "widely used with metaphorical associations in the ancient world."

[35] While it is not certain that the weak and strong of 14:1–15:13 allude to the Jews and Gentiles inside the Roman house churches, it is a likely identification, especially in light of the conclusion of the passage (15:7–13) which focuses on that particular problematic. By law, Jews were not required to abstain completely from meat and wine, but they would sometimes do so when they lived in an environment where they could not be sure of the provenance of the food and drink. This might have been the case for the Jewish-Christian community in Rome, which was perhaps forced, after the return from the exile demanded by Claudius, to live in unfamiliar parts of the city. See Moo, *Romans*, 829; Fitzmyer, *Romans*, 687; Johnson, *Reading Romans*, 210; Francis Watson, *Paul, Judaism and the Gentiles: A Sociological Approach* (Cambridge: Cambridge University Press,

hortation to practice genuine love is actualized in welcoming each other. Acceptance should be the characteristic attitude inside the community.[36] In a community composed of Jews and Gentiles, this welcoming has to take into account the problems of diversity and unity. As Johnson argues, Paul here attempts to deal with an issue of multiculturalism:[37] how does one create a united community out of individuals with different cultural commitments, without asking them to abandon their particular cultural "selves"? In that regard, 14:1 functions as a title for the entire passage (14:1–15:13). The welcoming in question has to demonstrate genuine love and cannot contain a hidden purpose, such as judging. It is done out of concern for the other person and does not simply amount to tolerating the other, but rather accepting them as true members of the community, almost as family members.[38] In this welcoming and in refraining from judging, the members of the Roman house churches embody a behavior which contrasts with the judging attitudes condemned in chapter 2 by Paul (see 2:1 in particular: there is no excuse for judging).

The exhortation to welcome is developed in three stages. In 14:1–23, Paul justifies his demand mainly through a reference to the identity of the Christ believer (14:4.7–8). In 15:1–6, Paul supports it through an appeal to the good of the community and finally, in 15:7–13, Paul uses the example of Christ as the main justification for his call to unity.

1986), 94–95; Engberg-Pedersen, *Paul and the Stoics*, 278; Grieb, *The Story of Romans*, 126–127. For a contrary position, see Robert J. Karris, "Romans 14:1–15:13 and the Occasion of Romans," in Donfried, *The Romans Debate*, 65–84. Karris (68–69) cites Max Rauer, *Die "Schwachen" in Korinth und Rom nach den Paulusbriefen* (Freiburg im Breisgau: Herder, 1923) as a monograph that defends the identification of the "weak" with Gentile Christians but he is not convinced by this reconstruction either. For him, "Rom. 14:1–15:13 is a generalized adaptation of a position Paul had earlier worked out respecting actual known situations, especially in Corinth." (71) Lopez, *Apostle to the Conquered*, insists that it is necessary to obtain a better definition of who the Gentiles were. For her, the Gentiles, in Roman imperial ideology, included all nations that had been conquered, thus also the Jews. The opposition, for her, is not so much between Jews and Gentiles, but between nations and empire (see in particular 22–25 and chap. 4).

[36] See Johnson, *Reading Romans*, 213: "The community, in short, should act with a bias toward acceptance rather than toward rejection ..." Mutual acceptance is often described as the purpose of this section; see Moo, *Romans*, 826; Fitzmyer, *Romans*, 687 speaks of a "plea for unity."

[37] See Johnson, *Reading Romans*, 212.

[38] See Moo, *Romans*, 835: "To 'receive' the 'weak' is not simply to accord them official recognition as church members. The verb means 'receive or accept into one's society, home, circle of acquaintance,' (BAGD) and implies that the Roman Christians were not only to 'tolerate' the 'weak' but that they were to treat them as brothers and sisters in the intimate fellowship typical of the people of God."

Rom 14:1–23: Welcome Each Other Because of the Identity God Gave You
The general exhortation of 14:1 requests Paul's addressees to embody two
types of behaviors: they need to be welcoming of the weaker brother and
they need to avoid quarreling over opinions. These two attitudes are at the
center of what follows and Paul will justify them in two ways. His first
reason is theological.[39] This welcome is demanded because God has received the members of the community (14:3a). If God has welcomed each
one among them in the community, then the members of the community in
rejecting some are acting against God's will and usurping God's place as
the one who decides whether someone can be included in the community
or not (see 9:15.16.18; 11:23.32). Among the community, differences have
to be accepted because only God is in the position to judge (14:4), a point
already prepared in chapter 2 (see 2:1–11). As long as each member of the
community acts in a way that she believes honors God (14:6) and is convinced that what she does is the right thing (14:5, see also 14:22.23), the
rest does not matter. The members of the Roman community need to focus
on their own relationship with God, on who they are, rather than worry
about the practices of others.

In keeping with his insistence on each person's relationship to God,
Paul, in his discussion of two concrete cases (14:2–6),[40] does not empha-

---

[39] See Moo, *Romans*, 838: "At the end of the verse, Paul states the ultimate reason
why such mutual criticism is out of place: 'God has received him.' Here we find Paul's
theological 'bottom line' in this whole issue, one that he elaborates in vv. 4–9 and states
again at the climax of his argument (15:7). Christians have no right to reject from their
fellowship those whom God himself has accepted." See also Meeks, "Judgment and the
Brother," 295: "The first apostrophe introduces the dominant theological warrant for
Christians' not judging one another; more precisely, it specifies the context of the warrant already stated in v. 3: 'God has received' the other precisely as the ultimate Judge,
before whom each 'stands or falls'."

[40] If one compares this passage with Paul's other thorough discussion of diet habits in
1 Cor 8–10, it is clear that the section in Romans is less developed, probably because
Paul has not heard of a crisis of the same dimension than in Corinth. Thus he might write
to the Romans because he fears that a similar situation could develop amidst their community. However, this does not mean that Paul's discussion in these chapters have no
connection at all to the Roman situation. Because the question of the relationship between Jew and Gentile and the exhortation to create a harmonious community are prominent in Romans, it is possible to argue that Paul is aware of delicate relationships between Jews and Gentiles in Rome. See Moo, *Romans*, 826–833; Käsemann, *Romans*,
364–365: "As a postulate we might venture the thesis that Paul presupposes or suspects
the existence of contending groups at Rome and that this is important for his concerns in
writing;" Grieb, *The Story of Romans*, 126; Fitzmyer, *Romans*, 687. For a contrary position, see Johnson, *Reading Romans*, 211: "In contrast [to 1 Cor 8–10], nothing in Paul's
description of the situation or his response to it suggest that here he has been informed of
a local crisis and is seeking to remedy it. It appears far more likely that Paul used his

size the actual practice and does not commend one behavior against another. Rather, he focuses on what each person believes (14:2 πιστεύει) or discerns (14:5 κρίνει; 14:6 ὁ φρονῶν) about what she does. Paul avoids centering the discussion on which side is right or wrong[41] but focuses instead on how to handle the differences. Paul is not trying to get some to change their diets; rather he wants both sides to avoid passing judgment on each other and accept one another in their differences, in order to create a harmonious community.[42] It is a matter of embodying the same kind of welcome that God has shown to them.[43]

Each member's relationship with God needs to define how one understands oneself and how one behaves inside the community (14:7–12). The key to the identity of the members of the community is the fact that they belong to the Lord (14:7–8). [44] They can no longer organize their lives and actions around themselves, in a selfish and self-absorbed manner. Their freedom is limited because of their commitment to Christ and all the aspects of who they are (in life and death) are in the hands of their master (see Rom 6:16.17.19.22). Christ believers need to realize that they do not hold the ultimate control over their lives, but that they have accepted to represent their master through their lives, and thus need to act according to their master's standards.[45] As a consequence, Christ believers can no longer

---

experience of the Galatian and Corinthian controversies as a backdrop for a reflection on the dimensions of 'life together' in a culturally pluralistic world."

[41] The qualifying adjective ἀσθενῶν does carry a judgmental nuance, but Paul does not focus on this – even though he identifies himself with the strong – in the rest of the discussion. Rather, it functions as a descriptive, perhaps coming from the manner in which the "strong" describe the other party. See Moo, *Romans*, 835–836. The reader might nonetheless get the feeling that Paul wishes the community would unite around the strong. See Moo, *Romans*, 836: "Paul's decision to use the pejorative phrase 'weak in faith' makes clear where his sympathies lie. We cannot avoid the impression (though his pastoral concerns lead him to keep it implicit) that Paul would hope that a growth in Christ would help those who were 'weak' become 'strong'."

[42] The issue is about attitude related to practice and not actual practice. See Johnson, *Reading Romans*, 212: "Paul pays practically no attention to the actual differences in practice, indicating to his readers at once that this is not the real issue. Instead he focuses on the attitudes accompanying the actions." Also Grieb, *The Story of Romans*, 127.

[43] See Minear, *The Obedience of Faith*, 15.

[44] I do not believe it matters to decide whether κύριος in 14:7–8 refers to God or to Christ. If the addressees belong to Christ (the most likely explanation because of 14:9, see Moo, *Romans*, 845 n. 86), then, through him, they also belong to God. In terms of identity however what matters is to see that the members of the Roman house churches cannot live for themselves. They are devoted to another.

[45] This is where the metaphor of slavery used by Paul might again be very powerful. The ideal Roman slave should conform her or his will to her or his master. See Harrill, *Slaves in the New Testament*, 21, 23 and 29.

pass judgment (14:10) because God is the only judge (14:10b–11) and to God they are now accountable (14:12).

The second reason highlights the good and the edification of the community (14:19). For the good of the community, Paul indicates that the weak always come first (14:13–23). In this regard, the strong carry a heavy responsibility towards the unification of the community. It is the strong who need to restrict their freedom.[46] First, the stronger brother needs to restrict his freedom in order to not tempt a weaker brother into a behavior that the weaker brother considers wrong (14:23). The strong should not try to convince someone of the truth of their position, rather they should act in a manner that is respectful of the doubts of the weaker members of the community (14:15), thus abstaining from some behaviors if necessary. Second, the stronger brother also needs to protect the weaker brother from judging. If the weaker member sees the strong eat something that the weaker member considers unclean, it might push the weaker member to judge the strong (14:16), which leads the weaker member to sin. The strong need to understand that, inside the community, it is not a matter of being right, but a matter of establishing good relationships.[47] In all cases, the good of the community needs to come first and this good resides in peace and edification (14:19). When the members of the community remember the welcoming of God and the need to place the community first, they embody the love that defines them (14:15a).

Rom 15:1–6: Welcome Each Other for the Good of the Community
Building on what he said in 14:13–23, Paul insists that the good of the neighbor is more important than one's own good (15:1–2). Chapter 15 opens with ὀφείλομεν, indicating that what follows is another exemplification of owing nothing but love to one another (13:8). It is the responsibility of the strong to take on themselves the failings of the weaker members of the community.[48] It is not just about tolerating the failings of the weak; it

---

[46] See Moo, *Romans*, 832: "And [Paul] makes clear that those who pride themselves on being the 'strong' have a special responsibility toward this end. It is they, those who truly sense their liberty on these matters, who are to put their exercise of that liberty in perspective and to subordinate it to the far more important 'good' of their fellow believers' edification and salvation (14:15–21)."

[47] See Johnson, *Reading Romans*, 215: "Paul's focus here, however, is not on the rightness or wrongness of the individual's actions – that is for God to judge – but on the righteousness of community relations."

[48] The translation of βαστάζειν by "to put up" in the NRSV suggests that the strong have to tolerate the weaker members' lack of faith. I think Paul has in mind a more active attitude which the translation "to bear" or to "take on" renders in a better manner. See Johnson, *Reading Romans*, 217; Moo, *Romans*, 864 and 866: "Paul is not urging the 'strong' simply to 'bear with,' to 'tolerate' or 'put up with,' the 'weak' and their scru-

is about being in solidarity with the weak in order to build up (οἰκοδομή) the neighbor (see 14:13). The example of Christ (15:1–3) though not developed in detail provides a basis for an attitude of embrace towards the weak. In particular, it confirms that the attitude of the strong towards the weak is more than simple tolerance. One is expected to intervene actively for the other (see the quotation of Ps 68:10 [LXX]) in the same manner than Christ has taken on himself insults that were not even directed towards him. What was said about Christ's attitude of sacrifice (15:3 but see as well 3:24–25 and 5:6) should also be true of the members of the Roman communities.

The final purpose of this attitude of welcome is foremost concerned with an attitude of the mind (15:5 φρονεῖν). The members of the Roman churches have to reach an attitude of common thought and understanding. To help them reach this unity of thought, Paul indicates that the person of Christ Jesus should serve as the factor bringing them together (15:5). Unity of thought should define the community. This purpose is in accordance with the beginning of chapter 12 (12:2.3) in which Paul exhorted his addressees to think humbly and to renew their minds. Once the members of the Roman house churches reach a common understanding, they can attain the final goal – to glorify God (15:6). It is important to notice that the members of the Roman house churches not only demonstrate proper relationships towards each other but also display the proper attitude towards God. In both ways, they fulfill what humanity could not do in the beginning of the letter. What Paul described as life in the spirit (see chapter 8) is actualized among the members of the Roman house churches.

Rom 15:7–13: Welcome Each Other Because of Christ's Example
Paul now moves into language about welcoming each other (ἀλλήλους) indicating that both weak and strong have a responsibility towards each other.[49] If the members of the Roman house churches show hospitality towards each other, they demonstrate that the differences and particularities among themselves do not matter and that what matters is their ability to give glory to God for what God has done among them. Differences are not erased, but they no longer function as what defines the believers in their most basic identity.

---

ples. For Paul uses this same verb in Gal. 6:2 (and cf. 6:5) in a similar way, urging believers to 'bear one another's burdens and so fulfill the law of Christ [i.e., love for one another; cf. Gal 5:14]."

[49] See Meeks, "Judgment and the Brother," 291: "The ἀλλήλους of v.7 thus replaces the qualification of 14:1, which has been superseded by the preceding appeals for reciprocal acceptance." Many commentaries also remark on this: Moo, *Romans*, 873; Wilckens, *Der Brief an die Römer*, 3:105; Dunn, *Romans*, 2:845.

The expression εἰς δόξαν τοῦ θεοῦ in 15:7 also explains what Christ has done for the Roman communities: Christ has welcomed them for the glory of God. This ambiguity should not be removed, especially since Christ is here used as an example to encourage a certain type of behavior among the members of the Roman churches. They are to show welcome to each other, because that is what Christ has shown to them; and both actions of welcome are done towards the glory of God. In imitating the behavior of Christ, they glorify God, embodying what should be the proper purpose of creation. Their glorification of God also indicates that they have now reversed what was at the root of the problem of humanity as described in 1:21 which indicates that human beings did not honor God in the proper manner. In their present state, however, Christ believers can do what they were once unable to do. In addition the language of 15:7 echoes 4:20, where Paul describes Abraham as glorifying God. The Christ believers are joined with Abraham through their attitude of obedient faith. Paul's demand is justified through the direct reference to Christ's example, reminding Paul's addressees that they are to welcome each other not just because of Paul's demand, but because their behavior and their moral orientation should now reflect Christ's.

Paul elaborates on the way in which Christ is an example of welcome in 15:8–9, two verses that are often seen as the summary of chapters 9–11.[50] In 15:8–9, Paul insists on the connection between the mission to the Gentiles and the mission to Israel, interlocking both in the role of Christ. In 15:8, Paul indicates that Christ has come to serve the Jews in accordance with the truth of God and in order to fulfill the purpose of the scriptures. It is only in 15:9 that Paul mentions the second purpose of Christ's coming, namely the participation of the Gentiles in the glorification of the God of Israel. It is through Christ's service for the Israelites that the Gentiles are able to glorify God for God's mercy towards them (see 11:11–32, in particular 11:30–31). The Gentiles are reminded of their subordinate role in relationship to Israel. The gift of Christ is not just a gift of mercy for the Gentiles; it is a sign of God's faithfulness towards Israel.

Because of Christ's mission to the Jews and because of its connection with the inclusion of the Gentiles among the children of God, Paul is able to insist on the importance of unity between Jews and Gentiles inside the Roman house churches. The members of the Roman community need to come together as one people, so as to implement among themselves the

---

[50] See Meeks, "Judgment and the Brother," 291–292: "This extraordinarily compact statement [15:8–9] constitutes a reprise of the themes Paul has developed in chaps 9–11 and, more than that, in the whole letter, leading up to Paul's restatement of the goal of his own mission, which follows in the remainder of this chapter ..."; Grieb, *The Story of Romans*, 131; Dunn, *Romans*, 2:844–845.

plan of God for Jews and Gentiles – a plan that Paul has presented in 9–11. This unity does not suppress the differences between Jews and Gentiles; it does not create a third people which would have the characteristics neither of Jews nor of Gentiles. Rather, it invites the members of the Roman house churches to think, imagine and realize a unity which is welcoming of differences of opinion and of actions, just as Christ was able to welcome both Jews and Gentiles. If Paul's addressees understand the story right, they can see that this story means something good for both Jews and Gentiles and that their fates as different nations are now connected in the fate of the children of God.

Paul has now reached his final point concerning the *ēthos* of the community at Rome. If the members of the community heed to Paul's exhortation and become a welcoming community, demonstrating harmony and unity between Jews and Gentiles, then they have become the kind of community – and the kind of individuals inside this community – that can and will help Paul in his own effort to continue the proclamation of the gospel to the Gentile world.

B. *Ēthos* of the Community in its Relationship with Paul (15:14–16:27)

In 15:7–13, Paul explained how the destinies of Jews and Gentiles are connected. Here he reaffirms the importance of his own work among the Gentiles while at the same time connecting it to his plans concerning the community in Rome.

1. Rom 15:14–16:2: Involvement of the Roman Community in Paul's Mission

In the first verse of this section, Paul is careful to place the members of the Roman house churches on equal footing with him. They are "full of goodness, filled with all knowledge and able to instruct one another." (15:14) The story of 1:18–8:39 stands behind this favorable description and Paul has written to remind them of this (15:15). Paul can describe them in such a manner because of God's intervention on their behalf through the death of Christ. As such, they also are people capable of reflecting Christ's behavior in their own actions and thus should demonstrate this behavior towards Paul's requests. In this regard, 15:16 plays a special role in Paul's argument. He describes himself as accomplishing the work of a priest and bringing in the offering of the Gentiles, an offering which is acceptable (εὐπρόσδεκτος) and made holy by the spirit. These terms remind one of the work of the spirit described in chapter 8, but also of the language of 12:1, which demanded of Paul's addressees to present their entire person as a sacrifice, pleasing to God (εὐάρεστον) and holy. In his letter, Paul has encouraged the members of the Roman churches to become precisely the type of Gentile sacrifice that Paul is appointed to present in his priestly service of the gospel (15:16). Since the work of Paul is to create this type of holy community, which can become sacred offering, he can boast in his mission (15:17–21), because his work reflects the demand of the gospel of God.

The understanding of the Gentile community as holy sacrifice creates a bond between Paul and the Roman house churches, even if Paul has not founded them or has not yet met them personally. Through Paul's mission, they are connected. Nonetheless, Paul knows that his relationship to the Roman house churches is somewhat different than the ones he has with churches he has founded elsewhere. The visit to Rome is not an evangelization visit. It is a visit for the purpose of receiving support for the mission to Spain. However, for Paul, this support can and will only be given to him if the members of the Roman churches practice the type of love and welcome exemplified by Christ, a type of love and welcome he has encouraged them to inhabit like a second nature particularly in the preceding chapters (12:1–15:7, see 13:14). In order to create this specific community, Paul feels he has written boldly (15:15). He justifies this boldness through the importance of the mission he has to accomplish (15:16). If through his boldness he has reminded the Romans of the story that stands behind their identity (1:18–8:39) and of what this identity means for their *ēthos* (12:1–15:13), Paul should be able to have his requests granted, for these requests are concerned above all with welcome.

The type of community that he hopes to find in Rome, that is, a community "full of goodness, filled with all knowledge and able to instruct one another," (15:14) is bound to welcome him (15:24b) and Phoebe (16:1–2). This welcoming is not passive tolerance, as 14:1–15:7 has already made clear. Rather it is active involvement for the benefit of the one requiring welcome. In the case of Paul, it means help – financial and strategic – for his mission to Spain (15:24b), and prayers concerning his voyage to Jerusalem (15:30–31). If the Roman house churches implement among themselves the kind of unity between Jews and Gentiles that the collection is meant to symbolize (15:27), they are contributing also to what the collection represents. In addition, their prayers on Paul's behalf would indicate their commitment to his mission and bide well for Paul's future involvement with the Roman communities.

Concerning Phoebe, it means assisting her in whatever she might need (16:1–2). The request for welcoming Phoebe is not elaborated. Whatever it is that Phoebe might need (shelter, money, food, personal support), the welcome that the Roman community offers to her should manifest the welcome that they need to practice towards each other. In particular, they should support her but also refrain from condemning her if on some matters she shows different convictions than the members of the Roman churches. In these concrete requests for help, Paul is giving an occasion to the Christ believers in Rome to embody the kind of behavior that is demanded of them because of their identity of children of God.

2. *Rom 16:3–27: Salutations and Ultimate Recommendations*

As a way of reinforcing his argument about unity in the community, Paul puts together a list of salutations (16:3–16) which refers to both Jewish and Gentile converts. The Gentile churches are indebted not only to Prisca, perhaps a Gentile woman,[51] but also to Aquila, a Jew (16:3). Together, they saved Paul's life. If one accepts that Prisca is a Gentile, then Prisca and Aquila are an example of the good that can come from the collaboration of Jews and Gentiles in general.[52] When asking the Roman communities to "greet" (ἀσπάσασθε) Prisca and Aquila, Paul might also expect his addressees to include the welcoming that he has asked from them earlier, concerning Phoebe and himself. In the list of names that follows, Paul insists on the work each individual accomplishes (16:3.6.9.12) and especially on each person's belonging to, or relationship with, Christ (16:3.5.7–13).[53] It allows Paul to emphasize the common elements and what properly defines each person, independently from ethnic or gender differences. As in the entire letter, Paul insists on the relationship to Christ as what ultimately decides the identity of an individual. If one focuses on that, then the differences that might have threatened the unity of the community (such as the conflict between weak and strong, Jews and Gentiles) recede into the background. They do not disappear, but they are not what makes or breaks the community. What makes or breaks the community is its belonging to Christ and the fact that it reflects the *ēthos* of Christ.

The importance of this conviction for Paul is reflected in the next section (16:17–20), which appears to be in sharp contrast with what comes

---

[51] See Jewett, *Romans*, 955: "In the case of Aquila, the evidence in Acts indicates that he was probably a freedman of Jewish origins. The fact that Aquila, not his wife, was identified as a Jew from Pontus (Acts 18:2) has led some researchers to infer that she was not a Jew. Her name and other details point to a freeborn origin in the noble Roman family of Acilius." See also, Peter Lampe, "Prisca/Priscilla," *ABD* 5:467–468, here 467.

[52] See Minear, *The Obedience of Faith*, 25: "Both by their [Prisca and Aquila's] work in Corinth and Ephesus and by their co-operation with Paul, they had demonstrated how crucial was the interdependence of Jews and Gentiles."

[53] See Minear, *The Obedience of Faith*, 27: "When we ask what accent recurs most frequently in this list, the answer is clear: 'for Christ,' 'in the Lord,' 'of Christ'."

before.[54] The change of tone can be explained if one takes into account that Paul is now reaching the end of the letter and has argued in different ways for the harmony of the community. The content of this final admonition is in keeping with Paul's purpose of emphasizing unity in the community. His addressees are to avoid those who create "dissensions and offenses," (16:17 σκάνδαλα; see 14:13) because they do not serve the Lord but focus on their own desires (16:18). This parallels 14:15–21 in which Paul asked the Christ believers to restrain from destroying the other for the sake of food or drink. In addition, 16:18 also insists that those who create occasions of scandal (16:17 and 14:13) are no longer serving Christ (16:18 οἱ γὰρ τοιοῦτοι τῷ κυρίῳ ἡμῶν Χριστῷ οὐ δουλεύουσιν; see the language of chapter 6 and 14:7–9). They have rejected the self-understanding given to them and, thus, they are nullifying the gift given to them in Christ's death and acting against God's work (see 14:20). The language and urgency of 16:17–20 testifies to the importance of the message of mutual welcome and of genuine love for Paul.

The letter closes with the habitual greetings from the sender's friends and from the scribe of the letter (16:21–23). Because of the debate surrounding the authenticity of the final doxology (16:25–27), it is best not to base arguments on it. If one considers it authentic, however, it is interesting to note that the final purpose of the disclosure of the mystery – namely the union of Jews and Gentiles – is the obedience of faith (see 1:5), a theme that has traversed the entire epistle and has been illustrated in the *ēthos* of Christ, precisely the *ēthos* that the members of the Roman house churches are invited to adopt and display in their relationships to each other and to Paul.

---

[54] Some scholars (Karl Erbes, "Zeit und Zeil der Grüsse Röm 16,3–15 und der Mitteilungen 2 Tim 4,9–21," *ZNW* 10 (1909): 146; O'Neill, *Romans*, 252–253; Schmithals, *Der Römerbrief*, 550–551), because of that sharp contrast, argue that these verses do not belong to the letter. However there is no textual evidence for omitting these verses. See Moo, *Romans*, 928.

C. How Story Constructs Self

My reading of Romans shows that *ēthos* is at the center of the manner in which Paul works on the identity of his addressees. Using Ricœur's work in *Oneself as Another* allows me to specify how story constructs self, and see how this applies to Paul's narrative strategy in Romans. In this section, Ricœur's thought and the concepts he develops allow translating Paul's work on the identity of his addressees in philosophical language. Ricœur's narrative theory is employed as a tool to prepare the discussion between Foucault and Paul in the final chapter.

1. Ricœur's Narrative Theory

In the fifth and sixth studies in *Oneself as Another*, Ricœur puts into place a reflection on the self and narrative identity.[55] In his analysis of the constitution of the self in relationship with the constitution of action, Ricœur works with the triad: description, story-telling and prescription. For the French philosopher, the art of story-telling can only fulfill its mediation function if it is clear that story-telling already includes "the broadening of the practical field and the anticipation of ethical considerations."[56] He sees stories as always being ethically involved. In fact, for him, literature functions as a laboratory in which judgments are exercised. This leads him to state that: "narrativity serves as a propædeutic to ethics."[57] Thus story-telling is more than just describing; it already serves to construct moral judgment. This connection of narrative theory with ethics will play an important role again when Ricœur discusses the ethical consequences of his narrative understanding of identity.

Ricœur carefully presents the manner in which narrative theory addresses the problem of personal identity. For Ricœur, the difficulties about personal identity are related to the fact that personal identity is the privileged place in which the confrontation between identity understood as sameness (*idem* identity) and identity understood as selfhood (*ipse* identity) emerges.[58] This confrontation surfaces first when personal identity is confronted

---

[55] See Ricœur, *Oneself as Another*, 140–168.

[56] Ricœur, *Oneself as Another*, 115.

[57] Ricœur, *Oneself as Another*, 115: "Literature is a vast laboratory in which we experiment with estimations, evaluations, and judgments of approval and condemnation through which narrativity serves as a propædeutic to ethics." This approach focuses on the effects texts have on readers, and recognizes the rhetorical dimension of texts. See for a similar discussion of texts, Stichele and Penner, *Contextualizing Gender in Early Christian Discourse*, 192–193.

[58] See Ricœur, *Oneself as Another*, 115–116: "The problem of personal identity constitutes, in my opinion, a privileged place of confrontation between the two major uses of

to the problem of permanence in time.[59] At first, it seems that time is mainly an issue for identity understood as sameness. Identity understood as sameness (or *idem* identity) refers to the traits of character that allow one to re-identify a person as being the same individual over time. Ricœur indicates that time represents a threat for identity because it brings with it the possibility of change. In reaction to that threat, the problem of personal identity is to find what Ricœur calls a "relational invariant," something that remains stable despite changes, which would give permanence in time to identity.[60]

Ricœur proposes two models of permanence in time. One involves character and the other involves keeping one's word. In the case of character, Ricœur argues that, in the permanence of character, *idem* identity and *ipse* identity coincide with each other. *What* one is, in one's characteristics and habits, is *who* one is. Our traits of characters make us who we are. In contrast, the notion of permanence in relation to one's faithfulness to one's word shows the extreme difference between permanence understood in terms of selfhood and permanence understood in terms of sameness. Keeping one's word implies that despite changes in one's character or despite unexpected events in one's life, one will still fulfill the promise one has made. The selfhood, the *who*, remains, despite changes in the character, changes in the *what*. Selfhood remains, even without the support of sameness. The role of narrative identity will be to keep the two together, in a mediating function.[61] Ricœur explains how the dialectic between permanence in time in terms of character (continuity of sameness) and *maintien de soi*[62] at the level of *ipse* identity happens.

At one pole of the dialectic, character covers all of the dispositions that allow one to recognize a person.[63] In this understanding, *idem* identity and *ipse* identity tend to be undistinguishable: my character is me, myself, *ipse*.

---

the concept of identity, which I have evoked many times without ever actually thematizing them. Let me recall the terms of the confrontation: on one side, identity as *sameness* (Latin *idem*, German *Gleichheit*, French *mêmeté*); on the other, identity as *selfhood* (Latin *ipse*, German *Selbstheit*, French *ipséité*)."

[59] See Ricœur, *Oneself as Another*, 116: "Indeed, it is with the question of *permanence in time* that the confrontation between our two versions of identity becomes a genuine problem for the first time."

[60] See Ricœur, *Oneself as Another*, 118.

[61] See Ricœur, *Oneself as Another*, 118–119.

[62] *Maintien de soi* is translated either by self-maintenance (119 for example) and by self-constancy (123 for example). Self-constancy is closer to Ricœur's use, but it does not quite have the same nuance as *maintien*. I will thus use *maintien de soi* to mark the particular meaning of this term for Ricœur.

[63] See Ricœur, *Oneself as Another*, 121: "Character, I would say today, designates the set of lasting dispositions by which a person is recognized."

As Ricœur puts it, in this case, "*ipse* announces itself as *idem*."[64] However, Ricœur indicates that one should be aware of the temporal dimension of disposition. Dispositions are connected to habits. Each habit, once it is ac-quired, becomes a trait of character, through which one is able to re-identify a person as the same person.[65] At the same time, dispositions also introduce the notion of otherness (*altérité*) in character. A person's identity or a community's identity is made of this person's, this community's iden-tification with values, norms, ideals, models even heroes.[66] For Ricœur, the otherness is clearly present in the identification to heroic figures, but he also indicates that it is already implicitly present in the decision of choos-ing one value and giving it more importance than one's own life for exam-ple. In this case, permanence in time is already associated to faithfulness to one's values, to one's word and touches on *maintien de soi* rather than on sameness. This brings Ricœur to observe that *ipse* identity, even when it is recovered by *idem* identity, cannot be suppressed in a person.[67] However, the permanence in time that comes through acquired habits and internal-ized identifications is mainly marked by sameness. In this case, identity is not the answer to the question "*who* am I?" but rather "*what* am I?"[68]

At the other pole of identity, Ricœur sees the notion of identity con-tained in the idea of keeping one's word. For him, this model of perma-nence in time reveals the *ipseity* of the self without the support of same-ness. In fact, being faithful to one's word indicates what Ricœur calls a *maintien de soi* that is not inscribed, like character, in the dimension of the something but uniquely in the dimension of the *who*.[69] In this way, remain-ing faithful to one's promise is a "challenge to time" and a "denial of change."[70] Ricœur writes: "even if my desire were to change, even if I

---

[64] See Ricœur, *Oneself as Another*, 121.

[65] See Ricœur, *Oneself as Another*, 121: "Each habit formed in this way, acquired and become a lasting disposition, constitutes a *trait* – a character trait, a distinctive sign by which a person is recognized, reidentified as the same – character being nothing other than the set of these distinctive signs."

[66] See Ricœur, *Oneself as Another*, 121.

[67] See Ricœur, *Oneself as Another*, 121.

[68] See Ricœur, *Oneself as Another*, 122: "Character is truly the 'what' of the 'who.' ... Here it is a question of the overlapping of the 'who' by the 'what,' which slips from the question 'Who am I?' back to the question 'What am I?'"

[69] See Ricœur, *Oneself as Another*, 123: "There is, in fact, another model of perma-nence in time besides that of character. It is that of keeping one's word in faithfulness to the word that has been given. I see in this keeping the emblematic figure of an identity which is the polar opposite of that depicted by the emblematic figure of character. Keep-ing one's word expresses a *self-constancy* which cannot be inscribed, as character was, within the dimension of something in general but solely within the dimension of 'who?'"

[70] Ricœur, *Oneself as Another*, 124.

were to change my opinion or my inclination, 'I will hold firm'."[71] Even though my character might change completely, I will remain the same, in faithfulness to my promise. Permanence in time through *maintien de soi* implies one's relationship to others. One behaves in a manner that allows others to count on her. Ricœur sees it as an answer to the question "Where are you?" This question is asked by another, who needs me. And the answer given to this question is "Here I am!" an answer which, for Ricœur, indicates *maintien de soi*.[72] In this model of identity, ispeity and sameness no longer coincide.

For Ricœur, this tension between ipseity and sameness constitutes a dialectic, which opens up a gap of meaning[73] that narrative identity is able to address. He argues that narrative identity walks between two limits. On the one hand, it takes into account an inferior limit in which permanence in time is expressed in the confusion of *ipse* and *idem*, in the notion of character. On the other hand, it also integrates a superior limit in which *ipse* addresses the question of identity without the help and support of *idem*.[74] According to Ricœur, narrative identity accomplishes two things. First, the notion of emplotment[75] applied to narrative and to characters in a plot allows integrating into permanence in time what seems to be its opposite in the mode of sameness-identity, namely discontinuity.[76] Second, the notion of emplotment when it is transferred to characters in a plot creates a dialectic in the character which is precisely a dialectic between sameness and ipseity.[77]

---

[71] Ricœur, *Oneself as Another*, 124.

[72] Ricœur, *Oneself as Another*, 165: "Self-constancy is for each person that manner of conducting himself or herself so that others can *count on* that person. Because someone is counting on me, I am *accountable for* my actions before another. The term 'responsibility' unites both meanings: 'counting on' and 'being accountable for.' It unites them, adding to them the idea of a *response* to the question 'Where are you?' asked by another who needs me. This response is the following: 'Here I am!' a response that is a statement of self-constancy."

[73] See Ricœur, *Oneself as Another*, 124: "an interval of sense."

[74] Ricœur, *Oneself as Another*, 124: "… we will not be surprised to see narrative identity oscillate between two limits: a lower limit, where permanence in time expresses the confusion of *idem* and *ipse*; and an upper limit, where the *ipse* poses the question of its identity without the aid and support of the *idem*."

[75] Emplotment translates the notion of *mise en intrigue*. See *Soi-même comme un autre*, 167 (*Oneself as Another*, 140).

[76] See Ricœur, *Oneself as Another*, 140: "First, I shall begin by showing, in a continuation of the analyses in *Time and Narrative*, how the specific model of the interconnection of events constituted by emplotment allows us to integrate with permanence in time what seems to be its contrary in the domain of sameness-identity, namely diversity, variability, discontinuity, and instability."

[77] See Ricœur, *Oneself as Another*, 140–141.

Using his work in *Time and Narrative* on the notion of *mimesis*, Ricœur repeats that the notion of emplotment, through configuration, creates concordance out of discordance. What is decisive for narrative identity is to move from plot to character, and demonstrate that the same movement of configuration is at work in the characters of a story. The notion of emplotment is transferred from the story to the characters.[78] Through that transfer, Ricœur shows that characters in a plot experience the dialectic between concordance and discordance, or continuity and discontinuity, in a very specific manner. On the one hand, characters are recognizable as totality, inscribed in time. It is what makes one character different from all others, and allows this character to be recognizable throughout the story.[79] On the other hand, however, this totality is threatened by discordance. This discordance is represented by the break that unpredictable events can create in the story, threatening the unity of a character's life. As the story is created through various events, so is the identity of the characters in the story.[80]

The concordance/discordance at work in the characters of a story is at odds with the request for permanence in time inscribed in the question of identity. Ricœur argues that the dialectic of the character of a plot creates a mediation between the two poles of permanence in time. For him, this is attested in what he calls the "imaginative variations" created by a story around the notion of identity.[81] According to Ricœur, literature can be seen as a laboratory that, through a plot, tests the resources of narrative identity.[82] An extreme case of this testing occurs in what Ricœur calls limit cases, for example fictions that tell of one's loss of identity. Read in the light of the dialectic between *ipse* and *idem*, these fictions can be interpreted as "exposing selfhood [*ipséité*] by taking away the support of the sameness."[83] The character is no longer identifiable through the permanence of her characteristics. We have a "self deprived of the help of sameness."[84] Without the support of sameness, there are no longer answers to the ques-

---

[78] See Ricœur, *Oneself as Another*, 143.

[79] See Ricœur, *Oneself as Another*, 147: "... following the line of concordance, the character draws his or her singularity from the unity of a life considered a temporal totality which is itself singular and distinguished from all others."

[80] See Ricœur, *Oneself as Another*, 147.

[81] See Ricœur, *Oneself as Another*, 148: "This mediating function performed by the narrative identity of the character between the poles of sameness and selfhood is attested to primarily by the *imaginative variations* to which the narrative submits this identity."

[82] See Ricœur, *Oneself as Another*, 148: "In this sense, literature proves to consist in a vast laboratory for thought experiments in which the resources of variation encompassed by narrative identity are put to the test of narration."

[83] Ricœur, *Oneself as Another*, 149.

[84] Ricœur, *Oneself as Another*, 166.

tions "what am I?" or "who am I?" It is as if only the "who?" remains.[85] This nakedness of ipseity, as Ricœur calls it, creates a problem for the readers, at an ethical level.

If one accepts, as Ricœur argues, that story-telling stands between describing and prescribing,[86] then one of the ethical consequences of story is that it can exercise a transformation in the feelings and actions of its readers.[87] When the notion of identity as sameness tends to disappear at a narrative level, how can one maintain a self at the ethical level? Ricœur writes: "how can one say at one and the same time 'Who am I?' and 'Here I am!'?"[88] For Ricœur, this tension between narrative dissolution and ethical affirmation can be positive and accomplishes two things. First, the affirmation "Here I am!" puts an end to the countless possibilities offered in the various models of identities present in narratives. The ethical responsibility contained in the act of promise grounds the subject in a form of permanence. It puts an end to endless imaginative variations.[89] Ricœur expresses it in the following manner: "Between the imagination that says 'I can try anything' and the voice that says 'Everything is possible but not everything is beneficial (understanding here, to others and to yourself),' a muted discord is sounded. It is this discord that the act of promising transforms into a fragile concordance: 'I can try anything,' to be sure, but 'Here is where I stand!'."[90]

At the same time, the fact that the proud declaration "Here I am!" is always seen as an answer to the anguishing question "Who am I?" indicates the humbleness of the notion of *maintien de soi*.[91] The question becomes: "Who am I, so inconstant, that *notwithstanding* you count on me?"[92] Because one knows, even if only secretly, the distance between the narrative variations of imagination and the responsibility of the self on whom someone else is counting, the notion of *maintien de soi* can only be marked by humbleness.[93]

---

[85] See Ricœur, *Oneself as Another*, 167.

[86] See Ricœur, *Oneself as Another*, 152.

[87] See Ricœur, *Oneself as Another*, 161–163. Ricœur is conscious of the difficulties related to the notion of applying fiction to one's life. He answers several objections: since one is not the author of a work of fiction how can that story contribute to one's understanding of one's own life? For Ricœur, the reader co-authors the meaning of a story through her act of reading. In addition, fiction helps us organize our real life in a narrative unity, addressing for example the issues of beginning and end of life that are out of our control. Story engages the reader in retrospection and prospection.

[88] Ricœur, *Oneself as Another*, 167.

[89] See Ricœur, *Oneself as Another*, 167.

[90] Ricœur, *Oneself as Another*, 167–168.

[91] See Ricœur, *Oneself as Another*, 168.

[92] See Ricœur, *Oneself as Another*, 168.

[93] See Ricœur, *Oneself as Another*, 168.

2. Romans in View of Ricœur's Narrative Theory

When Paul tells their story to the members of the Roman churches, he explains to them how their *ēthos*, their character, has been completely changed. In fact, he indicates that the various traits of their character (that is their body, their mind, their sense of belonging to a community and to a nation, as well as their moral sense) have been transformed and called into question. They have died with Christ (6:3–4), their old self is no longer (6:6) and they have received a new identity of children of God (8:14.16) which modifies the traits of their character and is translated in a new *ēthos* (chapter 8, and 12–15). Their old traits of character, despite the fact that they still exist (the Christ believers still have a body, a mind, a moral sense), need to be completely reconfigured. Through their character, the Christ believers need to embody new habits and new customs. Their lives need to reflect a new *ēthos*. Using Ricœur's categories, it is possible to say that the sense of *idem* identity of Paul's addressees has been deeply challenged, perhaps even destroyed. In *Oneself as Another*, Ricœur mentions conversion as a typical event which threatens the self in suppressing the notion of sameness. Ricœur describes it as the experience of *Ichlosigkeit*.[94] For the new Christ believers, when they died with Christ, their *idem* identity died with them. They have lost the support of sameness in their self-understanding and are confronted with the nakedness of their ipseity. The question then becomes: how is the identity of the self maintained?

The self maintains itself in its ethical engagement. Despite all the changes and all the possibilities opened up through the conversion experienced by the Christ believers, their self can maintain itself in the faithfulness to the choices made in the acceptance of the promise offered to them through Christ. In their belonging to Christ, their identity as ipseity is maintained. The affirmation "Here I am!" for the Christ believers corresponds to their faithful obedience to Christ as their new master. Their *maintien de soi* is tied to their ethical behavior and to the limits they place on their new freedom because of the choice they have made in becoming slaves of God. The multiple narrative identities offered to them in the dissolution of their *idem* identity are limited by the necessity for them to reflect the *ēthos* of Christ and to pursue the good of the community. The Christ believers maintain themselves and their identity through faithfulness to their responsibilities. For Paul, however, this faithfulness also takes on concrete qualities or traits of character. Hence the need for him to reconstruct the *ēthos* of his addressees by redefining their understanding of body, mind, moral sense, community and people. At the same time, the

---

[94] See Ricœur, *Oneself as Another*, 166 and 167: "So many conversion narratives attest to such nights of personal identity."

Christ believers, because of the loss of *idem* identity, are reminded of the humble modesty involved in *maintien de soi*. They can be faithful and keep their promises only because God has taken their side through Christ and through the spirit.

In this context, the story that Paul tells his addressees can be seen as redeploying the manner in which the Romans became who they are. It allows the members of the Roman churches to make sense of the discordance they experienced in their life through their conversion to Christ and to integrate the dimension of change into the continuity of life. Because story stands between describing and prescribing, it prepares Paul's readers for the move to ethical constitution of the self. In the final chapters of the letter, Paul is preoccupied in showing to his addressees how they can make their *idem* identity and their *ipse* identity coincide again. In his ethical injunctions, Paul is reconstructing the *idem* identity of his addressees so that it reflects their new found *ipse* identity. To say it differently, Paul is concerned with making *what* they are match *who* they are.

D. Categories of the Self in Romans

1. Ipse *Identity of the Christ Believers*

In Ricœur, we have seen that selfhood, or *ipse* identity, is expressed in the affirmation "Here I am!". Ricœur, even if he does not make this reference explicit in *Oneself as Another*, is working with biblical echoes. The two most prominent biblical references that come to mind in this case are Moses' answer when confronted with the burning bush (Ex 3:4), and Abraham's self-identification at the beginning of the story of the binding of Isaac (Gen 22:1). Both stories shed a particular light on Ricœur's use of "Here I am!". When Moses answers "Here I am!" this launches a change of identity. God demands that Moses become the leader of the Israelites. Moses' reticence (Ex 3:11.13; 4:1.10.13) indicates the depth of the change involved for Moses and the fear that goes with it. In Abraham's case, his "Here I am!" binds him to his word in an unbreakable promise. His willingness to answer God demands of him absolute faithfulness. Abraham is the example of faithfulness to one's word *par excellence*, despite the circumstances of life. Loss of a previous identity and faithfulness to one's word are integral part of the "Here I am!" that defines *ipse* identity. In the biblical world, "Here I am!" is the model response for the faithful servant of God.

This "Here I am!" is what gives some continuity also to the self of the Christ believers in Romans, despite the fact that their old person (ὁ παλαιὸς ἄνθρωπος) was destroyed (6:6). The "Here I am!" is an opportunity for self-affirmation in a time of change. Paul suggests several ways in which this self-affirmation is offered to the Christ believers. At the beginning of the letter, he indicates that the purpose of his work is to bring the obedience of faith to his addressees (1:5). Their ethical faithfulness is expressed in the obedience of faith, but also in the identity of slave that now defines both Paul and the Christ believers (1:1; 6:17.19.22). Despite all the accidents and chance events of their life, they need to be defined by their allegiance to their master. They belong to him (14:7–8) and thus they need to remain faithful to the word given to their master.

The weight of their obedience and of their faithfulness is however not put solely on the shoulders of the Christ believers. Rather, behind the possibility for the Christ believers to affirm "Here I am!" Paul sees the intervention of God in the world, through the death and resurrection of Christ and through the gift of the spirit. Christ, in displaying perfect obedience, restored peace between human beings and God (5:1.2.10.11) and provided human beings with the possibility of ethical behavior (6:2.3.4). The spirit is the force that energizes this changed behavior in human beings (8:13.16) and helps them in their new identity (8:26). For Paul, Christ and the spirit together make it possible for human beings to articulate the "Here I am!" that qualifies the children of God and makes them faithful servants. The new self of the Christ believers is marked by responsibility, the responsibility of the obedience of faith. Through this responsibility, Paul puts limits to all the possibilities opened up by the destruction of the old self. The story told by Paul, which destroyed the *idem* identity of his addressees, offered every kind of possibilities to his readers (we find here the "Everything is possible" of Ricœur). Through the obedience of faith, through this "Here I am!" Paul limits these possibilities (and here we have the "but not everything is beneficial" of Ricœur[95]) and these limits will bring about a metamorphosis of the character of the self (12:2). These limits are set in chapters 12–15, in which one can see Paul trying to make the character, the *ēthos* of his addressees, align with their new *ispe* identity.

2. Idem *Identity of the Christ Believers*

The *ēthos* of the Christ believers needs to be transformed at various levels, and all the dimensions of the *ēthos* need to reflect the new *ispe* identity of the believers. In the work Paul does on the character of his addressees, *ipse* identity and *idem* identity coalesce. The characteristics of human beings – what constitute their *idem* identity – remain the same attributes, but they now have to be used in agreement with the new *ipse* identity. In this sec-

---

[95] It is clear that this formula in Ricœur echoes Paul's writing in 1 Cor 6:12 and 1 Cor 10:23, thus it should not be a surprise that it helps us understand Paul's thought.

tion, I show how the *idem* identity of the believers is transformed, through the new use of human beings' attributes, to match their *ipse* identity. In Paul, the character of the believers is dependent upon various elements that all constitute *what* the person is, its *idem* identity. The *ēthos* of the believers is apparent first and perhaps most obviously in the manner in which they use their body. For Paul, the new ipseity of the believers is an embodied ipseity. Second the *ēthos* of a person also affects her inner abilities, namely everything that touches upon the mind, but also the heart and the rational and moral capacities of a person. Finally, *ēthos* is also seen in the manner one relates to others, inside a community and in relationship to one's sense of belonging to a particular nation or people. In Romans, *ēthos* in this case is affected by a person's understanding of particularism, in relationship to one's being Jewish or Gentile.

Body
When Paul thinks about the body in Romans, he uses two key concepts: σῶμα and σάρξ. Despite the fact that σάρξ is used more often in Romans,[96] σῶμα is the governing concept for Paul's understanding of the body. Σάρξ is part of σῶμα but σῶμα cannot be limited to σάρξ. In fact, Paul can write that the Christ believers have a σῶμα (12:1; 8:11) but that they are no longer providing for the σάρξ (13:14). In their unredeemed state, the bodies of human beings could be equated with flesh. In the redeemed state, even though the Christ believers are no longer worried for the flesh, they are still understood as being embodied. The body is an integral part of who the Christ believer is, even if flesh is not. The body might become unnecessary only once salvation is complete (8:23) but even then, the restoration of the body might not necessarily mean the disappearance of the body. For Paul, human life, restored or not, is embodied life.

The body in Paul is understood as subjected body.[97] It is dependent upon a master, and the master decides how the individual can use her body (6:12.13.19).[98] Because the life of the individual is embodied life, and thus happens in the world and in everyday life, the body – and the actions taken by the body – reveals which master the individual is serving. When the

---

[96] Σάρξ is used 25 times in Romans, whereas σῶμα occurs 13 times.

[97] See Moxnes, "Asceticism and Christian Identity in Antiquity," 20: "The male body is not a subject of its own; it is not under the control of man."

[98] A similar point is made by Moxnes, "Asceticism and Christian Identity in Antiquity," in which he analyzes a passage in 1 Corinthians, 20: "[Paul] obviously assumes that the human body is transformable. Moreover, the body receives its identity by entering into relations with other bodies, and it is by deciding which relations to enter into that men shape and determine the identity of their bodies, that is, themselves." and 23: "Paul's appeal is not to show self-mastery, but to realize that the male body is always engaged in relations, and is defined and given its identity by these relations."

body is subjected to sin, the only life the person can lead is κατὰ σάρκα (8:5). As a result, the body becomes a burden, and can even be described as a prison for the person (see chapter 7, in particular 7:18.23.24), making the person unable to act in the manner that she would want. At the same time, in the life according to the flesh, there is an unbridgeable distance between the person and God (8:7–8). For Paul, the body, because it cannot be controlled properly, reveals the fact that the person is not in the right relationship with God (1:24). In that case, the body is an instrument of sin and can only lead to death (6:13; 7:5; 7:24; 8:6). The body's subjection to sin makes it a negative force which needs to be destroyed (6:6).

When the body is subjected to Christ (or to God, or to righteousness; see 6:18.22; 14:7–8), the only life the person can lead is κατὰ πνεῦμα (8:5). The body is still part of who the person is, but now it can be used to accomplish the law (8:4). As a result, the person can enjoy life and peace (8:6), two gifts closely associated with the reconciliation that happened through Christ's death and resurrection (5:1; 6:4). The body itself does not need to be destroyed. In fact God has the power to give life (ζῳοποιήσει, see 8:11) to the body that was previously rendered dead because of sin. In the actions of the redeemed person's body, one needs to see the influence of the spirit and be able to recognize the lordship of God over that body (8:9–10; 12:1). The body becomes a tool for the service of God.

For Paul, the body is an essential part of who the redeemed person is, in its new *ēthos*. As such, it needs to reflect the new selfhood of the believer. The freedom that is given to the Christ believers through the death and resurrection of Christ and through the gift of the spirit is an embodied freedom. This has two important consequences for the way in which Paul understands the role of the body in the redeemed person.

First, the body is the location in which the self can and needs to try out its new self-understanding as child of God. Being a child of God is not just a decision of the mind or a spiritual endeavor. Rather, Paul insists that this self-understanding should be revealed in a person's everyday actions.[99] Grieb describes this embodied freedom in this manner: "what we do with our lives, our embodied existence and the materiality of daily decision making, inevitably reveals the extent of the lordship of Jesus Christ in our lives."[100] In particular, because the selves of the redeemed Christ believers

---

[99] For a similar point about the importance of the body, see Moxnes, "Asceticism and Christian Identity in Antiquity," 23: "to 'glorify God' was not just a spiritual or intellectual exercise; it actually happened through the use of the body ..."

[100] Grieb, *The Story of Romans*, 119. In this regard, I think that Jewett's assessment of the use of the body in 12:1 is too limitative. He writes: "In this letter, that purpose is the enlisting of the bodies of the Romans for the cause of righteousness and holiness (cf. Rom 6:19) for a mission project." (Jewett, *Romans*, 729) In my opinion, Paul, even if he

are embodied, the relationships these Christ believers have with others and with the world are especially important. Thus, when Paul asks his address-ees to place the weak first or to not be conformed to the world, he is not just constructing an ethical system but he is also showing concrete ways in which a Christ-like identity can be embodied.

Second, because, at least in this world, freedom can only be embodied, there are limits to what Christ believers can achieve. Salvation is not com-plete (5:9–10; 8:24). The body is not yet restored (8:23). According to Paul, the Christ believers are limited in what they can accomplish and thus exhortation remains a pertinent tool. The limits that are corollary of an embodied freedom also remind the addressees that their body is a subjected body, dependent on the will of the master (12:2). For Paul, the freedom given to the Christ believers needs to serve the will of the master and finds its limit in seeking "what is good and acceptable and perfect" for God. It is only in that subjection to the master that freedom can be possible for hu-man beings. Thus for Paul subjection is an integral part of the embodied lives of human beings. It is seen in a negative manner, when the master is sin, but Paul understands it as something powerfully positive when the master is God. In this case, subjection leads to freedom.

Abilities of Human Beings
When Paul thinks about the body, he sees it as being subjected to a particu-lar master. This subjection works either for good or bad. In Romans, the two masters who are opposed are sin and God;[101] both are powers distinct from the person herself. In their rule over the person, they decide how much and what this person can accomplish. Thus, Paul does not see the person's mind, or soul, or rational abilities as masters that would rule over the body. Rather, the master rules not only the body but also the person's inner abilities, her mind, her soul or her spirit. For Paul, there are no dif-ferences here between body and soul. The master does not only affect use of the body, but it also affects the use of human beings' abilities.[102]

---

includes the project of the mission, has a much wider understanding of the use of the body, which precisely involves very mundane tasks.

[101] The opposition is actually a bit more complex, since sin, at least in chapter 6, is al-so opposed to obedience (6:16), and to righteousness (6:18.19). From the entire letter, it seems clear however that the master at work behind the concepts of obedience and right-eousness is God.

[102] Chapter 7 seems to suggest a dualism between body and soul. The dualism appears here because Paul is developing a mythological world in which a mythological drama takes place. In this drama, we witness a battle between Sin, Law and Man. In this mytho-logical world, Man as a character is symbolically divided between the forces of Evil and Good. His mind is on the side of Good and his body is on the side of Evil. In addition, if one accepts the hypotheses that Paul is using a Hellenistic rhetorical device (*prosōpopoi-*

These abilities in Romans include human beings' rational capacities –
their power to think and reason – notions connected to Paul's use of νοῦς
and φρον- language, as well as vocabulary connected to λογίζομαι (for example: 1:20–21.28; 2:3; 6:11; 7:23.25; 11:20.25; 12:2.3.16.17; 15:5). Human beings are also able to discern and to judge, as κρίνω and συνείδησις
language makes clear (see for example 2:1.3.15; 9:1; 14:1). Finally, human
beings experience emotions and feelings (καρδία: for example 5:5; 8:27;
10:1.8–10), and they are able to have spiritual experiences (πνεῦμα: for example 1:9; 8:4–6.9.13.15.16). For Paul, the use of these capacities is limited by the way human beings perceive reality. If human beings have the
wrong master, they perceive reality (and their own person) in a distorted
way and use their various abilities in a misguided manner. However, once
they serve the proper master, human beings also benefit from correct self-
perception and become able to use their abilities properly. This correct
self-perception consists in realizing that Christ believers have no longer
any sort of relationship with sin, but rather they now have dedicated their
life to God (6:11). Human beings are freed, but for something else, which
could be summarized as the obedience of faith (6:18 and 1:5).

For Paul, correct self-perception cannot be reached through human
achievement.[103] It is dependent upon the death and resurrection of Christ

---

ia) and that the mythological figure of Medea stands behind at least parts of the discussion in chapter 7 (7:14–25 in particular; see Stowers, "Romans 7:7–25 as Speech-in-
Character (*prosōpopoiia*);" also Édart, "De la nécessité d'un sauveur." For Medea as the
figure behind Rom 7, see also Muriel Schmid, "Illusion et passion dans l'expérience humaine: essai anthropologique en regard de Rm 7" [Mémoire de diplôme de spécialisation
en Nouveau Testament, University of Neuchâtel, 1992]), it is possible to argue that in
this case Paul also uses a Hellenistic view of the relationship of body and mind, in which
the mind is a positive force opposed to the body. This language does not appear elsewhere in the letter; however it points out the fact that Paul is aware of the difficulty of
doing what is right, even when one *knows* what is right. For him however, ultimately this
difficulty does not come from a division between mind and body, but from the hold of sin
on human beings.

[103] In 2:13–16, Paul seems to entertain the possibility that some might actually be able
on their own to respect the law. In opposition to what he has shown in the opening pages
of his letter, he does recognize here the actual possibilities of some Gentiles respecting
the law. This comment might be aimed more particularly at Jews who might have thought
that they could exclude themselves from Paul's accusation in 1:18–2:12. Clearly, for the
needs of his story, Paul darkens the picture of humanity, and insists on the utter failure of
human beings to grasp the will of God. In reality, however, he leaves open the possibility
that some people sometimes respect the law. Nonetheless, even in that case, he points out
that these people will not escape God's final judgment and this judgment will reveal the
"secret thoughts of all." (2:16) No one should think that she can be a law unto herself and
everyone should remember that God will judge in the end. Therefore, Paul can conclude
his accusation with the statement that "all are under the power of sin," (3:9) confirming

and the gift of the spirit (8:2). The rational abilities of human beings, as well as their moral, spiritual and emotional achievements, are not enough to allow human beings to save themselves. It is the outside authority of God, mediated through Christ and the spirit, which restores human beings to themselves. Human beings' ability to know and understand things, their thirst for knowledge, even their capacity for introspection are not sufficient to bring human beings to a proper understanding of themselves and of their place in the world. Paul affirms the need for an outside revelation in order to bring any sort of empowerment in the lives of human beings.

For Paul, human beings are never characterized by an absolute freedom of choice. Both the hold of sin and the ultimate sovereignty of God limit what the human mind can achieve. Once human beings have been transformed by the power of the spirit and serve the right master, they do have a responsibility to use all of their abilities for good (12:1–15:13) and to think of themselves as transformed (6:11). Thus for Paul, being clothed in Christ (13:14) does not mean giving up one's rational abilities. Rather, human beings are invited to use their inner capacities to their full potential in order to embody the kind of obedience that God requires. To use a reflection put into place by Slavoj Žižek, in this case, freedom needs to be understood as a gift from grace. Paul does not see freedom and salvation as opposed; rather, they work together allowing human beings to act.[104]

Paul mentions several concrete results of this transformation through the spirit. First, the spirit enables human beings to think of themselves as serving God (8:9) and empowers them to use their abilities to the fullest, both in body and mind. At the level of their personal identity, human beings are able to understand themselves and their role in the world in a better manner. They are given a purpose and an identity that allow them to bridge the distance that sin opened between their body and their mind (see 7:14–25). Their relationship to themselves is no longer a field given over to a battle between evil and good. In the redeemed state, human beings are able to use their bodies in accordance with their inner will, because of the presence of the spirit in them.

But, for Paul, the transformation of the Christ believers' mind (12:2) also signifies that their relationship to God is restored; this allows human beings to use their mind and their rational abilities to determine the will of

---

his general conviction that human beings, under the power of sin, cannot use their inner abilities fully.

[104] See Žižek, *The Puppet and the Dwarf*, 159: "This, perhaps, is also the most important ethics lesson of the twentieth century: we should abandon all ethical arrogance, and humbly acknowledge how lucky we are to be able to act ethically. Or, to put it in theological terms: far from being opposed, autonomy and grace are intertwined – we are blessed by grace when we are able to act autonomously as ethical agents."

God and to live in accordance with that will, as well as to respect the law (8:4). In addition, in respect to their relationship with others, inside or outside the community, Christ believers are now able to move away from their self-absorption in order to embrace others, even in their weaknesses (15:1). The relationship of Christ believers with others, especially in their differences, is marked no longer by judgment or contempt (14:1.3.13) but by respect and concern (14:13.14) and the possibility of building a community defined by love. The center of the world is no longer themselves, rather it is the community that they are now serving.[105]

Moreover, through this new understanding of their relationship with themselves, with others and with God, Paul sees human beings as invited to live in a state of freedom from the world (12:2; 13:14). The criteria of the world no longer decide who they are or what they can accomplish. The standards of the world should not represent what Christ believers are seeking. In fact, Christ believers should be prepared to face difficulties (8:35) but at the same time, they can also be confident that their identity is anchored in a reality that will never pass and that guarantees the strength of the foundation on which their identity is built (see 8:31–39). In this identity, Paul does not claim that human beings are given a new body or a new mind. Rather, they are now able to use both body and mind to the fullest of their capacities, through the work of the spirit in them. It is understood in both cases that mind and body can only be used fully once human beings are redeemed. And it is made clear that once human beings are redeemed, they are able to take into account the needs of others and to limit their own self-absorption through the preeminence given to the community.

The New Οἶκος of God

For Paul, once human beings are redeemed through Christ's obedience, they belong to what can be defined vaguely as a new group. I am using the language of οἶκος to name this group. Even though this language does not appear in Romans, I think the idea of family, of common household, of οἶκος, can be gathered from Paul's usage of language related to sonship (8:16–17) and to slavery (6:15–22) This new group can be described as a family for the believers (8:14–17).[106] The common ancestor is Abraham (4:11.16) and the members of the family or of the οἶκος should know that

---

[105] See Grieb, *The Story of Romans*, 121: "The renewed mind also sees itself not as an isolated individual around which the world revolves (the star of our own show) but as part of a larger community with legitimately competing needs and interests that have to be taken into account if the community is to live in peace."

[106] See Grieb, *The Story of Romans*, 67: "Paul is saying that those baptized into the death of Christ have died to the power of Sin over them because they have a new family head, a new ruler or Lord."

they are children and heirs of God (8:16.17), thus sharing in Christ's status. In this new οἶκος, God is the *pater familias*. Thus, family ties and kinship are no longer about being Jewish and having Jewish brothers and sisters or about being Gentile and having Gentile brothers and sisters. It is about God. One's family is now the family of God. Paul argues that this new sense of kinship changes several things for the Christ believers.[107]

For Paul, when one belongs to the family of God, one belongs to something new (6:4). This community did not exist before. It is perhaps even a foretaste of the new creation (8:19–23). It is not that this household is created entirely from scratch. Rather, God, through Christ's faith and the spirit, uses the old to form something new (6:6). The community itself, even though it brings together things from the past (like sinners) with particular characteristics (Jews, Gentiles, weak and strong), is actually something new that did not exist before. In its present form, it owes its existence to God.

In this new entity, God brings together people normally separated, such as Jews and Gentiles.[108] Uniting Jews and Gentiles challenges an ingrained way of defining one people against the other. In the new household of God, Paul sees Jews and Gentiles as united in a new people. They do not cease to be Jewish or Gentile, but they are brought together in order to form something new. Paul shows that the union of Jews and Gentiles in a new community was God's plan from the very beginning. In fact, for Paul, it goes back to Abraham (4:11). The reference to Abraham as being the ancestor of both circumcised and uncircumcised individuals places the unity of Jews and Gentiles at the beginning of times, and indicates that it was part of God's original design for humanity. This is confirmed by the role of Christ (15:8–9). It is not only that two different people are brought together in the family of God, but for Paul each people needs the other in order to be reconciled to God (see 11:11–12.17.25–32). In the new entity created through Christ's work (15:8–9), ethnic particularities do not disap-

---

[107] deSilva, *Honor, Patronage, Kinship and Purity*, 199–239 offers a discussion of kinship in the New Testament. He notes that Christ believers created a new family, marked by belonging to Christ (*Honor, Patronage, Kinship and Purity*, 200), which accomplishes several things: "it gives the early church a sense of shared identity and binds the members together in the solidarity of the kinship bond; it provides them with a legitimate connection to the promise of God recounted in the Jewish Scriptures; it speaks of the profound honor and privilege that has come to them by virtue of attachment to the Christian community, and the coming manifestation of that honor, such that perseverance with the group remains an attractive option even when the pressure to defect is high." deSilva also notes how belonging to the household of faith has important ethical consequences (*Honor, Patronage, Kinship and Purity*, 212–225).

[108] For the separation of Jews and Gentiles as a traditional value of the ancient Mediterranean world, see deSilva, *Honor, Patronage, Kinship and Purity*, 49.

pear (see 14:2.5.21) but they no longer need to exclude. Differences do not need to be suppressed, but they do need to be negotiated (12:1–15:13), in order for the community to reach harmony and unity.

According to Paul, a sense of unity and harmony is central to the household of God (14:1; 15:5.7). The members of the household have the same master (6:22), thus what unites them is stronger than the particularities that might separate them (14:7–12). In Paul's eyes, nothing can be more important than the shared lordship of God over each member of the community. The members might be aware of the differences that separate them, but these differences need not imperil the unity of the community. Because they share in the household of God, Christ believers can work and live together for the same good, even though their actual practices might be different. They share the same ultimate purpose, which is to serve the Lord (16:8). In addition, for Paul, their belonging to God insures that they can be welcoming differences without being threatened in who they are. Thus differences do not need to be suppressed. The tie that the Christ believers all share with God through Abraham and Christ is not only what guarantees their unity and founds their harmony but it is also what makes the strength of the οἶκος. Their bond with God assures them that nothing can threaten who they are as a community. This is true both of outside forces (8:31–39) but also of inside differences, in faith and in practice (see chapters 14 and 15).

For Paul, human beings lead lives that are deeply embedded in communities. In the community, the person shares characteristics that mark who one is and make one easily recognizable. This sense of community does not disappear when Paul describes the redeemed lives of the Christ believers. Rather, salvation is understood as belonging to the οἶκος of God, as being part of that new family.[109] For Paul, salvation is not an individualistic concept, in the sense that it would only concern the life and state of a particular person, or only a future condition (such as heaven or hell). Rather, it involves the person in her relationship with others. The relationships one has with the master of the οἶκος and with the other members of the οἶκος define who one is and give one its sense of self. Again here, the identity of slave of God is central. The particularities of each individual are relativized. They do not disappear but they do not define who the per-

---

[109] See Johnson, *Reading Romans*, 27: "There is no sign in Romans itself that Paul conceived of 'salvation' as something that pertained mainly to individuals or to their respective destinies ('heaven' or 'hell')... Paul thinks of salvation here in social rather than individual terms, and that it is something that occurs in this life. In effect ..., 'salvation' in Romans means something close to 'belonging to God's people'." This point is also made about the concrete implications of salvation in Paul's letters by Lopez, *Apostle to the Conquered*, 146–153.

son is. For Paul, the person is defined by its master, and thus shares the identity of all the other slaves that serve the same master. The family one has is the family of God, and that is who the individual can depend upon. In this context, differences can be seen as strength (12:5–6) and set one person apart, while at the same time affirming its deep-rootedness in the community.

Who the Christ believers are in their ipseity is not threatened by the particularities of their character and ethnicity – their *idem* identity. For Paul, their belonging to God diminishes the importance of their ethnic characteristics when it comes to self-definition. What matters is one's identity as a child of God.

3. The Constitution of the Ethical Subject in Romans

To conclude and sharpen the manner in which I understand how Paul constructs the self of his addressees in Romans, it might be helpful to move from a ricœurian analysis of identity towards a more foucaultian exploration of the same topic. Foucault was willing to see his writings as a toolbox,[110] in which his readers could look for a device that they could use in their own analyses. Thus, Moxnes in his discussion of 1 Corinthians uses Foucault's ethical categories to discuss the manner in which Paul shapes his addressees into ethical subjects.[111] These ethical categories, which I will present below, can be seen to relate to what Ricœur calls *idem* identity, namely the characteristics of human beings, which I have defined by the way human beings use their body, their inner abilities and their way of relating to a community. For Foucault, the manner in which these catego-

---

[110] See Paul Veyne, *Foucault: sa pensée, sa personne* (Paris: Albin Michel, 2008), 126: "[Foucault] n'avait pas oublié que nul homme ne saurait préjuger de son éventuelle destinée posthume: il envisageait une possibilité plus empirique. Quand il disait et répétait que ses livres n'étaient que 'des boîtes à outils,' ce n'était pas pour convenir modestement qu'ils ne contenaient pas de trésors; il entendait par ces mots qu'il souhaitait avoir des élèves (aurait-il dit en style universitaire), et il invitait ses lecteurs de bonne volonté à utiliser ses méthodes et à continuer son entreprise, de même qu'un physicien a des élèves qui sont ses continuateurs." Foucault uses the toolbox reference in an 1975 interview with the French newspaper *Le Monde*; see Michel Foucault, "Des supplices aux cellules," in *Dits et écrits*, 2:716–720: "Tous mes livres, que ce soit l'*Histoire de la folie* ou celui-là [*Discipline and Punish*], sont, si vous voulez, des petites boîtes à outils. Si les gens veulent bien les ouvrir, se servir de telle phrase, telle idée, telle analyse comme d'un tournevis ou d'un desserre-boulon pour court-circuiter, disqualifier les systèmes de pouvoir, y compris éventuellement ceux-là même dont mes livres sont issus ... eh bien, c'est tant mieux!"

[111] Moxnes, "Asceticism and Christian Identity" proposes a similar move for his reading of 1 Cor 6:12–20. I propose an analysis of the categories of foucaultian ethics for Romans 12:1–15:13.

ries are negotiated by human beings defines the relationship they can have to themselves as ethical subjects.

For Foucault, it is important to emphasize that morality or ethics is not primarily about obedience to a set of rules; rather it needs also to be understood, in pagan antiquity in particular, as a way of shaping and transforming oneself, as a manner to create an ethical subject.[112] In the domain of ethics, Foucault chooses to focus on the way in which an individual constitutes herself as a subject for her actions, rather than on behavior or rules: "the kind of relationship you ought to have with yourself, *rapport à soi*, which I call ethics, and which determines how the individual is supposed to constitute himself as a moral subject for his own actions."[113] For Foucault, there are four areas that one can analyze in order to understand the manner in which an individual constructs herself in an ethical subject.

First, one has to look for ethical substance – what part of the human being is concerned when talking about morals. Foucault explains that for our society this ethical substance is foremost feelings, but that, for Kant, for example, it was intention, and for the Christians it was desire, concupiscence.[114] Second, it includes a specific *mode d'assujettissement* – a type or mode of subjection. One needs to reflect on the principle (or principles) that justifies the respect of certain moral obligations.[115] The third aspect is concerned with the means one uses to become an ethical subject, to fit inside the moral code, to be normal.[116] Foucault refers to this third dimension as the practice of the self, or *askēsis*,[117] understood in a broad sense. Finally, the fourth dimension of an ethics of the self concerns the moral teleolo-

---

[112] See Moxnes, "Asceticism and Christian Identity in Antiquity," 9.

[113] Foucault, "On the Genealogy of Ethics," 352. This is also developed in the third chapter of *History of Sexuality vol. 2*, 25–32. See also Moxnes, "Asceticism and Christian Identity in Antiquity," 12.

[114] Foucault, "On the Genealogy of Ethics," 352–353.

[115] See Foucault, "On the Genealogy of Ethics," 353: "The second aspect is what I call the mode of subjection (*mode d'assujettissement*), that is, the way in which people are invited or incited to recognize their moral obligations. Is it, for instance, divine law, which has been revealed in a text? Is it natural law, a cosmological order, in each case the same for every living being? Is it rational rule? Is it the attempt to give your existence the most beautiful form possible?"

[116] See Foucault, "On the Genealogy of Ethics," 354: "The third one is: What are the means by which we can change ourselves in order to become ethical subjects? ... What are we to do, either to moderate our acts, or to decipher what we are, or to eradicate our desires, or to use our sexual desire in order to obtain certain aims like having children, and so on – all this elaboration of ourselves in order to behave ethically? ... That's the third aspect, which I call the self-forming activity (*pratique de soi*) or *l'ascétisme* – asceticism in a very broad sense."

[117] In my transliteration, I will use *askēsis*. However, when the word is used in quotes, I will respect the transliterations that the authors preferred.

gy, the *telos*, which considers what type of human being one wants to become through one's moral behavior, what goal one wants to reach.[118]

In Paul's letter to the Romans, the ethical substance on which Paul's addressees need to work can be defined, broadly speaking, as their identity, what makes them who they are. They have to give shape to the content of their *idem* identity, thus the Pauline injunction to shape the body and the inner abilities, and to work on the manner in which they relate to the community. Through the work on this ethical substance, they can transform the way they relate to themselves, to others, to the world and to God. Everything in who they are and what they do needs to be used in order to become the type of ethical subjects that Paul wants them to be. It would be a mistake to want to restrain the breadth of the ethical substance in Paul. It cannot be narrowed down to a particular dimension or characteristic. Rather the ethical work really concerns the person in its entirety, in its relationship to herself but also to others and to God.

This work on the ethical substance is made possible in human beings because they now belong to a new master, God (Rom 6:22). The mode of subjection is characterized by knowledge and respect for the will of God (Rom 12:2). The members of the Roman house churches have a responsibility to act in a manner that reflects the ways of the spirit, and their belonging to the household of God. Even though the guiding category for the mode of subjection is the will of God and is based on the slavery metaphor, the mode of subjection should not be equated to servile obedience. Rather, the obedience demanded of the Christ believers is made possible only though the union with Christ (Rom 6:4) and through the workings of the spirit (8:2). Through the presence of the spirit in each individual, obedience to the will of God also implies imagination and creativity in the use of one's body and one's mind (12:1–2). What is at stake here is creative decipherment of and obedience to the will of the master, not servile compliance to a body of laws.

In agreement with that notion of creative obedience, Paul, in Romans, does not give precise indications concerning the *askēsis* that his addressees have to practice on themselves in order to transform themselves. He does not provide rules or laws. Rather, the practice of the self that he encourages has to do broadly with proper use of the body (12:1) and renewal of the mind (12:2); both aimed at proper worship of God and proper grasp and respect of God's will.[119] In addition, respect of the other, and of the

---

[118] See Foucault, "On the Genealogy of Ethics," 355: "The fourth aspect is: Which is the kind of being to which we aspire when we behave in a moral way? For instance, shall we become pure, or immortal, or free, or masters of ourselves, and so on?"

[119] In that way, the Christ believer can be said to fulfill the demands of the law (8:4), since its basic orientation reflect Christ's *ēthos*.

weaker other in particular, is also central to this practice of the self (14:1–15:7). One of the guiding principles for selecting appropriate behavior is tied to deferral to the needs of the weaker other. In addition, as I have already noted, the *askēsis* that will lead to creative decipherment of and obedience to God's will is only possible after salvation has occurred for the believers. The union with Christ in baptism and the gift of the spirit allows one to begin the slow transformative work that is demanded of the believers in chapters 12–15. This saving event marks the beginning of a new life, in which ethical work and constitution of the self as an ethical subject are possible and necessary.

In Paul's construction of his readers as ethical subjects, the *telos* is the good of the community, the creation of a community marked by peace and harmony, a community in which people are united spiritually and intellectually in one mind that reflects the mind of Christ (15:5). In that harmony, and in the welcoming of differences, Paul's addressees also reflect the *ēthos* of Christ himself. Thus, the *telos* combines the good of the community and the shaping of the person into a Christ-like individual. The constitution of the self as an ethical subject is central to the purpose of the letter to the Romans, but this work on the self is possible only because Paul's addressees have received a new self-understanding from God, translated in their identity of children of God. The gift of this self-understanding makes it possible for Paul and for his addressees to form their self into a new ethical subject. Even though the task of creating a harmonious community and of embodying a Christ-like identity is central to Paul's construction of the self, it is never reached completely in this life time. His letters testify to the fact that the ethical work he asks of his communities is never perfected but is a goal towards which his addressees should work tirelessly and which is worth pursuing.

The new understanding does not magically transform the individual into a new person. Rather, the individual always has to work in order to implement and embody the new understanding. Baptism and the gift of the spirit do inaugurate a new era for the individual, but she still has to fulfill the abilities and potentialities given to her in the gift of the spirit and the union with Christ. To return, once more to ricœurian language, the person is indeed given a new *ipse* identity characterized by a commitment to Christ, but she is still in need to shape her *idem* identity so that it reflects her new *ipseity*. At the same time, *what* the Christ believers are no longer defines *who* they are, but what they are can still be used in their new lives in Christ. The *telos* is to have both identities correspond. Once the individual has shaped itself in an ethical subject that reflects the *ēthos* of Christ, *idem* and *ipse* identities coincide and the Christ believers lead a life characterized by peace. In foucaultian categories,[120] Paul is constructing a discourse that attempts to shape and influence the formation of his addressees' self.[121]

At the term of this work on the Pauline categories of the self, I am led to make one observation, which will prefigure my engagement with Foucault and Paul on the question of identity construction. In Rom 12:1–15:13, Paul constructs the self of his addressees and attempts to give some content to their identity now understood as the identity of children of God. He shapes the "Here I am!" that defines who they are and puts limits to the endless possibilities given to human beings in the destruction of their old self. The possibilities are limited because human beings are now slaves of God (6:22) and need to clothe themselves in Christ (13:14). They belong to a master who defines a basic identity for them, if only because they are now part of the household of God. There is an *ipse* identity to which they need to remain faithful, and this *ipse* identity defines the core content of their person. Thus we can see the presence of a concept of essence given to human beings that define who they are. The abilities of the individuals do not change *per se* but, because of the new self-understanding of human beings, they are able to explore new possibilities for their actions. In all this, their understanding of themselves as children of God needs to be key to who they are.

In contrast, Foucault understands human beings as constantly creating themselves, in a movement of permanent change. He is wary of the idea of essence. His ethical ideal of an "aesthetics of existence" is constructed to escape the notion of an essence of the subject, especially the notion of an essence given to human beings. The category of change and the responsibility for the self to create itself anew is at the heart of Foucault's reflection on the self and his entire thought is a plea for individual invention of the self, in order to escape given identities. Change is embraced and becomes a sought-after category, not something one should seek to domesticate, control or avoid. For Foucault, the notions of essence and of given

---

[120] As I will discuss below, Foucault cannot envision the concept of an *ipse* identity for the individual. For him, it is never a question of making some characteristics coincide with a core identity to which one has to remain faithful. However, despite this difference, it is interesting to see that, both in ricœurian and foucaultian terms, there is a necessity for creative work on the capacities of human beings.

[121] Moxnes, "Asceticism and Christian Identity in Antiquity," 28 makes a similar observation about Paul's discourse in 1 Cor 6: "This passage is not a moral treatise in a traditional sense, discussing moral norms or rules. Nor is it a description of moral behaviour; although Paul speaks of Christians who visit prostitutes, it does not give sufficient information for an empirical study of sexual behaviour among Christians in Corinth. It seems much more appropriate to understand the discourse as Paul's attempt to shape, or to influence the self-formation of, Christian men in Corinth as ethical subjects."

identity need to be criticized in order to remind his readers that even a system whose purpose is to liberate the individual might well end up tying the self to an identity which can then again be experienced as subjection.

Chapter 4

Categories of the Self in Michel Foucault

Introduction

Michel Foucault's works, as is well known, are difficult to classify and do not rest easily within a traditional definition of philosophy. He ventured into topics that one does not necessarily associate with philosophy, such as the study of prisons, of madness, of sexuality.[1] Foucault himself was not particularly comfortable with being called a philosopher. In a 1975 interview with Roger Pol-Droit, he refuses to be called a philosopher or a historian, two designations often used to describe him. Rather, he would want to be perceived as "un artificier": "Je fabrique quelque chose qui sert finalement à un siège, à une guerre, à une destruction. Je ne suis pas pour la destruction, mais je suis pour qu'on puisse passer, pour qu'on puisse avancer, pour qu'on puisse faire tomber les murs."[2] The work of destruction, not for the sake of destruction itself but in order to create a passage through which one can progress, unites the very different domains that Foucault explored in his career. Three areas constitute the field in which this siege took place: knowledge, power and ethics or relationship to one's self.[3]

---

[1] Early in his career (early 1950s) Foucault worked with Jacqueline Verdeaux on translating Ludwig Binswanger's *Traum und Existenz*, for which Foucault would end up writing a long preface (see Didier Éribon, *Michel Foucault* [trans. B. Wing; Cambridge, Mass.: Harvard University Press, 1991], 44–49). In fact, his first teaching appointments were in psychology (he taught psychology at the École Normale Supérieure from the fall of 1951 to the spring of 1955, and when he was appointed at Lille in October 1952, it was as "assistant in psychology," see Éribon, *Michel Foucault*, 50 and 61.) and when he was elected to the Collège de France, his chair was named "History of systems of thought."

[2] "Je suis un artificier," in *Michel Foucault, entretiens* (ed. R.-P. Droit; Paris: Odile Jacob, 2004), 90–135, here 92. Artificier in French refers to two worlds of meaning. In the civil, it is used to speak of someone who is responsible for preparing fireworks. In the military world, the word "artificier" refers to someone in charge of ammunitions, both the preparation and the launching.

[3] See the categories that Bernauer, *Michel Foucault's Force of Flight*, 4 and 5, uses to discuss Foucault's work. See also Frédéric Gros, "Course Context," in Michel Foucault, *The Hermeneutics of the Subject: Lectures at the Collège de France: 1981–1982* (trans. G. Burchell; New York: Picador, 2005), 507–550, here 512. Arnold I. Davidson, "Ar-

In each of these areas, no matter the particular topic, Foucault is seeking to create space in which one can move and think anew, thus delineating spaces of resistance. Simultaneously, as one seeks to create spaces of resistance, one is also acutely aware of the fact that individuals are being confined. To spaces of resistance inevitably correspond confinements. Identifying and challenging these confinements, finding the spots in which his mortar charges have to be placed, defines Foucault's work in its entirety. However, Foucault has done this work of destruction differently in various periods of his career, as James W. Bernauer indicates:

> While all three dimensions of this humanistic confinement are implicitly at work throughout Foucault's writings, a primacy was exercised by one of them at each general stage of his thought. Thus in the 1960s, it was principally philosophical confinement that he sought to illuminate... In the 1970s, his examination of power-knowledge relations focused on political confinement... In the 1980s, Foucault developed an ethical thinking that would propose a critique of and an alternative to modern self-subjugation.[4]

Scholars often charged that Foucault was betraying himself every time he explored a new space of confinement.[5] However, Foucault saw his own

chaeology, Genealogy, Ethics," in *Foucault: A Critical Reader*, (ed. D. Couzens Hoy; London: Basil Blackwell, 1986), 221–233, here 221 proposes the same threefold division between knowledge, power and self. Foucault himself divides his work in three parts: see Foucault, "Afterword: The Subject and Power," in Dreyfus and Rabinow, *Michel Foucault: Beyond Structuralism and Hermeneutics*, 208–226, here 208: "My work has dealt with three modes of objectification which transform human beings into subjects. The first is the modes of inquiry which try to give themselves the status of sciences; for example, the objectivizing of the speaking subject in *grammaire générale*, philology and linguistics... In the second part of my work, I have studied the objectivizing of the subject in what I shall call 'dividing practices.' The subject is either divided inside himself or divided from others... Finally, I have sought to study – it is my current work – the way a human being turns him- or herself into a subject. For example, I have chosen the domain of sexuality – how men have learned to recognize themselves as subjects of 'sexuality';" also Foucault, "On the Genealogy of Ethics," 351: "Three domains of genealogy are possible. First, a historical ontology of ourselves in relation to truth through which we constitute ourselves as subjects of knowledge; second, a historical ontology of ourselves in relation to a field of power through which we constitute ourselves as subjects acting on others, third, a historical ontology in relation to ethics through which we constitute ourselves as moral agents."

[4] Bernauer, *Michel Foucault's Force of Flight*, 9.

[5] See Colin Gordon, "Afterword," in Michel Foucault, *Power/Knowledge: Selected Interviews and Other Writings, 1972–1977*, (ed. C. Gordon; trans. C. Gordon et al.; New York: Pantheon Books, 1980), 229–259, here 244: "It is sometimes supposed hat Foucault's subsequent thematisation of power tacitly jettisons as obsolete the ambitious methodological edifice of the *Archaeology*." Also, to some degree, Dreyfus and Rabinow, *Michel Foucault: Beyond Structuralism and Hermeneutics*, 100: "Near the end of the *Archaeology*, when Foucault considers the possibility that archaeology might not turn out to be the stable and autonomous discipline he had hoped, he notes that in such a case the problems it deals with and the tools it introduces might be 'taken up later elsewhere,

work as being part of a process of change, an attempt to escape the confinement to which his own thought process might lead him. One of the ways in which he explains the work he does in his books is through the concept of experience. In a 1978 interview, he describes the role Nietzsche, Bataille and Blanchot played in the development of his thought, by providing him an alternative to the construction of a system and allowing him to focus on the "construction of a personal experience."[6] In each book that he writes, Foucault argues that he is trying to create this experience: "The idea of a limit-experience that wrenches the subject from itself is what was important to me in my reading of Nietzsche, Bataille, and Blanchot, and what explains the fact that however boring, however erudite my books may be, I've always conceived of them as direct experiences aimed at pulling myself free of myself, at preventing me from being the same."[7] At the same time, Foucault hopes that his books also contribute to change his readers, helping both the author and the readers "establish new relationships with the subject at issue,"[8] no matter what the subject is. In the end, thus it is not the truth of the historical facts discussed in a particular book which matters; rather it is the experience that the book makes possible.[9]

---

in a different way, at a higher level, or using different methods' (*AK* 208). These possibilities were more imminent than Foucault realized at the time. Just a few years later he himself took up this task and thus showed himself to be one of those rare thinkers, like Wittgenstein and Heidegger, whose work shows both an underlying continuity and an important reversal not because their early efforts were useless, but because in pushing one way of thinking to its limits they both recognized and overcame those limitations."

[6] See Foucault, "Interview with Michel Foucault," 241: "What struck me and fascinated me about those authors [Georges Bataille, Friedrich Nietzsche, Maurice Blanchot, Pierre Klossowski], and what gave them their capital importance for me, was that their problem was not the construction of a system but the construction of a personal experience."

[7] Foucault, "Interview with Michel Foucault," 241–242.

[8] Foucault, "Interview with Michel Foucault," 242: "... my problem is not to satisfy professional historians; my problem is to construct myself, and to invite others to share an experience of what we are, not only our past, but also our present, an experience of our modernity in such a way that we might come out of it transformed. Which means that at the end of a book we would establish new relationships with the subject at issue..."

[9] See Foucault, "Interview with Michel Foucault," 243: "For one to be able to have that experience through the book, what it says does need to be true in terms of academic, historically verifiable truth. It can't exactly be a novel. Yet the essential thing is not in the series of those true or historically verifiable findings but, rather, in the experience that the book makes possible."

All of his work, even his return to the Greeks for which he was criticized,[10] reflects that desire to create spaces of resistance, limit-experiences, that change writer and readers, particularly in their understanding of what human beings are: "The readers have ... found themselves involved in a process that was under way – we could say, in the transformation of contemporary man with respect to the idea he has of himself. And the book worked toward that transformation. To a small degree, it was even an agent in it. That is what I mean by an experience book, as opposed to a truth book or a demonstration book."[11] In these spaces of resistance and this will to construct the self through experiences, I think it is possible to find the concepts central to Foucault's understanding of the self.

A. Spaces of Resistance in Foucault's Thought

1. Resistance and Knowledge: Archaeology

Foucault's early work, perhaps including his inaugural lecture at the Collège de France (*The Discourse on Language*),[12] can be seen as leading

---

[10] See Mark Poster, "Foucault and The Tyranny of Greece," in Couzens Hoy, *Foucault: A Critical Reader*, 205–220, here 206: "Many readers will be disappointed by the recently published volumes," and 208: "In this regard, Foucault is unable to sustain the level of analysis of his earlier works. There is simply too much discourse and not enough practice." At the same time, Poster also recognizes the merits of Foucault's work in *History of Sexuality* (207, 208, 209).

[11] Foucault, "Interview with Michel Foucault," 246.

[12] The works covered in this section go from 1954, with the publication of *Maladie mentale et personnalité* (Paris: Presses Universitaires de France, 1954), (later republished in a revised edition as *Maladie mentale et psychologie* [Paris: Presses Universitaires de France, 1962], translated as *Mental Illness and Psychology* [trans. A. Sheridan Smith; New York: Harper and Row, 1976]), to *L'archéologie du savoir* (Paris: Gallimard, 1969), (*The Archaeology of Knowledge* [trans. A. Sheridan Smith; New York: Harper Colophon, 1976]). In addition to many interviews and articles, major works during that time include: *Folie et déraison: histoire de la folie à l'âge classique* (Paris: Plon, 1961), (*Madness and Civilization: A History of Insanity in the Age of Reason* [trans. R. Howard; New York: Pantheon, 1965]), *Naissance de la clinique: une archéologie du regard médical* (Paris: Presses Universitaires de France, 1963), (*The Birth of the Clinic: An Archaeology of Medical Perception* [trans. A. Sheridan Smith; New York: Pantheon, 1973]), *Raymond Roussel* (Paris: Gallimard, 1963), (*Death and the Labyrinth: The World of Raymond Roussel* [trans. Ch. Ruas; New York: Doubleday, 1986]), *Les mots et les choses: une archéologie des sciences humaines* (Paris: Gallimard, 1966), (*The Order of Things*). For the inaugural lecture at the Collège de France: *L'ordre du discours* (Paris: Gallimard, 1971), ("Orders of Discourses," *Social Science Information* (1971), republished as "The Discourse on Language," in appendix to the *Archaeology of Knowledge*,

to the methodological articulation of archaeology in *The Archaeology of Knowledge*. *The Order of Things* for example introduces many of the issues that the methodological articulation of *The Archaeology of Knowledge* will take up.[13]

As a method, archaeology[14] in Foucault's thought puts into place what can be called thinking from without.[15] At first the aim of archaeology can be seen as descriptive.[16] However, because Foucault in his archaeological method focuses on the conditions that make necessary the appearance and existence of certain statements, such description also includes the potential to call into question traditional presentations of ideas and thoughts. Because archaeology strives to think differently, beyond and outside of set limits, it also carries a potential for transgression. It intends to develop "dissonant thinking"[17] and focuses on integrating discontinuity in the way

---

215–237). For a complete chronological list of Foucault's books, articles and interviews, see Bernauer, *Michel Foucault's Force of Flight*, 231–254.

[13] Bernauer, *Michel Foucault's Force of Flight*, 89 sees *The Order of Things* as a cathartic moment in the development of Foucault's thought. This cathartic moment is articulated methodologically in *The Archaeology of Knowledge*.

[14] As Bernauer, *Michel Foucault's Force of Flight*, 45 indicates, Foucault traces the paternity of his use of the word "archaeology" to Kant: "Years later, Foucault will point out that he owes the word 'archaeology' to Kant, who employed it to designate the investigation of that which renders necessary a certain form of thought." The text to which Bernauer refers is Michel Foucault, "Monstrosities in Criticism," *Diacritics* 1 (1971), a response to some of his critics. It is reedited and translated in French in "Les monstruosités de la critique," in *Dits et écrits*, 2:221: "Même chose pour le mot 'archéologie.' Ce mot doit bien se situer quelque part, pense M. Steiner. Attribuons-le à Freud. M. Steiner ignore que Kant utilisait ce mot pour désigner l'histoire de ce qui rend nécessaire une certaine forme de pensée."

[15] See Bernauer, *Michel Foucault's Force of Flight*, 54: "As a result of his study of madness and the clinic, Foucault has glimpsed the difficult place in which man's thought is located. We exist within codes that structure the 'dark, but firm web of our experience.' Capacities and perspectives that seem so self-evident, the power of observation, the reality of disease, are not immemorial but temporary experiences that owe their specific character to certain operative structures and codes. This is the 'within' in which thought finds itself enclosed. The ability to identify this enclosure, however, implies a certain power to reflect from without upon these parameters of thought." See also 58: "Fundamental thinking is a 'thinking from without.' Although this 'pensée du dehors' is the title of one of Foucault's articles, it represents the culmination of the intellectual journey in which he had been engaged since 1954."

[16] See Davidson, "Archaeology, Genealogy, Ethics," 223: "Foucault's aim, in those of his books that worked out his archaeological method, was a thoroughly descriptive one."

[17] See Bernauer, *Michel Foucault's Force of Flight*, 91: "In place of the smooth concord that is imposed on a multiplicity of separate occurrences by the desire for sameness, [Foucault] wishes to place before the mind a constantly sounding dissonance. His earlier work has cleared the way for dissonant thinking, which will become the inspiration of the 'philosophy of event' emerging in this period as the horizon for archaeology." It is inter-

one thinks about history. In the introduction to *Archaeology of Knowledge*, Foucault writes: "discontinuity was the stigma of temporal dislocation that it was the historian's task to remove from history. It has now become one of the basic elements of historical analysis."[18] By integrating discontinuity in the analysis of history, Foucault transforms what used to be an obstacle into what is central to the work itself. Discontinuity no longer marks the end or the failure of the historical enterprise. Rather, it determines what the object of history should be and how history should be analyzed.[19] Integrating discontinuity into history also calls into question the idea of teleology, the belief that all of the events occurring can be strung together through a series of causes.[20] In contrast, Foucault's historical project deploys "the space of a dispersion."[21] One can see this at work in the manner in which discourse is handled by Foucault. Because archaeology seeks to take into account also the discourses that can no longer be ours, that are marked by otherness,[22] it insists on the dimension of difference: "it establishes that we are difference, that our reason is the difference of discourses, our history the difference of times, our selves the differences of masks. That difference, far from being the forgotten and recovered origin, is this dispersion that we are and make."[23] As such it goes against the desire for sameness

---

esting to notice that at the same time as Foucault is developing this form of thinking, he is in close contact with contemporary musicians working with serial and twelve-tone music. For Foucault, this opened up the possibility of seeing new possibilities in thought. See Éribon, *Michel Foucault*, 66–68.

[18] Michel Foucault, *The Archaeology of Knowledge* (trans. A. Sheridan Smith; 1976; repr., New York: Pantheon Books, 1982), 8.

[19] See Foucault, *The Archaeology of Knowledge*, 9: "One of the most essential features of the new history is probably this displacement of the discontinuous: its transference from the obstacle to the work itself; its integration into the discourse of the historian, where it no longer plays the role of an external condition that must be reduced, but that of a working concept; and therefore the inversion of signs by which it is no longer the negative of the historical reading (its underside, its failure, the limit of its power), but the positive element that determines its object and validates its analysis."

[20] Foucault, *The Archaeology of Knowledge*, 9–10.

[21] Foucault, *The Archaeology of Knowledge*, 10.

[22] This is why archives play an important role in Foucault's work. See *The Archaeology of Knowledge*, 130: "The analysis of the archive, then, involves a privileged region: at once close to us, and different from our present existence, it is the border of time that surrounds our presence, which overhangs it, and which indicates it in its otherness; it is that which, outside ourselves, delimits us. The description of the archive deploys its possibilities (and the mastery of its possibilities) on the basis of the very discourses that have just ceased to be ours; its threshold of existence is established by the discontinuity that separates us from what we can no longer say, and from that which falls outside our discursive practice; it begins with the outside of our own language (*langage*); its locus is the gap between our own discursive practices."

[23] Foucault, *The Archaeology of Knowledge*, 131.

that Foucault sees as dominating traditional history and that seeks to suppress and erase difference.

Through this quest for dissonance, or transgressive thinking, Foucault highlights the fact that particular time and space shape particular discourses, make some possible and exclude some. As Bernauer writes, the archaeological method is particularly attentive to the rarity of discourse: "its [archaeological's] curiosity is aimed at the rarity (*rareté*) of what is said, at the fact that within the wealth of rule and vocabulary language provides, relatively few things are actually stated."[24] Such attentiveness means that archaeology will also focus on what institutions, what circumstances, what practices make certain discourses not only possible but also worth preserving. There are rules that govern what can be said and what will be kept in collective memory. In that way, "the practice of discourse is a 'violence' done to things, not by virtue of men's ideas nor through the grammatical systems of language, but by a set of rules that determine what can be stated at a particular time and how these statements are related to others."[25] Statements are organized in discursive practices because of the rules governing their formation, and the archaeological method highlights these rules of formation, and organizes statements in relationship to these rules. Foucault designates as *savoir* these discursive practices, namely the "conditions that are necessary in a particular period for this or that type of object to be given to *connaissance* and for this or that enunciation to be formulated."[26] Archaeology goes behind the obvious, in order to reveal what is the *savoir* that lies behind domains of knowledge and systems of thoughts.

In its uncovering of the conditions behind discourse, archaeology creates spaces of resistance at several levels. First, by indicating what makes certain statements possible at certain times in history, the archaeological method works against the assumption that discourse proceeds from the creative genius of a single mind. It insists rather on the fact that discourse is dependent on various discursive practices that allow some statements to exist and others to disappear. As such, it calls into question the division that the history of ideas puts into place between statements that reflect the traditional way of seeing a field and statements that in comparison seem new.[27] Archaeology does not see history as a succession of moments of

---

[24] Bernauer, *Michel Foucault's Force of Flight*, 105.

[25] Bernauer, *Michel Foucault's Force of Flight*, 107.

[26] See note 2 in the English translation of *L'archéologie du savoir*: Foucault, *The Archaeology of Knowledge*, 15, n. 2. Also Bernauer, *Michel Foucault's Force of Flight*, 109 and 216, n. 118.

[27] See Bernauer, *Michel Foucault's Force of Flight*, 111–112: "One of the devices by which anthropological thinking continues to exert its pressure on contemporary thought is revealed in those attempts to reduce the specific existence of discourse to a movement

normalcy interrupted by sudden and individualistic bursts of genius. Rather it works with the assumption that "each statement effects the violence of a discursive practice."[28] This violence does not come from the mind of human beings but is organized through a set of rules that determine what can be said by whom at a particular time.[29] Statements are dependent upon an institutional hierarchy, which plays a role in what can and cannot be said.

Second, the archaeological method concerns itself with the contradictions inherent to discourse. Foucault writes that, for archaeology, "contradictions are neither appearances to be overcome, nor secret principles to be uncovered."[30] Rather, "they are objects to be described for themselves, without any attempt being made to discover from what point of view they can be dissipated, or at what level they can be radicalized and effects become causes."[31] According to Foucault, the history of ideas is focused on finding coherence in the discourses it analyzes, dealing with contradictions in a twofold way. First, it tries to resolve apparent contradictions in the "profound unity of discourse."[32] When the history of ideas finds statements that are irregular, it seeks "at a deeper level, a principle of cohesion that organizes the discourse and restores to it its hidden unity."[33] Small discrepancies and irregularities do not matter, because they can be resolved in the larger succession of causes that the history of ideas puts into place. Because of the particular point of view that the history of ideas chooses, it neglects differences and contradictions, and it works with the assumption that when men "speak, and if they speak among themselves, it is rather to overcome these contradictions, and to find the point from which they will be able to be mastered."[34] The purpose of the history of ideas is to find the

---

of subjective life, to read what is said in terms of creative contributions as opposed to standard and everyday functioning. This anthropological shackle is evident in the tendency of the history of ideas to treat all discourse as a domain with only two values. Does the particular object of study represent something new in the field of thought, or does it still function within the old pattern?"

[28] Bernauer, *Michel Foucault's Force of Flight*, 112.

[29] See Bernauer, *Michel Foucault's Force of Flight*, 107.

[30] Foucault, *The Archaeology of Knowledge*, 151.

[31] Foucault, *The Archaeology of Knowledge*, 151.

[32] Foucault, *The Archaeology of Knowledge*, 151.

[33] Foucault, *The Archaeology of Knowledge*, 149.

[34] See Foucault, *The Archaeology of Knowledge*, 149: "This law of coherence is a heuristic rule, a procedure obligation, almost a moral constraint of research: not to multiply contradictions uselessly; not to be taken in by small differences; not to give too much weight to changes, disavowals, returns to the past, and polemics; not to suppose that men's discourse is perpetually undermined from within by the contradiction of their desires, the influences that they have been subjected to, or the conditions in which they live; but to admit that if they speak, and if they speak among themselves, it is rather to

"hidden unity" behind the illusion of contradictions.[35] But contradictions can also be suppressed at another level.

In this other case, the history of ideas, at the end of the analysis, finds contradiction to be the ultimate organizing principle. It is the secret revealed at the end of the analysis, which explains discourse's existence itself: "such a contradiction, far from being an appearance or accident of discourse, far from being that from which it must be freed if its truth is at least to be revealed, constitutes the very law of its existence: it is on the basis of such a contradiction that discourse emerges."[36] At this level, contradiction is a foundation, "which gives rise to discourse itself"[37] and, also, keeps producing discourse, in order for discourse to translate and overcome contradiction.

In contrast, the archaeological method describes contradiction, without trying to suppress it. As a result, discourse is no longer seen as a process from which continuity emerges, rather it is a "space of multiple dissensions."[38] Resistance in this case opens up spaces for difference and for irregularities, for recognizing the wild dimension of change. Foucault is careful to indicate that he does not want to substitute one category of explanation for another. Rather, discontinuity has to be understood as the play of interrelated transformations.[39]

---

overcome these contradictions, and to find the point from which they will be able to be mastered."

[35] See Foucault, *The Archaeology of Knowledge*, 150: "Contradiction is the illusion of a unity that hides itself or is hidden: it has its place only in the gap between consciousness and unconsciousness, thought and the text, the ideality and the contingent body of expression. In any case, analysis must suppress contradiction as best it can."

[36] Foucault, *The Archaeology of Knowledge*, 150–151.

[37] Foucault, *The Archaeology of Knowledge*, 151.

[38] Foucault, *The Archaeology of Knowledge*, 155: "A discursive formation is not, therefore, an ideal, continuous, smooth text that runs beneath the multiplicity of contradictions, and resolves them in the calm unity of coherent thought; nor is it the surface in which, in a thousand different aspects, a contradiction is reflected that is always in retreat, but everywhere dominant. It is rather a space of multiple dissensions; a set of different oppositions, whose levels and roles must be described."

[39] See Michel Foucault, "Réponse à une question," in *Dits et écrits*, 1:673–695, here 1:677: "Mon problème: substituer à la forme abstraite, générale et monotone du 'changement,' dans laquelle, si volontiers, on pense la succession, l'analyse de *types différents de transformation*. Ce qui implique deux choses: mettre entre parenthèses toutes les vieilles formes de continuité molle par lesquelles on atténue d'ordinaire le fait sauvage du changement (tradition, influence, habitudes de pensées, grandes formes mentales, contraintes de l'esprit humain), et faire surgir au contraire, avec obstination, toute la vivacité de la différence: établir, méticuleusement, l'écart. Ensuite, mettre entre parenthèses toutes les explications psychologiques du changement (génie des grands inventeurs, crises de la conscience, apparition d'une nouvelle forme d'esprit); et définir avec le plus grand soin les transformations qui ont, je ne dis pas: provoqué, mais *constitué* le chan-

Through all this, archaeology creates a space to see what could have been said, to recognize the constructed character of knowledge and also what stands behind discursive practices. Foucault, when talking about his work in the 1960s, explains the purpose of his enterprise in the following manner: "déterminer, dans ses dimensions diverses, ce qu'a dû être en Europe, depuis le 18ᵉ siècle, le mode d'existence des discours, et singulièrement des discours scientifiques (leurs règles de formation, avec leurs conditions, leurs dépendances, leurs conditions, leurs transformations), pour que se constitue le savoir qui est le nôtre aujourd'hui et d'une façon plus précise le savoir qui s'est donné pour domaine ce curieux objet qui est l'homme."[40] Discursive practices are not analyzed to find who is expressing herself in them. Rather, they are pondered in order to highlight the limits and the necessities created by practices, quietly erasing the importance of the author behind them.[41] At the same time, when archaeology focuses on defining the power of the systems, it also creates potentiality for a form of thought willing to reintroduce difference, and thus some freedom, inside the systems that control knowledge.

If one wants to establish how Foucault's reflecting about knowledge affects his understanding of self, I suspect one could say that this constructed aspect of discourse, with discourse being sensitive and subjected to principles of organization and of limitation, indicates how the self, especially when it tries to express itself in language, is limited in its attempts to be independent or original. The self is inscribed in a discursive world, and in

---

gement" and 1:680: "Vous le voyez : absolument pas question de substituer une catégorie, le 'discontinu,' à celle non moins abstraite et générale du 'continu.' Je m'efforce au contraire de montrer que la discontinuité n'est pas entre les événements un vide monotone et impensable, qu'il faudrait se hâter de remplir (deux solutions parfaitement symétriques) par la plénitude morne de la cause ou par l'agile ludion de l'esprit; mais qu'elle est un jeu de transformations spécifiées, différentes les unes des autres (avec, chacune, ses conditions, ses règles, son niveau) et liées entre elles selon les schémas de dépendance."

[40] Foucault, "Réponse à une question," 1:694. See also Bernauer, *Michel Foucault's Force of Flight*, 86.

[41] See Foucault, "Réponse à une question," 1:694: "Je sais presqu'autant qu'un autre ce que peuvent avoir d''ingrat' – au sens strict du terme – de pareilles recherches. Ce qu'il y a d'un peu grinçant à traiter les discours non pas à partir de la douce, muette et intime conscience qui s'y exprime, mais d'un ensemble de règles anonymes. Ce qu'il y a de déplaisant à faire apparaître les limites et les nécessités d'une pratique, là où on avait l'habitude de voir se déployer, dans une pure transparence, les jeux du génie et de la liberté … Ce qu'il y a d'insupportable enfin, étant donné ce que chacun veut mettre, pense mettre de 'soi-même' dans son propre discours, quand il entreprend de parler, ce qu'il y a d'insupportable à découper, à analyser, à combiner, à recomposer tous ces textes maintenant revenus au silence, sans que jamais s'y dessine le visage transfiguré de l'auteur … Le discours, en sa détermination la plus profonde, ne serait pas 'trace'."

its action of speaking, it fits itself in these discursive practices, even while it also does violence to them. In any case, it cannot find itself outside of these discursive practices, and presume that it starts speaking as though it were a supreme consciousness, standing at the origin of discourse.[42] Rather it is dependent upon all the voices that came before and will come after it.[43]

2. Resistance and Power: Genealogy

Power already plays a role in Foucault's analysis of the systems presiding over the creation and the preservation of knowledge through discursive practices, but it takes a central role in his writings in the 1970s, writings in which he challenges the ways power is understood, experienced and resisted in his contemporary society.[44] His inaugural lecture at the Collège de

---

[42] In this regard, the beginning of "The Discourse on Language" is representative of that feeling of fitting oneself in a discourse that is already taking place. Foucault, "The Discourse on Language," in *The Archaeology of Knowledge*, 215–237, here 215: "I would really like to have slipped imperceptibly into this lecture, as into all the others I shall be delivering, perhaps over the years ahead. I would have preferred to be enveloped in words, borne way beyond all possible beginnings. At the moment of speaking, I would like to have perceived a nameless voice, long preceding me, leaving me merely to enmesh myself in it, taking up its cadence, and to lodge myself, when no one was looking, in its interstices as if it had paused an instant, in suspense, to beckon to me. There would have been no beginnings; instead, speech would proceed from me, while I stood in its path – a slender gap – the point of its possible disappearance." This is then followed by an allusion to Beckett's play, *Molloy*, insisting on how preceding discourse already repeats what is about to be said.

[43] In the "Discourse on Language," Foucault insists on all the words that precede the beginning of his own discourse. I think it is also possible to see the enveloping notion of discourse in the way Foucault speaks of his own work as toolboxes, designed to be used, modified and transformed through the work of others. In that way, discourse is also dependent on what comes after it.

[44] The major works for this period are: *L'ordre du discours*, (English: "The Discourse on Language"); *Moi, Pierre Rivière, ayant égorgé ma mère, ma sœur et mon frère* (Paris: Gallimard, 1973), (English: *I, Pierre Rivière, having slaughtered my mother, my sister and my brother* [trans. F. Jellinek; New York: Pantheon, 1975); *Surveiller et punir: naissance de la prison* (Paris: Gallimard, 1975), (English: *Discipline and Punish: The Birth of the Prison*); *Histoire de la sexualité vol. 1: la volonté de savoir* (Paris: Gallimard, 1976), (English: *History of Sexuality vol. 1: An Introduction* [trans. R. Hurley; New York: Pantheon Books, 1978). In addition, a great number of interviews and articles are published at the same time, something that also reflects Foucault's involvement in the political scene at the time. See Éribon, *Michel Foucault*, who titles the last part of his book, covering the years 1970 until Foucault's death in 1984: "Militant and Professor at the Collège de France." It is interesting to note that Foucault's involvement with politics and resistance movements was happening even as he was nominated at one of France's most prestigious academic institution, the Collège de France. Militantism and participa-

France in 1970 provides one of the early landmarks in Foucault's analysis of power. In *The Discourse on Language*, Foucault, pushing further the insights he developed in *The Archaeology of Knowledge*, analyzes the relationship between discourse and power, working with the assumption that "in every society the production of discourse is at once controlled, selected, organised and redistributed according to a certain number of procedures, whose role is to avert its powers and its dangers, to cope with chance events, to evade its ponderous, awesome materiality."[45] In *The Discourse on Language*, Foucault's understanding of power is still very much characterized by seeing power as mainly a repressive force.

In the course of the inaugural lecture, for example, Foucault distinguishes between several groups of systems that exercise some control over discourse. First, he sees systems that are "to some extent, active on the exterior; they function as systems of exclusion; they concern that part of discourse which deals with power and desire."[46] Through such systems one is concerned with limiting the power contained in discourse. But Foucault also identifies another group: "internal rules, where discourse exercises its own control; rules concerned with the principles of classification, ordering and distribution."[47] Through these rules, power functions as an entity that limits discourse, for example by creating disciplines. In disciplines, a system of control for the production of discourse is put into place. What one can say and how one can say it is restricted. Finally, Foucault defines a third group of rules: "here, we are no longer dealing with the mastery of the powers contained within discourse, nor with averting the hazards of its appearance; it is more a question of determining the conditions under which it may be employed, of imposing a certain number of rules upon those individuals who employ it, thus denying access to everyone else."[48] In this last process, one witnesses a "rarefaction among speaking subjects."[49] Not everyone can access all discourses. In some cases – and academic discourse is a good example of this – one needs particular qualifications to receive the authorization to speak on some topics and must be recognized as an expert.[50] Nor do all areas of discourse have the same status:

---

tion in the life of the institution were never separated for Foucault. In this, he actively embodied his own description of power and of resistance to power.

[45] Foucault, "The Discourse on Language," 216.

[46] Foucault, "The Discourse on Language," 220.

[47] Foucault, "The Discourse on Language," 220.

[48] See Foucault, "The Discourse on Language," 224.

[49] See Foucault, "The Discourse on Language," 224.

[50] Edward W. Said, *Representations of the Intellectual: The 1993 Reith Lectures* (New York: Vintage Books, 1994), 77 also sees expertise as one of the pressure exercised on intellectuals: "If specialization is a kind of general instrumental pressure present in all

"not all areas of discourse are equally open and penetrable; some are forbidden territory (differentiated and differentiating) while others are virtually open to the winds and stand, without any prior restrictions, open to all."[51]

For Foucault, despite our civilization's apparent reverence for discourse, its seeming logophilia,[52] the rules that have been put into place around discourse to limit and to control it, reveal in fact a "profound logophobia, a sort of dumb fear of these events, of this mass of spoken things, of everything that could possibly be violent, discontinuous, querulous, disordered even and perilous in it, of the incessant, disorderly buzzing of discourse."[53] At the level of methodology, Foucault explains that he uses four principles in order to analyze how this fear of discourse came into being and what effects are attached to it.[54] First, he speaks of a "principle of reversal," which calls into question the idea that our civilization put into place rules for the multiplication of discourse and rather recognizes "the negative activity of the cutting-out and rarefaction of discourse."[55] This principle of reversal is implemented in a critical analysis which considers the process of rarefaction of discourse. This side of the analysis focuses on the repressive dimension of power, how power limits discourse and exercises pressures to rarefy discourse.

The three other principles pertain to genealogy, and bring into light a more productive side of power. Foucault first sets up a principle of discontinuity, to avoid imagining that, once one has moved beyond the systems of repression, one finds vast amounts of discourse that were once repressed, that should now be liberated and to which one can now return a speaking voice. Rather, Foucault wants to treat discourse as "a discontinuous activity, its different manifestations sometimes coming together, but

---

systems of education everywhere, expertise and the cult of the certified expert are more particular pressures in the postwar world."

[51] See Foucault, "The Discourse on Language," 225.

[52] See Foucault, "The Discourse on Language," 228: "what civilization, in appearance, has shown more respect towards discourse than our own? Where has it been more and better honoured? Where have men depended more radically, apparently, upon its constraints and its universal character? But, it seems to me, a certain fear hides behind this apparent supremacy accorded, this apparent logophilia. It is as though these taboos, these barriers, thresholds and limits were deliberately disposed in order, at least partly, to master and control the great proliferation of discourse, in such a way as to relieve its richness of its most dangerous elements; to organize its disorder so as to skate round its most uncontrollable aspects. It is as though people had wanted to efface all trace of its irruption into the activity of our thought and language."

[53] Foucault, "The Discourse on Language," 229.

[54] These four principles are presented in Foucault, "The Discourse on Language," 229.

[55] Foucault, "The Discourse on Language," 229.

just as easily unaware of, or excluding each other."[56] Thus, he warns against the illusion of trying to find some "unsaid thing, or an unthought"[57] that would bring together everything that has been said or written. There is no hidden treasure that would unite all discourses. To this, he adds a principle of specificity, stating that one should not see discourse as corresponding to a previously known system of meaning, as if discourse merely reflected what we already know and naturally proceeded from our knowledge or our experience of the world. For Foucault, "we must consider discourse as a violence that we do to things, or, at all events, as a practice we impose upon them."[58] In fact, through discourse, one imposes a regularity on events, and this regularity should not be seen as something given to one in advance.[59] It is something one creates, through discourse. Finally, the fourth principle is one of exteriority: rather than to look for the deep meaning of discourse, hidden in its core, one needs to pay attention to the external conditions that made this discourse possible.[60] How and why was this particular discourse possible and acceptable at the time in which it was produced?

Foucault sees these three last principles having to do with genealogy. They are concerned with how discourse is produced inside, or in spite of, the systems of constraint. It seeks to show "what were the specific norms for each, and what were their conditions of appearance, growth and variation."[61] Foucault is here moving towards the productive side of power, touching upon the things that power can create and bring to life. Foucault is aware that, even though methodologically critical analysis and genealogy can be distinguished, they should in fact not be separated. Critical analysis looks at the way in which power limits discourse. It attempts "to mark out and distinguish the principles of ordering, exclusion and rarity in discourse."[62] On the other side, genealogy is more interested in the productive means of discourse, in the circumstances that stand at the origin of dis-

---

[56] See Foucault, "The Discourse on Language," 229.

[57] See Foucault, "The Discourse on Language," 229.

[58] See Foucault, "The Discourse on Language," 229.

[59] See Foucault, "The Discourse on Language," 229: "... we should not imagine that the world presents us with a legible face, leaving us merely to decipher it; it does not work hand in glove with what we already know; there is no pre-discursive fate disposing the word in our favour."

[60] See Foucault, "The Discourse on Language," 229: "The fourth principle, that of *exteriority*, holds that we are not to burrow to the hidden core of discourse, to the heart of the thought or meaning manifest in it; instead, taking the discourse itself, its appearance and its regularity, that we should look for its external conditions of existence, for that which gives rise to the chance series of these events and fixes its limits."

[61] See Foucault, "The Discourse on Language," 232.

[62] Foucault, "The Discourse on Language," 234.

course, and in the fact that these origins are inevitably enmeshed with "domination, subjugation, the relationship of forces – in a word, power."[63] Genealogy "deals with series of effective formation of discourse,"[64]focusing on what relations of power stand behind the appearance of particular discourses. In this interplay between critical analysis and genealogy one sees that discourse participates in the imposition of a mechanism of rarefaction, even while also carrying "a fundamental power of affirmation."[65]

While developing this genealogical study, Foucault became deeply involved with the way power was conceived and how it functioned. *The Discourse on Language* is still very much focused on describing power as a repressive force. The productive energy of power appears only in the shadows. Foucault will become increasingly dissatisfied with viewing power as something that only limits and represses.[66] His work after *The Discourse on Language* employs itself in teasing out the productive aspects of power. For Foucault, this is nowhere more apparent than when power becomes associated with knowledge.

When discourse is taken over by an institution, or when various systems of production of discourse control it, whether in the institution or not, the connection between power and knowledge becomes most apparent. Foucault maintains that, as soon as one tries to establish a particular discourse as science, several mechanisms of power are put into motion that try to establish one type of knowledge as dominant and unifying, and exclude other types of knowledge and other speaking subjects.[67] In contrast, genealogy, when it recovers what Foucault calls "local, discontinuous, disqualified, illegitimate knowledges,"[68] disturbs and challenges the association of pow-

---

[63] Davidson, "Archaeology, Genealogy, Ethics," 225.

[64] Foucault, "The Discourse on Language," 234.

[65] Foucault, "The Discourse on Language," 234.

[66] See Bernauer, *Michel Foucault's Force of Flight*, 122: "[Foucault's] most significant presupposition regarding the political realm was a conception of how power operated. The clearest formulation of his assumption is the consideration in *L'ordre du discours* ... of our culture's logophobia in the face of discourse. Whether through rules of exclusion or principles of limitation and constraint, discourse is conceived of as controlled and forced into submission by a power that functions repressively. Foucault's recognition of this assumption and his evaluation of its basic inadequacy for a study of power in modern society provide the most characteristic traits of his political analysis."

[67] See Michel Foucault, "Two lectures," in Gordon, *Power/Knowledge*, 78–108, here 84–85: "It is surely the following kinds of question that would need to be posed: What types of knowledge do you want to disqualify in the very instant of your demand: 'Is it a science'? Which speaking, discoursing subjects – which subjects of experience and knowledge – do you then want to 'diminish' when you say: 'I who conduct this discourse am conducting a scientific discourse, and I am a scientist'?"

[68] See Foucault, "Two lectures," 83: "It is not therefore via an empiricism that the genealogical project unfolds, nor even via a positivism in the ordinary sense of that term.

er and knowledge. Knowledge does not develop in a vacuum, immune to the effects and pressure of power, rather, it is defined, limited, disciplined by various relationships of power that weigh on it. Scientific discourse produces a type of knowledge that in turn exercises power on which discourses are acceptable and is at the origin of new power relationships. In the first pages of *Discipline and Punish*, Foucault provides a first formulation of his basic assumption about the relationship between power and knowledge:

> Perhaps, too, we should abandon a whole tradition that allows us to imagine that knowledge can exist only where the power relations are suspended and that knowledge can develop only outside its injunctions, its demands and its interests. Perhaps we should abandon the belief that power makes mad and that, by the same token, the renunciation of power is one of the conditions of knowledge. We should admit rather that power produces knowledge (and not simply by encouraging it because it serves power or by applying it because it is useful); that power and knowledge directly imply one another; that there is no power relation without the correlative constitution of a field of knowledge, nor any knowledge that does not presuppose and constitute at the same time power relations.[69]

As Colin Gordon points out, Foucault, when he talks about power/ knowledge, is not mainly interested in showing what kind of false knowledge might be at work in human relations of power. Rather, Foucault seeks to highlight "the role of knowledges that are valued and effective because of their reliable instrumental efficacy."[70] Power is able to use knowledges that in turn produce effects of power.

From there on and up to the publication of the first volume of *The History of Sexuality*, Foucault is preoccupied with presenting a new theory, or rather a new analytics,[71] of power. This need for a new understanding comes from his own frustration with not only traditional ways of understanding power in terms of sovereignty but also with his own preliminary approach, evidenced in *The Discourse on Language*, that understood power in terms of war/repression, with the opposition between struggle and submission attached to that schema.[72] As a result, Foucault works on de-

---

What it really does is to entertain the claims to attention of local, discontinuous, disqualified, illegitimate knowledges against the claims of a unitary body of theory which would filter, hierarchise and order them in the name of some true knowledge and some arbitrary idea of what constitutes a science and its objects."

[69] Foucault, *Discipline and Punish*, 27.

[70] Gordon, "Introduction," xviii.

[71] Foucault, *History of Sexuality*, 82: "The aim of the inquiries that will follow is to move less toward a 'theory' of power than toward an 'analytics' of power: that is, toward a definition of the specific domain formed by relations of power, and toward a determination of the instruments that will make possible its analysis."

[72] See Foucault, "Two lectures," 92: "Thus we have two schemes for the analysis of power. The contract-oppression schema, which is the juridical one, and the domination-repression or war-repression schema for which the pertinent opposition is not between

veloping a dynamic understanding of power, marked by several characteristics. In a lecture given in 1977 – a year after the publication of the first volume of *The History of Sexuality* – he proposes four methodological moves which are necessary in order to advance beyond an understanding of power as a repressive, static entity in the hand of a sovereign opposed to obedient subjects.

First, he claims that the study of power "should be concerned with power at its extremities, in its ultimate destinations, with those points where it becomes capillary, that is, in its more regional and local forms and institutions."[73] Looking for power "at the extreme points"[74] takes one away from the legal apparatuses of power and focuses one's attention on smaller, regional institutions, on local techniques of power and on particular instruments of power. Such an approach needs to focus on actual, embodied practices of power rather than on the theory behind them.

Second, the study of power should not concentrate on the "level of conscious intention or decision," thus asking the question "who has power and what does one intend to do with that power?" Rather, it needs to take into account the "external visage" of power, the point where it actually concretely has an effect on its objects, thus asking how subjects are created through mechanisms of power. What is needed is to "grasp subjection in its material instance as a constitution of subjects."[75] Power needs to be apprehended as numerous strategies and mechanisms which contribute to the constitution of a subject.

Third, power should not be seen as a force that one individual (or a group of individuals) exercises over another, as if one group had all the power and was opposed to another group with no power at all. Rather, power needs to be apprehended as something fluid; it circulates. It should not be localized in a particular spot; rather "power is employed and exercised through a net-like organisation."[76] In this organization, individuals are at the same time submitted to power, but also in a position where they can exercise it. Foucault writes that, even while individuals are actually an

---

the legitimate and illegitimate, as in the first schema, but between struggle and submission. It is obvious that all my work in recent years has been couched in the schema of struggle-repression, and it is this – which I have hitherto been attempting to apply – which I have now been forced to reconsider, both because it is still insufficiently elaborated at a whole number of points, and because I believe that these two notions of repression and war must themselves be considerably modified if not ultimately abandoned."

[73] Foucault, "Two lectures," 96.
[74] Foucault, "Two lectures," 97.
[75] For all the quotes in this paragraph, see Foucault, "Two lectures," 97.
[76] Foucault, "Two lectures," 98.

effect of power, they are also "the vehicles of power, not its points of application."[77]

Finally, Foucault is wary of assuming that, because power is conceived as a network, it should be assumed that it is distributed everywhere in the same manner.[78] Rather than trying to establish how power is distributed from top to bottom, one needs to "conduct an *ascending* analysis of power."[79] Thus one should start with small – Foucault calls them infinitesimal – manifestations of power and should determine their particularities, and only then proceed to see how these micro-manifestations of power are being swallowed up in ever more global forms of power.

These methodological reflections on power, which were at work in most of Foucault's work in the 1970s and are recapitulated in this 1977 lecture, lead to a formulation of the workings of power in the first volume of his *History of Sexuality*. In *History of Sexuality*, Foucault starts by carefully establishing what power is not, or in other words, from what conception of power he wants to move away. This conception of power is what he describes as "juridico-discursive."[80] Juridico-discursive power is inherited from the monarchical institution, but Foucault sees it as the main frame of reference used in his contemporary world to understand power. In relationship to sex, it is characterized by the following features.[81] It is negative – being able to only say "no" to sex – and engages in a cycle of prohibitions whose goal is to make sex renounce itself, leading to its disappearance, at least in discourse: "the logic of power exerted on sex is the paradoxical logic of a law that might be expressed as an injunction of nonexistence, nonmanifestation, and silence."[82] In addition, juridico-discursive power is perceived as being uniform, as exercising its hold everywhere on everyone in the same manner.[83] The main characteristic of power thus conceived is law. Confronted with this power, the individual is understood as subject –

---

[77] Foucault, "Two lectures," 98.

[78] See Foucault, "Two lectures," 99: "when I say that power establishes a network through which it freely circulates, this is true only up to a certain point. In much the same fashion we could say that therefore we all have a fascism in our heads, or, more profoundly, that we all have a power in our bodies. But I do not believe that one should conclude from that that power is the best distributed thing in the world, although in some sense that is indeed so."

[79] See Foucault, "Two lectures," 99.

[80] Foucault, *History of Sexuality vol. 1*, 82.

[81] Foucault describes these four characteristics in relationship to sex, but he does indicate that this representation of power "is much more general; one frequently encounters it in political analyses of power, and it is deeply rooted in the history of the West." (*History of Sexuality vol. 1*, 83)

[82] Foucault, *History of Sexuality vol. 1*, 84.

[83] Foucault, *History of Sexuality vol. 1*, 84: "it operates according to the simple and endlessly reproduced mechanisms of law, taboo, and censorship."

the one who is subjected and has to obey.[84] For Foucault, this understanding of power is limited and unsatisfying. It sees power as "poor in resources, sparing of its method, monotonous in the tactics it utilizes, incapable of invention, and seemingly doomed always to repeat itself."[85] In addition, this power displays no productive force.

In contrast, Foucault aims to develop an analytics of power that would be liberated from understanding it in terms of law. Foucault's analytics of power focuses on power relationships, rather than on a static understanding of power as being held by one (or a group of) person(s) and imposed on other(s). Power in fact is the "multiplicity of force relations."[86] Because it is understood as forces at play between different points, power does not reside somewhere or in someone. Rather we are in the presence of "states of power": "it is the moving substrate of force relations which, by virtue of their inequality, constantly engenders states of power, but the latter are always local and unstable."[87] These states of power, constantly created and modified, lead to what Foucault calls the "omnipresence of power."[88] This omnipresence does not refer to the fact that power concentrates everything in one point and radiates from there; rather power is omnipresent "because it is produced from one moment to the next, at every point, or rather in every relation from one point to another. Power is everywhere; not because it embraces everything, but because it comes from everywhere."[89] Through the distinction that Foucault puts into place between these two conceptions of power, he is able to oppose a static and a dynamic representation of power, one that contrasts power understood as an institution, and power understood as the name "that one attributes to a complex strategical situation in a particular society."[90]

An analytics of power proposes a number of things concerning power. One should abandon the notion that power is something that can be "acquired, seized, or shared." Rather power is something happening in numer-

---

[84] See Foucault, *History of Sexuality vol. 1*, 85: "Confronted by a power that is law, the subject who is constituted as subject – who is subjected – is he who obeys."

[85] Foucault, *History of Sexuality vol. 1*, 85. This also gives Foucault the opportunity to express clearly what power is not: "By power, I do not mean "Power" as a group of institutions and mechanisms that ensure the subservience of the citizens of a given state. By power, I do not mean, either, a mode of subjugation which, in contrast to violence, has the form of rule. Finally, I do not have in mind a general system of domination exerted by one group over another, a system whose effects, through successive derivations, pervade the entire social body." (*History of Sexuality vol. 1*, 92)

[86] Foucault, *History of Sexuality vol. 1*, 92.

[87] Foucault, *History of Sexuality vol. 1*, 93.

[88] Foucault, *History of Sexuality vol. 1*, 93.

[89] Foucault, *History of Sexuality vol. 1*, 93.

[90] Foucault, *History of Sexuality vol. 1*, 93.

ous places, "in the interplay of nonegalitarian and mobile relations." Because power lives inside of relations, one can no longer assume a simple opposition between rulers and ruled in which power is applied from the top down. Rather "power comes from below;"[91] it is active in a variety of relationships of force, at the level of families and groups, and institutions, which then form the basis for wider effects of domination.[92] If power does not belong to one particular person, or group of persons, then it should also be assumed that power can both be "intentional and nonsubjective."[93] One can understand tactics of power not because there is an instance behind them that would have invented them and would stand responsible for them. Rather, tactics of power, at the small level on which they are inscribed, have aims and intentions. They collaborate with each other and end up "forming comprehensive systems" whose logic, albeit perfectly clear, remains anonymous.[94]

Finally, and perhaps most importantly for my present purpose, an analytics of power affirms that "where there is power, there is resistance,"[95] but this resistance never stands outside of power. Rather it develops from every point of the network created by relationships of power. This means that one needs to abandon the idea of one single place from which all revolt, all rebellion emerges. In its place, Foucault envisions "a plurality of resistances, each of them a special case: resistances that are possible, nec-

---

[91] For the three last quotes, see Foucault, *History of Sexuality vol. 1*, 94.

[92] See Foucault, *History of Sexuality vol. 1*, 94: "there is no binary and all-encompassing opposition between rulers and ruled at the root of power relations, and serving as a general matrix – no such duality extending from the top down and reacting on more and more limited groups to the very depths of the social body. One must suppose rather that the manifold relationships of force that take shape and come into play in the machinery of production, in families, limited groups, and institutions, are the basis for wide-ranging effects of cleavage that run through the social body as a whole ... Major dominations are the hegemonic effects that are sustained by all these confrontations."

[93] Foucault, *History of Sexuality vol. 1*, 94.

[94] Foucault, *History of Sexuality vol. 1*, 94–95: "power relations are both intentional and nonsubjective. If in fact they are intelligible, this is not because they are the effect of another instance that 'explains' them, but rather because they are imbued, through and through, with calculation: there is no power that is exercised without a series of aims and objectives. But this does not mean that it results from the choice or decision of an individual subject."

[95] Foucault, *History of Sexuality vol. 1*, 95. See Bernauer, *Michel Foucault's Force of Flight*, 150: "The other side of power's pervasiveness is precisely the omnipresence of the resistance it discovers." See also Michel Foucault, "Non au sexe roi," in *Dits et écrits*, 3:256–269, here 3:267: "Je ne pose pas une substance de la résistance en face de la substance du pouvoir. Je dis simplement: dès lors qu'il y a un rapport de pouvoir, il y a une possibilité de résistance. Nous ne sommes jamais piégés par le pouvoir: on peut toujours en modifier l'emprise, dans des conditions déterminées et selon une stratégie précise."

essary, improbable; others that are spontaneous, savage, solitary, concerted, rampant, or violent; still others that are quick to compromise, interested, or sacrificial; by definition, they can only exist in the strategic field of
power relations."[96] Because points of resistance are inscribed in the network of power, are its indispensable counterpart, they share in the characteristics of power. Resistance is like power.[97] Points of resistance are "distributed in irregular fashion: the points, knots, or focuses of resistance are
spread over time and space at varying densities, at times mobilizing groups
or individuals in a definitive way, inflaming certain points of the body,
certain moments in life, certain types of behavior."[98] Foucault recognizes
that "great radical ruptures" happen occasionally, but he insists that volatile and mobile points of resistance take place more often, redistributing
the balance of power, modifying groups and individuals, sometimes "cut-
ting them up and remolding them, marking off irreducible regions in them,
in their bodies and minds."[99]

Foucault's own role as an intellectual inscribes itself in these spaces of
resistance and aims to embody the task of modifying the relations of power
in which he moved.[100] He envisions his role in the figure of the "specific
intellectual," whose role is not to dictate what others should think or how
they should behave, but who needs, precisely through his understanding of
the functioning of power in his specific institution, to ask questions about
its way of using power. [101] The specific intellectual finds herself in a posi-

---

[96] Foucault, *History of Sexuality vol. 1*, 96.

[97] Foucault, "Non au sexe roi," 3:267: "Pour résister, il faut qu'elle [la résistance] soit
comme le pouvoir. Aussi inventive, aussi mobile, aussi productive que lui. Que, comme
lui, elle s'organise, se coagule et se cimente. Que, comme lui, elle vienne d'en bas et se
distribue stratégiquement."

[98] Foucault, *History of Sexuality vol. 1*, 96.

[99] Foucault, *History of Sexuality vol. 1 Introduction*, 96.

[100]See Bernauer, *Michel Foucault's Force of Flight*, 150: "the political function of the
intellectual is tied to this task of modification."

[101] There are several articles and interviews in the late 1970s where Foucault puts into
place this contrast between the specific and the universal intellectual. For example, see
Michel Foucault, "Questions à Michel Foucault sur la géographie," in *Dits et écrits,*
3:28–40, here 3:29 : "Or, cette position d'arbitre, de juge, de témoin universel, est un rôle
auquel je me refuse absolument, car il me paraît lié à l'institution universitaire de la philosophie." Also: Foucault, "Non au sexe roi," 3:268: "D'une façon générale, je pense que
les intellectuels – si cette catégorie existe ou si elle doit encore exister, ce qui n'est pas
certain, ce qui n'est peut-être pas souhaitable – renoncent à leur vieille fonction prophé-
tique. Et, par là, je ne pense pas seulement à leur prétention à dire ce qui va se passer,
mais à la fonction de législateur à laquelle ils ont si longtemps aspiré: 'Voilà ce qu'il faut
faire, voilà ce qui est bien, suivez-moi. Dans l'agitation où vous êtes tous, voici le point
fixe, c'est celui où je suis.' Le sage grec, le prophète juif et le législateur romain sont
toujours des modèles qui hantent ceux qui, aujourd'hui, font profession de parler et
d'écrire." See also, Michel Foucault, "Truth and Power," in Gordon, *Power/Knowledge,*

tion of perpetual dissent and discomfort, always on the alert for too easily obtained evidences and universalizing statements:

> Je rêve de l'intellectuel destructeur des évidences et des universalités, celui qui repère et indique dans les inerties et contraintes du présent les points de faiblesse, les ouvertures, les lignes de force, celui qui, sans cesse, se déplace, ne sait pas au juste où il sera ni ce qu'il pensera demain, car il est trop attentif au présent; celui qui contribue, là où il est de passage, à poser la question de savoir si la révolution, ça vaut la peine, et laquelle (je veux dire quelle révolution et quelle peine), étant entendu que seuls peuvent y répondre ceux qui acceptent de risquer leur vie pour la faire.[102]

This uncomfortable position, one of rupture and of exile,[103] does not mean that the intellectual should stand outside of any and all institutions, in the margins, so to speak. Rather, and Foucault's own career exemplifies this, the specific intellectual should use her privileged place in the institution, her privileged knowledge of how power functions in her own institution, so as to implement strategic spaces of resistance inside the network of power. For example, by illuminating the relations of power at work behind the production of truth and of discourses of truth, the specific intellectual challenges the way the institution sustains specific relations of power. Certainly, Foucault embodied this type of intellectual in his own academic career, inside the institution of the Collège de France.[104]

If Foucault's work on discourse and knowledge depletes contemporary thinking about the self from the supposition that the subject reigns supreme over discourse and shows that, rather, the individual always inscribes herself in previous discourses, and is limited by circumstances and systems of

---

109–133, here 126: "For a long period, the 'left' intellectual spoke and was acknowledged the right of speaking in the capacity of master of truth and justice. He was heard, or purported to make himself heard, as the spokesman of the universal. To be an intellectual meant something like being the consciousness/conscience of us all." Contra seeing Foucault as a specific intellectual, see Paul Rabinow, introduction to *The Foucault Reader*, 3–27, here 23: "But Foucault is not a biologist or a physicist, a man of science, either. Such scientists occupy the key positions of the 'specific intellectual'." Rabinow sees Foucault as one of "these founders of discursivity." (26) He sees him as maintaining, with Max Weber for example, "a heroic refusal to sentimentalize the past in any way or to shirk the necessity of facing the future as dangerous but open. Both have committed their lives to a scrupulous, if unorthodox, forging of intellectual tools for the analysis of modern rationality, social and economic organization, and subjectivity." (27)

[102] Foucault, "Non au sexe roi," 268–269.

[103] See Said's description of the intellectual in *Representations of the Intellectual*, 52.

[104] His opening lecture at the Collège is an example of inserting oneself in the functioning of an institution and calling it into question precisely through the type of discourse that the institution demands. See Foucault's reference to the "theatre" within which he will be working: "The Discourse on Language," 216: "here then is the hypothesis I want to advance, tonight, in order to fix the terrain – or perhaps the very provisional theatre – within which I shall be working." Also, the reference to Beckett at the beginning of the lecture: "The Discourse on Language," 215.

organization, Foucault's work on power and resistance deprives the self from her feeling of absolute freedom (or, correlatively, absolute subjection). The individual can never stand outside of relations of power, nor should she wish to do so. Rather, her responsibility is to understand the workings of power and to construct, inside of them, small, punctual, "spontaneous, savage, solitary, concerted, rampant, or violent"[105] strategies of resistances. The opposition between freedom and power is thus also redelineated. In particular, it is no longer possible to understand freedom as the state of being immune to the influence of power. Neither absolute freedom, nor absolute power, truly exists. The individual exists in a network of relations of power to which she also contributes, while at the same time being able to call it into question through her own expertise.

Foucault's own reflections on the subject and power indicate how his analysis of power plays a fundamental role in his discussions concerned with the manner in which "human beings are made subjects."[106] In the context of power, "subject" comes to mean two things: "there are two meanings of the word *subject*: subject to someone else by control and dependence, and tied to his own identity by a conscience or self-knowledge. Both meanings suggest a form of power which subjugates and makes subject to."[107] At the level of the first meaning, Foucault works with the notion of government, indicating that the focus should not necessarily be only on the state, but also on "those men who orient our daily lives either through administrative acts or through direct or indirect influences, for example, the influences of the media."[108] Foucault sees a disciplining of human beings happening in the practices that a government uses to control its population. He calls these techniques of power governmentality.[109] The human being becomes a significant element for the state; and in France and in Germany, from the 16th to the 18th century, Foucault finds this governmentality, this form of power, exemplified in what Foucault reconstructs as the police. In this context, police represents "the specific techniques by which a government in the framework of the state was able to govern people as individuals significantly useful for the world."[110] He defines it as bio-power, a power which exercises a disciplining and normalizing function on human beings. For Foucault, bio-power's principal purpose is "to take care of men

---

[105] Foucault, *History of Sexuality vol. 1*, 96.

[106] Foucault, "Afterword: The Subject and Power," 208.

[107] Foucault, "Afterword: The Subject and Power," 212.

[108] Foucault, "Interview with Michel Foucault," 283.

[109] See the title of an essay given in the context of the course "Security, Territory, and Population" at the Collège de France in the 1977–1978 academic year. Re-published as "Governmentality," in Faubion, *Power: Essential Works of Foucault,* 201–222.

[110] Michel Foucault, "The Political Technology of Individuals," in Faubion, *Power: Essential Works of Foucault,* 403–417, here 410.

as a population."[111] Through the police, "it wields its power over living beings as living beings, and its politics, therefore, has to be a biopolitics."[112]

In reaction to this, Foucault sees the necessary development of an "art of not being governed," at least not like that.[113] In this refusal of being governed, subjects have a duty and a right to embody "voluntary nonservitude," "considered non-docility."[114] Although Foucault never masks the hold of this power on the subject, he also refuses to say that human beings are simply in states of domination *vis-à-vis* this power. Rather, human beings' responsibility, as was already pointed out, is to find spaces of resistance in relationship to this binding to one's identity: "Maybe the target nowadays is not to discover what we are, but to refuse what we are. We have to imagine and to build up what we could be to get rid of this kind of political 'double bind,' which is the simultaneous individualization of the modern power structures."[115] In this refusal of a "subject identity," the struggle is not so much a matter of destroying the state and the institutions. Rather, it has to do with mechanisms and techniques of power attached to the state: "The conclusion would be that the political, ethical, social, philosophical problem of our days is not to try to liberate the individual from the state, and from the state's institutions, but to liberate us both from the state and from the type of individualization which is linked to the state. We have to promote new forms of subjectivity through the refusal of this kind of individuality which has been imposed on us for several centuries."[116] Foucault finds that possibility of freedom inside relationships of power in the relation of the self to itself, in ethics.[117]

3. Resistance and the Self: Ethics

Through his work on knowledge and power, Foucault reveals an individual made subject by outside forces. Both discourse and power constitute the subject and bind the individual to an identity given to her by techniques of domination (power) or by discursive practices (knowledge). In contrast,

---

[111] Foucault, "The Political Technology of Individuals," 416.

[112] Foucault, "The Political Technology of Individual," 416.

[113] See Gordon, "Introduction," xxxix, who quotes Michel Foucault, "Qu'est-ce que la critique? Critique et *Aufklärung*," *Bulletin de la Société Française de Philosophie* 84.2 (April–June 1990): 35–63. This text was not re-published in *Dits et écrits*.

[114] See Gordon, "Introduction," xxxix.

[115] Foucault, "Afterword: The Subject and Power," 216.

[116] Foucault, "Afterword: The Subject and Power," 216.

[117] See Michel Foucault, "The Ethics of the Concern for Self as a Practice of Freedom," in Rabinow, *Ethics: Subjectivity and Truth*, 281–301, here 284: "… for what is ethics, if not the practice of freedom, the conscious [*réfléchie*] practice of freedom?"

when working with the concept of ethics, Foucault presents a subject constituting itself through specific practices.[118] In the analyses concerned with
ethics, Foucault concentrates on texts that are used as practical devices
which enable individuals to "question their own conduct, to watch over
and give shape to it, to shape themselves as ethical subjects."[119] For Foucault, the relationship to oneself, defined through the four aspects of ethical substance, mode of subjection, *askēsis* and *telos*, is a central part of an
analysis of morality. In particular, Foucault insists that even though one
might be able to see remarkable similarities between moral codes – he argues for that similarity between classical and Hellenistic philosophers and
Christian writers – the relationship to oneself, the ethics of the self, is in
fact different.

This reflection on an ethics of the self also emerges as a possible option
for resisting the disciplining and normalizing effects of bio-power.[120] As
Bernauer indicates, Foucault's reflections on ethics of the self introduce
the positive side of resistance. After highlighting the need to "refuse what
we are," Foucault is looking for ways in which the subject can constitute

---

[118] These practices are often referred to as techniques of the self. Technologies of the
self become important in Foucault's work in the 1980s. They are the object of many interviews, articles, seminars and lectures at the Collège de France. Some of the most important works include: "Afterword: The Subject and Power"; "On the Genealogy of Ethics"; *Histoire de la sexualité vol. 2: L'Usage des Plaisirs*, Paris: Gallimard, 1984 (English translation: *History of Sexuality vol. 2: The Use of Pleasure*); *Histoire de la sexualité
vol. 3: Le souci de soi*, Paris: Gallimard, 1984 (English translation: *History of Sexuality
vol. 3: The Care of the Self*); "What is Enlightenment?"; *L'herméneutique du sujet: cours
au Collège de France, 1981–1982* (Paris: Gallimard – Le Seuil, 2001) (English translation: *The Hermeneutics of the Subject: Lectures at the Collège de France, 1981–1982*);
*Le courage de la vérité: le gouvernement de soi et des autres II: cours au Collège de
France, 1984* (Paris: Gallimard – Le Seuil, 2009). Foucault even states that the topic of
the subject is at the heart of all of his work. See Gros, "Course Context," in Foucault, *The
Hermeneutics of the Subject*, 512: "Soon he maintains that this problem of the subject,
and not that of power, is his main concern, and has been for more than twenty years of
writing: the emergence of the subject from social practices of division (*Madness and Civilization* and *Discipline and Punish* – on the construction of the mad and criminal subject); emergence of the subject in theoretical projections (*The Order of Things* – on the
objectification of the speaking, living, and working subject in the sciences of language,
life, and wealth); and finally, with the 'new formula' of *History of Sexuality*, the emergence of the subject in practices of the self. This time the subject [constitutes] itself by
means of techniques of the self, rather than being constituted by techniques of domination (Power) or discursive techniques (Knowledge)."

[119] Foucault, *History of Sexuality vol. 2*, 12

[120] See Bernauer, *Michel Foucault's Force of Flight*, 182: "Foucault's *History of Sexuality* points to the ethical task of detaching ourselves from those forces that would subordinate human existence to biological life. His 'aesthetics of existence' would be in resistance to a 'science of life'."

itself, can invent itself.[121] The analyses concerned with classical and Hellenistic thought allow Foucault to think about the creativity involved in making one's life a work of art.[122]

However, Foucault is well aware that one cannot simply return to the Greeks and hope to find there the solution to the problems that plague the contemporary world. In a published interview that results from discussions with Hubert Dreyfus and Paul Rabinow in April 1983, Foucault is asked whether he thinks that "the Greeks offer an attractive and plausible alternative" to contemporary problems and his answer is unambiguous: "No! I am not looking for an alternative; you can't find the solution of a problem in the solution of another problem raised at another moment by other people."[123] In his answer, Foucault reaffirms his distrust for prescriptions and prefabricated solutions. Rather, he is interested in thinking about similar problems, not in presenting a history of solutions. The Greeks confronted a problem that, for Foucault, is similar to the one he is addressing:

I wonder if our problem nowadays is not, in a way, similar to this one, since most of us no longer believe that ethics is founded in religion, nor do we want a legal system to intervene in our moral, personal, private life. Recent liberation movements suffer from the fact that they cannot find any principle on which to base the elaboration of a new ethics. They need an ethics but they cannot find any other ethics than an ethics founded on so-called scientific knowledge of what the self is, what desire is, what the unconscious is, and so on.[124]

For Foucault, problematization is what matters. The main task of thinking for him lies in the attention given to the configuration of problems. Thus, it prevents the danger of rushing into solutions that carry with them the potential to become immediately normalized and disciplined by knowledge.

---

[121] See Bernauer, *Michel Foucault's Force of Flight*, 183.

[122] Foucault's analyses have been criticized for suggesting that the work of the self in the Greeks had an art of existence as its goal (see for example Bartsch, *The Mirror of the Self*, 253: "the aesthetic dimension of Stoic self-cultivation has little support in the sources, even if on a few occasions Seneca uses the language of molding or shaping the self into its more sagelike manifestation. On the contrary, it seems clear that while allowances could be made for different personal strengths and aptitudes in the individual seeking to transform himself via a regimen of *meditation*, the goal of this practice remained essentially the same for everyone who embarked on it: to align one's belief structures with the tenets of Stoicism so as [to] bring to full fruition one's inherent capacity for rational agency.") Even if this criticism is justified, I believe it actually matters little whether Foucault is correct or not in his analyses of Greek thought. As with his other books, what matters is what he *sees* in the texts he is reading and what it allows him to think (and to make others think) in relationships to these texts. It is in that way that his books are truly "experience books" (see Foucault, "Interview with Michel Foucault," 239–240).

[123] Foucault, "On the Genealogy of Ethics," 343.

[124] Foucault, "On the Genealogy of Ethics," 343.

As Dreyfus and Rabinow write, "any new ethical system will presumably bring new dangers which it will be the job of interpretive analysis to recover and to resist."[125] Even though the Greeks do not provide Foucault with a magical solution to the question of ethics, they give him tools with which he can reflect. The Greeks are thinking about a problem that echoes Foucault's own questions and they give it a particular solution. This solution should not be transposed in our own world, but the way in which the Greeks posit the problem and work on the solution offers new perspectives on our own questions.[126]

It is not that one can draw lessons from classical or Hellenistic Greece, but, in the articulation of ethics, one can identify a different relationship between desire and pleasure. For the Greeks, pleasure, and how human beings use and master it, plays an important role in the constitution of an ethical subject.[127] In contrast, Foucault argues that everybody today insists on the concept of desire, and rejects the notion of pleasure. The difference between the classical age and our own time calls into question the historical necessity behind the separation of pleasure and desire; it challenges the fact that this separation is seen as something necessary or connected to human nature.[128] In asking his readers to look at a historical development seen as ineluctable and question it, Foucault remains faithful to the principles of archaeology and genealogy, insisting that there are different ways of explaining the coming into being of a certain situation.

His interest in the constitution of the ethical subject leads Foucault to take into account the concept of the *technē tou biou*,[129] a sort of art of

---

[125] Hubert L. Dreyfus and Paul Rabinow, "Foucault's Interpretive Analytic of Ethics," in *Michel Foucault: Beyond Structuralism and Hermeneutics*, 253–264, here 263.

[126] See Dreyfus and Rabinow, "Foucault's Interpretive Analytic of Ethics," 257: "Foucault is emphatical that this elaborate analysis does not offer any solutions or alternatives. It shows, however, that an ethical problem similar in form to our own has been confronted before in our history, and his analysis thus gives us a new perspective on our problem."

[127] See Foucault, "On the Genealogy of Ethics," 347: "I think there is no exemplary value in a period which is not our period... it is not anything to get back to. But we do have an example of an ethical experience which implied a very strong connection between pleasure and desire."

[128] See Foucault, "On the Genealogy of Ethics," 347: "If we compare that to our experience now, where everybody – the philosopher or the psychoanalyst – explains that what is important is desire, and pleasure is nothing at all, we can wonder whether this disconnection wasn't a historical event, one which was not at all necessary, not linked to human nature, or to any anthropological necessity."

[129] In my use of the word, I will use the transliteration *technē*. However, when the word is used in quotes, I will respect the choices made by the authors. In Foucault's own work, the transliteration is rarely consistent.

life.[130] He mentions two things in particular which help problematize the question of an ethics of the self and provide preliminary elements to think about the way the individual constitutes herself as an ethical subject. First, Foucault is fascinated by the Greek idea that life can be "a material for an aesthetic piece of art."[131] He argues that, in the modern understanding of art, the notion of work of art applies first and foremost to something that is independent from its creator, and will survive that creator.[132] In contrast, Foucault maintains that the Greeks see the entirety of one's life as a material for a work of art. Ethics provides a foundation for an aesthetics of life; it gives it a frame that is "without any relation with the juridical *per se*, with an authoritarian system, with a disciplinary structure."[133]

Second, Foucault insists on an evolution in the role that care of the self plays in the *technē tou biou*. In classical and Hellenistic antiquity, Foucault agrees that care of the self plays an important role for the art of life. But, for Socrates, and classical antiquity, the care of the self is mainly aimed at preparing the subject to rule others. If one is able to rule oneself in the correct manner, one will then be able to rule over others. Foucault argues that in classical Greece the government of others is the main purpose of the care of the self. In contrast, Foucault sees Hellenistic antiquity as developing a concern for care of the self in itself. It is no longer to rule over others that one has to take care of oneself, but taking care of oneself becomes an end in itself. It is both the means and the end.[134]

As is well known, in his work on *technē tou biou* and technologies of the self, Foucault identifies three periods worth analyzing in the evolution of ethics. In volume two of *The History of Sexuality*, Foucault focuses on care of the self as understood in classical Greece. In volume three, he focuses on the same topics as they appear in Hellenistic Greece. In what

---

[130] See Foucault, "On the Genealogy of Ethics," 348: "What I want to show is that the general Greek problem was not the *techne* of the self, it was the *techne* of life, the *techne tou biou*, how to live." For my purpose, I do not think it is very important to know if Foucault privileged the notion of *technē* of the self or the notion of *technē tou biou*. In fact, it seems that *technē* of the self can be seen as a part of *technē tou biou*. See Foucault, "On the Genealogy of Ethics," 348: "[The Greeks and Romans] had a *techne tou biou* in which the economy of pleasure played a very large role. In this 'art of life' the notion of exercising a perfect mastery over oneself soon became the main issue."

[131] See Foucault, "On the Genealogy of Ethics," 348.

[132] See Foucault, "À propos de la généalogie de l'éthique," 615: "Pour nous, il n'y a d'œuvre et d'art que là où quelque chose échappe à la mortalité de son créateur." To my knowledge, this sentence does not figure in the English version of the interview.

[133] See Foucault, "On the Genealogy of Ethics," 348.

[134] See Foucault, *The Hermeneutics of the Subject*, 111–112: "in short, people were no longer told what Socrates told Alcibiades: If you wish to govern others, take care of yourself. Now it is said: Take care of yourself, and that's the end of it."

should have been volume four of *The History of Sexuality*, Foucault discusses the changes that occur with early Christianity.[135]

Ethics of the Self in Classical Greece

In the second volume of *The History of Sexuality*, Foucault focuses his analyses on classical Greece. The volume is divided in two main sections. The first eighty pages are given over to establishing the framework in which the reflection on ethics of the self takes place. It covers the ethical substance, the *mode d'assujettissement* or the type of subjection, the means used to mold oneself in an ethical subject (*askēsis*) and finally the *telos* that one attains through the practices. In the second part, Foucault shows how these four elements of the ethics of the self are put into practice in three main domains: diet, domestic and political economics and erotic relationships with young boys.[136] In these three fields, Foucault insists that the reflection belongs to the realm of ethics; it is a way for the individual to establish a relation to himself which allows him to be the subject of his moral behavior.[137]

Throughout his analysis of classical writers, Foucault intends to show that, even though the Greeks might have shared the austere rules that also characterize Christian morality, the structure and motivations behind the moral rules are vastly different. According to Foucault, the early Christians are concerned with putting into place a hermeneutics of desire, in which the individual has to tell the truth about him or herself, whereas the writers in classical Greece want to provide their students and themselves with the tools to fashion life in a work of art, to put into place an aesthetics of existence. For Foucault, it is not the case that early Christianity develops a strict moral concerning sex that would be in sharp contrast with the indifference of the Ancients.[138] Rather, Foucault argues that the difference concerns the ethics of the self, including the four elements he presented earlier: the ethical substance, the type of subjection, the means or *askēsis*, and

---

[135] This volume was entitled *Les aveux de la chair* and was never published due to Foucault's premature death. Nevertheless, its contents were discussed by Foucault in lectures, interviews and articles. See Foucault, *History of Sexuality vol. 2*, 12.

[136] Foucault, *History of Sexuality vol. 2*, 36.

[137] In this case, it is necessary to use the gendered language man/he/him, since only men were considered as free or thought as able to exercise proper control over their desires. Foucault insists on the gendered aspect of this ethics: see Foucault, *History of Sexuality vol. 2*, 22: "This is doubtless one of the most remarkable aspects of that moral reflection: it did not try to define a field of conduct and a domain of valid rules – subject to the necessary modulations – for the two sexes in common; it was an elaboration of masculine conduct carried out from the viewpoint of men in order to give form to *their* behavior."

[138] See Foucault, *History of Sexuality vol. 2*, 14–15, also 249–250.

the *telos*.[139] For his study, thus, Foucault explains that he does not focus on the moral codes, and on what the Christians might have borrowed from the Greeks. Instead, "it seemed more pertinent to ask how, given the continuity, transfer, or modification of codes, the forms of self-relationship (and the practices of the self that were associated with them) were defined, modified, recast, and diversified."[140] Foucault's purpose is to trace the different ways in which the ethical subject is constituted, in the four aspects he defined.

In classical Greece, Foucault sees *aphrodisia* as forming the ethical substance.[141] For Foucault, this covers "the acts, gestures, and contacts that produce certain form of pleasure."[142] Foucault notes that, for the Ancient Greeks, acts, desire and pleasure, although not identified with one another, are closely connected to one another. In fact, Foucault argues that it is precisely "their close linkage that constituted one of the essential characteristics of that form of activity."[143] The ethical substance is precisely the "dynamics that joined all three in a circular fashion."[144] In contrast, for Foucault, Christianity dissociates pleasure and desire. Pleasure is "elided" by the Christian clergy when it argues for the practice of sexuality as a means of procreation only and calls into question the pursuit of pleasure as a goal of sexual practice. According to Foucault, desire also becomes increasingly problematic for the Christians, since it is the mark of a fallen humanity.[145]

For classical Greece, sexual activity, and the pleasure associated with it, is not understood as something inherently bad. Rather, Foucault presents it as the object of "moral differentiation and valuation."[146] Concerning *aphrodisia*, the two main forms of immorality that men are wont to commit are "excess and passivity."[147] Excess means that one self-indulges in pleasures and acts not evil in themselves, but that need to be carried out in modera-

---

[139] See Foucault, *History of Sexuality vol. 2*, 250: "… isn't it the case that the philosophical, moral, and medical thought that formed in their midst formulated some of the basic principles that later ethics – and particularly those found in the Christian societies – seem to have only had to revive? We cannot stop there, however; the prescriptions may be formally alike, but this actually shows only the poverty and monotony of interdictions. The way in which sexual activity was constituted, recognized, and organized as a moral issue is not identical from the mere fact that what was allowed or prohibited, recommended or discouraged is identical."

[140] Foucault, *History of Sexuality vol. 2*, 32.
[141] Foucault, *History of Sexuality vol. 2*, 37.
[142] Foucault, *History of Sexuality vol. 2*, 40.
[143] Foucault, *History of Sexuality vol. 2*, 42.
[144] Foucault, *History of Sexuality vol. 2*, 43.
[145] See Foucault, *History of Sexuality vol. 2*, 42.
[146] Foucault, *History of Sexuality vol. 2*, 47.
[147] Foucault, *History of Sexuality vol. 2*, 47.

tion. Self-restraint thus becomes central in relationship to the *aphrodis-ia*.[148] Passivity is traditionally associated with the feminine role in the sexual act. Being passive is the role of the woman during sexual intercourse. But for the Greeks, and the Romans, anyone that submits to penetration endorses the passive role in sexual relationships. This role could be forced on another man, who is then "reduced to being the object of the other's pleasure" or it could be the position willingly assumed by a young boy or a man who lets himself be penetrated.[149] This passive role creates a problem for men in general and for free men in particular, who should never accept it in sexual intercourse. At the same time, women should never attempt to take the active role in sexual relationships.[150] Maintaining the proper status relationships inside the sexual act is critical to the proper enjoyment of the *aphrodisia*.

For Foucault, the moral valuation of the *aphrodisia* shows that the sexual act itself, as well as sexual desire and sexual pleasure, is considered natural and indispensable, but it becomes the object of moral concern regarding "the proper degree and extent to which it could be practiced"[151] and regarding the position one assumes during intercourse. The same concern for moderation is shown in the treatment of one's use of food and drink. In all three cases, Foucault argues that the Greeks see natural forces at play, but that these forces "always tended to be excessive and they all raised the same question: how could one, how must one 'make use' (*chrēsthai*) of this dynamic of pleasures, desires, and acts?"[152]

The mode of subjection, and the principles related to it, guarantees the proper use of pleasure.[153] For Foucault, the Greeks are not concerned with developing a systematic code of behavior; rather they are intent on "work-

---

[148] See Foucault, *History of Sexuality vol. 2*, 44–45.

[149] Foucault, *History of Sexuality vol. 2*, 46.

[150] Foucault talks at length about the gender implications of sexuality in *History of Sexuality vol. 2*. This theme is also central to Moore's reading of Romans in *God's Beauty Parlor*. Moore notes the importance of penetration to "express social relations of honor and shame, aggrandizement and loss, domination and submission, or, more generally, movement up or down that treacherously slippery social ladder whose greased rungs marked discrete levels of status and prestige" (146) and the importance of the active/passive antithesis for the definition of gender, thus remarking that the opposition is not so much between man and woman than between man and unman (136 and 140, for the importance of the active/passive antithesis, 142–146).

[151] Foucault, *History of Sexuality vol. 2*, 48.

[152] Foucault, *History of Sexuality vol. 2*, 52.

[153] Foucault, *History of Sexuality vol. 2*, 53: "How does a man enjoy his pleasure 'as one ought'? To what principles does he refer in order to moderate, limit, regulate that activity? What sort of validity might these principles have that would enable a man to justify his having to obey them? Or, in other words. what is the mode of subjection that is implied in this moral problematization of sexual conduct?"

ing out the conditions and modalities of a 'use'; that is to define a style for what the Greeks called *chrēsis aphrodisiōn*, the use of pleasures."[154] It is less a question of what is permitted or forbidden than a question of "prudence, reflection and calculation in the way one distributed and controlled his acts."[155] The mode of subjection is not dependent on a clearly defined moral code that delimits which pleasures and desires are acceptable and which need to be suppressed. Rather, in order to evaluate the best way to relate to pleasures, one has to take into account natural necessity or need, timeliness, which covers both time and circumstances, and the status of the various individuals involved.

The satisfaction of need functions as its internal limit. One has to provide only "what [is] necessary to the body and [is] intended by nature, and nothing more."[156] For Foucault, this understanding of need as a limitative principle means that moderation is not a matter of obeying a code of law, nor of suppressing pleasure altogether, but rather it is an "art, a practice of pleasures that was capable of self-limitation through the 'use' of those pleasures that were based on need."[157] Timeliness translates a preoccupation with finding the opportune time, the *kairos*, for a particular action.[158] This cannot be accomplished by following a set of rules. One has to decipher the right time, a practice that Foucault also understands as an art.[159] Finally, the use of pleasure has to take into account the status of the user. Foucault argues that in classical Greece, "standards of sexual morality were always tailored to one's way of life, which was itself determined by the status one had inherited and the purposes one had chosen."[160] Not all acts are judged in the same manner for all persons. In particular, if one leads a public life and has some amount of authority on others, one needs to keep higher standards of morality, in order for one to shape one's life in a work of art.[161] In the analysis of the mode of subjection, Foucault concludes that Ancient Greeks are far from proposing a universal law. Rather, moral decisions are a "matter of adjustment, circumstance, and personal position."[162] A rigid code of laws is unhelpful in this case; rather what is needed is "a *technē* or 'practice,' a *savoir-faire*."[163] This *technē* can take into account general principles, but has to integrate circumstances, time,

---

[154] Foucault, *History of Sexuality vol. 2*, 53.
[155] Foucault, *History of Sexuality vol. 2*, 54.
[156] Foucault, *History of Sexuality vol. 2*, 56.
[157] Foucault, *History of Sexuality vol. 2*, 57.
[158] Foucault, *History of Sexuality vol. 2*, 57.
[159] See Foucault, *History of Sexuality vol. 2*, 58.
[160] Foucault, *History of Sexuality vol. 2*, 60.
[161] Foucault, *History of Sexuality vol. 2*, 60.
[162] Foucault, *History of Sexuality vol. 2*, 62.
[163] Foucault, *History of Sexuality vol. 2*, 62.

status and purpose to really allow the self to construct itself in an ethical subject.

This *technē*, the means to form the proper ethical subject, is characterized by *enkrateia*, a concept which, according to Foucault, refers "in general to the dynamics of domination of oneself by oneself and to the effort that this demands."[164] *Enkrateia* implies a combative relationship with desires and pleasures. In order to become moderate, one has to confront and fight pleasures and desires; otherwise, because they are lower driving forces, they always have the potentiality to take over and control the person. Pleasures and desires are perceived as "a formidable enemy force,"[165] residing inside the person. Foucault insists that, for the ancient Greeks, the battle is not with an other who tries to tempt the person from the outside. Rather, it is a battle with one's own self.[166] In this combat within the self, Foucault argues that victory is sometimes seen as the suppression of all desires, but most often, it consists in establishing a "solid and stable state of rule of the self over the self."[167] Desire is still present, but the self masters it well enough so as not to be submerged by violent and passionate emotions. In fact, *enkrateia* is seen by the Greeks as all the more remarkable if there is still some desire remaining which the person needs to fight.[168]

Foucault defines the "virtuous and moderate subject" in classical Greece as an individual who "has to construct a relationship with the self that is of the 'domination-submission,' 'command-obedience,' 'mastery-docility' type ... This is what could be called the 'heautocratic' structure of the subject in the ethical practice of the pleasures."[169] For Foucault, the classical Hellenic model contrasts with the Christian model, which aims for an "'elucidation-renunciation,' 'decipherment-purification'" structure.

In the quest for *enkrateia*, Foucault notes that the individual is equipped with a specific training – much like an athlete or a warrior is trained in his

---

[164] Foucault, *History of Sexuality vol. 2*, 65.

[165] Foucault, *History of Sexuality vol. 2*, 66.

[166] Foucault, *History of Sexuality vol. 2*, 68. For Foucault, this is in contrast with the "Christian ethics of the flesh," which first introduced the idea of an outside enemy. In fact, it seems clear that, for Paul at least, sin is not understood as a power outside of the person, but rather as a force that resides inside the person and takes her over. In that sense, Paul remains close to the understanding developed by the ancient Greeks.

[167] Foucault, *History of Sexuality vol. 2*, 69.

[168] See Foucault, *History of Sexuality vol. 2*, 69.

[169] Foucault, *History of Sexuality vol. 2*, 70. For Foucault, this structure was implemented in two models: the household and civic life. In both cases, what was needed was a master able to preserve proper order and to rule over inferiors (be it servants, or the population).

specific art – an *askēsis*.[170] This *askēsis* is formed of several practices and exercises, techniques that allow one to take proper care of one's self, before one attends to the needs of others. It includes the principle of knowing oneself (knowing one's nature, being aware of one's lack of knowledge) but it also comprises the need to "exercise and transform oneself."[171] For Foucault, it is important to reclaim the practical side of care of the self. Foucault indicates that the principle of "knowing oneself" is the dominant notion when one thinks of philosophy in classical Greece. However, Foucault maintains that one should re-appropriate the practical and physical dimension of care of the self in the analyses of Greek and Roman ethics.[172] Foucault insists that this transformation of the self is, in classical Greece, always related to the practice of virtue that enables one to become a perfect citizen and to play a role in the life of the city.[173] The care of the self, the *epimeleia heautou*, is a preliminary step towards the final goal of taking care of others and governing them.

For Foucault, the *telos* of this ethics of the self resides in *sōphrosynē*, "characterized as freedom."[174] Foucault is careful to point out that this freedom should not be understood as "the independence of a free will;"[175] rather it needs to be associated with independence from one's pleasures and desires. It is a freedom from enslavement – the possibility of not being dependent upon one's passions, but of mastering them and thus of displaying self-control. In addition, Foucault argues that once one possesses this type of freedom over one's self, then one can also exercise power over others. For Foucault, this mastery over one's self, which parallels the mastery one has to embody in one's house or in one's city, is a virile characteristics, virile in the sense that "self-mastery was a way of being a man with respect to oneself; that is, a way of commanding what needed commanding, of coercing what was not capable of self-direction, of imposing principles of reason on what was wanting in reason; in short, it was a way of being active in relation to what was by nature passive and ought to remain so."[176]

---

[170] See Foucault, *History of Sexuality vol. 2*, 72.

[171] See Foucault, *History of Sexuality vol. 2*, 73.

[172] See Foucault, *The Hermeneutics of the Subject*, 12.

[173] See Foucault, *History of Sexuality vol. 2*, 76–77.

[174] See Foucault, *History of Sexuality vol. 2*, 78.

[175] Foucault, *History of Sexuality vol. 2*, 79.

[176] Foucault, *History of Sexuality vol. 2*, 82–83. Foucault adds that this does not mean that women were not capable of *sōphrosynē*, but even for women this virtue remained virile, because the woman, in order to be moderate, had to establish a relation of control over herself that was understood as virile. Thus, a man who was not able to display moderation and self-control was seen as effeminate.

Foucault also indicates that the freedom associated with self-mastery is closely connected to truth, to *logos*. Truth for Foucault constitutes an essential element of the quest for moderation and self-mastery, but it plays a role not as a "form of decipherment of the self by the self."[177] It does not lead to a "hermeneutics of desire" that forces the individual to speak the truth about him or herself and his or her desires; rather truth is an instrument that helps the self constitute itself as an ethical subject. It leads to an "aesthetics of existence."[178] For Foucault, this means that the value of one's life does not come from following a set body of laws, or from an effort of purification.

It is inside this aesthetics of existence that Foucault sees the "themes of sexual austerity"[179] developing. For Foucault, these themes are evident in the practices used by men to shape and transform their conduct. They are associated with diet, with domestic government, and with erotic relationships with young boys. Foucault insists that in these three domains, the purpose is not to elaborate a set of rules to codify behaviors; rather it is a matter of "stylizing"[180] one's behavior through various practices and through an understanding of how one fits in one's family and one's city. Whether it is about dietetics, or private and public economics, or relationships with boys, what matters is enabling the person to make the right decisions. The texts concerned with diet, with public and private economics, and with erotic relationships provide what Foucault calls "strategic principles" that each individual needs to adapt to his own situation.[181] Because they are not a set of rules, they give the person the possibility and responsibility to conduct his life in agreement with the principles, while at the same time making room for particular circumstances (such as time, space and status). As a goal, the person needs to aim at an "aesthetics of life." The moral value of this way of life is related to the respect and the use of certain general principles.[182]

---

[177] See Foucault, *History of Sexuality vol. 2*, 89.

[178] Foucault, *History of Sexuality vol. 2*, 89.

[179] Foucault, *History of Sexuality vol. 2*, 93.

[180] Foucault, *History of Sexuality vol. 2*, 93.

[181] See Foucault, *History of Sexuality vol. 2*, 111: "the almanac is thus not to be read as a set of imperative recipes but as strategic principles that one must know how to adapt to circumstances."

[182] See Foucault, *History of Sexuality vol. 2*, 89: "Now, while this relation to truth, constitutive of the moderate subject, did not lead to a hermeneutics of desire, it did on the other hand open onto an aesthetics of existence. And what I mean by this is a way of life whose moral value did not depend either on one's being in conformity with a code of behavior, or an effort of purification, but on certain formal principles in the use of pleasures, in the way one distributed them, in the limits one observed, in the hierarchy one respected."

Foucault claims that the ethics of the self in classical Greece, and its way of constituting the ethical subject, differs from the structure of Christian ethics. He admits that, concerning austerity about the body, marriage and the love of boys, Christianity and classical Greece share similar precepts and interdictions.[183] However, Foucault insists that the four aspects of the ethics of the self change. For Christianity, the ethical substance is no longer the *aphrodisia*. Foucault defines it "by a domain of desires that lie hidden among the mysteries of the heart, and by a set of acts that are carefully specified as to their form and their conditions."[184] Desire becomes the central element; it needs to be deciphered and suppressed. Once desire is suppressed, the sexual act itself needs to be performed in a neutral manner, with no pleasure attached to it.[185] The mode of subjection is characterized not by a *technē* or a *savoir-faire*, but by the "recognition of the law and an obedience to pastoral authority."[186] For Foucault, since the focus is on law and authority, the virile activity of mastery of one's self over one's self no longer accompanies obedience. The *askēsis* is characterized by "self-renunciation" and the *telos* lays in "a purity whose model was to be sought in virginity."[187] To attain purity, Foucault argues that Christianity has to highlight two practices: the "codification of sexual acts" and the development of a "hermeneutics of desire," marked by "procedures of self-decipherment."[188] For Foucault, the move from an aesthetics of existence to a hermeneutics of desire already begins with some changes attested in the works of the moralists, philosophers and doctors of the first and second centuries CE.[189]

---

[183] See Foucault, *History of Sexuality vol. 2*, 92: "As we shall see, this moral reflection developed themes of austerity – concerning the body, marriage, and love of boys – that show a resemblance to the precepts and interdictions that were to appear later on. But we must not let this apparent continuity obscure the fact that the ethical subject would no longer be constituted in the same manner." See also, Foucault, "On the Genealogy of Ethics," 361: "What interests me about the classical concept of care of the self is that we see here the birth and development of a certain number of ascetic themes ordinarily attributed to Christianity. Christianity is usually given credit for replacing the generally tolerant Greco-Roman lifestyle with an austere lifestyle marked by a series of renunciations, interdictions, or prohibitions. Now, we can see that in this activity of the self on itself, the ancients developed a whole series of austerity practices that the Christians later directly borrowed from them. So we see that this activity became linked to a certain sexual austerity which was subsumed directly into the Christian ethic. We are not talking about a moral rupture between tolerant antiquity and austere Christianity."

[184] See Foucault, *History of Sexuality vol. 2*, 92.

[185] See Foucault, "On the Genealogy of Ethics," 359.

[186] See Foucault, *History of Sexuality vol. 2*, 92.

[187] Foucault, *History of Sexuality vol. 2*, 92.

[188] Foucault, *History of Sexuality vol. 2*, 92.

[189] See Foucault, *History of Sexuality vol. 2*, 254.

Ethics of the Self in Hellenistic Writers
The Care of the Self, volume three of *The History of Sexuality*, looks at the period that Foucault identifies as coming between the classical age and early Christianity. Hellenistic philosophy is analyzed on its own terms, but also to highlight the shifts, changes, transformations that occur in relationship to classical age and to early Christianity. The book can be divided in two main sections, with the three first parts putting into place the comparison with classical antiquity and providing some elements particular to the Hellenistic period. The three last parts take up the three concrete domains that were at the center of *The Use of Pleasure*'s analysis of classical ethics (sexual pleasures, relationship to the household in general and to one's wife in particular, and the love of boys) and develop them in relationship to their destiny in Christian morals. In contrast to what he does in *The Use of Pleasure*, Foucault does not elaborate separately on the four domains (ethical substance, type of subjection, *askēsis*, and *telos*) of ethical construction of the self. These four areas are discussed in the body of the analysis, often to contrast them with the manner in which they were conceived in classical Greece or early Christianity.

To summarize, for Foucault, the ethical substance remains the same in classical and Hellenistic moral reflections. Both focus on *aphrodisia* in their articulation of pleasure, desire and act. Foucault argues that *askēsis* is also similar. One has to construct an art of living, marked by aesthetic principles, but this art of living concerns itself more heavily with self-knowledge.[190] For Foucault, the difference with classical antiquity appears mainly in the type of subjection asked of the individual and in the *telos* of the ethical practices. The type of subjection is no longer a choice to lead an aesthetic life, both in private and in public. Rather Foucault argues that, especially in Stoic circles, it depends upon the respect of a universal law, valid for all rational human beings.[191] The *telos* of the ethical practices still aims at creating an individual master of himself or herself,[192] but this mas-

---

[190] See Foucault, *History of Sexuality vol. 3*, 67–68.

[191] See Foucault, "On the Genealogy of Ethics," 354 and 356.

[192] Foucault does not comment on the applicability of Hellenistic ethics to women (something for which feminists have often reproached him. See for example Lin Foxhall, "Pandora Unbound: A Feminist Critique of Foucault's *History of Sexuality*," in *Rethinking Sexuality: Foucault and Classical Antiquity* [ed. D. H. J. Larmour, P. A. Miller, C. Platter; Princeton: Princeton University Press, 1998], 122–137 and Amy Richlin, "Foucault's *History of Sexuality*: A Useful Theory for Women?" in Larmour, Miller and Platter, *Rethinking Sexuality*, 138–170). He sees Greek and Roman ethics in general as the product of male reflections for male individuals. However, I think that Hellenistic ethics, which seems to be less focused on hierarchical relationships and on the need to govern oneself in order to govern others, might more easily be appropriated by women. Whether

tery becomes a goal in and for itself. It is no longer directly related to one's involvement in the political life of the city.[193] The self, and one's relation to one's self, becomes increasingly important in Hellenistic times. In that focus on the self, and on self-mastery for the sake of self-mastery, it might be possible to see a shift from classical antiquity to the Hellenistic period. In classical antiquity, the focus seems to be more on the natural dimensions related to the use of pleasure. One should be able to use pleasure in a moderate way, as a manner to satisfy the body and keep it healthy. In Hellenistic philosophy, one witnesses a slight move towards attention to the self and its passions, for itself. Foucault does not insist on this, but recognizes that one moves towards more self-examination, in order to control one's passions and emotions. One could argue that there is more anxiety related to care of the self in Hellenistic times, thus opening the door to what Foucault describes as happening in Christianity.

In *The Care of the Self*, Foucault also develops the differences between Christianity and Hellenistic philosophy. Again, he concentrates on the ethical substance, the type of subjection, the means to form one as an ethical subject and the *telos* behind the ethical enterprise. In the final pages of *The Care of the Self*, Foucault recognizes that, in the treatment of sex, of marriage and of relationships to boys, Hellenistic philosophy and Christianity are rather similar in their precepts.[194] But he insists that the "modalities of the relation to self"[195] are different. The ethical substance in Christianity is based on desire, understood as something that needs to be purged because of the fall. The type of subjection is divine law. It implies "obedience to a general law that is at the same time the will of a personal god."[196] Even the *askēsis* developed in Christianity departs from the Hellenistic practices. It might include similar exercises, but it centers on self-decipherment, an examination and interpretation of desires. Finally, the *telos* includes immor-

---

this was actually true is difficult to evaluate but there are some indication that it might have been the case. See for example Musonius Rufus' indications about the necessity of studying philosophy for women (Musonius Rufus, *Fragment 3 [That Women Too Should Study Philosophy]* as quoted in Abraham J. Malherbe, *Moral Exhortation: A Greco-Roman Sourcebook* [Philadelphia: Westminster Press, 1986], 132–134).

[193] See Foucault, "À propos de la généalogie de l'éthique," 621: "En gros, on peut dire que la maîtrise de soi était restée longtemps liée à la volonté d'exercer un ascendant sur les autres. De plus en plus, dans la pensée morale des deux premiers siècles, la souveraineté sur soi a pour fin d'assurer son indépendance à l'égard des événements extérieurs et du pouvoir des autres." I do not think these sentences are found in the English version. For a similar point, see Foucault, "On the Genealogy of Ethics," 355–356.

[194] See Foucault, *History of Sexuality vol. 3*, 239: "Thus, as the arts of living and the care of the self are refined, some precepts emerge that seem to be rather similar to those that will be formulated in the later moral systems."

[195] Foucault, *History of Sexuality vol. 3*, 239.

[196] Foucault, *History of Sexuality vol 3*, 239.

tality and purity but also self-renunciation.[197] Thus, Foucault repeats that the divergence between Christianity and the Greek world (both classical and Hellenistic) does not reside in the content of the moral codes, with Christianity inaugurating an age of austerity after the moral tolerance of antiquity. Rather, "between paganism and Christianity, the opposition is not between tolerance and austerity, but between a form of austerity which is linked to an aesthetics of existence and other forms of austerity which are linked to the necessity of renouncing the self and deciphering its truth."[198]

In *The Care of the Self* and in Foucault's lectures at the Collège de France, the ethics of the self put into place by Hellenistic philosophy is also presented in its own right, with less emphasis put on the relationship with classical Greece and Christianity. Foucault is particularly interested in the creation of "an art of existence dominated by self-preoccupation."[199] Foucault insists that the *telos* of the Hellenistic philosophers is to achieve "pure enjoyment of oneself."[200] In this context, the techniques of the self play an important role. Foucault analyzes these practices in several articles and devotes a course at the Collège de France to that particular topic. These practices aim at an observation of soul and body, so that one can reinforce the rational principles used to lead a life characterized by wisdom.[201] Mastery is important, but it is not only mastery of outside forces or of desires. It is a way to be in harmony with oneself, at peace with oneself so that one is not only in control of oneself, but can also enjoy oneself.

Foucault insists that care of the self is not simply an attitude but a concrete practice, translated in various actions. Foucault remarks that *epimeleia* is a very concrete and practical word: "*Epimeleia heautou* is a very powerful word in Greek which means working on or being concerned with something ...; it describes a sort of work, an activity; it implies atten-

---

[197] See Foucault, *History of Sexuality vol. 3*, 240 and "On the Genealogy of Ethics," 366: "This new Christian self had to be constantly examined because in this self were lodged concupiscence and desires of the flesh. From that moment on, the self was no longer something to be made but something to be renounced and deciphered."

[198] Foucault, "On the Genealogy of Ethics," 366.

[199] See Foucault, *History of Sexuality vol. 3*, 238.

[200] See Foucault, *History of Sexuality vol. 3*, 238.

[201] See Foucault, *History of Sexuality vol. 3*, 62: "The purpose of the examination is not therefore to discover one's own guilt, down to its most trifling forms and its most tenuous roots. If one 'conceals nothing from oneself,' if one 'omits nothing,' it is in order to commit to memory, so as to have them present in one's mind, legitimate ends, but also rules of conduct that enable one to achieve these ends through the choice of appropriate means. The fault is not reactivated by the examination in order to determine a culpability or stimulate a feeling of remorse, but in order to strengthen, on the basis of the recapitulated and reconsidered verification of a failure, the rational equipment that ensures a wise behavior."

tion, knowledge, technique."[202] Knowledge is a part of this practice of care of the self. Foucault argues that it involves knowledge of oneself (the famous *gnôthi seauton*), but the precept of knowing oneself is subordinated to the need for care of the self.[203] Even in the *Apology*, Socrates is described first and foremost as "the person whose essential, fundamental, and original function, job, and position is to encourage others to attend to themselves, take care of themselves, and not neglect themselves."[204] If knowledge of the self certainly plays a role in the care of the self, Foucault remarks that knowledge also refers to "knowledge of a number of rules of acceptable conduct or of principles that are both truths and prescriptions."[205] This knowledge of truth, of the principles that will help one know how to behave in certain circumstances, requires practicing certain techniques that allow the truth to inhabit the individual.

Foucault defines these techniques in the following manner: "the procedures, which no doubt exist in every civilization, suggested or prescribed to individuals in order to determine their identity, maintain it, or transform it in terms of a certain number of ends, through relations of self-mastery or self-knowledge."[206] Foucault identifies several characteristics regarding these techniques. They include various concrete exercises that need to be

---

[202] Foucault, "On the Genealogy of Ethics," 359–360.

[203] See the distinction Foucault puts into place at the beginning of his course on *The Hermeneutics of the Subject*, 2–3: "It is somewhat paradoxical and artificial to select this notion when everyone knows, says, and repeats, and has done so for a long time, that the question of the subject (the question of knowledge of the subject, of the subject's knowledge of himself) was originally posed in a very different expression and a very different precept: the famous Delphic prescription of *gnōthi seauton* ('know yourself'). So, when everything in the history of philosophy – and more broadly in the history of Western thought – tells us that the *gnōthi seauton* is undoubtedly the founding expression of the question of the relations between subject and truth, why choose this apparently rather marginal notion – that of the care of oneself, of *epimeleia heautou* – which is certainly current in Greek thought, but which seems not to have been given any special status?" and 4–5: "Now not always, but often, and in a highly significant way, when this Delphic precept (this *gnōthi seauton*) appears, it is coupled or twinned with the principle of 'take care of yourself' (*epimeleia heautou*). I say 'coupled,' 'twinned.' In actual fact, it is not entirely a matter of coupling. In some texts, to which we will have to return, there is, rather, a kind of subordination of the expression of the rule 'know yourself' to the precept of care of the self. The *gnōthi seauton* ('know yourself') appears quite clearly and again in a number of significant texts, within the more general framework of the *epimeleia heautou* (care of oneself) as one of the forms, one of the consequences, as a sort of concrete, precise, and particular application of the general rule: you must attend to yourself, you must not forget yourself, you must take care of yourself."

[204] Foucault, *The Hermeneutics of the Subject*, 5.

[205] See Foucault, "The Ethics of the Concern for Self," 285.

[206] Michel Foucault, "Subjectivity and Truth," in Rabinow, *Ethics: Subjectivity and Truth*, 87–92, here 87.

practiced during one's entire life – not just during an educational period in one's youth. Care of the self should be a constant occupation.[207] The purpose of the practices themselves, according to Foucault, is not to know everything about a vast array of topics. Rather, it is to know what is necessary to insure self-control in the face of various unpredictable events.[208] The familiarity one needs with the *logoi* necessary to ensure self-control is not simply of the order of memorization. Rather, these *logoi* need to properly be within someone, to become part of him or her, so as to be always at hand when one needs them.[209] The practices' aim is not to rediscover a truth hidden inside the person; rather the person needs to internalize "accepted truth through an increasingly thorough appropriation."[210] In the end, the purpose, for the Stoics in particular is, as Foucault indicates, to arm "the subject with a truth that he did not know and that did not dwell within him; it involves turning this learned and memorized truth that is progressively put into practice into a quasi-subject that reigns supreme within us."[211]

For Foucault, three methodological elements are important for this practice of "'ascesis' of truth."[212] First, the practice of listening is central to learning the principles of truth. Second, writing plays an important role in the practice of the self. It takes the shape of personal writing: "taking notes on the reading, conversations, and reflections that one hears or engages in

---

[207] See Michel Foucault, "Course Summary," in *The Hermeneutics of the Subject*, 491–505, here 494: "Attending to the self is not therefore just a brief preparation for life; it is a form of life ... One should be one's own object for oneself throughout one's life." The course summary was also published in another translation in Rabinow, *Ethics: Subjectivity and Truth*, 93–106.

[208] See Foucault, "Course Summary," in *The Hermeneutics of the Subject*, 498: "We must train like an athlete; the latter does not learn every possible move, he does not try to perform pointless feats; he practices a few movements that are necessary for him to triumph over his opponents in the fight. In the same way, we do not have to perform feats on ourselves (philosophical ascesis is very mistrustful of those characters who draw attention to their feats of abstinence, their fasts, and their knowledge of the future). Like a good wrestler, we should learn only what will enable us to resist possible events; we must learn not to let ourselves be disconcerted by them, not to let ourselves be carried away by the emotions they may arouse in us."

[209] See Foucault, "Course Summary," in *The Hermeneutics of the Subject*, 499: "To protect ourselves from an unexpected event or misfortune we must be able to call upon the appropriate true discourses. They must be available to us, within us. The Greeks had a common expression for this: *prokheiron ekhein*, that the Latins translate as: *habere in manu, in promptu habere* – to have ready to hand. It should be understood that this involves something very different from a simple memory that one would recall should something occur."

[210] Foucault, "Course Summary," in *The Hermeneutics of the Subject*, 500.

[211] Foucault, "Course Summary," in *The Hermeneutics of the Subject*, 501.

[212] Foucault, "Course Summary," in *The Hermeneutics of the Subject*, 500.

oneself;" but it also involves the creation and keeping of "notebooks on important subjects" – the *hupomnēmata*. [213] In these notebooks, one collects various thoughts and maxims, which one is able to reread occasionally, in order to "reactualize their contents."[214] Third, as Marcus Aurelius' *Meditations* make clear, the individual is also supposed to take stock of him or herself at the end of the day. The purpose here is to go through what one has learned and thus (re)-commit it to memory.

In these methodological elements, the practice of the self appears as a rather spiritual and intellectual endeavor, an exercise of thought over itself. This is confirmed by the various concrete practices that have been transmitted, in particular the *praemeditatio malorum* (the meditation on future evils), practices that involve the control of representations and the *meletē thanatou* (meditation on or training for death).[215] But at the same time, Foucault is careful to emphasize the bodily dimension of the care of the self. One has to pay attention to the various needs and functionings of the body – as is clear from his analyses in the third volume of *History of Sexuality* – and some exercises are practices on the body: "exercise of abstinence, privation, or physical resistance."[216] However, even for these bodily practices, the purpose is to test "the individual's independence in relation to the external world."[217]

In the concrete practices that the various writings about care of the self prescribe to their readers, Foucault sees an "etho-poetic" function. Foucault argues that they are "'practical texts,' which are themselves objects of a 'practice' in that they were designed to be read, learned, reflected upon, and tested out, and they were intended to constitute the eventual framework of everyday conduct."[218] Their purpose is to shape the individual as an ethical subject. As Frédéric Gros writes, Foucault's interest lies with that etho-poetic truth: "a truth such as is read in the weft of accomplished actions and physical postures, rather than as deciphered in the secrets of conscience or worked out in the chambers of professional philosophers."[219] The learned truth, the assimilated logos, needs to become the "spontaneous form of the acting subject."[220] In the opposition between a truth that becomes embodied in the individual and a truth that needs to be

---

[213] Foucault, "Course Summary," in *The Hermeneutics of the Subject*, 500.

[214] Foucault, "Course Summary," in *The Hermeneutics of the Subject*, 500.

[215] See Foucault, "Course Summary," in *The Hermeneutics of the Subject*, 501, 503 and 504.

[216] Foucault, "Course Summary," in *The Hermeneutics of the Subject*, 502.

[217] Foucault, "Course Summary," in *The Hermeneutics of the Subject*, 502.

[218] Foucault, *History of Sexuality vol. 2*, 12–13.

[219] Gros, "Course Context," in Foucault, *The Hermeneutics of the Subject*, 528–529.

[220] Gros, "Course Context," in Foucault, *The Hermeneutics of the Subject*, 529, quoting Foucault's notes in a dossier called "Government of the self and others."

deciphered, one encounters again the opposition that Foucault has been drawing out in *History of Sexuality*, between Hellenistic Greece and Christianity. I will have to return to this opposition, especially also to reflect on its elision of Paul, but it is necessary first to analyze the last dimension of the care of the self touched upon by Foucault, the necessity of the other in order to establish a proper relationship to oneself.[221]

This need for the other, for a master, is at the center of Foucault's last lectures given in 1984 at the Collège de France, on *Le Courage de la vérité*, but it is also a theme touched upon in all of his works on the Greeks. Foucault insists that the work on the self cannot happen without the help of someone else. He explains that in classical Greece, the master-student relationship often develops in an erotic context, between an older and a younger man, but it needs to differ from the relationship between two lovers. For Foucault, Socrates and Alcibiades exemplify that relationship. He argues that it is distinct from three other types of relationship, which can also be the context of activities related to care of the self: "the activities of the doctor, the head of the household, and the lover."[222] Foucault argues that if, in the care of the self, one does need a master, "the master's position is defined by that which he cares about, which is the care the person he guides may have for himself."[223] This position differs from the doctor, since the doctor is only concerned about the body, it is separated from the head of the household, whose concern is property, and it is different from the position of the lover, who is interested in his own benefit when loving a boy. In contrast, the master loves the boy disinterestedly, and can thus be "the source and model for the care the boy must have for himself as subject."[224]

For Foucault, this notion of the master as model persists throughout antiquity. In the care of the self, the master does not only have the responsibility of speaking the truth but the master also needs to inhabit the truth that he is speaking – the notion of *parrhēsia*. The master can only be an *exemplum* if he commits to *parrhēsia*, to an *adæquatio* between the truth he speaks and the truth he lives:

---

[221] Foucault, "Course Summary," in *The Hermeneutics of the Subject*, 496: "In the first and second centuries, the relation to the self is always seen as having to rely on the relationship with a master, a guide, or anyway someone else. But the need for this relationship was increasingly independent of the love relationship. Not being able to take care of oneself without the help of someone else was a generally accepted principle."

[222] Foucault, *The Hermeneutics of the Subject*, 57. Plato's *Alcibiades* plays an important role in Foucault's genealogy of techniques of the self. He sees it as a moment of "fairly profound reorganization" of technologies of the self (see *The Hermeneutics of the Subject*, 50–51).

[223] Foucault, *The Hermeneutics of the Subject*, 58.

[224] Foucault, *The Hermeneutics of the Subject*, 59.

"[*parrhēsia*] is speech that is equivalent to commitment, to a bond, and which establishes a certain pact between the subject of enunciation and the subject of conduct. The subject who speaks commits himself. At the very moment he says 'I speak the truth,' he commits himself to do what he says and to be the subject of conduct who conforms in every respect to the truth he expresses. It is in virtue of this that there can be no teaching of the truth without an *exemplum*. There can be no teaching of the truth without the person who speaks the truth being the example of this truth, and this is also why the individual relationship is necessary..."[225]

Foucault indicates that slowly, throughout Greek, Hellenistic and Roman history, the care of the self slowly separates from the erotic relationship.[226] In addition, for Hellenistic writers, care of the self becomes the occupation of a life time. Foucault describes it as a "form of life," no longer just "a brief preparation for life."[227] The relationships formed with the master are therefore often relationships that span a lifetime. If it is possible to practice the care of the self in schools and with private counselors, other forms of guidance are put into place, which are less formal. These relationships can be familial, or involve a protective aspect, but they can also be a friendship bond between two persons of similar age, status and culture.[228] In this case, the master in the care of the self relationship can be anybody. One does not need any specific qualifications to become involved in a care of the self relationship with someone else.[229] In fact, Foucault argues that the only requirement in order to become involved in a relationship of care of the self is the willingness to practice *parrhēsia* and to lead the other towards a practice of truth-telling.

In this truth-telling practice, the subject of the care of the self does not need to tell the truth about himself – as will be the practice, Foucault notes, in Christian confession – rather, he needs to be able to speak the truth, to

---

[225] Foucault, *The Hermeneutics of the Subject*, 406.

[226] Foucault, *The Hermeneutics of the Subject*, 60.

[227] Foucault, "Course Summary," in *The Hermeneutics of the Subject*, 494.

[228] See Foucault, "Course Summary," in *The Hermeneutics of the Subject*, 497.

[229] See Foucault, *Le courage de la vérité*, 7: "Cet autre si nécessaire pour que je puisse dire le vrai sur moi-même, cet autre dans la culture antique peut être un philosophe de profession, mais aussi n'importe qui." Foucault contrasts this "blurry" figure, who has no particular status or diplomas, with the more institutionalized versions known in our contemporary society: confessor, or counselor, doctor, psychiatrist, psychologist, psychoanalyst (see *Le courage de la vérité*, 7). For him, the study of *parrhēsia* and of the figure of the parrhesiast is like a prehistory of the practices that are created later around religion, medicine, psychiatry, psychology and psychoanalysis: "L'étude de la *parrêsia* et du *parrêsiastês* dans la culture de soi au cours de l'Antiquité est évidemment une sorte de préhistoire de ces pratiques qui se sont organisées et développées par la suite autour de quelques couples célèbres: le pénitent et son confesseur, le dirigé et le directeur de conscience, le malade et son psychiatre, le patient et le psychanalyste. C'est bien cette préhistoire, en un sens, que j'ai essayé d'[écrire]." (see *Le courage de la vérité*, 9)

inhabit the truth which the *parrhēsiast* is trying to transmit to him or her.[230] Because of that purpose, the relationship with the other in the care of the self is characterized by the need for the *parrhēsiast* to let the other become the subject of his own truth-telling. Through the master's *parrhēsia*, the disciple can appropriate the truth discourse and become his own "subject of veridiction."[231] If the discourse of the master is truly marked by *parrhēsia*, it becomes a discourse that "the disciple's subjectivity can appropriate and by which, by appropriating it, the disciple can reach his own objective, namely himself."[232] The final purpose of *parrhēsia* is to free the person to whom one is speaking, so that this person can enter in his or her own relationship to truth and constitute him or herself as a true subject: "it is insofar as the other has given, has conveyed a true discourse to the person to whom he speaks, that this person, internalizing and subjectivizing this true discourse, can then leave the relationship with the other person."[233] The role of truth, and truth-telling, is to seal "the autonomy of the person who received the speech from the person who uttered it."[234] For Foucault, through *parrhēsia*, one constitutes free subjects, armed with a truth that will enable them to act ethically.

Ethics of the Self in Christianity

One of the driving forces in the two last volumes of the *History of Sexuality* lies in Foucault's intent to contrast classical and Hellenistic ethics of the self with Christian ethics of the self. As I have already noted, Foucault insists that, if the moral precepts remain remarkably similar throughout the periods he chooses to examine, the relationship to the self is rather different. For him, the modality of the relation to the self in Christianity is characterized by a hermeneutics of desire, whose ultimate purpose is to renounce the self in the endless decipherment of its desires. Even though Foucault died before being able to publish the fourth volume of *History of Sexuality* – the Christian book as he jokingly calls it in an interview[235] –

---

[230] See Foucault, *The Hermeneutics of the Subject*, 365: "And I think that one of the most remarkable features of the practice of the self in this period is that the subject must become a subject of truth. He must be concerned with true discourse. He must therefore carry out a subjectivation that begins with listening to the true discourses proposed to him. He must therefore become the subject of truth: he himself must be able to say the truth and he must be able to say it to himself. In no way is it necessary or indispensable that he tell the truth about himself."

[231] Foucault, *The Hermeneutics of the Subject*, 368.

[232] See Foucault, *The Hermeneutics of the Subject*, 368.

[233] Foucault, *The Hermeneutics of the Subject*, 379.

[234] Foucault, *The Hermeneutics of the Subject*, 379.

[235] Foucault, "On the Genealogy of Ethics," 358: "In the Christian book – I mean the book about Christianity! – I try to show that all this ethics has changed."

certain elements of his reflections on Christianity are already present in volumes two and three of *History of Sexuality* and in a number of articles and interviews.[236]

In this context, I am interested in two questions. First, I would like to reflect on what is at stake for Foucault in the opposition he draws between Christianity and Hellenistic thought. This opposition mirrors the 19th century debate in biblical studies concerning the New Testament's relationship to Hellenistic philosophy, a debate mentioned by Foucault at the end of *The Care of the Self*.[237] Second, I want to consider the seeming elision of Paul by Foucault in relationship to that moment. It seems that Paul could function as a helpful link between Hellenistic morals and later Christianity, yet Foucault does not make use of the apostle. I want to take this into account briefly.

When Foucault talks about Christianity, as Moxnes remarks, his presentation is "surprisingly static."[238] Christianity seems to include a large historical period and lumps together Christian thought in the first centuries and in the twentieth century. It is presented as a religion strongly marked by confession, penance and the belief and obedience in a set of laws.[239] The opposition of Christianity and antiquity can be summarized by this statement: "From Antiquity to Christianity, we pass from a morality that was essentially a search for personal ethics to a morality as obedience to a system of rules."[240] Even if this statement is nuanced in Foucault's more complete analyses of the relationship between Christianity and antiquity, he does see Christianity as introducing a major shift in the ethics of the self, particularly in one's relationship to one's self. For Foucault, the purpose of Christian ethics is, once one has told the truth about one's self

---

[236] Moxnes makes the same observation in his article. See "Asceticism and Christian Identity in Antiquity," 11.

[237] See Foucault, *History of Sexuality vol. 3*, 236–237. I am thankful to Dr. Ward Blanton at the University of Glasgow for bringing this to my attention.

[238] See Moxnes, "Asceticism and Christian Identity in Antiquity," 15. It is difficult to pinpoint what "Christianity" historically represents for Foucault. As Moxnes notes, Foucault's sources for his study of Christianity were limited which might have led to a simplified presentation of Christianity in contrast with antiquity. See Moxnes, "Asceticism and Christian Identity in Antiquity," 16: "One reason for this simplified position may be that Foucault's own studies of Christian sources were limited to a few authors in late antiquity (Cassian and Augustine) and the mediaeval period (in particular penitence handbooks)."

[239] See Michel Foucault, "Technologies of the Self," in Rabinow, *Ethics: Subjectivity and Truth*, 223–251, here 242–243.

[240] Michel Foucault, "An Aesthetics of Existence," in *Politics, Philosophy, Culture: Interviews and other Writings of Michel Foucault, 1977–1984* (ed. L. D. Kritzman; New York: Routledge, 1998), 47–56, here 49.

through confession and later through penance, to renounce that self.[241] Foucault sees that purpose as being in strong contrast with antiquity. However, Foucault's presentation of Christianity, and especially early Christianity, as characterized by an ethics of obedience to a set of rules can be called into question. As Moxnes remarks, "Foucault's thesis that Greek ethics was a search for personal morals, whereas Christian ethics consisted in obedience towards a set of rules, does not seem to be well founded."[242]

Regardless of the correctness of Foucault's views on Christian ethics and on the relationship between Christianity and antiquity, I am more interested in seeing what is at stake for Foucault in this particular reconstruction of the genealogy of morals and why he is eager to maintain a form of discontinuity between the Greeks and the Christians.[243] The conclusion to *The Care of the Self* is particularly interesting in that regard. In these final pages, Foucault lingers on the relationship between Hellenistic philosophy and early Christianity. He asks whether one has to recognize in the ethics of the Hellenistic philosophers "the lineaments of a future ethics, the ethics that one will find in Christianity."[244] He recognizes the history of the problem and refers to the debates in biblical studies about the relationship between the Stoics in particular and the New Testament writers. In this debate, Foucault mentions that "the participants granted, in a relatively confused way, three presuppositions." First, Foucault argues that the debaters recognized that the "essential component of an ethics is to be sought in the code elements it contains." Second, the continuity between Christianity and Hellenistic morals is located in its severe precepts. This austerity represents "an almost complete break with the previous tradition,"[245] as it was transmitted by classical authors. Finally, the comparison between Christianity and certain philosophers of antiquity is best done in terms of "loftiness and purity."[246]

Foucault, however, is dissatisfied with this state of affair and proceeds to deconstruct it, in order to reconfigure the relationships between classical antiquity, Hellenistic philosophy and Christianity. On a general level, his

---

[241] See Foucault, "On the Genealogy of Ethics," 362.

[242] Moxnes, "Asceticism and Christian Identity in Antiquity," 16.

[243] For that matter, the same is true of Foucault's presentation of ancient and Hellenistic philosophy. It is not so important to know whether Foucault is right or not in his presentation, rather, it matters to see why he constructs both systems in the way he does.

[244] Foucault, *History of Sexuality vol. 3*, 235. In the same sentence, he describes the Christian ethics in these – rather unflattering – terms: "the ethics that one will find in Christianity, when the sexual act itself will be considered an evil, when it will no longer be granted legitimacy except within the conjugal relationship, and when the love of boys will be condemned as unnatural."

[245] For these three last quotes, see Foucault, *History of Sexuality vol. 3*, 236.

[246] Foucault, *History of Sexuality vol. 3*, 237.

reconfiguration – as I have shown – insists on the fact that, if there is continuity in the domain of the moral rules,[247] there is however discontinuity at the level of ethics, in the relationship one has with one's self when one constitutes oneself as an ethical subject. Foucault starts by deconstructing the argument that the austerity of Hellenistic philosophy and Christianity can be contrasted with a so-called libertinism of classical antiquity. For him, the precepts of classical antiquity are no less demanding than the rules of Hellenistic philosophy or Christianity.[248] Thus, for Foucault, it is necessary to abandon the supposed contrast between classical authors and Hellenistic philosophers. The break in this continuity is related to the "development of an art of existence dominated by self-preoccupation,"[249] not to a modification of the moral codes. But Foucault also remarks that the focus on moral codes constructs a deceptive continuity between classical antiquity, Hellenistic philosophy and Christianity. The moral codes might be similar, but they "derive from a profoundly altered ethics and from a different way of constituting oneself as the ethical subject of one's sexual behavior."[250]

---

[247] See Foucault, "On the Genealogy of Ethics," 361: "... we can see that in this activity of the self on itself, the ancients developed a whole series of austerity practices that the Christians later directly borrowed from them. So we see that this activity became linked to a certain sexual austerity which was subsumed directly into the Christian ethic. We are not talking about a moral rupture between tolerant antiquity and austere Christianity."

[248] Foucault, *History of Sexuality vol. 3*, 237: "One has to bear in mind, first, that the principles of sexual austerity were not defined for the first time in the philosophy of the imperial epoch. We have encountered in Greek thought of the fourth century B.C. formulations that were not much less demanding."

[249] Foucault, *History of Sexuality vol. 3*, 238.

[250] Foucault, *History of Sexuality vol. 3*, 240. Foucault reaches a very similar conclusion at the end of the second volume of *History of Sexuality vol. 2*, 249: "... It is important to recognize that the principle of a rigorous and diligently practiced sexual moderation is a precept that does not date either from Christian times, obviously, or from late antiquity, or even from the rigorist movements – such as were associated with the Stoics, for example – of the Hellenistic and Roman age. As early as the fourth century [BCE], one finds very clearly formulated the idea that sexual activity is sufficiently hazardous and costly in itself, and sufficiently linked to the loss of the vital substance, to require a meticulous economy that would discourage unnecessary indulgence." and 253–254: "Taking a very schematic, bird's eye view of the history of this ethics and its transformation over a long period of time, one notes first of all a shift of emphasis... But there was also a 'practical' unification that recentered the different arts of existence around the decipherment of the self, purification procedures, and struggles against concupiscence. So that what was now at the core of the problematization of sexual conduct was no longer pleasure and the aesthetics of its use, but desire and its purifying hermeneutics. This change was the result of a whole series of transformations. We have evidence of the beginnings of these transformations, even before the development of Christianity, in the reflection of the moralists, philosophers, and doctors of the first two centuries of our

I want to think about the reasons behind Foucault's support of the desire to keep Hellenistic philosophy and Christianity separate, at least in their constitution of an ethical subject. In part, as I have already mentioned, it stems from his interest in reconstructing the genealogy of the modern self. For that purpose, Foucault does not need – indeed, he does not want – to reflect accurate scholarship, whether it be about the biblical texts or about early Christian writers. Rather, his use of the Church fathers in particular allows him to construct his own version of Christianity, so as to be able to deconstruct the traditional reading of the relationships between Hellenistic philosophy and early Christianity, and present a new understanding of these relationships focused more clearly on the constitution of an ethical subject. In this case, as in many places in Foucault's work, actual historical facts do not matter as much as the elaboration of a plausible alternative way of seeing history. The experience of this history is more important than the historically verifiable findings.[251]

In addition, in this case, I suspect that Foucault's own use of the sources has to do with his attempt to provide a space of resistance inside ethics, using the Greeks as a starting point for his creation of an ethics not based on law but understood as an art of existence. Foucault insists that the Greeks do not offer an alternative, or a ready-made solution to our own ethical difficulties. I do not think he wants to simply transpose the ethics of the Greek to his time period in order to liberate human kind from an ethics based on law or religion, but the Greeks do allow him to think about ethics in a different manner.[252] Remaining faithful to his attempt to do a genealogy of ethics, the return to the Greeks emphasizes the constructed aspect of a Christian system based on endless decipherment of desires and self-renunciation. From that perspective, the contrast that Foucault constructs between the Greek ethics and the Christian ethics allow him to underline the malleability of ethics, and therefore the possibility of change. In particular, he can show that a hermeneutics of desire is not necessary to the construction of an ethical system. From thereon, he can fight for a space of resistance that would reclaim the value of existence understood as work of art. The contrast between Hellenistic philosophy and Christianity

---

era." The distinction between Hellenistic philosophy and Christianity will be marked more strongly in *The Care of the Self*.

[251] See Foucault, "Interview with Michel Foucault," 243.

[252] See Foucault, "On the Genealogy of Ethics," 343. See also Moxnes, "Asceticism and Christian Identity in Antiquity," 28: "[Foucault] did not see the actual forms of life in antiquity, with subordination of women and slaves, as an ideal for modern society. But he was concerned to identify the forces and structures that determined the formation of moral discourses, and he found in the 'search for a personal ethics' a form of moral work that he apparently regarded as an ideal also for today."

allows him to highlight the importance of relation to self in the constitution of an ethical identity.

I would like to argue that this might also explain his lack of engagement with the figure of Paul. It is evidently pretty futile to speculate on the reasons behind Foucault's elision of Paul in his discussion of Christianity, but I do find it surprising that Foucault never engages Paul in his own writing.[253] It seems Paul would have fitted very well as one stop in Foucault's discussion of the evolution of ethics from Hellenistic philosophy to Christianity. He could be the missing link between Hellenistic ethics and a Christian morality based on law. Perhaps this is precisely one of the reasons why Paul does not present any interest for Foucault. Indeed, I tried to show that Paul, particularly in his letter to the Romans – but Moxnes shows that the same is true for ethical discussions in Corinthians – does not provide his readers with a body of rules and precepts.[254] Rather Paul is preoccupied with equipping his addressees with the identity and the self-understanding that will help them become ethical subjects. As Moxnes notes, "[f]or Paul, the moral obligation was not an external law but a question of identity."[255] It is the identity given to them through the dying with Christ, an identity which brings about the bodily union with Christ, which has to determine how Paul's addressees use their bodies and their selves.[256] If one understands Paul in this manner, then he does not fit easily in the genealogy of ethics that Foucault reconstructs in his late works and which describes Christian ethics as focused mainly on sets of rules.

However, when Foucault identifies the *telos* of Christian ethics as self-renunciation, he throws a new light on a central category for Christian identity, one upon which Moxnes also insists, the bodily participation of the Christ believer in Christ. Moxnes writes that "Foucault does not seem to grasp the importance of divine presence in the Christians' lives for their understanding of identity."[257] In contrast, I believe that Foucault's analyses of self-renunciation do take into account the concept of the divine presence in Christians. In fact, I think Foucault's discussions of self-renunciation

---

[253] Foucault does mention Paul very briefly at the end of his 1984 lectures at the Collège de France, see *Le courage de la vérité*, 301, where he discusses the way in which *parrhēsia* is used in the New Testament.

[254] Indeed, he seems comfortable – to a certain degree – with the slogan "All things are lawful." (1 Cor 10:23)

[255] Moxnes, "Asceticism and Christian Identity in Antiquity," 25.

[256] See Moxnes, "Asceticism and Christian Identity in Antiquity," 23–24: "… the primary determination of the male body is that it is a member of Christ's body. This is not understood intellectually, in terms of world-view, but in terms of an inclusion into another corporeal existence. And it is this participation in Christ's body that Paul wants his readers to recognize as the main determining factor of their identity."

[257] Moxnes, "Asceticism and Christian Identity in Antiquity," 16.

can be used to critically point out the potential dangers attached to the importance of the concept of bodily participation in Christ for the construction of Christian identity. In Foucault's understanding, the participation in Christ amounts to returning to the concept of an essence given to the subject, the poisonous gift of an identity to which one needs to remain faithful – a subjection, if you will, which echoes the language of slavery predominant in Romans. I will get back to this in my last chapter. In light of Foucault's discussion of ethics, it seems appropriate to offer some comments on the spaces of resistance that Foucault carves in his presentation.

Spaces of Resistance in Ethics
When reflecting upon his career towards the end of his life, Foucault describes his work as centered on the question of the subject; his books represent efforts to reflect on the various ways the individual can be constituted as subject.[258] I see his work on ethics as the positive side of this reflection on the constitution of the subject. It does not present a solution, nor endorse a model to follow in order to produce a free responsible subject. Foucault intends to stay away from the role of the intellectual as a prescriber of solutions.[259] However, his works on the self delineates a task that anyone can take up on one's own. In the interview in which Foucault traces and, to some degree, retells, the story of what his work has been about, he wonders why everyone's life could not become a work of art.[260] In this longing for a life lived as a work of art, I believe one can hear the echo of the reflections Foucault developed in dialogue with his readings of Nietzsche, Bataille and Blanchot. Almost five years earlier,[261] Foucault indicated the importance of these writers in the conception of his own thought and in finding ways to embody the task he once defined as the work "to refuse what we are."[262] Foucault rejects prescriptions that indicate what needs to be done, step by step. Rather, he thinks about a new idea of the subject, and his work with the Greeks gives the starting impulse for that thinking.[263] This new idea of the subject should not be understood as the

---

[258] See Foucault, "Afterword: The Subject and Power," 208 and 209.

[259] This theme is constant in his interviews when asked about the role of the intellectual. See for example, Foucault, "Non au sexe roi," 3:268. See also, Foucault, "Truth and Power," 126.

[260] See Foucault, "On the Genealogy of Ethics," 350.

[261] See Foucault, "Interview with Michel Foucault," 239–297. See the discussion of the philosophical engagement of the subject in chapter 1.

[262] See Foucault, "Afterword: The Subject and Power," 216.

[263] See Gros, "Course Context," in Foucault, *The Hermeneutics of the Subject*, 527: "Foucault is far from considering these practices of the self as a philosophical fashion; they are rather the spearhead of a new idea of the subject, far from transcendental constitutions and moral foundations." See also what Foucault says in "On the Genealogy of

sudden discovery of a free subject, "a free subject creating itself in the ahistorical ether of a pure self-constitution,"[264] as if Foucault suddenly cancels the years he spent working on the concept of power and its ramifications.

Rather, technologies of the self underline the fact that the subject constitutes its relationship to itself in a historical setting, in which power relationships also play a role: "now, precisely what constitute the subject in a determinate relation to himself are historically identifiable techniques of the self, which combine with historically datable techniques of domination."[265] The process of the constitution of the subject happens in worlds marked by various techniques of subjection; it fits itself inside the techniques of domination current around it. For Foucault, because of that historicity, and because of the interconnectedness with techniques of domination, "the subject is not tied to his truth according to a transcendental necessity or inevitable destiny."[266] Rather, the task of creating one's self anew is a daily challenge that is never finished, or fixed in an essence. In a sense, it corresponds to the genealogical enterprise, which seeks to always call into question the naturalness and necessity of things. In the creation of the subject, nothing is taken for granted. Because the subject is always enmeshed in relationships of power and anchored historically, Foucault underlines the fragility of the subject, and the constant efforts it takes to avoid the petrifaction of the subject in an identity to which it feels necessarily attached and bound.

Foucault has often been criticized for describing the task of the subject as one akin to an art of existence, to the creation of an aesthetics of existence. It carries with it the danger of narcissism or dandyism, of an empty and endless quest for a subject perpetually seeking beauty in transgression.[267] However, Foucault's reflections on ethics do not prescribe a vacu-

---

Ethics," 362: "We have hardly any remnant of the idea in our society that the principal work of art which one has to take care of, the main area to which one must apply aesthetic values, is oneself, one's life, one's existence. We find this in the Renaissance, but in a slightly academic form, and yet again in 19th century dandyism, but those were only episodes."

[264] See Gros, "Course Context," in Foucault, *The Hermeneutics of the Subject*, 525. As Gros notes as well, this is precisely what Foucault reproached to Sartre.

[265] Gros, "Course Context," in Foucault, *The Hermeneutics of the Subject*, 526.

[266] See Gros, "Course Context," in Foucault, *The Hermeneutics of the Subject*, 526.

[267] See Gros, "Course Context," in Foucault, *The Hermeneutics of the Subject*, 530: "It has been said, here and there, that in the face of the collapse of values, Foucault, in appealing to the Greeks, gave in to the narcissistic temptation. That he proposed an 'aesthetics of existence' as an alternative ethic, indicating to each the path to personal fulfillment through a stylization of life, as if halting thought, fixed at the 'aesthetic stage' with all its narcissistic avatars, could disguise the loss of meaning. Or else it is said that Foucault's morality consists in a call to systematic transgression, or in the cult of a cher-

ous moral of aesthetics. On the contrary, even though Foucault recognizes his debt to a form of dandyism[268] (through the figure of Baudelaire) and to the potential of transgression (through Blanchot and Bataille), I believe that in constructing his ethical reflections he avoids the dangers of narcissism and of empty transgression.

First, it is important to take into account Foucault's reflections on the concept of limit when he elaborates his ethos. In "What is Enlightenment?," he defines philosophical ethos as a *limit-attitude*.[269] The task is not one of rejection, but it is one of standing at the frontiers, and "analyzing and reflecting upon limits."[270] His genealogical method in particular allows thinking of limits and of transgression of limits in a careful and nuanced way. Genealogy identifies the contingency behind what seems established and thus gives the possibility to call into question that contingency: "This critique will be genealogical in the sense that it will not deduce from the form of what we are what it is impossible for us to do and to know; but it will separate out, from the contingency that has made us what we are, the possibility of no longer being, doing, or thinking what we are, do, or

---

ished marginality. These generalizations are facile, excessive, but above all wrong, and in a way the whole of the 1982 course is constructed in opposition to these unfounded criticisms. Foucault is neither Baudelaire nor Bataille. There is neither a dandyism of singularity nor a lyricism of transgression in these final texts." While I agree with Gros's analysis, I suspect Foucault's relationship to transgression is complicated. I believe that the concept of transgression might play a fundamental role in helping Foucault criticize any system that establishes itself and subjects the individual to him or herself. See Michel Foucault, "A Preface to Transgression," in *Bataille: A Critical Reader* (ed. F. Botting and S. Wilson; Oxford: Blackwell Publishers, 1998), 24–40. First published in English in *Language, Counter-Memory, Practice* (ed. D. F. Bouchard; Ithaca: Cornell University Press, 1977), 29–52.

[268] I do not think Foucault develops a form of dandyism in the commonly accepted meaning of the term (as the attitude of one concerned with appearances, elegance, and critical of the masses). However, dandyism as defined by Baudelaire plays an important role in Foucault's understanding of life as a material for art. See Foucault, "What is Enlightenment?" 41–42: "To be modern is not to accept oneself as one is in the flux of the passing moments; it is to take oneself as object of a complex and difficult elaboration: what Baudelaire, in the vocabulary of his day, calls *dandysme*. Here I shall not recall in detail the well-known passages on 'vulgar, earthly, vile nature'; on man's indispensable revolt against himself; on the 'doctrine of elegance' which imposes 'upon its ambitious and humble disciples' a discipline more despotic than the most terrible religions; the pages, finally, on the asceticism of the dandy who makes of his body, his behavior, his feelings and his passions, his very existence, a work of art. Modern man, for Baudelaire, is not the man who goes off to discover himself, his secrets and his hidden truth; he is the man who tries to invent himself. This modernity does not 'liberate man in his own being'; it compels him to face the task of producing himself." This understanding of dandyism has much influence on Foucault's own understanding of the ethical task.

[269] Foucault, "What is Enlightenment?" 45.

[270] Foucault, "What is Enlightenment?" 45.

think."[271] Genealogy shows that things are contingent for a reason, but this reason is not necessity. Once one challenges that necessity, it is possible to show the intelligibility of the contingency, "and deny its necessity."[272] The next step is to realize that "what exists is far from filling all possible spaces."[273] Thus, the genealogical critique "transform[s] the critique conducted in the form of necessary limitation into a practical critique that takes the form of a possible crossing-over [*franchissement*]."[274]

For Foucault, what is at stake is not just the rejection of limits, the perpetual critique of limits and their endless transgression in a rebellious attitude; rather, it is also about giving a positive content to the transgression, in the notion of *franchissement* of limit. Foucault explains this *franchissement* as an experimental attitude, marked by immanence and inscribed in history: "I shall thus characterize the philosophical ethos appropriate to the critical ontology of ourselves as a historico-practical test of the limits we may go beyond, and thus a work carried out by ourselves upon ourselves as free beings."[275] Foucault insists that this work is precisely not about (re)discovering who one is, beyond and perhaps against the limits of necessity. It has to be a work of invention and creativity. If it is simply seen as the needs of recovering something that has been lost, or in liberating human beings from repressive forces, it "runs the risk of falling back on the idea that there exists a human nature or base that, as a consequence of certain historical, economic, and social processes, has been concealed, alienated, or imprisoned in and by mechanisms of repression."[276]

Liberation is not sufficient to implement "practices of freedom." Practices of freedom can only be the result of creativity and invention and are also the only freedom-producing strategies that can function inside of relationships of power. For Foucault, it is illusory to hope that power relationships will be completely suppressed – or should be completely suppressed – rather, practices of freedom give one the rules of the game, "the ethos, the practice of the self, that will allow us to play these games of power with as little domination as possible."[277] Thus, practices of freedom cannot

---

[271] Foucault, "What is Enlightenment?"46.

[272] See Michel Foucault, "Friendship as a Way of Life," in Rabinow, *Ethics: Subjectivity and Truth*, 135–140, here 140. This interview was published in April 1981, in the French magazine *Gai Pied*. It is republished as "De l'amitié comme mode de vie," in *Dits et écrits*, 4:163–167.

[273] See Foucault, "Friendship as a Way of Life," 140.

[274] Foucault, "What is Enlightenment?" 45.

[275] Foucault, "What is Enlightenment?" 47. I think that here the influence of Baudelaire's dandy is clear.

[276] Foucault, "The Ethics of the Concern for Self," 282.

[277] Foucault, "The Ethics of the Concern for Self," 298. In that understanding, practices of freedom could be the heirs to the punctual and very concrete strategies of resistance

be given a program, a predetermined content which would dictate for all the right way to become oneself and to behave ethically. They can only function as a personal choice; and it is everyone's responsibility, in a constant daily practice, to give a positive content to the *franchissement* of limit.

Foucault discusses a concrete example of this creative work of the self on the self through his reflections on the manner in which homosexuality invents, or should invent, new relationships. In discussing homosexuality, Foucault brings up the notion of asceticism, and defines it in terms resounding with echoes of his work on the Greeks: "it's the work that one performs on oneself in order to transform oneself or make the self appear which, happily, one never attains."[278] For Foucault, homosexuality, understood as the use of one's sexuality to create new forms of relationships, can be a form of ascesis "that would make us work on ourselves and invent– I do not say discover – a manner of being that is still improbable."[279] Homosexuality should be understood as a mode of life, and, as a mode of life, it "can yield intense relations not resembling those that are institutionalized."[280] In this case, being gay is not so much about one's sexuality, than about being able to see things differently, and being willing to invent and create new ways of being and of relating to other persons. Foucault writes: "Homosexuality is a historic occasion to reopen affective and relational virtualities, not so much through the intrinsic qualities of the homosexual but because the 'slantwise' position of the latter, as it were, the diagonal lines he can lay out in the social fabric allow these virtualities to come to light."[281]

For an ethics in which the purpose is to make one's life a creation, homosexuality is an opportunity to invent new relationships, to create slanted ways of understanding reality and history, and to queer one's perspective on the world. But this creation is each individual's responsibility. One cannot repeat enough that this creation cannot be about following precepts and a program, even a program of perpetual rejection or transgression.

---

that Foucault was advocating in his work on power. I think, however, that practices of freedom might include the dimension of the relationship to oneself more predominantly than strategies of resistance.

[278] Foucault, "Friendship as a Way of Life," 137.
[279] Foucault, "Friendship as a Way of Life," 137.
[280] Foucault, "Friendship as a Way of Life," 138.
[281] Foucault, "Friendship as a Way of Life," 138.

For each person, it is a practical embodiment of the theoretical content of genealogy, a form of life that calls into question contingencies, invents new forms of life, and imagines unseen possibilities.[282] Thus, Foucault's work of destruction, as he states, is not for destruction's sake, but its purpose is truly to make room for passages and to offer opportunities to create something new.[283]

B. Categories of the Self in Foucault

Central to Foucault's understanding of philosophy and of his role as an intellectual – for lack of a better term – is the conviction that it is futile to try to replace a certitude by another. As a corollary, Foucault is deeply wary with injunctions to find an identity and with demands to constantly break this identity. Both feel abusive because they assume in advance what one needs to be. Rabinow quotes an excerpt of "For an Ethics of Discomfort," where Foucault writes: "The demand [*exigence*] for an identity and the injunction to break that identity, both feel, in the same way, abusive."[284] For Rabinow, "such demands are abusive because they assume in advance what one is, what one must do, what one always must be closed to, which side one must be on. [Foucault] sought not so much to resist as to evade this installed dichotomy."[285] Foucault insists on the fact that each individual has his or her own way of changing: "my way of being no longer the same is, by definition, the most singular part of what I am."[286]

Foucault therefore does not provide his readers with an anthropology or with an ethical system which could orient them. He focuses on experiences and on specific transformations, and quoting Merleau-Ponty approvingly, he defines the task of philosophy in the following manner: "never to consent to being completely comfortable with one's own presuppositions."[287] This task of philosophy can only be taken up individually, through a prac-

---

[282] Paul Rabinow makes a similar remark: "The challenge is not to replace one certitude (*évidence*) with another but to cultivate an attention to the conditions under which things become 'evident,' ceasing to be objects of our attention and therefore seemingly fixed, necessary and unchangeable." (See Paul Rabinow, Introduction to *Ethics: Subjectivity and Truth* [ed. P. Rabinow], xi–xlii, here xix.)

[283] See Foucault, "Je suis un artificier," 92.

[284] Published in a slightly different translation in Faubion, *Power: Essential Works of Foucault*, 443–448, here 444: "The insistence on identity and the injunction to make a break both feel like impositions, and in the same way." I quote Rabinow's translation in Rabinow, "Introduction," in Rabinow, *Ethics. Subjectivity and Truth*, xix.

[285] See Rabinow, "Introduction," in Rabinow, *Ethics: Subjectivity and Truth*, xix.

[286] Foucault, "For an Ethics of Discomfort," 444.

[287] See Foucault, "For an Ethics of Discomfort," 448.

tice. Philosophy, for Foucault, is "a practice and an ethos, a state or condition of character, not detached observation and legislation."[288] I believe that it is in this practice that one is best able to reconstruct Foucault's categories of the self, as they appear in his ethics in particular.

1. Remarks About the Idem/Ipse Distinction and Foucault

Ricœur and Foucault, albeit contemporary, never really engaged in discussion with each other or with each other's works. It is not that they ignored each other, or were hostile towards each other. Rather it seems that they never were in position to have a true encounter, either in person or through their ideas.[289] At the level of their understanding of the subject, I am simply interested in remarking that the distinction between *idem* and *ipse* identity that I have successfully employed to talk about Paul's concept of the subject cannot be applied to Foucault's thought. In a way, it can simply not exist in Foucault's thought; it has no ground on which to stand because of two reasons in particular. First, the distinction between *idem* and *ipse* identity in Ricœur comes from a concern with permanence in time. One of the questions that matters to Ricœur in his construction of the *idem/ipse* distinction concerns the way an individual can remain the same despite the

---

[288] Rabinow, "Introduction," in Rabinow, *Ethics: Subjectivity and Truth*, xx.

[289] Ricœur expresses reservations about Foucault's thought, in particular in the findings of *The Order of Things* (See Paul Ricœur, *La critique et la conviction: Entretien avec François Azouvi et Marc de Launay* [Paris: Calmann-Lévy, 1995], 122–123). He also indicates that he discusses *The Archaeology of Knowledge* in his own *Temps et récit vol. 3: Le temps raconté* (3 vols.; Paris: Seuil, 1983–1985). Finally, he recognizes that a true encounter between him and Foucault never took place: "C'est dans la mesure où Foucault s'est éloigné de lui-même, avec ses deux derniers livres, que je me suis senti plus proche de lui: mais sans avoir l'occasion de le lui dire. C'est une rencontre qui n'a pas eu lieu. Certainement que lui n'en attendait rien, et moi j'étais sur des chemins où je le rencontrais peu, sinon par des intersections très ponctuelles." (See Ricœur, *La critique et la conviction*, 123) A little bit later in the interview, he elaborates on the reasons behind the fact that he did not engage some authors and indicates that he can only speak about writers with whom he can experience productive conflicts (See Ricœur, *La critique et la conviction*, 124: "De façon plus générale, je ne parle que des auteurs que je peux accompagner assez loin pour pouvoir dire que la séparation d'avec eux m'est coûteuse, mais qu'elle m'est aussi profitable parce que je suis passé par l'école de leur adversité. Ceux avec lesquels je n'ai pas ce rapport de conflictualité productive, je n'en parle pas. Ce qui explique nombre de mes silences, qui ne sont ni d'ignorance, ni de mépris, ni d'hostilité; ils viennent seulement de ce que je ne *rencontre* pas ces auteurs … ils sont là où je ne passe pas."). It seems that Foucault might precisely have stood somewhere where Ricœur did not walk. Foucault does not discuss Ricœur at length either. He mentions his name in "Structuralism and Post-Structuralism," in *Aesthetics, Method, and Epistemology: Essential Works of Foucault* (ed. J. D. Faubion; vol. 2 of Rabinow, *Essential Works of Foucault, 1954–1984*), 433–458, here 436.

passing of time. However, Foucault's major concern with the self is marked by the need for change, the need for creating new forms of being and acting. In such a perspective, permanence in time has very little importance.

Second, Ricœur notes that in the concept of *ipse* identity, the individual can show some form of resistance to change through the affirmation "Here I am!" The ethical affirmation made in the promise provides a core to the person, and faithfulness to that promise is indispensable in the construction of the person's identity. In contrast, Foucault rejects the notion of a core identity in the person. In agreement with his conviction that the task of the self is to constantly re-invent itself, Foucault argues that an identity is never given to the self, thus there is no possibility for authenticity or for faithfulness to something previously received. The subject is either constituted by power or knowledge, and in this case the individual needs to work towards resisting the subjection effected by power or knowledge, or the subject has the possibility to constitute itself, through various practices of the self, and ethical work. In this case, the task remains a perpetual self-creation, which never quite attains its goal. In such a conception, the notion of *ipse* identity, of a permanence in time attained through faithfulness to an engagement, has no place. This is not to say that Foucault abandons the question of how to behave towards others, of how to put into place relationships that are respectful of others, but the motivation behind his concern for others does not lie in the need to remain faithful to an identity pre-given in the act of promise.[290] The categories of the self in Foucault's work need to be reconfigured on his own terms.

2. Categories of the Self

The notion of the creation of the self as a work of art has traversed my presentation of Foucault's thought. The perpetual task of change and self-creation opens up spaces of resistance in many of the domains that Foucault analyzes. In the rejection of the notion of a subjected identity, it creates cracks in the hold of relationships of power. In challenging the necessity of some discursive constructions, it traces gaps in which a different genealogy can be assembled. When it looks at the subject, it calls for a constant work of transformation on the self. Change and inventiveness are constant categories in Foucault's description of one's task as a subject. In order to understand what this means for an understanding of the subject, I

---

[290] I do not believe that Ricœur simply proposes slavish respect of a promise. Faithfulness to one's engagement can also – and probably should – include creativity and inventiveness. But I do think that Foucault and Ricœur have a very different premise on which they then construct the tasks, responsibilities and possibilities of the ethical self.

propose to unpack the various dimensions of this notion of creation of the self through the concept of experience. Foucault places experience at the center of his work as a thinker:

What I think is never quite the same, because for me my books are experiences, in a sense, that I would like to be as full as possible. An experience is something that one comes out of transformed. If I had to write a book to communicate what I'm already thinking before I begin to write, I would never have the courage to begin. I write a book only because I still don't exactly know what to think about this thing I want so much to think about, so that the book transforms me and transforms what I think. Each book transforms what I was thinking when I was finishing the previous book. I am an experimenter and not a theorist. I call a theorist someone who constructs a general system, either deductive or analytical, and applies it to different fields in a uniform way. That isn't my case. I'm an experimenter in the sense that I write in order to change myself and in order not to think the same thing as before.[291]

The concept of experience is central to Foucault's work as a philosopher; and manifests itself foremost in the way he describes the task of thinking and writing. As the previous quote indicates, the purpose of writing for Foucault has nothing to do with sharing ready-made results, which would elaborate a system in the safety of which he could instruct his readers or his students. Rather, what is involved in creating a book, in the work of thinking, is constant change, a constant calling into question of what one believes. As Rabinow notes, "privileging experience over engagement makes it increasingly difficult to remain 'absolutely in accord with oneself,' for identities are defined by trajectories, not by position taking."[292] In the task of critical thought, the self is anchored in practices, in an active experience that challenges what seems necessary or evident, rather than in a "vantage point," whose purpose would be to appoint evidences.[293] Rather, experiences transform one's relationship with a particular topic.

When Foucault describes his work in *Madness and Civilization* or in *Discipline and Punish*, he insists that the books do no attempt to establish a "historical truth." These books play a game between the notion of experience, "something that one fabricates oneself, that doesn't exist before and will exist afterward," and "verifiable findings."[294] In this game, the books simultaneously use historical documents but also bring about an experience that has some bearing on the contemporary world in which one lives and the way in which one understands this world: "The book [here *Discipline and Punish*] makes use of true documents, but in such a way that through them it is possible not only to arrive at an establishment of truth but also to experience something that permits a change, a transformation of the rela-

---

[291] Foucault, "Interview with Michel Foucault," 239–240.

[292] Rabinow, "Introduction," in Rabinow, *Ethics: Subjectivity and Truth*, xix.

[293] Rabinow, "Introduction," in Rabinow, *Ethics: Subjectivity and Truth*, xix.

[294] For the three last quotes, see Foucault, "Interview with Michel Foucault," 245.

tionship we have with ourselves and with the world where, up to then, we had seen ourselves as being without problems – in short, a transformation of the relationship we have with our knowledge."[295] Each book can be seen as inaugurating or launching a new trajectory, in which the self has to loose and re-find itself. In this thought marked by experience, I aim to explore three categories, which construct a figure of the self as ever-changing: curiosity, invention and pleasure.

Curiosity

In the practice of a thought centered on experience and transformation, Foucault praises the notion of curiosity. In his introduction to *The Use of Pleasure*, Foucault mentions that curiosity is behind the major reorganization of *The History of Sexuality*. He writes: "As for what motivated me, it is quite simple; I would hope that in the eyes of some people it might be sufficient in itself. It was curiosity – the only kind of curiosity, in any case, that is worth acting upon with a degree of obstinacy: not the curiosity that seeks to assimilate what it is proper for one to know, but that which enables one to get free of oneself."[296] Curiosity is the motivation to see if one can think differently, if one dares to travel far away from what one knows and recognizes. Foucault admits that this form of curiosity may bring about an ironic result: "There is irony in those efforts one makes to alter one's way of looking at things, to change the boundaries of what one knows and to venture out a ways from there. Did mine actually result in a different way of thinking? Perhaps at most they made it possible to go back through what I was already thinking, to think it differently, and to see what I had done from a new vantage point and in clearer light. Sure of having travelled far, one finds that one is looking down on oneself from above. The journey rejuvenates things, and ages the relationship with oneself."[297] Curiosity is not a guarantee that entirely new things will be produced, but it is a guarantee that one will go through one's own thoughts and try to think them anew, thus at least changing one's relationship with oneself, a notion at the center of Foucault's understanding of the ethical subject. For Foucault, curiosity can be a tool to reconstruct the self and reconfigure knowledge. One more quote, taken from a 1980 anonymous interview with *Le Monde*, should make this clear:

Curiosity is a vice that has been stigmatized in turn by Christianity, by philosophy, and even by a certain conception of science. Curiosity is seen as a futility. However, I like the word; it suggests something quite different to me. It evokes 'care'; it evokes the care one takes of what exists and what might exist; a sharpened sense of reality, but one that

---

[295] Foucault, "Interview with Michel Foucault," 244.

[296] See Foucault, *History of Sexuality vol. 2*, 8.

[297] See Foucault, *History of Sexuality vol. 2*, 11.

is never immobilized before it; a readiness to find what surrounds us strange and odd; a certain determination to throw off familiar ways of thought and to look at the same things in a different way; a passion for seizing what is happening now and what is disappearing; a lack of respect for the traditional hierarchies of what is important and fundamental. I dream of a new age of curiosity. We have the technical means; the desire is there; there is an infinity of things to know; the people capable of doing such work exist.[298]

In the notion of care, one is reminded of Foucault's interest in the care of the self as practiced by the Greeks. Curiosity is not a futile waste of time; it represents a way to "care," not just about oneself, but about one's perception of the world. Once more, Foucault's reader is returned to a genealogical perspective on the world, a perspective that sees the functioning of power-relationships in established knowledges, and imagines new ways to envisage reality inside these power relationships. Curiosity stands behind the critical stance that Foucault puts into place in his writings. It is the condition necessary so that the work of deconstruction that grounds genealogy can take place. The subject as understood by Foucault is willing to gaze at the world in a slightly skewed perspective. The individual is always askance in the world, ready to challenge the order of things. Curiosity reflects this need for a queer perspective on the world. Curiosity is a way for the individual to embody a constant resistance to the immobilism and petrification embedded in power and in power relationships. In order for this bent perspective to never be disciplined and straightened out, the subject must practice this curiosity in perpetual movement.

The refusal of immobility is fundamental to Foucault's perception of the self, and to the task of this self. In the domain of thinking, eternal mobility implies that one can never consider that one has "arrived," or that one has finally reached the point where one can look back on one's work and feel that one's task is accomplished. On the contrary, the task of philosophy is "the critical work that thought brings to bear on itself."[299] This critical task is never over, and thus, one never attains a form of thought in which one can rest, and in which one could potentially distribute lessons to others. One is always *en route*, knowing neither the itinerary, nor the final goal. For Foucault, thought is characterized both by curiosity and constant movement. It traces the image of a subject deeply committed to questioning reality, knowledge and what is, intent to look for the unseen. The quest of the unseen cannot be done without invention.

---

[298] Michel Foucault, "The Masked Philosopher," in Rabinow, *Ethics. Subjectivity and Truth*, 321–328, here 325–326.

[299] Foucault, *History of Sexuality vol. 2*, 9. This definition is also completed by an answer of Foucault in the same anonymous interview with *Le Monde*: "The displacement and the transformation of frameworks of thinking, the changing of received values and all the work that has been done to think otherwise, to do something else, to become other that what one is – that, too, is philosophy." (See "The Masked Philosopher," 327)

Invention

I have repeatedly emphasized that Foucault insists on the necessity of *creating*, of *inventing* the self, not just discovering or re-discovering some secret identity that had been lost until now. In this perpetual invention of the self, Foucault sees the possibility of modeling one's life as a work of art, of creating an aesthetic experience out of one's life. In the discussion of spaces of resistance connected to ethics, I have argued that the aesthetics of life of which Foucault thinks is not narcissism, nor is it a gratuitous transgression of limits, for the sake of transgression. Rather, it is closely connected to Foucault's involvement in political action. Foucault did not believe in political programs and he saw the danger in practices of liberation that quickly turn into systems running the risk of fossilizing in apparatuses that subject the individual to a particular identity. A good part of his work is about identifying these systems, which not only create a certain amount of knowledge about a particular topic, but also constitute a subject around that knowledge and put into place systems of exclusion.[300]

In contrast to these systems, Foucault poses problems, seeing his books as gestures to invite reflection and to avoid simplistic and bureaucratic solutions. The problems need to be perceived as complex, and thus "through concrete questions, difficult cases, movements of rebellion, reflections, and testimonies, the legitimacy of a common creative action can also appear."[301] This action is marked by on the spot inventiveness, thus making the practice of resistance a messy business, which always needs to be begun anew again. It is not about philosophical programs, but about concrete and partial transformations: "I prefer the very specific transformations that have proved to be possible in the last twenty years in a certain number of areas which concern our ways of being and thinking, relations to authority, relations between the sexes, the way in which we perceive insanity or illness; I prefer even these partial transformations, which have been made in the correlation of historical analysis and the practical attitude, to the programs for a new man that the worst political systems have repeated throughout the twentieth century."[302] In this partial and practical work, the individual is responsible for thinking beyond her own limits, and in the work that she accomplishes on herself, she is able to create small spaces of resistance. For Foucault, this is not only a responsibility one has as a hu-

---

[300] This qualifies the work Foucault did on madness, on the punitive system and on discursive practices. In this work, Foucault tried to show "how the subject constituted itself, in one specific form or another, as a mad or healthy subject, as a delinquent or nondelinquent subject, through certain practices that were also games of truth, practices of power, and so on." (See Foucault, "The Ethics of the Concern for Self," 290)

[301] Foucault, "Interview with Michel Foucault," 288.

[302] Foucault, "What is Enlightenment?" 46–47

man being, it is the content of "the philosophical ethos appropriate to the critical ontology of ourselves."[303]

I believe that the notion of constant invention is Foucault's answer to the danger he perceives in political programs or philosophical systems that threaten to bind the individual to an identity she can then no longer escape. In contrast, Foucault might be said to embrace a sort of fluidity, a constant movement.[304] Experience is marked by invention, and functions as an appropriate category to implement change. If curiosity characterizes the critical work necessary for the practice of genealogy and deconstruction, invention marks the creative side of the deconstructive project. The deconstruction is not done in order to simply destroy. As I have argued, through the figure of the *artificier*, Foucault is eager to open up new ways for creating one's self and for implementing new relationships. It is not about destroying *per se*, it is about clearing space for new areas of creativity. For that project, invention is necessary. It characterizes the constructive side of Foucault's reflection.

In addition, through the category of invention, Foucault can position his understanding of the subject in relationship to power. For Foucault, power relationships are never completely absent of our world. In fact, they contribute to its proper functioning. With the notion of invention, Foucault is able to define a subject that needs to imagine ways of being and living inside relationships of power that, simultaneously, use these relationships of power in respectful manners, and can also envision a perpetual mutability in these relationships. Foucault is suspicious of the many ways in which power relationships can present themselves as necessary and unalterable, so much so that they always have the potential of becoming oppressive systems. In the face of such a danger, the subject, through invention, has the possibility – and the responsibility – of maintaining movement inside power relationships, ever modifying them, and ever resisting their potential

---

[303] See Foucault, "What is Enlightenment?" 47: "I shall thus characterize the philosophical ethos appropriate to the critical ontology of ourselves as a historico-practical test of the limits we may go beyond, and thus as work carried out by ourselves upon ourselves as free beings."

[304] The concept of fluidity is mentioned in a quote by Renée Green in Bhabha, *The Location of Culture*, 4: "I wanted to make shapes or set up situations that are kind of open... My work has a lot to do with a kind of fluidity, a movement back and forth, not making a claim to any specific or essential way of being." See also Vander Stichele and Penner, *Contextualizing Gender in Early Christian Discourse*, 23: "...people frequently have multiple identities that issue forth in a variety of performative acts and situations, and often these can interact with and shape one another. The point, then, is that identity itself (and gender, sex, and sexuality in particular) is not fixed – it is, rather, fluid. It can shift and morph throughout one individual's lifetime or even during the course of one day, depending on the different social contexts one inhabits."

immobilization in a system of oppression. The inventive subject supple-
ments liberation and ensures, through practices of freedom, that relationships of power remain flexible and susceptible to resistance.

Pleasure
Pleasure is not a very well defined category in Foucault's literary corpus.
It plays a role in the *History of Sexuality* as one of the elements that should
be recovered in the passage through the Greeks; or at least, in discussion
with Greek thought, the current separation between pleasure and desire is
challenged.[305] Foucault argues that, for the classic philosophers, the control
and proper enjoyment of pleasure is closely connected to their work on the
self. For the Hellenistic philosophers, once they have reached the right relationship with themselves, they are in a position to enjoy that self, to take
pleasure in the company of their own self. The relationship between pleasure and desire, as well as the notion of taking pleasure in one's own self,
has little to do with hedonism. Pleasure is not sought in its own right. Rather, it comes as "an accompaniment to other activities."[306] In relationship
to experience, pleasure is a consequence of the work on does on one's
self.[307] It is related to concrete practices.

For Foucault, work, and the work of thought in particular, can result in
pleasure. When defining "work" for a possible new collection Foucault
was proposing to the Parisian publishing house, Le Seuil, Foucault describes work as "that which is susceptible of introducing a meaningful difference in the field of knowledge, albeit with a certain demand placed on
the author and reader, but with the eventual recompense of a certain pleasure, that is to say of an access to another figure of truth."[308] In this defini-

---

[305] See Foucault, "On the Genealogy of Ethics," 347: "... [W]e do have an example of
an ethical experience which implied a very strong connection between pleasure and desire. If we compare that to our experience now, where everybody – the philosopher or the
psychoanalyst – explains that what is important is desire, and pleasure is nothing at all,
we can wonder whether this disconnection wasn't a historical event, one which was not
at all necessary, not linked to human nature, or to any anthropological necessity." Also,
in the same interview, 359: "... I could say that the modern 'formula' is desire, which is
theoretically underlined and practically accepted, since you have to liberate your own
desire. Acts are not very important, and pleasure – nobody knows what it is!" Foucault
sees Deleuze as being much more interested in desire than he is and indicates that this is
one thing that distinguishes them; see Foucault, "Structuralism and Post-Structuralism,"
in Faubion, *Aesthetics, Method, and Epistemology*, 446.
[306] Rabinow, "Introduction," in Rabinow, *Ethics: Subjectivity and Truth*, xxxvii.
[307] See Rabinow, "Introduction," in Rabinow, *Ethics. Subjectivity and Truth*, xxxvii:
"Foucault's pleasure is embedded in a practice, in an *askēsis*."
[308] Michel Foucault, "Des travaux," in *Dits et écrits*, 4:366–367, here 4:367: "Travail:
ce qui est susceptible d'introduire une différence significative dans le champ du savoir,
au prix d'une certaine peine pour l'auteur et le lecteur, et avec l'éventuelle récompense

tion, pleasure is connected to two elements. It is a by-product of making a difference in a certain field of knowledge, and it is defined as the access to another figure of truth. At the intellectual level, Foucault's genealogy seeks to hunt down the contingent and challenge it, thus inserting a small wedge in the domain of knowledge, and opening up the possibility for seeing new truths. For Foucault, pleasure resides in this constant challenge to the contingent, in the hope of creating something new. In that sense, the genealogical method is a practice of pleasure. Pleasure is found in the work accomplished to think differently, in the experiences crafted to live differently and to act differently. At the same time, as Rabinow indicates, the relationship might be inversed: where there is pleasure, there might be experiences worth exploring and reconfiguring.[309]

The work of thought, and the task of philosophy, coalesces with pleasure for Foucault. The practice of curiosity and invention creates pleasure for the person who is practicing them. But pleasure should not be seen as related only to the realm of intellectual life. Just as, for Foucault, thought and philosophy are always experiences embedded in practices, the pleasure of thinking differently can also be embodied in new ways of living. The gay experience, and what Foucault says of it, reflects one of the ways in which pleasure comes from creating and inventing new forms of relationships. Foucault reflects that the problem confronting gays might not be the liberation of desire, but the invention and creation of new pleasures: "what we must work on, it seems to me, is not so much to liberate our desires but to make ourselves infinitely more susceptible to pleasure [*plaisirs*]."[310] This openness to pleasure is not the quest for perpetual pleasure; rather, it is a willingness to invent new forms of relationships that help to create pleasure: "we must escape and help others to escape the two readymade formulas of the pure sexual encounter and the lovers' fusion of identities."[311] Foucault notes that this can be done in friendship, as long as friendship is understood as "the sum of everything through which [two

---

d'un certain plaisir, c'est-à-dire d'un accès à une autre figure de la vérité." Here I am quoting Rabinow's translation; See Rabinow, "Introduction," in Rabinow, *Ethics: Subjectivity and Truth*, xxi.

[309] See Rabinow, "Introduction," in Rabinow, *Ethics: Subjectivity and Truth*, xxxvii: "For [Foucault], pleasure seems to function as a kind of ethical heuristic, in the sense that he suggests that where one encounters pleasure, one will be in the vicinity of experiences worthy of further reflection, experimentation, and reformulation."

[310] Foucault, "Friendship as a Way of Life," 137. Foucault also notes the scarcity of real pleasure; see Michel Foucault, "An Interview by Stephen Riggins," in Rabinow, *Ethics: Subjectivity and Truth*, 121–133, here 129.

[311] Foucault, "Friendship as a Way of Life," 137.

men] can give each other pleasure."[312] In the necessity to create new forms
of relationship, queerness can extend beyond the homosexual world, and
be a practice of pleasure available to anyone. A subject in quest of pleasure
for Foucault is willing to look at things with a new perspective, to challenge what is in place as well as what she herself already is, and to be open
to new forms of thinking, of living and of relating to people.

The pleasure that accompanies the invention of new relationships and
new ways of thinking is another sign of the embodiment and practicality of
Foucault's thought. His ethics, understood in terms of the relationship the
self should have with one's self, is not only an intellectual endeavor, and is
not governed by laws or by a religion to which one needs to conform. It is
constructed on the premise that human beings can and should be responsible in making their lives into a work of art, and should do so in practices of
freedom that construct relationships of power in which as little domination
as possible is applied.[313] I suspect that pleasure might function as an appropriate indicator of practices of freedom, in thinking and in life. Pleasure, in Foucault, should flow both for the one implementing a practice of
freedom, concretely and locally, and for the one benefiting from it. In that
connection with practices of freedom, the notion of pleasure loses its individualistic connotation and is able to open up on a community, even
though this community is always reconfigured and refuses to name and/or
identify itself. It does, however, indicate that Foucault's ethics is not just a
personal endeavor, with no implications for others. On the contrary, in the
work one does on one's life, concern for the other, and for the limitation of
the devastating effects of relationships of power, is corollary of the inventiveness required to create new ways of being.

The work of thought, which expresses itself in curiosity, invention and
pleasure, is a category that helps to understand the manner in which Foucault conceived of experience. Through the concept of experience, and
through these three notions attached to it, Foucault's readers encounter, as
if in muted colors, a figure of the self in perpetual movement, a form more
than a substance and a form which is "not primarily or always identical to
itself."[314] Changeability in the relationship to oneself is perhaps the most
fundamental characteristic of Foucault's subject:

You do not have the same type of relationship to yourself when you constitute yourself as
a political subject who goes to vote or speaks at meeting and when you are seeking to

---

[312] Foucault, "Friendship as a Way of Life," 136. In the context of the interview, this
definition of friendship refers to the relationship that a younger and an older man need to
invent in order to make sense of their experience of attraction. I think that it can be
broaden however, and used as a tool for thinking about Foucault's definition of pleasure.

[313] See Foucault, "The Ethics of the Concern for Self," 298.

[314] See Foucault, "The Ethics of the Concern for Self," 290.

fulfill your desires in a sexual relationship. Undoubtedly there are relationships and interferences between these different forms of the subject; but we are not dealing with the same type of subject. In each case, one plays, one establishes a different type of relationship to oneself.[315]

Inside this changeability, the work of constituting oneself as a subject is constant. Identity is never a given, for Foucault. Rather, Foucault wants to highlight the ways in which, historically, the subject has constituted itself, or, in some case, has been constituted as a subject, by various practices. These practices can be the result of new fields of knowledge – as is the case for the mad subject for example – but are also historical models, that one can find in one's society and culture – as is the case for practices of the self.[316] If identity is not a given, the subject has to do its work on itself inside a historical context, within particular relationships of power, and in the midst of cultural obligations and expectations. Creation and invention are not *ex-nihilo*. They are embedded in the world in which the subject lives, but are all the more essential because of that embeddedness. The task of the self is to deconstruct and reconstruct itself, in relationship to the various contingencies it encounters. Foucault insists that this task takes time and hard work: "I am sure of this that this change does not take the form of a sudden illumination in which "one's eyes are opened," nor of a permeability to all the movements at work in the present; I would like it to be an elaboration of self by self, a studious transformation, a slow, arduous process of change guided by a constant concern for truth."[317]

---

[315] See Foucault, "The Ethics of the Concern for Self," 290.

[316] See Foucault, "The Ethics of the Concern for Self," 291: "If it is indeed true that the constitution of the mad subject may be considered the consequence of a system of coercion – this is the passive subject – you know very well that the mad subject is not an unfree subject, and that the mentally ill person is constituted as a mad subject precisely in relation to and over against the one who declares him mad. Hysteria, which was so important in the history of psychiatry and in the asylums of the nineteenth century, seems to me to be the very picture of how the subject is constituted as a mad subject. And it is certainly no accident that the major phenomena of hysteria were observed precisely in those situations where there was a maximum of coercion to force individuals to constitute themselves as mad. On the other hand, I would say that if I am now interested in how the subject constitutes itself in an active fashion through practices of the self, these practices are nevertheless not something invented by the individual himself. They are models that he finds in his culture and are proposed, suggested, imposed upon him by his culture, his society, and his social group."

[317] See Michel Foucault, "The Concern for Truth," in Kritzman, *Politics, Philosophy, Culture*, 255–268, here 264.

This constant transformation marks the self, as Rabinow points out, as being in *égarement*, as "straying afield of himself."[318] I find that this notion of *égarement*, of "straying afield of oneself," also resonates with the concept of experience, and the notion of limit-experience elaborated with Bataille and Blanchot. In the genealogical movement as defined by Foucault, it is the will not to deceive oneself,[319] the meandering necessary to avoid and transform "historical constituted obstacles." As Rabinow writes, it is also a "patient disentanglement from the encumbrances of contingency."[320] In and through experience, the self is constituted as an ethical subject capable of implementing new relationships and new ways of thinking.

3. The Constitution of the Ethical Subject in Foucault

I have used Foucault's four modes of the relationship of the self to itself to summarize the way in which Paul constitutes his readers as ethical subjects in his letter to the Romans. The same exercise can be done – and has been done[321] – on Foucault's thought. Foucault himself did not elaborate his thought in these categories, but one can use this tool from his toolbox to organize some of his reflections, even if in a limitative and somewhat distorting way, since one always runs the risk of privileging some aspects over others. However, the exercise, albeit artificial, serves as a good introduction to my final chapter, and sketches the broad lines of a conversation between Foucault and Paul on the theme of the constitution of the self.

Rabinow defines the ethical substance – "the prime material of moral conducts"[322] – as the will to truth. The will to truth is not defined in a very precise manner by Foucault. Thus, in making it the concept behind the ethical substance, one still has the burden to develop what this will to truth covers. I choose a sentence of the *Discourse on Language* as one of the more helpful mentions of the will to truth in relationship to Foucault's un-

---

[318] See Rabinow, "Introduction," in Rabinow, *Ethics: Subjectivity and Truth*, xxxix, referring to the introduction to *The Use of Pleasure* (See Foucault, *History of Sexuality vol. 2*, 8).

[319] See Nietzsche's expression in *The Gay Science* (trans. J. Nauckhoff; Cambridge: Cambridge University Press, 2001), 200 and 201 (aphorism 344): "Consequently, 'will to truth' does *not* mean 'I do not want to let myself be deceived' but – there is no alternative – 'I will not deceive, not even myself'; *and with that we stand on moral ground.*" (italics original)

[320] For the two last quotes, see Rabinow, "Introduction," in Rabinow, *Ethics. Subjectivity and Truth*, xl.

[321] See Paul Rabinow's approach in his introduction to the first volume of Foucault's essential works; Rabinow, "Introduction," in Rabinow, *Ethics: Subjectivity and Truth*, xxvii–xl.

[322] Rabinow, "Introduction," in Rabinow, *Ethics: Subjectivity and Truth*, xxix.

derstanding of his own work.[323] Foucault writes in the *Discourse on Language*: "... [W]e are unaware of the prodigious machinery of the will to truth, with its vocation of exclusion. All those who, at one moment or another in our history, have attempted to remould this will to truth and to turn it against truth at that very point where truth undertakes to justify the taboo, and to define madness; all those, from Nietzsche to Artaud and Bataille, must now stand as (probably haughty) signposts for all our future work."[324] In this identification with Nietzsche, Artaud and Bataille, an identification conscious of its own limitations and failures, Foucault defines his work as the remolding of the will to truth, against truth itself.

From this, I argue that the ethical substance of Foucault's intellectual work is the will to truth in so far as it establishes systems of exclusion, and traces historical continuities, focused on the notion of essence and of truth as an unalterable from. It is also the ethical substance of Foucault's work because Foucault sees truth as inevitably enmeshed with systems of power, in regimes of truth which contribute to the production of truth.[325] Critiquing this exclusive power of the will to truth, "detaching the power of truth from the forms of hegemony, social, economic, and cultural, within which it operates at the present time,"[326] is essential to the task of the individual when she constitutes herself as an ethical subject.

The work one has to do on the will to truth is not related to any law, or science or doctrine.[327] In Foucault, I am tempted to say that the mode of subjection, the manner in which the subject recognizes that she is obligated to a certain work, has precisely nothing to do with obligation. Since Foucault refuses prescription, there is no general mode of subjection valid universally.[328] Rather, one can only see how this mode of subjection functions

---

[323] In this, I suspect I depart from Rabinow's understanding of the will to truth, but he also is vague in his own presentation of the concept.

[324] Foucault, "The Discourse on Language," 220.

[325] See Foucault, "Truth and Power," 131: "In societies like ours, the 'political economy' of truth is characterised by five important traits. 'Truth' is centred on the form of scientific discourse and the institutions which produce it; it is subject to constant economic and political incitement (the demand for truth, as much for economic production as for political power); it is the object, under diverse forms, of immense diffusion and consumption (circulating through apparatuses of education and information whose extend is relatively broad in the social body, not withstanding certain strict limitations); it is produced and transmitted under the control, dominant if not exclusive, of a few great political and economic apparatuses (university, army, writing, media); lastly, it is the issue of a whole political debate and social confrontation ('ideological' struggles)."

[326] Foucault, "Truth and Power," 133.

[327] See also Rabinow, "Introduction," in Rabinow, *Ethics: Subjectivity and Truth*, xxxi.

[328] This was precisely the problem that interested him in his work on the Greeks: how to elaborate an ethics which is not founded on science, religion or law. See Foucault, "On

for Foucault himself. For Foucault, the work on the self as critical work, although it can and should be practiced by anyone, needs to be part, at the very least, of the task of the intellectual and of the philosopher.[329] If one practices philosophy, one is called, in Foucault's understanding, to challenge limits and contingencies, to reflect critically on the world, in order to go beyond those limits. It might be possible to understand this work on the limits as an aesthetic principle of existence, orientated towards making one's life a work of art. Rabinow indicates that, in his reflection on Baudelaire and Kant in "What is Enlightnment?," Foucault develops an *ēthos* which would be "a practice of thought formed in direct contact with social and political realities."[330] The mode of subjection has to do with self-discipline, in thought and in practice. If thought is understood as a practice aimed at always reflecting upon the limits, then the aesthetic principle demands a practical work on the self, in order to go beyond what one is. What are the means that one can use to become that individual always working on limits and questioning certainties and necessities?

The work on the self and the molding of life as a work of art involves *askēsis*, understood in the broad sense of "the work that one performs on oneself in order to transform oneself."[331] As should be clear by now, this work for Foucault is the work of thought itself. It takes into consideration actions and questions them. It examines discursive practices and points out their mechanisms of exclusion. It looks at historical necessities and dismantles them and it takes place, in Foucault's writing, through genealogy.[332] But the work of thought is a practice as well. As ethical work, Rab-

---

the Genealogy of Ethics," 343. In his political actions as well, Foucault did not seek to prescribe solutions to those with whom or for whom he was working. Rather, he sought to give them a voice, to give them an opportunity to make their own voices heard, not to speak for them, but to give them a space in which they could speak. See Foucault, "Interview with Michel Foucault," 288–289: "I'd like to be able to participate in this work myself without delegating responsibilities to any specialist, including myself – to bring it about that, in the very workings of society, the terms of the problem are changed and the impasses are cleared. In short, to be done with spokesperons."

[329] See the preface to *The Use of Pleasure*; Foucault, *History of Sexuality vol. 2*, 8 and 9. See also his definition of himself as "un artificier," in "Je suis un artificier," 92. See finally, Foucault, "The Concern for Truth," 263–264: "This work of altering one's own thought and that of others seems to me to be the intellectual's *raison d'être*."

[330] Rabinow, "Introduction," in Rabinow, *Ethics: Subjectivity and Truth*, xxxii.

[331] Foucault, "Friendship as a Way of Life," 137.

[332] Rabinow quotes a definition of thought in Foucault in the following manner: "Thought is not what inhabits a certain conduct and gives it its meaning; rather, it is what allows one to step back from this way of acting or reacting, to present it to oneself as an object of thought and to question it as to its meaning, its conditions, and its goals. Thought is freedom in relation to what one does, the motion by which one detaches one-

inow points out, "it would be a disentangling and re-forming of the (power and thought) relationships within which and from which the self is shaped and takes shape."[333] In this context, Foucault's reflection on homosexuality as a form of life functions as concrete examples of the *askēsis* Foucault has in mind in his constitution of the ethical subject.

Finally, looking at Foucault's *telos* for the ethical subject is interesting. The *telos* as Foucault defines it concerns the type of persons one wants to become when one behaves in a moral way. Examples of *teloi* mentioned by Foucault include: purity, immortality, freedom, self-mastery.[334] All these *teloi* add qualities to the self. In contrast, in Foucault, the *telos* is precisely to break away from one's identity, the movement of detaching oneself from all the subjections created by practices of power. For Foucault, this does not equate renouncing the self, nor does it imply a movement of conversion. Rather, the detaching is also a constant remodeling, recreating, reinventing of the self by oneself. Thus in the detaching, the self is also created every day as a work of art.[335] The ethical responsibility of the subject for Foucault is to take the risk of "disassembling"[336] the self and of reconstructing it. For Foucault, this takes place precisely in the work one does to critique "the historical forms that, with all their constraints and their diversity, make us what we are, and the patient labor required to reformulate them."[337] I argue that, precisely because Foucault insists on the ethical constitution of a subject, his work, although it is started by deconstruction – attested in the explosive and destructive dimension of his writings – does not stop with deconstruction. The passages created through the work of the *artificier* are not dead-ends. They are truly new routes for thought and action. Transgression is not gratuitous rebellion; it carries with

---

self from it, establishes it as an object, and reflects on it as a problem." See Rabinow, "Introduction," in Rabinow, *Ethics: Subjectivity and Truth*, xxxv.

[333] Rabinow, "Introduction," in Rabinow, *Ethics: Subjectivity and Truth*, xxv–xxvi.

[334] See Foucault, "On the Genealogy of Ethics," 355.

[335] See Foucault, "On the Genealogy of Ethics," 362: "In the Californian cult of the self, one is supposed to discover one's true self, to separate it from that which might obscure or alienate it, to decipher its truth thanks to psychological or psychoanalytic science, which is supposed to be able to tell you what your true self is. Therefore, not only do I not identify this ancient culture of the self with what you might call the Californian cult of the self, I think they are diametrically opposed. What happened in between is precisely an overturning of the classical culture of the self. This took place when Christianity substituted the idea of a self which one had to renounce, because clinging to the self was opposed to God's will, for the idea of a self which had to be created as a work of art."

[336] See Rabinow's expression in "Introduction," in Rabinow, *Ethics: Subjectivity and Truth*, xxxviii.

[337] Rabinow, "Introduction," in Rabinow, *Ethics: Subjectivity and Truth*, xl.

it the painstaking and slow work of inhabiting the new spaces created by the *franchissement* of a limit.

At the same time, Foucault insists that this work is never finished; the new self is never completely attained, thus making the critique of limits permanently necessary. In transgression, the limit is always, again, reiterated.[338] Transgression is a constant work, necessary to resist power, and does not simply find its end in generalized negation: "contestation does not imply a generalized negation, but an affirmation that affirms nothing, a radical break of transitivity."[339] In this sense, Foucault's ethical *telos* is attained precisely when it is never reached, when it is always ahead, when it remains a *telos* pursued and never possessed. In the impossibility to ever possess the *telos*, Foucault provides a form of guarantee against the establishment of a fixed system of power and against the risk of subjecting the self to an unmovable identity. In this perpetual work resides the pleasure of forming one's life as a work of art. Foucault's constitution of an ethical subject reflects the malleability and the perpetual movement of his own thought, the refusal to dispense prescriptions, and a challenge to any system of thought that postulates the fact that an identity can be a given to which one owes faithfulness.

---

[338] See Fred Botting and Scott Wilson, Introduction to *Bataille: A Critical Reader*, 4: "… transgression requires that the meaning of the law it denies be equally intense; transgression has 'its entire trajectory, even its origin' in that form of negativity that is the law, the prohibition and taboo. It is not, therefore, a positive dialectical 'victory over limits' …, a juridico-political struggle against repressive laws or political injustice in the domain of sexuality (as important as that it), but rather the contestation of all limits in the affirmation of *the* limit, death."

[339] Foucault, "A Preface to Transgression," 29.

Chapter 5

Thinking with Romans and Foucault

A. Hermeneutical Position

In the dialogue between Foucault and Romans, I do not construct oppositions or highlight weaknesses and strengths in both authors. I suppose that
differences in corpuses, cultures, literary genres and time period make this
exercise rather futile. But even more importantly, I am convinced that this
is not the most fruitful manner of dialoguing with the two authors. Such a
presentation presumes that I, as the reader of Foucault and of Romans,
stand outside the discussion and function as a neutral observer, a judge or
referee, counting points and finally choosing the position which is worth
following. Rather, I would like to take full advantage of my position as an
interpreter in the midst of this discussion, involved on both sides and im-
mersed in both literary corpuses. My questions and my problems shape my
reading both of Foucault and of Paul. These same questions also influence
my construction of the topic that I see Foucault and Paul addressing, so
that I am far from being a neutral observer. On the contrary, I have prob-
lematized my reading of the two authors and centered it on the question of
the subject because of my own interests. Because of my reading of Paul, I
believe I illuminate aspects of Foucault that might have been neglected if I
had come to Foucault only from the side of philosophy. Evidently, the
same is true of my reading of Paul: Because I also read Foucault, I focus
on a different set of problems in Paul than I would have, had I remained
entirely inside the bounds of Pauline scholarship.

Thus, my position as an interpreter indicates that a critical reading is only complete when it also takes into account the relevance of past texts for
present conversations. In my interaction with the Paul of Romans and the
work of Michel Foucault, I would like to use the texts that I have analyzed
as "foils" for my own thinking, conversation partners that allow me to
challenge and revise my own assumptions about identity-construction.[1] If

---

[1] The approach is also advocated in Vander Stichele and Penner, *Contextualizing Gender*, 3–4: "Thus, with our students in view, we also want to push the edge of critical interaction with early Christian texts, making clear throughout that there is no critical
thinking that does not bear a marked relevance for our own time and place, for our own
thinking, ... In the end, then, this book is not about the ancient world; it is, rather, about

my engagement with these two thinkers modifies my own thoughts and challenges some of my ideas about the self and its identity, then, and only then, will the interpretative project have reached its end. Foucault and Paul's discourses are used to reflect about the problem at hand, and are not seen as offering convenient solutions.

Ironically, this can be seen as a foucaultian approach in itself since it focuses on the manner in which two authors have approached the *problem* of the construction of the self. In a way, my work, without relying on historical dependency, is about creating an embryonic discursive practice around the question of the self. Discourse creates a certain perspective on the world and produces particular knowledge about a topic. When I choose to link Foucault and Romans in my reflections on identity-construction, I create a particular way, through language, to look at the problem of the self. Discursive practices, as Foucault writes in "The Will to Knowledge," are "characterized by the demarcation of a field of objects, by the definition of a legitimate perspective for a subject of knowledge, by the setting of norms for elaborating concepts and theories."[2] Thus, because discursive practices are constructed around an object, around a field of knowledge, they do not necessarily "coincide with individual works."[3] In addition, they do not necessarily match "disciplines" and "sciences": "more often, it happens that a discursive practice brings together various disciplines or sciences, or it passes through a number of them and gathers several of their areas into a sometimes inconspicuous clutter."[4]

It would be too ambitious to say that my analysis gathers discursive practices around the question of the construction of the self.[5] However, I

---

rethinking our own world and our place in it through interaction with texts from long ago, including also the engagement of our own interpretative practices and disciplines. Thus, for us the challenge is to use the ancient world as a foil for interacting with our own, and, in the process, challenging our assumptions, values, and social-political identities."

[2] See Michel Foucault, "The Will to Knowledge," in Rabinow, *Ethics: Subjectivity and Truth*, 11–16, here 11.

[3] Foucault, "The Will to Knowledge," 11.

[4] Foucault, "The Will to Knowledge," 11–12.

[5] In particular, it does not take into account the institutional dimension of discourse, or the modes of transformation related to these practices. See Foucault, "The Will to Knowledge," 12: "Discursive practices are not purely and simply modes of manufacture of discourse. They take shape in technical ensembles, in institutions, in behavioral schemes, in types of transmission and dissemination, in pedagogical forms that both impose and maintain them. Finally, they have specific modes of transformation. One cannot reduce these transformations to a precise individual discovery; and yet one cannot merely characterize them as an overall change of outlook [*mentalité*], of collective attitude or state of mind. The transformation of a discursive practice is tied to a whole, often quite complex set of modifications which may occur either outside it (in the forms of produc-

believe I can use Foucault's reflections on discursive practices as a way of articulating my own engagement with various discourses on the question of the construction of the self, discourses that are not necessarily connected by their authors, their time period, their location or their discipline, but that are concerned with the construction of the self nonetheless. My idea of self-construction is deployed in dialogue with Paul and Foucault and seeks to illustrate how certain elements of the discussion about identity and personhood can successfully be articulated with the help of Paul and Foucault's discourses.

In this perspective, I would like to qualify my work on Foucault and Paul as a "thinking with," rather than a comparison or the constitution of a play of oppositions. As a result, I am not so much interested in determining which solution is the better one; rather, I want to underline the various ways in which the problem has been articulated,[6] as well as reflect on the manner in which these articulations help me develop my own reflection on the construction of the self. This reflection will take place in two steps. In a first section, I present the main areas of problematization that emerge when one looks at the question of identity construction with Foucault and Paul. In a second part, I move beyond Paul and Foucault, and I suggest ways in which the dialogue with Paul and Foucault helps me think about present issues, issues related in particular to Paul's status in current scholarship, and to hermeneutical decisions concerning the interpretation process.

B. Thinking about the Self with Paul and Foucault

To me, as an interpreter concerned with identity-construction, an unsuspected commonality emerges between Foucault and the Paul of Romans, despite all of their differences. In their thought, I believe that both Foucault and Paul (at least in Romans) are concerned primarily with the task of inventing new ways of being and of living in the world. Both conceive of this task differently and I suspect that the main divergence between Foucault and Paul in their construction of the self resides in their ac-

---

tion, in the social relations, in the political institutions), or within it (in the techniques for determining objects, in the refinement and adjustment of concepts, in the accumulation of data), or alongside it (in other discursive practices). And it is linked to them in the form not simply of an outcome but of an effect that maintains its own autonomy and a set of precise functions relative to what determines the transformation."

[6] See Foucault, "On the Genealogy of Ethics," 343: "You see, what I want to do is not the history of solutions, and that's the reason why I don't accept the word *alternative*. I would like to do the genealogy of problems, of *problématiques*."

ceptance or not of the notion of a given identity. The gift of being united with Christ allows a new self-understanding in Paul and stands behind the ability of the individual to constitute itself as an ethical subject. Foucault recognizes the potential of such an approach, particularly when he discusses the concept of conversion,[7] but he also rejects it, because, for him, it marks a return to a form of self-understanding in which an identity is given to the person and she finds herself trying to remain faithful to that identity, thus inscribing herself in a self-understanding marked by essence, and faithfulness to essence. Nonetheless, despite this disagreement – to which I will return below – I will argue that both are confronted with similar difficulties and have to negotiate similar elements in their construction of the self.

1. Power in the Construction of the Self

In Foucault' works, construction of the self is traversed through and through by the need to navigate relationships of power. The categories I have delineated in regard to Foucault's understanding of the self show this concern with power. Curiosity, invention and pleasure all function together in order for the self to deconstruct oppressive systems of power and reconstruct them in a manner that is more respectful of the other. For Foucault, the destructive and creative process happens at the level of discourse and knowledge, but it also takes place in the relationships the self can have with itself and with others. Thus, Foucault's thinking reflects the need to identify networks of power, as well as the perpetual effort to dismantle these apparatuses of power in order to invent new processes of thought and new forms of relationships. Curiosity and invention are demanded of the self in order to identify the various relationships of power in which it is enmeshed. It enables the genealogical process witnessed in Foucault's own thought. Pleasure not only accompanies this deconstructive and reconstructive process, but it is also a powerful motor to think beyond the obvious, and to create new forms of thoughts and new relationships.

Workings of power can also be identified in the ethical categories I have outlined to summarize the manner in which Foucault delineates the construction of an ethical subject. In the work on the will to truth, Foucault wants to expose the extent to which truth is embedded in relationships of power and how the production of truth – or of what is considered to be truth – depends on particular social, economic, political and cultural hegemonies. In this context, the task of the subject is to make herself aware of these hegemonies and of the way they relate to truth, in order to detach, as much as possible, truth from the workings of power. In going beyond

---

[7] See Foucault, "The Concern for Truth," 263.

the limits traditionally imposed upon knowledge in various disciplines, the self reflects critically on the world, but also agrees to put her person at stake in the reflection, and engages in a perpetual task of recreating herself, thus challenging any potential fossilization of power relationships. In the *askēsis* performed by the self upon itself, relationships of power are perpetually modified and boundaries are perpetually crossed, in order to create spaces of resistance, spaces where relationships of power are redefined, so that one can lead one's life with as little domination, and as much pleasure, as possible. Thus, it is not that power is eliminated in Foucault's open confrontation with it. Rather, Foucault aims to make power, in its different forms, apparent, and to acknowledge and highlight its workings even where one would rather keep it hidden and ignore its presence. Thus, he makes it possible to detach oneself from the various subjections created by the workings of power.

For me, the theme of power so prominent in Foucault's work is not absent from Paul's reflections about the manner in which the members of the Roman churches need to understand their own identity and the identity of the community to which they belong. Needless to say, a reflection on power is not developed in explicit terms in Paul's letter to the Romans. However, I cannot but help to see an awareness of power at work in the way Paul formulates his ethical injunctions to his addressees (Rom 12:1–15:13); especially when one reads these ethical injunctions in close relationship to the story Paul has told in the previous sections of the letter (Rom 1:18–8:39). In the first part of his letter, Paul has reminded his addressees of the story which made them become who they are now (beloved of God, called to be saints [1:7], full of goodness, filled with all knowledge [15:14]). In this story, he has developed two aspects of an identity grounded in Christ.

On the one hand, he has insisted on the strong foundation that a Christlike identity gives to Christ believers, providing them with an ethical grounding on which to construct their identity of children of God – the ricœurian "Here I am!". In this "Here I am!", the Christ believers are invited to put limits to the endless possibilities offered in the liberation from sin by embodying a Christ-like *ēthos* and placing the needs of the weaker member and of the community first. On the other hand, Paul has presented his addressees with dizzying possibilities about the ways they can use their bodily and inner abilities, arguing that the Christ believers are responsible for utilizing both their rational and physical abilities freely in order to attain proper God worship (12:1–2). Because of that tension, inherent to the concept of saved human beings, Paul is forced to negotiate the various ways in which his addressees can use the freedom which he insists has been given to them. In these negotiations, I maintain that Paul is not unaware of the workings of power. Rather, to use foucaultian language, he does inscribe his discussion of freedom and of liberation into networks of power and seeks to establish relationships of power which, though they do not suppress power, use it in respectful ways.

Paul is particularly conscious of the devastating power that sin can exercise on human beings. This power is not only absolute, it also has a deeply degenerating effect on human beings (see Rom 1:18–32) and creates devastating anxiety in them, rendering them unable to truly embrace who they are and what they do, and suppressing all possibilities of an authentic relationship to themselves (Rom 7:14–25). For Paul, sin as a power can only be defeated through divine intervention, thus restoring human beings to a proper relationship to themselves and to others around them. This liberation, however, does not mean the end of power relationships; power struggles remain a reality even in the life of the restored Christ believers. These power struggles occur at various levels and need to be navigated in a way that leaves the most space open for the workings of freedom to unfold, so that relationships of power remain fluid and do not fossilize themselves in mortiferous ways. I suspect we can identify several ways in which Paul, in Romans, negotiates the freedom that he believes is given to his addressees through the sacrifice of Christ.

Even though Paul is clear that the power of sin no longer has any hold on the Christ believers and that the Christ believers are now living in a different realm, ruled by a different master (Rom 6:11.13.18.22), Paul makes no mystery that Christ believers still lead their lives inside the structures of the world and inhabit mortal bodies (13:14).[8] Their freedom is embodied freedom, and this embodiment demarcates boundaries to what human beings can accomplish. The limitation related to embodiment does not define the body as a bad entity, or as something that human beings ultimately need to escape – in fact even restored life must be embodied life (8:23) – but it does describe the body as something that needs to be ruled by the proper master in order to be used fully. When God wields the power over the body, it can be used in a positive fashion. In this case, the type of relationship of power in which the person is involved decides whether the body can be used freely and positively (12:1–2). For Paul, it is not that power needs to be overthrown or suppressed, but it needs to be qualified as the right type of power in order for human beings to implement new ways of living and relating to each other. When human beings are established as slaves of God through Christ's death and the gift of the spirit (6:22), they are put in the hand of a power that has the potential to liberate them. When they recognize God as their rightful master, human beings enter into a relationship of power that frees them to act in ways that express the authentici-

---

[8] See Johnson, *Reading Romans*, 105.

ty and integrity of their self-understanding as children of God, thus minimizing abuses of power in their dealings with other. Through their subjection to God, they are empowered to act in ways respectful of those around
them.

In that context, inside the community of Christ believers, power relationships among community members are completely redefined. In the
community, Paul invites believers to establish relationships that embody
alternative modes of relating to each other, in which power relationships
are conceptualized in ways that are always respectful of the weakest members of the community. In the respect for the weakest members, Paul defines a principle that stands in contrast to the hierarchical organization of
the world around him – a point to which I will return later – and sketches
the outline of an alternative mode of being a community. Being a Christ
believer not only changes how one understands oneself, but, more importantly, changes how one relates to others in the world. Concrete actions
of solidarity and interconnectedness are needed in the community, in order
to truly embody the call of the Christ believers. A different community can
be, and needs to be, created among Christ believers. This community is
marked by clothing oneself in Christ and detaching oneself from the ways
of the world (13:14). Without making it explicit, Paul elaborates the possibility of putting into place a community characterized by an alternative
dynamic, in contrast to the dominant ideology of his time, symbolized by
the hierarchical organization of the Roman empire and of the Mediterranean world in general.

In contrast, Paul invites his addressees to implement creative ways of
fitting themselves in the body of Christ, without providing a predetermined
structure or hierarchy. The call to put on Christ should be understood as a
constant practice, which embodies relationships that contrast with the
power relationships put into place in the dominant surrounding milieus.[9]
Evidently, Paul is not about to advocate the over-throwing of the dominant
political setting in which he operates, but amidst this system, he seeks to
construct a community that personifies other types of relationships and
emphasizes concern for the weaker members of the community. In foucaultian language, one might say that inside power itself, Paul implements
strategies of resistance, spaces in which new modes of relating to each other can be put into place.

This however is not developed as a political program for Paul. Rather, it
is part of his ethical reflection, of his work to transform the *ēthos* of his
addressees. When he challenges the traditional ways of understanding
power relationships and incites his addressees to embrace a new *ēthos*,
Paul takes some risks. In that regard, I would like to retain the fact that the

---

[9] See the approach that Lopez develops in *Apostle to the Conquered*.

only time Paul is mentioned in Foucault's works (at least to my knowledge) is in relationship to Foucault's work on *parrhēsia*. Foucault writes
that for the New Testament, *parrhēsia* symbolizes trust in God but is also
"la marque de l'attitude courageuse de celui qui prêche l'Évangile."[10] Foucault sees Paul as an example of apostolic *parrhēsia*, speaking frankly and
openly to his addressees, even if it could put him in (sometimes mortal)
danger. For Foucault, the exercise of *parrhēsia* is intrinsically perilous because it is a form of truth-telling that is not abstract or theoretical but aims
to transform the *ēthos* of the person.[11] The figure of the *parrhesiast*, which
Foucault develops rather late in his life, is another personification of the
constant need to reflect on what seems given and natural in the world, in
order to challenge it.[12] The *parrhesiast* is involved in various power relationships and seeks to construct these relationships in a way that minimizes
abuses of power.

For that purpose, the *parrhesiast* not only seeks to tell the truth, but she
(more frequently, he, in the ancient world) also embodies this truth in her
own life and challenges the other person to enter in that truth as well. The
final purpose of *parrhēsia* is to free the person to whom one is speaking,
so that this person can actually enter in her own relationship to truth and
constitute herself as a true subject: "it is insofar as the other has given, has
conveyed a true discourse to the person to whom he speaks, that this person, internalizing and subjectivizing this true discourse, can then leave the
relationship with the other person."[13] The *parrhesiast* does not dispense
already made solutions; she sets the other in motion and creates possibilities for the other to constitute herself in a subject responsible for her own
ethical decisions. In addition, and Foucault develops this notion in particular through his work on the Cynics, the philosopher preoccupied with true
life leads what Foucault calls the life of a *militant* and her purpose is to
change the world: "C'est donc une militance qui prétend changer le monde, beaucoup plus qu'une militance qui chercherait simplement à fournir à

---

[10] Foucault, *Le courage de la vérité*, 301.

[11] See Frédéric Gros, "Situation du cours," in Foucault, *Le Courage de la vérité*, 314–
328, here 316: "C'est ainsi que le dire-vrai de la *parrêsia* – en tant qu'elle vise à la transformation de l'*êthos* de son interlocuteur, comporte un risque pour son locuteur, et
s'inscrit dans une temporalité de l'actualité – est distingué du dire-vrai de l'enseigne-
ment, de la prophétie et de la sagesse."

[12] This critical nature of the *parrhesiast* is also noted by Gros who defines truth-
telling as requiring "courage et surtout un souci du monde et des autres, exigeant
l'adoption d'une 'vraie vie' comme critique permanente du monde." (See Gros, "Situation du cours," in Foucault, *Le courage de la vérité*, 320)

[13] Foucault, *The Hermeneutics of the Subject*, 379

ses adeptes les moyens de parvenir à une vie heureuse."[14] In this identification of the true life, Foucault underlines the political dimension of practical action in his studies of the ancient world. In his work on the Cynics, he is able to reconcile the work on the self with the transformation of the world.[15]

In Paul's efforts to transform the person and consequently to transform the community in which the person lives, the same endeavor is apparent. Paul does not simply want to bring his addressees to a state of happiness, he wants them to embody among themselves modes of relationships that model Christ's spirit of sacrifice and emphasize the needs of the weakest members of the community. Even though neither Foucault nor Paul identify themselves in that manner, it is possible to see them both as *parrhesiasts* in their own right, engaged in the creation of spaces of resistance amidst relationships of power and using creativity and freedom to do so.

In the figure of the *parrhesiast* who deals with relationships of power, one is also reminded of the importance of practical work for Foucault. I have argued that Paul advocates strong practical embodiments of the freedom given to the Christ believers. Ethical self-construction means a deep involvement with others and an attention to community. One is thus reminded of Foucault's discreet but constant concern with the manner in which construction of the self also determines one's relationships with others. Foucault is sometimes portrayed as a pessimist, who advocates a nihilistic approach to things, destroying evidences and certitudes without worrying about the work of reconstruction, eager only to transgress limits.[16] In answer to such charges, Foucault insists that his argument, although it does not present one with solutions and political programs, is about finding spaces in which to anchor resistance: "nothing is more foreign to me than the idea of a master who would impose his law on one. I

---

[14] Foucault, *Le courage de la vérité*, 262. See Gros, "Situation du cours," in Foucault, *Le courage de la vérité*, 325: "Dans les derniers cours, ... Foucault montre comment cette vie autre constitue en même temps la critique du monde existant et soutient l'appel à un 'monde autre'."

[15] See Gros, "Situation du cours," in Foucault, *Le courage de la vérité*, 326: "Il demeure que ce souci de soi, essentiellement présenté dans sa version stoïcienne et épicurienne, faisait apparaître un jeu de la liberté où la construction intérieure primait sur la transformation politique du monde. L'introduction du concept de *parrêsia*, dans sa version socratique et cynique, devait apporter à cette présentation de l'éthique ancienne un rééquilibrage décisif."

[16] This, at least, is how Foucault sometimes understood that people depicted him. See Michel Foucault, "Polemics, Politics and Problematizations," in Rabinow, *Ethics: Subjectivity and Truth*, 111–119, here 113: "I think I have in fact been situated in most of the squares on the political checkerboard, one after another and sometimes simultaneously: as anarchist, leftist, ostentatious or disguised Marxist, nihilist, explicit or secret anti-Marxist, technocrat in the service of Gaullism, new liberal, and so on."

don't accept either the notion of mastery or the universality of law. On the contrary, I'm very careful to get a grip on the actual mechanisms of the exercise of power; I do this because those who are enmeshed, involved, in these power relations can, in their actions, their resistance, their rebellion, escape them, transform them, in a word, cease being submissive."[17]

Being conscious of relationships of power, for Foucault, is not about trapping people into closed systems. Rather, for Foucault, it is only by identifying mechanisms of power that one can also transform them. Foucault's stark diagnosis of reality is an optimism, deeply connected with the conviction that there is always something that can be done: "... if I don't say what needs to be done, it isn't because I believe there is nothing to be done. On the contrary, I think there are thousands things that can be done, invented, contrived by those who, recognizing the relations of power in which they are involved, have decided to resist them or escape them. From that viewpoint, all my research rests on a postulate of absolute optimism. I don't construct my analyses in order to say, 'This is the way things are, you are trapped.' I say these things only insofar as I believe it enables us to transform them. Everything I do is done with the conviction that it may be of use."[18] We are reminded that invention plays an important role in Foucault's thought, and that critical work is not just about challenging what is in place, but also about conceiving what could be instead of what is.

Paul's project with his communities is precisely a concrete and historical embodiment of this optimism. Even if Foucault himself did not call for new communities, both Foucault and Paul create new ways of thinking about communities. And these communities rather than being marked by belonging to a certain *ethnos*, or to a certain gender, or to a certain sexual orientation, or to a certain class, are created through concrete ethical practices, which can lead to new ways of understanding the subject and its task.[19] Inside these communities, relationships of power are acknowledged

---

[17] Foucault, "Interview with Michel Foucault," 294.

[18] Foucault, "Interview with Michel Foucault," 294–295.

[19] A similar reflection on citizenship is conducted by Bhaba, *The Location of Culture*, xvii–xviii: "Our nation-centered view of sovereign citizenship can only comprehend the predicament of minoritarian 'belonging' as a problem of ontology – a question of *belonging* to a race, a gender, a class, a generation becomes a kind of 'second nature,' a primordial identification, an inheritance of tradition, a *naturalization* of the problem of citizenship. The vernacular cosmopolitan takes the view that the commitment to a 'right to difference in equality' as a process of constituting emergent groups and affiliations has less to do with the affirmation or authentication of origins and 'identities,' and more to do with political practices and ethical choices. Minoritarian affiliation or solidarities arise in response to failures and limits of democratic representation, creating new modes of agency, new strategies of recognition, new forms of political and symbolical representation ... "

and engaged creatively, in order to avoid the risk of the fossilization of these same relationships. One of the ways in which this danger of fossilization is addressed by both thinkers is through the refusal of formulating concrete laws, the refusal to engage in casuistry.

2. Askēsis: *the Work on the Self*

In his description of Christianity, Foucault insists that the mode of subjection related to ethical practice is contained in the law: "the form of obligation was a legal form."[20] I have shown that Foucault's reconstruction of the genealogy of ethics hinges in part on the necessity to show the contrast between Christianity understood as obedience to a body of law, and Greek ethics as a quest for the construction of an ethical life. I have also discussed the fact that Paul, at least in the way he develops the ethical injunctions of Romans, does not in fact fit easily in this reconstruction. In Rom 12:1–15:13, Paul does not emphasize the need to follow a particular set of rules. In particular, when one looks at the manner in which he addresses concrete cases (for example the eating of vegetables or the distinction between certain days of the week, 14:2.5), Paul does not dispense rules concerned with proving a side right or wrong. Rather he insists on the importance of hospitality and on the need for welcoming the weaker members of the community. The precepts given to order conduct are general instructions (12:9–21; 13:8–9.12–14; 14:1.13.19; 15:1–2.7), which insist on each believer's responsibility to be a Christ-like person, attentive first and foremost to the needs of the community.[21] Paul's purpose is not to create community members that are tied down to legal prescriptions. Rather he constructs ethical subjects, who are invited to think about themselves, about others, about God and about their community in new and demanding ways. In the story that he has told the members of the Roman house churches, Paul is able to challenge the way in which members of the communities relate to each other and conceive their position in the world. The work that the addressees have to do on themselves is thus not related to law-observance. It is creative work, which engages the whole person and demands inventiveness in using the person's abilities in new ways.

Neither Foucault nor Paul engage in casuistry, rather both could be said to rely on imagination when conceiving the task of the ethical subject. In her work on Paul in relationship to Roman imperial ideology, Davina

---

[20] See Foucault, "On the Genealogy of Ethics," 356.

[21] In chapter 13, Paul might be seen as giving instructions with a more concrete content (13:7) but even in this context, the precise advice of the first part of the verse, about tax-paying, is generalized by the second part of the verse, which leaves the responsibility of deciding to whom honor is due in the hands of Paul's addressees.

Lopez distinguishes between the *imaginary* and *imagination*.[22] Using the work of Althusser on ideology,[23] she defines the imaginary in the following manner: "the *imaginary* designates what is created out of the presentation of knowledge as inevitable and universal. It is a relentless display of reality as unmediated and neutral and renders such reality invisible to criticism."[24] For Lopez, the imaginary functions as a barrier to real change and real transformation. She writes, "within the landscape of the imaginary, it is sufficient to just tweak, alter, and add: a wholesale transformation is neither desirable nor possible."[25] Because of the limits the imaginary poses to transformation, "it is not emancipatory."[26] Behind this critique of the imaginary, one hears echoes of Foucault's injunction to not take anything for granted, to engage in a constant work of critique and challenging, to bring to the surface different ways to read history and to understand reality.[27]

For Lopez, the counter-voices to the power of the imaginary, which silences attempts of critique sometimes through violence, "can be detected speaking out of what can be called *imagination*."[28] Imagination functions as a discourse that throws a challenge to what is established, while at the same time recognizing the imaginary as contingent and changeable. Imagination does not only function as an instrument of critique and challenge – even though it also does that – but it includes a productive force, an "ability to envision a different world when that task seems overwhelming, implausible and forbidden."[29] In that ability to see new things, to create new options for thinking and being, imagination is more than an opposition discourse. It is also a discourse that creates an alternative reality, which goes beyond what one can see. In Pauline language, imagination could be defined as hope, the ability to wait for what is still unseen, unheard of, perhaps even unimaginable (Rom 8:25), an ability exhibited in an exemplary fashion by Abraham (Rom 4:18), an ability which needs to characterize the doings of Paul's addressees.

In this need to imagine what is impossible, a body of laws cannot help. Rather, each individual, each Christ believer, has a responsibility to sketch

---

[22] See Lopez, *Apostle to the Conquered*.

[23] See Louis Althusser, *Lenin and Philosophy, and Other Essays* (trans. B. Brewster; New York: Monthly Review Press, 1971).

[24] Lopez, *Apostle to the Conquered*, 18.

[25] Lopez, *Apostle to the Conquered*, 18.

[26] Lopez, *Apostle to the Conquered*, 18.

[27] Evidently Althusser stands as an important figure in Foucault's own formation and these echoes are not surprising. Even if Lopez does not explicitly use Foucault in the construction of the opposition between imaginary and imagination, it is clear that she knows his work.

[28] Lopez, *Apostle to the Conquered*, 18.

[29] Lopez, *Apostle to the Conquered*, 18.

new ways of being, of relating to the world and to each other, ways that are not characterized by the expectations of the world, but rather are characterized by hope. In this context, the story effort in which Paul engages is not only about creating (perhaps imposing, as I will discuss below) a self-understanding for his addressees, it is also about challenging the manner in which his addressees act in the world. In particular, in the new self-understanding that Paul proposes to his addressees, he calls into question the relevance of the distinction between Jews and Gentiles. The way Paul's addressees understand kinship is challenged by the manner in which Paul constructs a new sense of kinship through the identity of children of God, co-heirs with Christ (see 8:17).[30] His story constructs a community in which Jews and Gentiles – although their differences are not suppressed – come together in one household, under the authority of God, thus creating a unified people. In this, community, Jews and nations share one common denominator that grounds their identity and minimizes the importance of their differences: they are slave to the same master, God. They share the identity of children of God. In the household of the Christ believers, the members are invited to embody an *ēthos* which aims to welcome Jews and non-Jews, in order to create a harmonious community.

The strategy that Paul uses to put into place this alternative community is not concerned with rules. Rather, when Paul encourages harmony and unity between Jews and nations, he modifies the narratives that Jews and Gentiles have been telling and which oppose the two entities. In the way Paul uses the Jewish traditions (in particular, the Abraham story), he re-stages the past, to use Homi Bhabha's expression,[31] and creates a new narrative that embraces the hybridity of a community composed of both Jews and Gentiles. Through this hybridity, which he himself embodies to a certain extent, Paul redefines the relationships between Jews and non-Jews.[32] In that redefinition, he opens up the door for new collaboration, and the creation of a community that embodies a new way of living. Rather than being marked by obedience to a body of laws, this endeavor can be read in light of Foucault's efforts to create new spaces for living and new ways of

---

[30] See deSilva, *Honor, Patronage, Kinship and Purity*, 199–239.

[31] See Bhabha, *The Location of Culture*, 3.

[32] See Bhabha, *The Location of Culture*, 2: "What is theoretically innovative, and politically crucial, is the need to think beyond narratives of originary and initial subjectivities and to focus on those moments or processes that are produced in the articulation of cultural differences. These 'in-between' spaces provide the terrain for elaborating strategies of selfhood – singular or communal – that initiate new signs of identity, and innovative sites of collaboration, and contestation, in the act of defining society itself." Bhabha does not have Paul in mind when he defines these "in-between" spaces, but I think that Paul's work with Jews and Gentiles can be seen as a moment that articulates cultural difference.

relating to others. In foucaultian language, Paul's work on the ethical substance can be seen as an adventure into creating alternative modes of relating to others.

I propose to see in this type of reconfiguration of relationships an example of Foucault's notion of resistance and of *franchissement* of limits.
Paul is calling into question the established order, pushing its limits, and
putting into place concrete, local and practical strategies which resist the
dominant ideology of separation between Jews and Gentiles. In the genealogy of the community as he tells it in Romans, Paul engages in a strategy
of resistance, which invents new relationships among peoples. This strategy of resistance works at two levels. First, it challenges national identity
and seeks to create a community that understands itself in an international
manner, and promotes the inclusion of Jews and non-Jews in its midst. Second, Paul also resists the hierarchy in place in the milieu in which he
lives. The care for the other, especially for the weaker individual, promot-
ed by Paul in the last chapters of Romans, puts into place a model that
challenges the hierarchical power relationships which were widespread in a
society based on patronage and slavery. In his community, Paul promotes
horizontal relationships of equality[33] marked by respect and love rather
than judgment and contempt. In particular, Paul insists on the necessity of
owing no one anything, except mutual love (13:8). In the injunction to mutual love, Paul distances himself from the patronage system, which also
took care of the less fortunate members of the community, but expected
something in exchange. Inside the community, the power dynamics are
displaced through the personal involvement of the Christ believers, at
small, concrete and local levels. In this context, invention, or imagination,
plays a critical role, in particular to avoid the fossilization of these living
and active practices into laws.

Thus, the prescriptive sections of Romans in particular and of Pauline
letters in general should neither be neglected nor turned into stagnant and
binding moral prescriptions. Behind Paul's efforts to construct the self of
his addressees, one does not need to see a desire for putting a new law into
place.[34] Rather, Paul is emphasizing concrete embodiments of an attitude

---

[33] See Lopez, *Apostle to the Conquered*, 146, 147, 148.

[34] This of course is in contrast to what Foucault sees happening in Christianity, which
for him precisely paralyzes practices of change into a system of obligations. For Foucault, a predominant example of obligation is the practice of confession, which makes
Christianity into a religion that imposes "obligations of truth on the practitioners" (see
Foucault, "Sexuality and Solitude," 178). For him, the practice of confession is also
strongly linked to the renouncing of the self: "The more we discover the truth about ourselves, the more we must renounce ourselves; and the more we want to renounce ourselves, the more we need to bring to light the reality of ourselves. That is what we would
call the spiral of truth formulation and reality renouncement which is at the heart of

marked by respect for the others. These embodiments are bound to change depending on the situations and on the people involved. They are practices of a freedom that has been reoriented and now takes into account the needs and limits of others. As such, imagination is a necessary tool to confront various situations. One needs to remember that imagination is not just the critique of a given situation but also the ability to think beyond necessities, beyond what seems natural and embedded in time. It has the potential to deconstruct what is given and to reconstruct something new, very much like Foucault's genealogical practices.

If one keeps in mind the importance of imagination and of thought in Paul's mission (see the use of φρον- [8:5; 11:20; 14:6; 12:3.16; 15:5], πνεῦμα [7:6; 8:2.4–6.9–11.13–16.23.26–27; 14:17; 15:13.16.30] and νοῦς [7:23; 12:2; 14:5] language in the letter), the role of the spirit can also be redefined. In ways that Paul might not be able to fully explain, the spirit functions as a productive force for practices of imagination that invent and create new ways of being a community (8:26). The spirit stands behind the practices of *askēsis* asked of the Christ believers. It contributes to the endless and tiring work of deconstructing and recreating a reality that portrays itself as natural and unchangeable. The spirit for Paul is a force that can nourish the practices of resistance central to the identity of the Pauline communities. In a context where the separation of Jews and Gentiles was a reality given as natural and immutable, Paul sees the spirit as a divine force that enables the work of imagination and nourishes the possibility of hope, even when it seems impossible to see – let alone implement – new ways of relating to one another (8:24–25). Foucault's categories of curiosity and change are not absent from Paul. They are highlighted in the necessary work that each believer has to do on herself in order to live in the hope of what cannot be seen. A focus on conversion and personal salvation should not obscure this patient, difficult and concrete work. In the critical and imaginative dimensions of this work, one comes close to the concrete, small, diverse and constant practices of transformation that Foucault sees at work in strategies of resistance.[35]

If Paul's work inside his communities is illuminated when one takes into account Foucault's work on imagination and practices of resistance, it also brings to light a dimension that is left practically untouched by Foucault in his reflections on power and in his construction of the ethical subject. In both cases, Foucault says very little about community, whether it be the role of community in practices of resistance or the manner in which practices of resistance can be consolidated in communities. I suspect that

---

Christian techniques of the self." I suspect that for Foucault this practice of the self cannot really make sense, since there is no concept of "reality of the self" in his thinking.

[35] See Foucault, *History of Sexuality vol. 1*, 96.

Foucault sees communities as potential spaces were practices of resistance can be fossilized in new systems of oppression. It can also be the privileged place in which authorities proclaim prescriptions and resolutions which are constructed as binding for certain individuals, thus limiting and impoverishing the ever-creative dimension of resistance. For Foucault, this dangerous potential is sufficient to make him suspicious of any kind of prescriptive power that could take a universal value.[36]

In contrast, Foucault advocates a stark individual *askēsis* that benefits from no outside help in the perpetual work of re-creation that it demands. The potential for cooptation is thus limited, but the dimension of community disappears. This does not mean, as I have noted, that Foucault ignores the needs of others or isolates himself in a narcissism concerned only with the aesthetic value of the individual life. Quite the contrary; for Foucault, the value of the *askēsis* comes precisely from the manner in which power relationship are shaped and reworked in order to provide freedom and respect for the others. However, the refusal of any kind of program or system does call into question the possibility for the establishment of a community, making the foucaultian *askēsis* a matter of self-discipline, independent from and impervious to any kind of allegiance to a master, but also deprived from the support that a community can offer.

3. Telos

The discussion of the practices of invention and of imagination that are at work in Foucault and Paul shows that both aim at carving spaces of resistance for their addressees. Despite this commonality, in the elaboration of the *teloi* that Foucault and Paul pursue when constructing the ethical subject, one encounters a tension that cannot and should not be resolved. For Foucault, I have argued that the *telos* to which his writings point is, in a sense, a continual escape from the self, a perpetual play with limits, a breaking away from oneself. It is marked by a refusal of the concept of a given identity, which has the potential to define the person and provide her with a basic direction to follow in order to truly become herself. I believe that the notion of becoming *truly* oneself is alien to Foucault's thought. One constantly moves away from oneself and is constantly called to shape and reshape oneself in a new work of art, which forever transgresses

---

[36] The fate of the church as an institution, and the destiny of Paul inside the church and traditional patriarchal exegesis, confirms that danger. Moore remarks on the conservative interpretations of Paul. In particular, he cites the commentary of Sanday and Headlam (William Sanday and Arthur C. Headlam, *A Critical and Exegetical Commentary on the Epistle to the Romans* [ICC 32; 3d ed.; New York: Scribners, 1897]) as an example of a commentary promoting a colonial and patriarchal interpretation of Romans (see Moore, *God's Beauty Parlor*, 158–159 and 163–165).

boundaries, whether it is in artistic endeavors, intellectual work, social relationships and practical actions. Each person is individually responsible
for the manner in which she uses her life to make it into a work of art.

In contrast, Paul, even though he also advocates a perpetual work on
oneself, elaborates a relationship to oneself in which Christ, and the characteristics of his life, plays the role of a model which needs to guide his
addressees (and Paul himself) in the construction of their selves. In Paul,
the *telos* is conforming one's identity to the *ēthos* of Christ. Christ believers need to answer a calling to become Christ-like. In that sense, they are
only truly themselves once they have completely embraced the identity of
co-heirs of God, with Christ. In Paul, I find not only the idea of a given
identity, which serves as a guide for the addressees in their ethical choices,
but also the possibility of becoming truly oneself. The true identity of the
Christ believers is not who they were before baptism – slaves of sin – but
who they become through baptism, and through self-transformation – children of God, serving God.

Paul – and this is also related to a specific cultural context – cannot envision the autonomy and freedom that Foucault sees as necessary for ethical construction. For Paul, true freedom can only occur in servitude to the
right master, God. This need for a master also guides the efforts of the
Christ believers to become Christ-like. In the task to become Christ-like,
Paul portrays himself as a model, or at least as someone engaged in the
same work, and who can be imitated. This role of Paul as a model and the
need to become Christ-like do not necessarily amount to a suppression of
differences.[37] Rather, Paul's way of imitating Christ is one way to become
Christ-like.[38] Christ functions as a formal model, infinitely flexible when it
comes to provide it with content. Each believer is responsible for putting
on Christ in the manner that fits her or him (13:14). The diversity of gifts
among believers can be and is recognized by Paul (12:3–8). Paul's call for
unity among Jews and nations insists that differences do not matter but,
precisely, because they do not matter, they do not need to be suppressed.
They should not divide, but neither do they need to disappear.[39] What really matters is the solidarity achieved in Christ.

---

[37] Contra Castelli, *Imitating Paul*.

[38] In this lack of autonomy, the self envisaged by Paul is in contrast with the modern
idea of the self. Gavin D. Flood, *The Ascetic Self: Subjectivity, Memory and Tradition*
(Cambridge: Cambridge University Press, 2004), 241 delineates a similar opposition between the ascetic self and the modern self: "For our purposes the important point is that
self-assertion both as autonomy and fulfillment erodes tradition-dependent ideas of the
ascetic self."

[39] The treatment of differences in Rom 12:1–15:15 reveal the Pauline attitude about
differences. Differences are respected, whether in the diversity of gifts, or of practices,
but they really do not matter.

If these two *teloi* cannot and should not be reconciled – and I will return to the impact of this difference below – I nonetheless want to insist on two commonalities that emerge especially when one focuses on the concrete practices in which one has to engage in order to construct one's self. First, I contend that both Foucault and Paul insist on the constant work involved in the transformation or the creation of the self. For both, the *telos* envisioned in their writings can never be achieved. In Foucault, this is actually part of the *telos* itself. Never quite attaining oneself is at the centre of the relationship that the self has with itself, as the last couple of sentences of the introduction to *The Archaeology of Knowledge* make clear:

> 'Are you already preparing the way out that will enable you in your next book to spring up somewhere else and declare as you're now doing: no, no, I'm not where you are lying in wait for me, but over here, laughing at you?'
>
> 'What, do you imagine that I would take so much trouble and so much pleasure in writing, do you think that I would keep so persistently to my task, if I were not preparing – with a rather shaky hand – a labyrinth into which I can venture, in which I can move my discourse, opening up underground passages, forcing it to go far from itself, finding overhangs that reduce and deform its itinerary, in which I can lose myself and appear at last to eyes that I will never have to meet again. I am no doubt not the only one who writes in order to have no face.[40]

Pleasure emerges precisely from the impossibility of achieving a *telos*, from having to start over and over again, perpetually. Never reaching one self, always having the possibility and the responsibility to change is intrinsic to the construction of the self. Foucault also insists that human beings usually inhabit various selves that can vary depending on the social and personal roles one is performing. Far from finding that fact distressing, Foucault argues that understanding the self as a form that can be molded and ever transformed in various figures – one could almost say incarnations – is part of the work involved in making one's life a work of art.[41] Part of the pleasure involved in the invention of the self is the ease with which one can navigate these different selves and identify how they were constituted historically. Foucault delineates an understanding of identity which is characterized by fluidity.[42] In order to maintain that fluidity, the

---

[40] Foucault, *The Archaeology of Knowledge*, 17. It seems that for those who are at pains to find a unity in Foucault's thought, the need to change and to surprise everyone, and particular himself, is a good candidate. See also his answer in "An Interview by Stephen Riggins," in Rabinow, *Ethics: Subjectivity and Truth*, 130–131. For a similar perspective on Foucault's inconsistency, see Page duBois, "The Subject in Antiquity after Foucault," in Larmour, Miller and Platter, *Rethinking Sexuality*, 85–103, here 98–99.

[41] See Foucault, "The Ethics of the Concern for Self," 290–291.

[42] For the understanding of identity as fluid, see also Vander Stichele and Penner, *Contextualizing Gender*, 23.

telos of becoming a self is necessarily unattainable. One has to start anew each day.

As I have argued, in contrast, Paul does give a concrete content for his *telos*, in the molding of a Christ-like identity and in the creation of a community marked by peace, harmony and solidarity, which thus glorifies God (Rom 15:5–7). However, this *telos* is only always an ideal which serves to orient the present behavior of the individuals in the community. Even in the case of the Romans, which Paul describes as "full of goodness, filled with all knowledge, and able to instruct one another," Paul writes in order to reactivate some elements that were known but perhaps not practiced (15:14). The task of becoming Christ-like as an individual and as a community only ends when final salvation is fulfilled (5:9.10; 8:23) and, for Paul, this can only happen when the full reconciliation between nations and Jews has taken place (11:25–26; 15:8–9), in the eschatological time.

As such, Paul's addressees are invited to tirelessly tend to this *telos*, but Paul is also convinced that this *telos* cannot be attained before the earth is restored and the true identity of human beings is revealed (8:19). The *telos* is also dependent upon the full inclusion of Israel (11:26), indicating that it is not attainable individually. Even the concept of imitation carries that dimension. When one imitates, one precisely never reaches the quality of the original. One only infinitely tends to becoming like the original and molds oneself for that purpose, without ever actually becoming the original. In Paul, this impossibility to reach the *telos* does no more bring despair than it does for Foucault. Rather, in both cases, it is an occasion for constant work and practices, aimed at shaping the self for a *telos* that can be understood as utopian in both cases. It emphasizes, once more, the need for invention in aiming towards a *telos* that one might not be able to quite see, but which is nonetheless worth pursuing.

In the constant work and in the constant mobility associated with the construction of identity, Foucault explicitly sees a location for pleasure and a guarantee against the establishment of a fixed system of power. It is not completely far-fetched to maintain that Paul also sees a dimension of pleasure, or at least satisfaction in the work, both accomplished and yet to be done, of constructing ethical subjects. He describes the fruits of the reconciliation with God as peace (Rom 5:1) and life (Rom 5:18), even new life (Rom 6:4), and speaks of the riches associated with the incorporation of the nations in the people of God (Rom 11:12). At the same time, he refuses to believe that these positive attributes are definite and final. Rather Paul's own insistence on the work still to be done and on what is still to come also functions as a warning against fossilizing the *telos* of becoming Christ-like in any kind of institution or system. For both thinkers, the *telos* is valuable and worth following precisely because it is always pursued, but never possessed. In addition, the unattainable character of the *teloi* also contributes to minimizing the risks for cooptation into abusive forms of power.

The second commonality surfaces when one reflects on the practical and embodied dimensions of the *teloi* of both writers. In both cases, there is a risk to interpret their *teloi* as personal goals, focused on the individual and having to do, in Foucault's case, with narcissistic pleasure, and in Paul's case, with individual, spiritual salvation. In both cases however, neither Paul nor Foucault is simply concerned with individual pleasure, or personal salvation, or aesthetic existence, or moral perfection. Both affirm the necessity for human beings to see themselves as embodied creatures, involved in the world that surrounds them, having responsibilities towards the other members of the community. They also recognize, and believe in, the capacity of each individual to translate these responsibilities into concrete practices without the support of a body of rules or prescriptions that would dictate their behavior.

In Paul, when one keeps in minds the importance of the games of power analyzed by Foucault, one cannot ignore the concrete, practical and political consequences of Paul's conception of salvation. In Romans, one of the effects brought about by the union of the believers to Christ is the liberation from the hold of sin. The Christ believers no longer lead their lives in the realm of sin. Traditionally, liberation from sin has been understood as having important personal consequences for the individual. It is seen as a theological concept that changes one's self-understanding and brings about an identity marked by peace and authenticity for the believers.[43] The believers are given a correct relationship to themselves, to God, to others and to the world. While I would not contest the validity of this claim – it seems clear to me that Paul did envision human beings as needing a restored relationship to themselves and to God – I maintain that Paul's thought is im-

---

[43] As is widely argued now, especially in the context of the new perspective on Paul, this interpretation owes much to Martin Luther's reading of Paul. It is also brought to New Testament studies through Søren Kierkegaard's philosophy and existentialist philosophy. See in particular Bultmann's presentation of Pauline anthropology in Bultmann, *Theology of the New Teswtament*. The journey of "man" is understood as the movement from a wrong self-perception to a correct one through the event of Christ (see *Theology of the New Testament*, 1:197: … man is a being who has a relationship to himself, and that this relationship can be either an appropriate or a perverted one; that he can be at one with himself or at odds; that he can be under his own control or lose grip on himself. In the latter case, a double possibility exists: that the power which comes to master him can make the estrangement within him determinative, and that would mean that it would destroy the man by entirely wresting him out of his own hands, or that this power gives him back to himself, that is, brings him to life."). For Lutheran interpretations of Paul, see Stephen Westerholm, *Perspectives Old and New on Paul: the 'Lutheran' Paul and his Critics* (Grand Rapids, Mich.: Eerdmans, 2004).

poverished if one neglects, as is often done, the dimension of the relationships with others and with the world and sees them as secondary consequences of Paul's major theological affirmation about the individual's personal salvation.[44]

Rather, I would like to argue that relationships with others and with the world are a central part of the concept of salvation. They are not simply consequences of personal salvation. They are part of what salvation is. In fact, the way Christ believers relate to others and handle differences is a practical and concrete embodiment of the salvation proclaimed to the believers. It gives substance and concrete incarnation to the news of salvation. Keeping this daily embodiment of salvation in mind wrestles Paul's writings from a conception that tends to see them as immortal theological treatises, whose bold and risky dimensions have long been domesticated.[45] When one begins to see salvation as more than a theological reality, one is able to delineate the resistance path taken by Paul, in his understanding of what forms a community, especially in his insistence that the community of Christ believers should include both Jews and pagan nations. When Paul describes his addressees as slaves (Rom 6:16.17.19.20.22), when he himself models the behavior of a slave (1:1), when he calls for understanding the family head as God, and constructs the family cell as uniting nations and Jews (Rom 8:14–17; 9–11; 15:7–13), he proposes a counter-narrative to dominant ways of understanding the world, whether it be inside the Jewish community or inside the Roman world at large.[46] Even though Paul is

---

[44] This secondary place is often reflected in the manner in which some commentaries analyze the role of chapters 12–16 in the structure of the letter to the Romans. They are often given less importance than the rest of the epistle. See for example the treatment of these chapters in Wilckens, *Der Brief an die Römer*. The last volume, which treats 12–16, is significantly shorter than the two first ones. For the view that 12:1–15:13 is an add-on not related to the theological core of the letter, see Dibelius, *From Tradition to Gospel*, 238. Lopez, *Apostle to the Conquered*, 4 challenges this traditional approach to Paul: "Could it really be that Paul's letters were all and only about the spread of a new form of personal faith to individuals who erroneously thought they would be justified by works of the law? Is it true that anything else is a wild dream, wishful thinking, or a figment of the imagination? It seems as if the history of New Testament interpretation would have it this way."

[45] In current scholarship on Paul, there is a trend in recovering the political dimension of Paul. This trend, although it sometimes insists too unilaterally on the political in Paul, challenges one to re-introduce Paul in his "real" world. See the work of Roland Boer, Neil Elliott and Richard Horsley (for a bibliography, see Lopez, *Apostle to the Conquered*, 178 and 179, n. 21, 180, n. 27).

[46] See Lopez, *Apsotle to the Conquered*, 153: "…S/he [Paul] advocates living into another world, the new creation, through inter-national community resistance and nonconformity to the Roman imperial structure, the metanarrative ordering the world and helping to keep peace at the time."

comfortable with staying inside these dominant ideologies (see Rom 13:1–7, or the recognition of Jewish privileges [Rom 3:2; 9:4–5]), at the same time, his mission imagines ways of living for his communities that are at odds with the world in which he evolves.[47]

Foucault could similarly be seen as overly focused on the individual and as engaging in a futile chase of pleasure that involves a perpetual and abusive crossing of limits. He himself always refused to develop universally valid prescriptions, leaving the door ajar for such misinterpretations. In particular, Foucault never elaborated what political consequences his writings could have. He never defined a political system, or political instructions that could be followed by a party or by voters – something that has often been reproached to him. Nonetheless, his analyses of the subject constituted by power relationships, by knowledge apparatuses, and his work on the self-constituted subject through technologies of the self all have consequences for the manner in which the individual behaves in a world traversed by political games. Construction of the self does imply the others, and Foucault often indicated that the purpose of ethical work is precisely to envision relationships in which power is negotiated in ways that are respectful of others. I would argue that precisely his refusal to engage in any kind of prescriptive discourse stems from a deep respect for the others, and their own capacity for ethical work. Foucault's aspiration to have his works become tool boxes used by others succinctly represents the way in which he felt his thought engaged with the world. Far from being detached from the world and indifferent to its difficulties, Foucault hopes that everyone will be able to engage both the world and self-construction in a manner that demonstrates not only an awareness of the pervasiveness of power relationships but also a willingness to engage these relationships in new, creative and respectful ways.

4. Summary

Above, I have emphasized the dimensions through which I believe a real dialogue between Paul and Foucault is possible. For me, reading Foucault and Paul together has raised three elements in relation to construction of

---

[47] See Lopez, *Apostle to the Conquered*, for example 8: "Paul's letters, then, can be re-read as a 'rhetoric of resistance'," also 119: "I contend that Paul, like many of the New Testament writers, provided intervention into Roman imperial ideology" and 120: "Paul works within his context from a marginalized position, using imagination to respond to this world."

the self. Both insist that self-construction necessarily means negotiating complex and multiple relationships of power, for the person herself, and for the community. Just because one works on personhood and on the self does not mean that power and power relationships are absent or do not play a role in the way one understands oneself. Rather, the work of constructing oneself, of negotiating one's personal freedom, is tightly woven with the need to engage in various power struggles and power relationships with others. In addition, both insist that these power struggles related to self-construction cannot be solved by a body of rules. Rather they demand creativity and inventiveness. Finally, both make one aware that the *telos* of self-construction can never be attained and even less possessed. It requires constant work and aspiration. This work involves a perpetual reorganization of both power relationships and self-construction.

These elements indicate, again, that Paul might be closer to the Hellenistic philosophers than to Christianity – at least in the way Foucault understands both of them. Despite these commonalities, I also want to think about differences, moving, eventually, beyond Paul and Foucault towards my own role as an interpreter.

C. Understanding of Identity

While highlighting similar concerns in the way Foucault and Paul reflect about the problems related to self-construction, I have also remarked that Foucault and Paul differ from each other when it comes to discussing the grounding of the subject in a possible given identity. On this topic, I believe Foucault and Paul's ways to look at the problem are irreconcilable, and it would be a mistake to try to make them agree. Rather, I think we can fruitfully explore this difference, in order to clarify what is involved in the construction of the self when one sees identity as given or not.

For Paul, the notion of an identity given to the Christ believers is tied to his understanding of baptism, and to what happens to the Christ believers in this event. Through baptism, the Christ believers experience the death and resurrection pattern that characterizes the life of Jesus,[48] and, through this experience, they can walk in the newness of life (6:3–4). Baptism symbolizes the entrance in something new, and starts something new in the life of the believers. It is an activation "within the community" of "the experience of Jesus' death and resurrection."[49] Baptism does not mean that their person *per se* has changed. I have noted that the Christ believers still

---

[48] See Johnson, *Reading Romans*, 102: "… for Paul, baptism was not a mere ritual of initiation but a powerful participation in the death and resurrection of Jesus."

[49] See Johnson, *Reading Romans*, 103.

have the same body, the same abilities, and that they still relate to the same persons, in the same world. However, as the use of Ricœur's thought has clarified, they have experienced a complete reconfiguration of their personhood. Possibilities that were unimaginable suddenly open up for them. They are asked to think of themselves in a new way, they are invited to leave behind a form of their self which was inhabited by sin and to embrace and fit themselves in a self that reflects their belonging to Christ.[50] It is not so much that the person receives a completely new and different identity, but she understands herself differently, and thus has new responsibilities in relationship to that new self-understanding. She is called to use her body and her abilities in a manner that reflects the fact that sin no longer lives in her; rather, she has to reveal in her actions that she is now clothed in Christ.

Paul's language of clothing oneself in Christ, of becoming Christ-like, as well as his use of the image of the family of God (8:14–17), in which believers belong to the master and thus have to act on his behalf, reveal that Paul is at ease with the idea that the Christ believers are not completely autonomous in the constitution of their selves, that they are not free to use their capacities in any way they want, but rather that they are responsible to conform to the *ēthos* of their master. In fact, that is the only worldview Paul can embrace: one can serve the wrong master and be limited in what one can accomplish, or one can serve the right master, and in that relationship, find the proper fulfillment of one's capacities, abilities and vocation (6:16).

In serving a new master, the believers are transformed in their self-understanding and subject themselves to the will of God. Their identity is shaped by their master, and they owe obedience to that master. For Paul, slavery to God is a powerful liberating event, which returns the individuals to their correct purpose and their correct place in the world. Once the

---

[50] In his philosophical commentary on Romans, Agamben proposes a reading of the concept of vocation which clarifies the relationship between old and new identity. It is not that the Christ believers receive an entirely new identity after baptism; rather, their identity is both cancelled and reclaimed. See Agamben, *The Time that Remains*, 41. In his interpretation of the "as not," Agamben is able to maintain the tension between what has disappeared in human beings through the union with the messiah, while at the same time arguing that it is not just a new identity that is given to human beings: "The coming of the Messiah means that all things, even the subjects who contemplate it, are caught up in the *as not*, called and revoked at the same time. No subject could watch it or act *as if* at a given point. The messianic vocation dislocates and, above all, nullifies the entire subject. This is the meaning of Galatians 2:20, 'It is no longer I that live [zō ouketi egō], but the Messiah living in me.' He lives in him precisely as the 'no longer I,' that dead body of sin we bear within ourselves which is given life through the Spirit in the Messiah (Rom 8:11)."

Christ believers have received a Christ-like identity in baptism, they need to conform to this identity and remain faithful to it. In addition, for Paul, it is also clear that without baptism, without the participation in Christ's *ēthos* and without the gift of the spirit, the transformation of the believers would be neither possible nor realizable. It is only because the Christ believers have clothed themselves in Christ (13:14) that they can leave behind the ways of the world and build a new type of community among believers, a community marked by solidarity and harmony, and not by competition and strife.

In contrast, when Foucault defines the task of each individual, through his notion of curiosity or invention, I understand him as opposing the notion that one can receive one's identity from someone or something else. On this he finds himself in agreement with Sartre. Both reject the "idea of the self as something that is given to us."[51] But Foucault pushes the argument further and argues that Sartre in fact returns, through the notion of authenticity, to the necessity of being truly oneself.[52] Notwithstanding whether or not Foucault represents Sartre rightly in this critique, it is important to see that, for Foucault, there is no interest in the notion of a self given to human beings, or even in the concept of a true self. For Foucault, "It [the subject] is not a substance. It is a form, and this form is not primarily or always identical to itself."[53] What primarily characterizes the subject is change. As such, identity is not something one can reach or someday attain, when all the changes are completed. Rather, identity is a constant work, which is never finished. Through the various forms the subject takes, a self is delineated, but this self is fluid, so much so that there is never an "I" which the person eventually reaches and which defines who the person is. The self is constructed each day and is changed each day, through the experiences one makes, the persons one encounters, and Foucault would add, the limits one transgresses.

The fundamental place given to change in Foucault's understanding of the subject also means it would be futile to look for an essence behind the concept of "man": "… In the course of their history, men have never ceased to construct themselves, that is, to continually displace their subjectivity, to constitute themselves in an infinite, multiple series of different subjectivities that will never have an end and never bring us in the presence of something that would be 'man.' Men are perpetually engaged in a process that, in constituting objects, at the same displaces man, deforms, transforms, and transfigures him as a subject."[54] In this context, the task

---

[51] Foucault, "On the Genealogy of Ethics," 351.

[52] See Foucault, "On the Genealogy of Ethics," 351.

[53] Foucault, "The Ethics of the Concern for Self," 290.

[54] Foucault, "Interview with Michel Foucault," 276.

for the subject is a perpetual recreation of itself, which defies the fossilization in an identity which defines who one truly is and to which one needs
to remain faithful. In addition, in Foucault, there is no room for a life-
changing, divinely induced, event that would define a path of transformations for the subject. Rather, each individual is solely responsible for
the slow and arduous work of change, made possible through small transformations and creative practices. The relationship one has with oneself
should be one of creative activity.[55] It does not depend from outside intervention, and it certainly has no basis in the gift of identity through a con-
version-like event. It is the responsibility, and perhaps also the pleasure, of
each individual to create her life as a work of art.

It is possible to oppose succinctly and bluntly the Paul of Romans and
Foucault on that question by saying that the former believes in the necessity of an identity given to the person and that the latter rejects this possibility. I believe that there are several elements at stake for each thinker in this
opposition and that these elements can help me conceptualize some of the
difficulties related to identity-construction.

In his work on the subject, Foucault emphasizes the various ways in
which the person can be made into a subject, through power relationships
or discursive practices. A foucaultian reading of Paul renders one attentive
to the potential alienation irremediably attached to a doctrine that equates
freedom and liberation with the necessity to submit to a higher power. The
mode of subjection in Paul's ethical construction of the subject is related to
the respect of God's will. In the respect of God's will, in the embracing of
the identity shaped by God's will, human beings find their purpose. If one
adopts a foucaultian perspective on Paul and reads his letter to the Romans
with a hermeneutics of suspicion, one can argue that Paul bonds the subject to a self-understanding to which she has the obligation of remaining
faithful, to which she needs to show loyalty. This self-understanding is
characterized first and foremost by obedience, an obedience modeled by
Christ, even unto his own death. For Paul, it is only this obedience that can
create true freedom and that can help human beings reach their true identity and their true purpose. In addition, this obedience, which grounds the
identity of the subject, is not the subject's own doing; it is created through
the outside intervention of a divine human being and imposed on the person. For Foucault, the idea of obedience, especially when it is connected

---

[55] See Foucault, "On the Genealogy of Ethics," 351: "In his analyses of Baudelaire,
Flaubert, etc. it is interesting to see that Sartre refers the work of creation to a certain
relation to oneself – the author to himself – which has the form of authenticity or of inau-
thenticity. I would like to say exactly the contrary: we should not have to refer the creative activity of somebody to the kind of relation he has to himself, but should relate the
kind of relation one has to oneself to a creative activity."

with the objective of the authentic realization of the human being, carries with it the potential of becoming a lethal form of alienation.[56]

Even if in Romans Paul shares a good news of restoration with his addressees and insists that they are now in a state that allows them to use their abilities to the fullest, there is a risk for this state to become petrified in a tradition and in a set of values to which one has to comply and that become the natural, established order of things. A foucaultian reading reminds one that even (or perhaps especially) a message which wants to free those to whom it is addressed and challenge the status quo runs the risk of solidifying itself in a new established order that is then also in need of being challenged. Foucault warns against the idea that any form of freedom can take place in a system which renders the individual subject to an identity she or he cannot escape. I maintain that Paul himself was intent on calling into question a conventional order of things and a traditional ideology. However, Foucault makes one acutely conscious and suspicious of the potential of fossilization contained in Paul's own writings.

Whether Paul himself was aware of this risk or not is of course extremely difficult to decide. On the one hand, he certainly did not write his letters with the idea that they would be included in a collection that would receive canonical authority in the centuries coming after him. On the other hand, the identity that Paul defines for his addressees is something that he is willing to shape and construct, sometimes also enforce, if needed, through his letters and through his authority as an apostle.[57] Even though I have

---

[56] Moore insists on the alienating dimension of that model of obedience, especially for the manner in which the Church has treated women. See Moore, *God's Beauty Parlor*, 156: "This universal sin is epitomized, or, better, synecdochically figured (the part standing in for the whole), by homoerotic sexual relations, especially between women, as we have seen. But why is *Jesus* the solution? Because Jesus submitted himself absolutely to God (cf. Phil. 2:5–8; Rom. 5:19), uniquely exemplifying the obedience to, and reverence for, God's authority that God demands of every human being. Stripped naked and spread out on the cross, run through with sundry phallic objects, Jesus in his relationship to God perfectly models the submissiveness that should also characterize the God-fearing female's proper relationship to the male. This is the sexual substratum of Paul's soteriology." and 159–160: "Mastery – of others, but most especially of oneself – was the supreme index of masculinity in the Greco-Roman intellectual milieu of the mid first century C.E., and had been for quite some time. Against this towering backcloth, it is hard to resist reading the Pauline Jesus' submission unto death as a bravura display of self-mastery, and hence a spectacular performance of masculinity." Also 162. Moore also suggests the possibility (albeit quickly stifled) of finding spaces of resistance inside Paul's rhetoric: see 167 and 168.

[57] See a point made by Caroline Vander Stichele and Todd Penner, "Paul and the Rhetoric of Gender," in *Her Master's Tools? Feminist and Postcolonial Engagements of Historical-Critical Discourse* (ed. C. Vander Stichele and T. Penner; Atlanta: Society of Biblical Literature, 2005), 287–310, here 291: "[i]t ... redirects the attention from the traditional image of Paul as pastor, who offers sublime guidance to his struggling com-

shown that Paul does not rely on a body of laws to outline the mode of subjection at work in his ethical construction on the subject, and that he encourages his addressees to develop their own embodiments of the identity of children of God, it is also true that, in some places, he does not shrink from using exhortative language much more forceful than what he writes in Romans. In these cases, he uses authoritative means to try to impose his point of view, through rhetorical moves, or through the appeal to apostolic and divine authority. In addition, tradition after him – and I will return to this – has quickly transformed Paul's writings in orthodoxy that becomes immutable and weighs down on efforts to challenge what is in place.

Foucault reminds one that workings of power are also active in Paul's own doctrine of liberation and reconciliation to God. I maintain that Romans can be read as a negotiating of power that limits the dangers of alienation, but Foucault invites us to not rest on those laurels and to give particular attention to the spaces in which power relationships go unnoticed. The power that Paul – consciously or not – wields over his communities needs to be seen as such. Even a liberating event can result in the binding of the individual to an alienating identity. As a tool of power, Paul's salvation doctrine can – and has – become an instrument for submitting others, for forcing them to fit in an identity marked by alienation and lack of autonomy. In these cases, challenge is necessary and new readings of Paul are demanded. I will discuss the possibilities for these new readings in the next section.

Reading with Paul also offers a new angle of approach on Foucault's discussion of identity. I do not pretend to know how Paul would have valued Foucault's work on the subject, but I think that for my purpose it might be possible to reflect on the manner in which Foucault's understanding of the subject would translate into Pauline categories. When one thinks with Paul's conceptual categories in mind, Foucault's position represents a self-grounding attempt to found the subject. Given his cultural and religious contexts, Paul cannot envision a form of thought that works with the assumption of the autonomy of the subject. For him, presuming that the subject can be its own foundation reveals an incorrect understanding of the world and its organization. It ignores the activity of the creator in the world. Such a misunderstanding is developed by Paul in the first chapter of Romans (1:18–32). It reflects foolishness (1:22) and a skewed perspective on the world (1:21). Paul can only conceive of it in terms of sin. For him, this self-reliance is not only arrogance – the arrogance of the human being who claims to be able to control her life and to make her own decisions – but it ultimately leads to anxiety. Paul discusses this anxiety in Rom 7. In

---

munities, to a founder seeking to shape, maintain, and, if necessary, enforce a strongly boundaried Christian identity."

this section of the letter, the false idea that one is in control of what one is doing is revealed as the product of sin. For Paul, the person might claim to know what she is doing but in reality, it is not her acting on her behalf. Rather, it is sin taking hold of her and controlling her actions. Presumably, at one moment or another, the person will end up divided against herself, and realize that she in fact is not in control of her actions; sin is. For Paul, nothing can liberate the person from this alienation, other than divine intervention through the death and resurrection of Christ.

Thus, in a perhaps surprising turn of event – but one that would not necessarily have offended Foucault – the edges of a possible alienating dimension in Foucault's thought emerge out of the shadows of reading Paul. The requirement for constant change ineluctably connected to the pursuit of spaces of resistance and to the crossing of limits sketches a figure of the subject who is, in a way, never at peace with itself and never liberated from the concern about the self. In fact, this is precisely what Foucault is after: unquietness. Only in an unquiet state is one prepared to challenge what is established and to engage in the necessary and perpetual work of deconstructing what is in place, in order to reconstruct what one cannot yet see. For Foucault, this is never seen as paralyzing or distressing. Rather it is the motor that allows the work to continue, through curiosity and innovation. In a Pauline perspective, however, this can be read as futile and anxiety-driven behavior by a person unable to understand, let alone accept, her proper position in the world. In the long run, this person is menaced by exhaustion, despair and the loss of herself.[58] In contrast, in Paul's thought, especially when one keeps in mind Ricœur's discussion of *idem* and *ipse* identity, the notion of commitment to one's word can be experienced as a freeing decision. It liberates from enslavement to constant change, from a necessity to never feel at ease with oneself and allows for serenity. Through this commitment, the self grounds itself strongly in a community and can stop worrying about itself, focusing instead on the needs of others in the community.

For me, this difference of perspective on the status of the person who self-reliantly grounds herself in her own abilities is at the core of not only the dialogue between Foucault and Paul, but also of the discussion about self-construction. These two positions are ultimately irreconcilable, and they each emphasize a completely different outlook on what the person

---

[58] In addition, this person is threatened by a lack of engagement with others around her and with community. Beverly W. Harrison sees this self-reliance and the freedom from dependence on others as the mark of a male dominated ethics. See her article "The Power of Anger in the Work of Love," *USQRSupplementary* 36 (1981): 41–57, here 51. In this perspective, Foucault's insistence on change can be seen as not only arrogant but also a way of creating a typical male identity.

should aim for in identity-construction. In a Pauline perspective, the person can be assured that, once she embraces the right perspective on the world, she will be liberated from the anxiety of becoming herself. In that regard, the fact that one of the results of the union with Christ is peace cannot be emphasized enough (5:1). Clearly peace defines first and foremost the person's relationship with God. But at the same time, I maintain that peace also defines the relationship the person can have with herself (8:6). It liberates her from the concern over herself. In contrast, Foucault precisely calls for discomfort and restlessness. In the perpetual movement away from oneself, one has the possibility to shape one's life in a work of art, which defies fossilized power-relationships and established boundaries. Whatever side is chosen, however, I would like to note that in both cases, peace and restlessness lead to concrete actions in the world, that seek to establish an ethics more respectful of the other. Neither one is attained (or precisely not attained) for its own sake.

D. Thinking Beyond Foucault and Paul

At the beginning of this chapter, I have insisted that my reading of Foucault and Paul did not exhaust its purpose in a confrontation between the two thinkers. Rather, it is a reading done in order to engage my own present and the questions related to the construction of the self.[59] The previous section has highlighted the issues and problems that emerge when one thinks about the self with Paul and Foucault. It has emphasized the impact of power relationships on the construction of the self, and delineated one major alternative in the definition of identity, by contrasting the concept of a given identity, maintained over time, with the notion of a created identity, ever changing. Now, in this final section, I am interested in seeing what this changes for me, how this challenges not only my understanding of what it means to be a subject, but also my status as an interpreter both of Paul and of Foucault.

I have emphasized throughout my reading of Romans that Paul presents his addressees with a story designed to underscore the remarkable liberation that the Christ believers experience in their baptism, while simultaneously insisting on the opportunities and need for concrete actions that are

---

[59] The title for this section is inspired from Vander Stichele and Penner, *Contextualizing Gender.* In their introduction, they explain their use of "thinking beyond" as denoting the need to "move 'beyond' the historical past, as much as we are also interested in that same past, but largely as a tool 'to think about' the present." For them, "this reconfigured paradigm means ... that we have one foot in the past and another in the present, trying to keep that balance, as delicate a balancing act as it may be." (7)

connected to this liberation. Although I am convinced that it is important to reclaim the liberating possibility contained in Paul's thought, Foucault, through his constant and relentless attentiveness to the imprisoning potentialities of systems of liberation, also calls into question the destiny of Paul in later interpretations and forces one to practice a hermeneutics of suspicion towards the apostle. Traditional interpretations have confirmed the suspicion that Paul's liberating action and mission could be transformed in alienating systems by later interpreters. Paul, through the misogynist and homophobic texts in his corpus – and a good part of his bad press is due to that – has been used to promote a universalism in which otherness is suppressed in the name of a oneness marked by masculinity, patriarchal values and refusal of differences. Because of the use of Paul by those seeking to maintain a dominant position, it has been very difficult for queer, feminist and postcolonial interpretations in particular to find any liberating value in Paul.[60] At the same time, Paul is often described in biblical studies as having a strictly theological program, thus political and/or social issues should not be associated with his work. This contributes to fitting Paul in a conservative framework, in which transgression, change, imagination and invention have little to do. In that case, it seems that the only option left for queer, feminist, gender-critical and postcolonial interpretations is to simply get rid of Paul and abandon him.

---

[60] See Lopez, *Apostle to the Conquered*, 167: "It is true that Paul uses the language of universalism, and this truth is unfortunately what has led to interpretations of Paul as a patriarch himself who conquers otherness in the name of oneness." That is the way Castelli portrays Paul in *Imitating Paul*, for example, 103: "'Become imitators of me' is a call to sameness which erases difference and, at the same time, reinforces the authoritative status of the model." See also Moore, *God's Beauty Parlor*, chapter 3 in particular. Lopez is aware of these interpretations of Paul and seeks to challenge them and to regain the resistance aspect of Paul; see *Apostle to the Conquered*, 15: "Feminist and queer biblical interpretations have evolved into multifaceted methodological tools for addressing biblical texts and contexts from the margins in the service of liberation. In both cases, however, Paul has been considered a major obstacle to true emancipatory re-readings of the New Testament due to his perceived insurmountable hatred of women and gay people, as well as his overall domineering masculine self-presentation and expectation of his communities. This is at least partly due to the reality that famous and enduring prooftexts for misogyny and homophobia are in Paul's letters. While I would not argue that Paul is perfect or even a feminist or gay man himself, I submit that characterizations of Paul as excessively dominating and irretrievably harmful suffer from a lack of complexity. Ancient Paul is not simply for or against contemporary women and LGBT people. As is the case with empire-critical and postcolonial interpretation, conflation of what is perceived to be *in* the text with the prejudices that have been *mapped onto it* in its 'captured' form throughout time, primarily by those who seek to maintain privilege, have prevented a thorough re-evaluation and re-imagination of Paul from feminist, gender-critical, and/or queer perspectives."

Abandoning Paul seems to be the natural option, the necessary option. Foucault's genealogical work however, and his analytics of power as well, reminds us of the constant need to see beyond contingencies and to find spaces of resistance inside power relations. Using imagination, one can implement Foucault's critical method. If we move away from a solely theological interpretation of Paul and see him as deeply involved in the political, cultural and religious world around him, it becomes possible to reclaim the potential for resistance contained in his writings. In particular, it invites the interpreter to look at Paul as enmeshed in a network of relationships of power, and inside this network, Paul can be seen as creating new forms of relationships which propose an alternative way of behaving towards others and implement small, local and concrete spaces of resistance.

In particular, I have mentioned several times that Paul imagines a new type of community. I have already discussed the images that Paul uses to define this community and its members, in particular his use of the image of family – which I have presented in terms of the household of God in chapter 3 – of the language of slavery and sonship. All these images carry with them a strong potential for alienation and can be critiqued as outlining an oppressive, paternalistic and male understanding of the community and the people who live in it. However, if one keeps in mind the milieu in which Paul lives, works and writes, I imagine that the liberating power of this imagery can be reclaimed. In establishing God as the new master of the Christ believers, as the *pater familias*, Paul reminds his addressees that the elements that divide Jews and nations – elements that seem so central to their self-understanding – fade when one takes into account the fact that Jews and pagans serve the same master and now belong to the same household. The universalism that Paul encourages is a universalism of solidarity, which should embrace the weakest of the community as the common denominator.[61] The language of slavery also reminds Paul's addressees that their rightful master is the God of Israel, and not the Roman emperor, as might have been claimed by Roman imperial ideology, which portrayed the nations (both Jews and non-Jews) as enslaved to Rome and to the emperor.

In addition, the language of slavery is not the only way in which Paul elaborates the identity of his addressees in Romans. In the ethical injunctions of chapters 12–15, and in the language of chapter 8, Paul moves away from the slave metaphor, and, in chapter 8 in particular, he privileges the language of sonship, which unites all peoples (both Jews and non-Jews) in a common household, and allows them to know God's will (Rom 12:2). In moving away from the language of slavery – a move made explicit in Gal 5:1 – Paul impresses on his addressees the awareness that they are already

---

[61] Lopez, *Apostle to the Conquered*, 168.

living in a new creation. In the concept of new creation, Paul does not simply unite Jews and non-Jews at a theological level, arguing that they are both saved; rather he envisions practical consequences to this affirmation, consequences that need to be drawn out on several levels: sociological, cultural, ethical, political and economic. In the creation of a community, here on earth, which embodies values that are in contrast to the dominant ideologies of the Greco-Roman and Jewish milieus surrounding the Christ believers, Paul makes clear that salvation is not simply a theological category, which insures one's future participation in heaven. The community that Paul founds in Romans through his narrative is called to display harmony and solidarity, between two people that were often understood as separated. In that call for solidarity, Paul creates a story that allows the invention of a counter-narrative to the forms of subjection represented by the dominant ideologies surrounding the Pauline community.

For the community to which he addresses himself, Paul, when he appeals to the renewing of the mind (Rom 12:2), opens up spaces for change, for challenge and for resistance. Through imagination and the type of story-telling that he exemplifies in the epistle to the Romans itself, Paul remodels and transforms the manner in which his addressees perceive their bodies, their inner abilities and their ethnic belonging. For me, this crossing of limits, which is highlighted in Foucault's thought, offers possibilities to use Paul in new, and perhaps subversive, ways, even among groups who might feel rejected or offended by his letters. In particular, I want to insist on the fact that Paul negotiates power, and he can be read as doing it in a modern, or even postmodern, manner. Evidently, Paul holds some power, and he is conscious of that power, of the responsibilities that come with it (see Rom 1:5.9.11.13–14) and of what is due to him because of that power (see Rom. 15:24.30–32; 16:1–2). In letters less polite and less collected than Romans, he is not afraid to use this power or to appeal to it, sometimes in harsh and menacing tones, especially when he has to deal with controversy. Power is not something that is suppressed in his dealings with the communities. Even in his ethical injunctions, he remains aware of the fact that power relationships are at work inside the communities, that some are stronger than others, and that these tensions and difficulties will not disappear. However, this power is not seen as something debilitating or paralyzing.

Rather, Paul is also at the origin of empowerment among his addressees. The tools he uses to construct the identity of the members of the communities are at the disposal of these members, in order for them to build authentic relationships with God, with themselves, and with others. I maintain that the conflicts that occur between Paul and his communities can happen precisely because his addressees, in the relationship with Paul, are given power to argue with power. After all, they too can boast in a Christ-like *ēthos* since that is precisely what Paul asks them to embody. Because Paul recognizes the existence of power relationships inside the community as well, these power relationships can remain dynamic, fluid, and sometimes even volatile. This explosive dimension leads the way for exposing artificial limits and opens up possibilities for creating new spaces of resistance.

If one remembers that the conversations that occur inside the Pauline communities were once living embodiments of fluid power relationships, and not fixed, fossilized, canonical writings that prescribe solutions, then I would hope that one can engage the Pauline texts in new and challenging ways, in order to redefine some contemporary power relationships and create the spaces of resistance one needs now. In that attempt, the burden lays on the interpreters to create new perspectives on Paul, in order to queer one's understanding of him, beyond the limitations necessarily related to his anchoring in his time period. If there is one thing that Foucault teaches interpreters, it is precisely to question the temporal roots of truths and necessities. If Paul, despite the limitations clearly present in his letters, is seen as implementing practices of freedom inside his communities and then negotiating the difficulties that arise when one actually lives inside this new found freedom, then nothing should keep interpreters from imagining new ways in which freedom can be negotiated today, through Pauline texts themselves. Paul challenges his addressees to construct new relationships with God, with themselves and with others. Through imagination, curiosity and invention, one can implement this challenge in one's own life, but also in one's own reading of Paul, hopefully constructing "an alternative image of Paul,"[62] as someone not afraid to cross boundaries and create new ways of living. Paul's own life illustrates this experience of tremendous change, which opens up new possibilities.

In that context, the opposition between given identity and created identity that I have outlined earlier loses some of its edge. In fact, I suspect that it is not impossible to integrate the notion of creativity in the Pauline understanding of identity. Perhaps it is precisely this foucaultian notion of creativity and invention that needs to give dynamism to the concept of given identity. If one keeps in mind the need for imagination and curiosity when it comes to the constitution of the self, one needs to question the understanding of baptism in Paul and the relevance of the concept of conversion. Baptism, and the notion of conversion associated with it, insists on the importance of a single life-changing event. Particularly in the European

---

[62] Lopez, *Apostle to the Conquered*, 19. This stands in contrast to approaches of Paul that see him as epitomizing the model of the Roman male. See for example, Moore, *God's Beauty Parlor*, 155, even though Moore notices that Paul's own portrayal as celibate contrasts with his depiction of God as the patriarchal Roman male in Rom 1:18–32.

and North-American world, conversion tends to be understood as a single event concerned with the individual.[63] After the work of Stendhal and of the new perspective, the notion of call might be more appropriate to describe the life of the Christ believers.[64] The call can be understood as the beginning of a long transformation that demands constant work. It does not particularly emphasize the call-launching event – even as it also recognizes its importance – but insists on the process inaugurated by the call.

In this process, invention and creativity need to play a role. The process, for Paul, cannot begin without the experience of being united to Christ. But the experience of being united to Christ should not be the ultimate *telos* for the Christ believers. It should be understood as what opens up endless possibilities for work in the present. The story that Paul tells in Romans and that allows the ethical injunctions of chapters 12–15, inscribes his letter in a process aimed at making his addressees imagine the practical consequences of their belonging to Christ and invent new ways in which they can embody these consequences in their relationships to each other. There are no reasons for this process of change, for the work of curiosity, for the daring crossing of boundaries to stop at any point in time. Again, we are reminded that the *telos* envisioned by Paul for the Christ believers will only be reached when creation is restored (8:21) and when the full number of the Gentiles and of Israel has joined the people of God (11:25–26). Thus, the responsibility to create anew is left to those reading Paul, today and tomorrow. Our own reading practices can become opportunities to create spaces of resistance and to cross boundaries.

E. Crossing Boundaries:
The Work of Hermeneutical Imagination

I suspect that resistance in my own work on Paul has functioned principally in my willingness to engage in interdisciplinary work, in giving equal importance to two very different voices that have shaped my own understanding of what it means to construct the self. My interest in the question of the construction of the self also creates certain pictures of Paul and of Foucault that function as muted backdrops for this study. Perhaps it is necessary to at last bring these backdrops to the fore so as to confront the risks of fossilization and cooptation present in my own work and to develop

---

[63] Lopez, *Apostle to the Conquered*, 121.

[64] See Stendhal, "Paul and the Introspective Conscience of the West," and Lopez's own reading of Paul's call in *Apostle to the Conquered*.

once again the spaces of resistance obstinately delineated in the dialogue
between these two men.

Writers are, in the end, only always what one reader makes of them –
my own work does not depart from this rule. The image that readers have
in their mind concerning an author might be infinitely more or infinitely
less than what the writer really is, but it is, in the end, the only one that really matters to the readers. The destiny of Paul has not been any different.[65] In my reading, I believe I have constructed the image of a talented
narrator, who cares deeply about the people to whom he writes, who tries,
with more or less success, to shape who these people would become by
reminding them of who they were and how they became these particular
individuals, beloved of God, called to be saints (Rom 1:7). I have highlighted the formidable freedom that Paul sees at work in human beings
once they accept to become servants of the right master and I have insisted
on the potential subjection that can hide behind this freedom. I have maintained the importance of challenging this potential subjection through attention to the subversive dimension of Paul's work and to the spaces of
resistance created in his own work. In that dimension more than any other,
the colors of Paul's portrayal have been influenced by the palette used in
Foucault's writings.

At the same time, concerning Foucault, I have created the portrayal of a
man for whom invention and creativity are primary categories for understanding the task of the individuals, for whom resistance inside relationships of power is not only always necessary but also always possible. I
have constructed a unity in his thought through the notion of resistance and
I have given credit to the manner in which the man himself summarizes his
work as deeply concerned with the subject and its constitution. I have used
aspects of Paul's thought to warn against the danger of ignoring the community dimension in Foucault's thought and transforming his philosophy
in narcissistic dandyism and empty arrogance.

In both cases, I believe that it is not extremely important to know
whether or not Foucault and Paul really match my portrayals of them. I am
able to portray them in that manner because of my own position as an interpreter and my own interest in a particular question (the construction of
the self). More than each other's palette, thus, my own colors seep into the
portrayals of these two men and impress my concerns over their own.
Their texts become tools for the construction of my own hermeneutics. If
need be, I can seek a justification in Foucault himself, and argue that I do
not seek solutions in the past as much as ways to problematize a question

---

[65] Paul has been portrayed as a caring pastor, a daring missionary, a chauvinistic pig,
a horrible conservative, a bold reformer, an awful homophobic... The list is long, and the
images called forward here are by no means exhaustive.

for my own time. In that problematization, imagination plays an important role.

My reading has been a space for an encounter between Foucault and Paul, between philosophical ways of reading texts, narrative ways of reading texts and historical-critical ways of reading texts. It has mixed various methodologies and various perspectives on two authors, not necessarily standing outside of these methods, but situating itself at the intersections, at the borders.[66] It has brought together two very different authors and in the difficulties of bringing together these two voices, I believe it has highlighted the risk of subjection always contained in discursive practices.[67] Through interdisciplinarity, one resists the disciplining effects of discourse because one necessarily stands somewhat outside of disciplines, at the juncture between one discipline and the other, in a hybrid space; in my case, neither properly New Testament exegesis, nor really postmodern philosophy. Interdisciplinarity can function as space for creativity, and marks a need for invention.[68] Interdisciplinarity challenges the firmness and certainty of the division between "traditional" and "non-traditional" approaches to the disciplines and seeks to open new routes for thought. It invites one to see what is not necessarily seen by the disciplines that one straddles in the practice of interdisciplinarity.[69]

---

[66] For the hermeneutics associated to a reading from the borders and its connection to imagination, see Hjamil A. Martínez-Vázquez, "Breaking the Established Scaffold: Imagination as a Resource in the Development of Biblical Interpretation," in Vander Stichele and Penner, *Her Master's Tools?* 71–91, also Hjamil A. Martínez-Vázquez, "The Postcolonizing Project: Constructing a Decolonial Imaginary from the Borderlands," *The Journal of World Christianity* 1 (2009): 1–28.

[67] Vander Stichele and Penner emphasize this as one of the dimensions of the postmodern project. See Caroline Vander Stichele and Todd Penner, "Mastering the Tools or Retooling the Masters? The Legacy of Historical-Critical Discourse," in Vander Stichele and Penner, *Her Master's Tools?* 1–29, here 23: "One ... finds discrete communities (past and present) and different experiences, which can only be brought into conversation with great difficulty, and then always at the risk of being subjected to one colonizing project/power or another."

[68] See Bhabha, *The Location of Culture*, 12: "...It is the space of intervention emerging in the cultural interstices that introduces creative invention into existence."

[69] While I do not pretend to have brought out completely neglected aspects of Paul or Foucault's thought, I think that the interdisciplinary approach I have practiced has forced me to move from the center and approach these two writers from a somewhat different perspective. See a reflection that Bhabha develops in relationship to his own experience with English literature: *The Location of Culture*, xi: "What was missing from the traditionalist world of English literary study, as I encountered it, was a rich and paradoxical engagement with the pertinence of what lay in an *oblique* or alien relation to the forces of centering. Writers who were off-center; literary texts that had been passed by; themes and topics that had lain dormant or unread in great works of literature – these were the angles of vision and visibility that enchanted me."

In the case of Paul, my interaction with the thought of Foucault has emphasized the creative dimension of Paul's work in the construction of the self and the possibility to see spaces of resistance in his writings, as well as the necessity to create new spaces of resistance in Pauline interpretation. It has looked for what is unseen, sometimes even un-hoped for, in Paul, namely practices of freedom that create new relationships between not only individuals, but peoples, and invite Christ believers to use their new-found freedom in ways that challenge the power relationships induced by differences in practices and in beliefs. In the case of Foucault, the community dimension central to Paul's work has reminded one that critical work does not happen in a vacuum, and that the other stands at the center when it comes to developing respectful power relationships. Paul's deep attention to the others reminds one that boundary crossing does not happen in a void.

When we cross limits, we are bound by our own engagements towards others: trespassing limits cannot and should not be done for the simple pleasure of transgression. It needs to inscribe itself in an ethical project that takes into account the other, and thus it becomes an *"ethical* task."[70] It is also, as I have noted, a never-ending task. As soon as a boundary is crossed, others are drawn and reconfigured. In the awareness of the fact that boundaries always recreate themselves, one also realizes that one's own way of thinking, one's own spaces of resistance, need to be open to questioning and challenge. Identifying and criticizing boundaries is not sufficient, one also needs to be willing to reconstruct ever-shifting spaces of resistance in one's own life and work, in order to avoid being imprisoned inside immobilizing relationships of power.[71]

Finally, this willingness to always remain in movement (at least metaphorically) modifies the traditional understanding of the scholar and of the intellectual. In the footsteps of Foucault, it invites one to move away from a picture of the intellectual as a provider of solutions for contemporary questions. Rather, it presents an image of the intellectual as someone who respects the fact that identity-construction is the task of each individual person. Thus, the most an intellectual can do is, while she herself uses the

---

[70] Vander Stichele and Penner, *Contextualizing Gender*, 234.

[71] I have shown that this idea is abundantly developed by Foucault in his reflection on his own work. It is also present in a similar reflection on boundary crossing in Vander Stichele and Penner, *Contextualizing Gender*, 234: "Boundary-crossing is an endless task, one in which we ourselves also ought to be challenged and provoked (and willingly so). Of course, boundaries are also fluid, they are not stable and static. Boundary-crossers, therefore, have to be attuned to the shifting and redrawing of boundaries in our own times and places, realizing that power comes through the ability to remap and to reconfigure speech and place, not simply through the description and analysis of those spaces and places."

tools of others, to provide tools with which others can tinker, in the hope of creating new spaces where one can think differently and in which one can move just a little bit more freely. And in the process, it also contributes to recreating the self, as constantly changing and narrating new stories.[72] Being on the border, in exile, as Edward W. Said puts it,[73] might sometimes be uncomfortable – as is straddling two disciplines – but it makes for new perspectives, and invites the imaginative creation of ever changing thoughts and behaviors, a practice of which I suspect Paul and Foucault – who were after all both *artificiers* in their own right – would approve.

---

[72] See Bhabha, *The Location of Culture*, 12.

[73] See Said, *Representations of the Intellectual*. The theme of the intellectual as a figure in exile traverses the entire book, but see especially 47–64, for example, 64: "The *exilic* intellectual does not respond to the logic of the conventional, but to the audacity of daring, and to representing change, to moving on, not standing still."

Bibliography

Λ. Philosophical Sources

Agamben, Giorgio. *Homo sacer: Il potere sovrano e la nuda vita*. Turin: Einaudi, 1995. English translation: *Homo Sacer: Sovereign Power and Bare Life*. Translated by Daniel Heller-Roazen. Stanford: Stanford University Press, 1998.
–. *Il tempo che resta: Un commento alla Lettera ai Romani*. Turin: Bollati Boringhieri, 2000. English translation: *The Time that Remains. A Commentary on the Letter to the Romans*. Translated by Patricia Dailey. Stanford: Stanford University Press, 2005.
–. *La comunità che viene*. Turin: Einaudi, 1990. English translation: *The Coming Community*. Translated by Michael Hardt. Minneapolis: University of Minnesota Press, 1993.
–. *Stato di eccezione*. Turin: Bollati Boringhieri, 2003. English translation: *State of Exception*. Translated by Kevin Attell. Chicago: University of Chicago Press, 2005.
Aristotle. *Poetics*. Edited and translated by Stephen Halliwell. Loeb Classical Library. Cambridge, Mass.: Harvard University Press, 1995.
Althusser, Louis. *Lenin and Philosophy, and Other Essays*. Translated by Ben Brewster. New York: Monthly Review Press, 1971.
Badiou, Alain. *L' être et l'événement*. Paris: Seuil, 1988. English translation: *Being and Event*. Translated by Oliver Feltham. London: Continuum, 2005.
–. *Logiques des mondes: l'être et l'événement 2*. Paris: Seuil, 2006. English translation: *Logics of Worlds: Being and Event 2*. Translated by Alberto Toscano. New York: Continuum, 2009.
–. *Manifeste pour la philosophie*. Paris: Seuil, 1989. English translation: *Manifesto for Philosophy*. Translated by Norman Madarasz. Albany, N.Y.: State University of New York Press, 1999.
–. *Saint Paul: la fondation de l'universalisme*. Paris: Presses Universitaires de France, 1997. English translation: *Saint Paul: The Foundation of Universalism*. Translated by Ray Brassier. Stanford: Stanford University Press, 2003.
–. *Théorie du Sujet*. Paris: Seuil, 1982.
Bhabha, Homi K. *The Location of Culture*. London: Routledge, 1994. Repr., London: Routledge, 2006.
Camus, Albert. *La Chute*. Paris: Gallimard, 1956.
Faubion, James D., ed. *Aesthetics, Method, and Epistemology: Essential Works of Foucault. Vol. 2 of Essential Works of Foucault, 1954–1984*. Edited by Paul Rabinow. New York: The New Press, 1998.
–. *Power: Essential Works of Foucault. Vol. 3 of Essential Works of Foucault, 1954– 1984*. Edited by Paul Rabinow. New York: The New Press, 2000.
Foucault, Michel. "A Preface to Transgression." Pages 29–52 in *Language, Counter-Memory, Practice*. Edited by Donald F. Bouchard. Ithaca: Cornell University Press,

1977. Repr. pages 24–40 in *Bataille: A Critical Reader*. Edited by Fred Botting and Scott Wilson. Oxford: Blackwell Publishers, 1998.

–. "À propos de la généalogie de l'éthique: un aperçu du travail en cours." Pages 609–631 in *Dits et écrits, 1954–1988*. Edited by Daniel Defert and François Ewald. Vol 4. of *Dits et écrits, 1954–1988*. Edited by Daniel Defert and François Ewald. Paris: Gallimard, 1994.

–. "Afterword: The Subject and Power." Pages 208–226 in *Michel Foucault: Beyond Structuralism and Hermeneutics*. Edited by Hubert L. Dreyfus and Paul Rabinow. 2d ed. Chicago: The University of Chicago Press, 1983.

–. "An Aesthetics of Existence." Pages 47–56 in *Politics, Philosophy, Culture: Interviews and other Writings of Michel Foucault, 1977–1984*. Edited by Lawrence D. Kritzman. New York: Routledge, 1998.

–. "An Interview by Stephen Riggins." Pages 121–133 in *Ethics: Subjectivity and Truth: Essential Works of Foucault*. Edited by Paul Rabinow. Vol. 1 of *Essential Works of Foucault, 1954–1984*. Edited by Paul Rabinow. New York: The New Press, 1997.

–. "Course Summary." Pages 491–505 in *The Hermeneutics of the Subject: Lectures at the Collège de France, 1981–1982*. Translated by Graham Burchell. New York: Picador, 2005.

–. "Des supplices aux cellules." Pages 716–720 in *Dits et écrits, 1954–1988*. Edited by Daniel Defert and François Ewald. Vol. 2 of *Dits et écrits, 1954–1988*. Edited by Daniel Defert and François Ewald. Paris: Gallimard, 1994.

–. "Des travaux." Pages 366–367 in *Dits et écrits, 1954–1988*. Edited by Daniel Defert and François Ewald. Vol. 4 of *Dits et écrits, 1954–1988*. Edited by Daniel Defert and François Ewald. Paris: Gallimard, 1994.

–. *Dits et écrits, 1954–1988. 4 vols*. Edited by Daniel Defert and François Ewald. Paris: Gallimard, 1994.

–. *Folie et déraison: histoire de la folie à l'âge classique*. Paris: Plon, 1961. English translation: *Madness and Civilization: A History of Insanity in the Age of Reason*. Translated by Richard Howard. New York: Pantheon, 1965.

–. "For an Ethics of Discomfort." Pages 443–448 in *Power: Essential Works of Foucault*. Edited by James D. Faubion. Vol. 3 of *Essential Works of Foucault, 1954–1984*. Edited by Paul Rabinow. New York: The New Press, 2000.

–. "Friendship as a Way of Life." Pages 135–140 in *Ethics: Subjectivity and Truth: Essential Works of Foucault*. Edited by Paul Rabinow. Vol. 1 of *Essential Works of Foucault, 1954–1984*. Edited by Paul Rabinow. New York: The New Press, 1997.

–. "Governmentality." Pages 201–222 in *Power: Essential Works of Foucault*. Edited by James D. Faubion. Vol. 3 of *Essential Works of Foucault, 1954–1984*. Edited by Paul Rabinow. New York: The New Press, 2000.

–. *Histoire de la sexualité vol. 1: la volonté de savoir*. Paris: Gallimard, 1976. English translation: *History of Sexuality vol. 1: An Introduction*. Translated by Robert Hurley. New York: Pantheon Books, 1978. Repr., New York: Vintage Books, 1990.

–. *Histoire de la sexualité vol. 2: l'usage des plaisirs*. Paris: Gallimard, 1984. English translation: *The History of Sexuality vol. 2: The Use of Pleasure*. Translated by Robert Hurley. New York: Pantheon Books, 1985.

–. *Histoire de la sexualité vol. 3: le souci de soi*. Paris: Gallimard, 1984. English translation: *The History of Sexuality vol. 3: The Care of the Self*. Translated by Robert Hurley. New York: Pantheon Books, 1986. Repr., New York: Vintage Books, 1988.

–. "Interview with Michel Foucault." Pages 239–297 in *Power: Essential Works of Foucault*. Edited by James D. Faubion. Vol. 3 of *Essential Works of Foucault, 1954–1984*. Edited by Paul Rabinow. New York: The New Press, 2000.

–. "Je suis un artificier." Pages 90–135 in *Michel Foucault, entretiens*. Edited by Roger-Pol Droit. Paris: Odile Jacob, 2004.

–. *L'archéologie du savoir*. Paris: Gallimard, 1969. English translation: *The Archaeology of Knowledge*. Translated by Alan Sheridan Smith. New York: Harper Colophon, 1976.

–. *L'herméneutique du sujet: cours au Collège de France, 1981–1982*. Paris: Gallimard – Le Seuil, 2001. English translation: *The Hermeneutics of the Subject: Lectures at the Collège de France, 1981–1982*. Translated by Graham Burchell. New York: Picador, 2005.

–. *L'ordre du discours*. Paris: Gallimard, 1971. English translation: "The Discourse on Language." Pages 215–237 in *The Archaeology of Knowledge*. Translated by Alan Sheridan Smith. New York: Harper Colophon, 1976. Repr., New York: Pantheon Books, 1982.

–. *Le courage de la vérité: le gouvernement de soi et des autres II: cours au Collège de France, 1984*. Paris: Gallimard – Le Seuil, 2009.

–. "Les monstruosités de la critique." Page 221 in *Dits et écrits, 1954–1988*. Edited by Daniel Defert and François Ewald. Vol. 2 of *Dits et écrits, 1954–1988*. Edited by Daniel Defert and François Ewald. Paris: Gallimard, 1994. English: "Monstrosities in Criticism." *Diacritics* 1 (1971).

–. *Les mots et les choses: une archéologie des sciences humaines*. Paris: Gallimard, 1966. English translation: *The Order of Things: An Archaeology of the Human Sciences*. Unidentified collective translation. New York: Pantheon Books, 1971. Repr., New York: Vintage Books, 1973.

–. *Maladie mentale et personnalité*. Paris: Presses Universitaires de France, 1954. Republished as *Maladie mentale et psychologie*. Paris: Presses Universitaires de France, 1962. English translation: *Mental Illness and Psychology*. Translated by Alan Sheridan Smith. New York: Harper and Row, 1976.

–. *Moi, Pierre Rivière, ayant égorgé ma mère, ma sœur et mon frère*. Paris: Gallimard, 1973. English translation: *I, Pierre Rivière, having slaughtered my mother, my sister and my brother*. Translated by Frank Jellinek. New York: Pantheon, 1975.

–. *Naissance de la clinique: une archéologie du regard médical*. Paris: Presses Universitaires de France, 1963. English translation: *The Birth of the Clinic: An Archaeology of Medical Perception*. Translated by Alan Sheridan Smith. New York: Pantheon, 1973.

–. "Non au sexe roi." Pages 256–269 in *Dits et écrits, 1954–1988*. Edited by Daniel Defert and François Ewald. Vol. 3 of *Dits et écrits, 1954–1988*. Edited by Daniel Defert and François Ewald. Paris: Gallimard, 1994.

–. "On the Genealogy of Ethics: An Overview of Work in Progress." Pages 340–372 in *The Foucault Reader*. Edited by Paul Rabinow. New York: Pantheon Books, 1984. Also: pages 229–252 in *Michel Foucault: Beyond Structuralism and Hermeneutics*. Edited by Hubert L. Dreyfus and Paul Rabinow. 2d ed. Chicago: The University of Chicago Press, 1983 and pages 253–280 in *Ethics: Subjectivity and Truth: Essential Works of Foucault*. Edited by Paul Rabinow. Vol. 1 of *Essential Works of Foucault, 1954–1984*. Edited by Paul Rabinow. New York: The New Press, 1997.

–. "Polemics, Politics and Problematizations." Pages 111–119 in *Ethics: Subjectivity and Truth: Essential Works of Foucault*. Edited by Paul Rabinow. Vol. 1 of *Essential Works of Foucault, 1954–1984*. Edited by Paul Rabinow. New York: The New Press, 1997.

–. *Power/Knowledge: Selected Interviews and Other Writings, 1972–1977*. Edited by Colin Gordon. Translated by Colin Gordon et al. New York: Pantheon Books, 1980.

–. "Qu'est-ce que la critique? Critique et Aufklärung." *Bulletin de la Société Française de Philosophie* 84.2 (April–June 1990): 35–63.

–. "Questions à Michel Foucault sur la géographie." Pages 28–40 in *Dits et écrits, 1954– 1988*. Edited by Daniel Defert and François Ewald. Vol. 3 of *Dits et écrits, 1954– 1988*. Edited by Daniel Defert and François Ewald. Paris: Gallimard, 1994.

–. *Raymond Roussel*. Paris: Gallimard, 1963. English translation: *Death and the Labyrinth: The World of Raymond Roussel*. Translated by Charles Ruas. New York: Doubleday, 1986.

–. "Réponse à une question." Pages 673–695 in *Dits et écrits, 1954–1988*. Edited by Daniel Defert and François Ewald. Vol 1. of *Dits et écrits, 1954–1988*. Edited by Daniel Defert and François Ewald. Paris: Gallimard, 1994.

–. "Sexuality and Solitude." Pages 175–184 in *Ethics: Subjectivity and Truth: Essential Works of Foucault*. Edited by Paul Rabinow. Vol. 1 of *Essential Works of Foucault, 1954–1984*. Edited by Paul Rabinow. New York: The New Press, 1997.

–. "Structuralism and Post-Structuralism." Pages 433–458 in *Aesthetics, Method, and Epistemology: Essential Works of Foucault*. Edited by James D. Faubion. Vol. 2 of *Essential Works of Foucault, 1954–1984*. Edited by Paul Rabinow. New York: The New Press, 1998.

–. "Subjectivity and Truth." Pages 87–92 in *Ethics: Subjectivity and Truth: Essential Works of Foucault*. Edited by Paul Rabinow. Vol. 1 of *Essential Works of Foucault, 1954–1984*. Edited by Paul Rabinow. New York: The New Press, 1997.

–. *Surveiller et punir: naissance de la prison*. Paris: Gallimard, 1975. English translation: *Discipline and Punish: The Birth of the Prison*. Translated by Alan Smith Sheridan. New York: Pantheon Books, 1978. Repr., New York: Vintage Books, 1995.

–. "Technologies of the Self." Pages 223–251 in *Ethics: Subjectivity and Truth: Essential Works of Foucault*. Edited by Paul Rabinow. Vol. 1 of *Essential Works of Foucault, 1954–1984*. Edited by Paul Rabinow. New York: The New Press, 1997.

–. "The Concern for Truth." Pages 255–268 in *Politics, Philosophy, Culture: Interviews and other Writings of Michel Foucault, 1977–1984*. Edited by Lawrence D. Kritzman. New York: Routledge, 1998.

–. "The Ethics of the Concern for Self as a Practice of Freedom." Pages 281–301 in *Ethics: Subjectivity and Truth: Essential Works of Foucault*. Edited by Paul Rabinow. Vol. 1 of *Essential Works of Foucault, 1954–1984*. Edited by Paul Rabinow. New York: The New Press, 1997.

–. "The Masked Philosopher." Pages 321–328 in *Ethics: Subjectivity and Truth: Essential Works of Foucault*. Edited by Paul Rabinow. Vol. 1 of *Essential Works of Foucault, 1954–1984*. Edited by Paul Rabinow. New York: The New Press, 1997.

–. "The Political Technology of Individuals." Pages 403–417 in *Power: Essential Works of Foucault*. Edited by James D. Faubion. Vol. 3 of *Essential Works of Foucault, 1954–1984*. Edited by Paul Rabinow. New York: The New Press, 2000.

–. "The Will to Knowledge." Pages 11–16 in *Ethics: Subjectivity and Truth: Essential Works of Foucault*. Edited by Paul Rabinow. Vol. 1 of *Essential Works of Foucault, 1954–1984*. Edited by Paul Rabinow. New York: The New Press, 1997.

–. "Truth and Power." Pages 109–133 in *Power/Knowledge: Selected Interviews and Other Writings, 1972–1977*. Edited by Colin Gordon. Translated by Colin Gordon et al. New York: Pantheon Books, 1980.

–. "Two lectures." Pages 78–108 in *Power/Knowledge: Selected Interviews and Other Writings, 1972–1977*. Edited by Colin Gordon. Translated by Colin Gordon et al. New York: Pantheon Books, 1980.

–. "What is Enlightenment?" Pages 32–50 in *The Foucault Reader*. Edited by Paul Rabinow. New York: Pantheon Books, 1984. Also pages 303–319 in *Ethics: Subjectivity and Truth: Essential Works of Foucault*. Edited by Paul Rabinow. Vol. 1 of *Essential Works of Foucault, 1954–1984*. Edited by Paul Rabinow. New York: The New Press, 1997. French: "Qu'est-ce que les Lumières?" Pages 562–578 in *Dits et écrits, 1954–1988*. Edited by Daniel Defert and François Ewald. Vol 4. of *Dits et écrits, 1954–1988*. Edited by Daniel Defert and François Ewald. Paris: Gallimard, 1994.

Gordon, Colin, ed. *Power/Knowledge: Selected Interviews and Other Writings, 1972–1977*. Translated by Colin Gordon et al. New York: Pantheon Books, 1980.

Kierkegaard, Søren. *Concluding Unscientific Postscript to Philosophical Fragments*. Edited by Walter Lowrie. Translated by David. F. Swenson. Princeton: Princeton University Press, 1944.

Kritzman, Lawrence D., ed. *Politics, Philosophy, Culture: Interviews and other Writings of Michel Foucault, 1977–1984*. New York: Routledge, 1998.

Malherbe, Abraham J., ed. *Moral Exhortation: A Greco-Roman Sourcebook*. Philadelphia: Westminster Press, 1986.

Nietzsche, Friedrich. *The Gay Science*. Translated by Josefine Nauckhoff. Cambridge: Cambridge University Press, 2001.

Rabinow, Paul, ed. *Ethics: Subjectivity and Truth: Essential Works of Foucault*. Vol. 1 of *Essential Works of Foucault, 1954–1984*. Edited by Paul Rabinow. New York: The New Press, 1997.

–, ed. *The Foucault Reader*. New York: Pantheon Books, 1984.

Ricœur, Paul. *La critique et la conviction: entretien avec François Azouvi et Marc de Launay*. Paris: Calmann-Lévy, 1995.

–. *La métaphore vive*. Paris: Seuil, 1975.

–. *Soi-même comme un autre*. Paris: Seuil, 1990. English translation: *Oneself as Another*. Translated by Kathleen Blamey. Chicago: Chicago University Press, 1992.

–. *Temps et récit. 3 vols*. Paris: Seuil, 1983–1985.

–. "The Narrative Function." *Semeia* 13 (1978): 177–202.

Rorty, Richard. *Contingency, Language and Solidarity*. Cambridge: Cambridge University Press, 1989.

Said, Edward W. *Representations of the Intellectual: The 1993 Reith Lectures*. New York: Vintage Books, 1994.

Sartre, Jean-Paul. *L'existentialisme est un humanisme*. Paris: Nagel, 1946. Repr., Paris: Gallimard, 1996.

Taubes, Jacob. *The Political Theology of Paul*. Translated by Dana Hollander. Stanford: Stanford University Press, 2004.

Žižek, Slavoj. *The Puppet and the Dwarf: The Perverse Core of Christianity*. Cambridge, Mass.: The MIT Press, 2003.

B. Secondary Literature

Adams, Edward. "Paul's Story of God and Creation." Pages 19–43 in *Narrative Dynamics in Paul: A Critical Assessment*. Edited by Bruce W. Longenecker. Louisville, Ky.: Westminster John Knox, 2002.

Barclay, John M. G. "Paul's Story: Theology as Testimony." Pages 133–156 in *Narrative Dynamics in Paul: A Critical Assessment*. Edited by Bruce W. Longenecker. Louisville, Ky.: Westminster John Knox, 2002.

Barr, James. *The Semantics of Biblical Language*. London: Oxford University Press, 1961.

Barrett, Charles K. *A Commentary on the Epistle to the Romans*. New York: Harper & Row, 1957.

Barth, Karl. *L'Épître aux Romains*. Translated by Pierre Jundt. Geneva: Labor et Fides, 1972.

Bartsch, Shadi. *The Mirror of the Self: Sexuality, Self-Knowledge, and the Gaze in the Early Roman Empire*. Chicago: The University of Chicago Press, 2006.

Bassler, Jouette M. *Divine Impartiality: Paul and a Theological Axiom*. Chico, Calif.: Scholars Press, 1982.

Bernauer, James W. *Michel Foucault's Force of Flight: Towards an Ethics for Thought*. London: Humanities Press, 1990.

Betz, Hans-Dieter. *Der Apostel Paulus und die sokratische Tradition: Eine exegetische Untersuchung zu seiner "Apologie" 2 Korinther 10–13*. Tübingen: Mohr, 1972.

Black, David A. "The Pauline Love Command: Structure, Style, and Ethics in Romans 12.9–21." *Filología Neotestamentaria* 1 (1989): 3–21.

Bonhöffer, Adolf Friedrich. *Epiktet und das Neue Testament*. Religionsgeschichtliche Versuche und Vorarbeiten 10. Giessen: Töpelmann, 1911.

Bornkamm, Günther. *Paul*. London: Hodder & Stoughton, 1971.

–. "The Letter to the Romans as Paul's Last Will and Testament." *Australian Biblical Review* 11 (1963–1964): 2–14. Repr. pages 16–28 in *The Romans Debate*. Edited by Karl P. Donfried. Rev. and enl. ed. Peabody, Mass.: Hendrickson, 1991.

Botting, Fred and Scott Wilson, eds. *Introduction to Bataille: A Critical Reader*. Oxford: Blackwell Publishers, 1998.

Brown, Michael Joseph. "Paul's Use of Δοῦλος Χριστοῦ Ἰησοῦ in Romans 1:1." *Journal of Biblical Literature* 120/4 (2001): 723–737.

Bruce, Frederick F. *The Letter of Paul to the Romans: An Introduction and Commentary*. Tyndale New Testament Commentaries. Rev. ed. Grand Rapids, Mich.: Eerdmans, 1985.

Bühler, Pierre. Introduction to *La narration: quand le récit devient communication*. Edited by Pierre Bühler and Jean-François Habermacher. Geneva: Labor et Fides, 1988.

Bultmann, Rudolf. "Autobiographical Reflections." Pages 335–341 in *Existence and Faith*. Edited and translated by Schubert M. Ogden. New York: Meridian Books, 1960.

–. *Der Stil der paulinischen Predigt und die kynisch-stoische Diatribe*. Göttingen: Vandenhoeck & Ruprecht, 1910.

–. *Existence and Faith*. Edited and translated by Schubert M. Ogden. New York: Meridian Books, 1960.

–. "Is Exegesis Without Presuppositions Possible?" Pages 342–351 in *Existence and Faith*. Edited and translated by Schubert M. Ogden. New York: Meridian Books, 1960.

–. "L'étrange de la foi chrétienne." Pages 229–246 in *Foi et compréhension: eschatologie et démythologisation*. Vol. 2 of *Foi et compréhension*. Translated by André Malet. Paris: Seuil, 1970.

–. "Le problème de l'herméneutique." Pages 599–626 in *Foi et compréhension: l'historicité de l'homme et de la révélation*. Vol. 1 of *Foi et compréhension*. Translated by André Malet. Paris: Seuil, 1969.

–. *Theology of the New Testament*. Translated by Kendrick Grobel. 2 vols. New York: Scribner, 1951–1955. Repr., Eugene, Oreg.: Wipf and Stock Publishers, 1997.

Burnett, Gary W. *Paul and the Salvation of the Individual*. Leiden: Brill, 2001.

Byrne, Brendan. *Romans*. Sacra Pagina 6. Collegeville, Minn.: Liturgical Press, 1996.

Campbell, William S. *Paul and the Creation of Christian Identity.* New York: T&T Clark, 2006.

Caputo, John D. and Linda Martín Alcoff, eds. *Saint Paul among the Philosophers.* Bloomington, Ind.: Indiana University Press, 2009.

Castelli, Elizabeth A. *Imitating Paul: A Discourse of Power.* Louisville, Ky.: Westminster John Knox, 1991.

Chrulew, Matthew. "The Pauline Ellipsis in Foucault's Genealogy of Christianity," *Journal for Cultural and Religious Theory* 11 (Winter 2010): 1–15. Cited 12 April 2012. Online: http://www.jcrt.org/archives/11.1/chrulew.pdf

Cohen, Anthony P. *Self Consciousness: An Alternative Anthropology of Identity.* London: Routledge, 1994.

Couzens Hoy, David, ed. *Foucault: A Critical Reader.* London: Basil Blackwell, 1986.

Cranfield, Charles E. B. *Romans: A Shorter Commentary.* Grand Rapids, Mich.: Eerdmans, 1985.

Davidson, Arnold I. "Archaeology, Genealogy, Ethics." Pages 221–233 in *Foucault: A Critical Reader.* Edited by David Couzens Hoy. London: Basil Blackwell, 1986.

deSilva, David A. *Honor, Patronage, Kinship and Purity: Unlocking New Testament Culture.* Downers Grove, Ill.: Intervarsity Press, 2000.

Di Vito, Robert A. "Old Testament Anthropology and the Construction of Personal Identity." *Catholic Biblical Quarterly* 61 (1999): 217–238.

Dibelius, Martin. *From Tradition to Gospel.* Translated by Bertram Lee Woolf. New York: Scribners, 1935.

Dodd, Charles. *The Epistle of Paul to the Romans.* Moffatt New Testament Commentary. New York: Harper and Bros., 1932.

Donfried, Karl P., ed. *The Romans Debate.* Rev. and enl. ed. Peabody, Mass.: Hendrickson, 1991.

Dreyfus, Hubert L. and Paul Rabinow. "Foucault's Interpretive Analytic of Ethics." Pages 253–264 in *Michel Foucault: Beyond Structuralism and Hermeneutics.* Edited by Hubert L. Dreyfus and Paul Rabinow. 2d ed. Chicago: The University of Chicago Press, 1983.

Dreyfus, Hubert L., and Paul Rabinow, eds. *Michel Foucault: Beyond Structuralism and Hermeneutics.* 2d ed. Chicago: The University of Chicago Press, 1983.

duBois, Page. "The Subject in Antiquity after Foucault." Pages 85–103 in *Rethinking Sexuality: Foucault and Classical Antiquity.* Edited by David H. J. Larmour, Paul Allen Miller and Charles Platter. Princeton: Princeton University Press, 1998.

Dunn, James D. G. *Romans.* Word Biblical Commentary 38A–38B. Dallas: Word Books, 1988.

–. "The Formal and Theological Coherence of Romans." Pages 245–250 in *The Romans Debate.* Edited by Karl P. Donfried. Rev. and enl. ed. Peabody, Mass.: Hendrickson, 1991.

–. "The Narrative Approach to Paul: Whose Story?" Pages 217–230 in *Narrative Dynamics in Paul: A Critical Assessment.* Edited by Bruce W. Longenecker. Louisville, Ky.: Westminster John Knox, 2002.

–. *The Theology of Paul the Apostle.* Grand Rapids, Mich.: Eerdmans, 1998.

–. "What Was the Issue Between Paul and 'Those of the Circumcision'?" Pages 295–312 in *Paulus und das antike Judentum.* Edited by Martin Hengel and Ulrich Heckel. Tübingen: Mohr Siebeck, 1991. Repr. pages 153–171 in *The New Perspective on Paul.* Rev. ed. Grand Rapids, Mich.: Eerdmans, 2008.

Édart, Jean-Baptiste. "De la nécessité d'un sauveur: rhétorique et théologie de Rm 7:7–25." *Revue Biblique* 105 (1998): 359–396.

Elliott, Neil. "Romans 13:1–7 in the Context of Imperial Propaganda." Pages 184–204 in *Paul and Empire: Religion and Power in Roman Imperial Society*. Edited by Richard A. Horsley. Harrisburg, Pa.: Trinity Press International, 1977.

–. *The Arrogance of Nations: Reading Romans in the Shadow of the Empire*. Paul in Critical Contexts. Minneapolis: Fortress Press, 2008.

–. *The Rhetoric of Romans: Argumentative Constraint and Strategy and Paul's "Dialogue with Judaism"*. Journal for the Study of the New Testament: Supplement Series 45. Sheffield: Sheffield Academic Press, 1990.

Engberg-Pedersen, Troels. *Paul and the Stoics*. Louisville, Ky.: Westminster John Knox, 2000.

Erbes, Karl. "Zeit und Zeil der Grüsse Röm 16,3–15 und der Mitteilungen 2 Tim 4,9–21." *Zeitschrift für die neutestamentliche Wissenschaft und die Kunde der älteren Kirche* 10 (1909): 146.

Éribon, Didier. *Michel Foucault*. Translated by Betsy Wing. Cambridge, Mass.: Harvard University Press, 1991.

Fitzmyer, Joseph A. *Romans: A New Translation with Introduction and Commentary*. Anchor Bible 33. New York: Doubleday, 1993.

Flood, Gavin D. *The Ascetic Self: Subjectivity, Memory and Tradition*. Cambridge: Cambridge University Press, 2004.

Foxhall, Lin. "Pandora Unbound: A Feminist Critique of Foucault's History of Sexuality." Pages 122–137 in *Rethinking Sexuality: Foucault and Classical Antiquity*. Edited by David H. J. Larmour, Paul Allen Miller and Charles Platter. Princeton: Princeton University Press, 1998.

Furnish, Victor P. *Theology and Ethics in Paul*. Nashville: Abingdon, 1968.

Gill, Christopher. *Personality in Greek Epic, Tragedy and Philosophy: The Self in Dialogue*. Oxford: Clarendon Press, 1996.

Gooch, Paul W. *Partial Knowledge: Philosophical Studies in Paul*. Notre Dame, Ind.: University of Notre Dame Press, 1987.

Goodenough, Ward H. *Culture, Language and Society*. Menlo Park, Calif.: Benjamin Cummings, 1981.

Gordon, Colin. "Afterword." Pages 229–259 in *Power/Knowledge: Selected Interviews and Other Writings, 1972–1977*. Edited by Colin Gordon. Translated by Colin Gordon et al. New York: Pantheon Books, 1980.

–. Introduction to *Power: Essential Works of Foucault*. Edited by James D. Faubion. Vol. 3 of *Essential Works of Foucault, 1954–1984*. Edited by Paul Rabinow. New York: The New Press, 2000.

Grieb, A. Katherine. *The Story of Romans: A Narrative Defense of God's Righteousness*. Louisville, Ky.: Westminster John Knox, 2002.

Gros, Frédéric. "Course Context." Pages 507–550 in *The Hermeneutics of the Subject: Lectures at the Collège de France, 1981–1982* by Michel Foucault. Translated by Graham Burchell. New York: Picador, 2005

–. "Situation du cours." Pages 314–328 in *Le courage de la vérité: le gouvernement de soi et des autres II: cours au Collège de France, 1984* by Michel Foucault. Paris: Gallimard – Le Seuil, 2009.

Harrill, Albert J. *Slaves in the New Testament: Literary, Social and Moral Dimensions*. Minneapolis: Fortress Press, 2006.

Harrison, Beverly W. "The Power of Anger in the Work of Love." *Union Seminary Quarterly Review Supplementary* 36 (1981): 41–57.

Hawkins, Faith K. "1 Corinthians 8:1 –11:1: The Making and Meaning of Difference." Ph.D. Diss., Emory University, 2001.

Hays, Richard B. *Echoes of Scripture in the Letters of Paul.* New Haven, Conn.: Yale University Press, 1989.

–. *The Faith of Jesus Christ: The Narrative Substructure of Galatians 3:1–4:11.* 2d ed. Dearborn, Mich.: Dove Booksellers – Eerdmans, 2002.

–. *The Moral Vision of the New Testament: Community, Cross, New Creation: A Contemporary Introduction to New Testament Ethics.* San Francisco: HarperSanFrancisco, 1996.

Hooker, Morna D. "Adam in Romans 1." Pages 73–84 in *From Adam to Christ: Essays on Paul.* Cambridge: Cambridge University Press, 1990.

Horrell, David G. "Paul's Narratives or Narrative Substructure: The Significance of 'Paul's Story'." Pages 157–171 in *Narrative Dynamics in Paul: A Critical Assessment.* Edited by Bruce W. Longenecker. Louisville, Ky.: Westminster John Knox, 2002.

Horsley, Richard A. *In the Shadow of Empire: Reclaiming the Bible as a History of Faithful Resistance.* Louisville, Ky.: Westminster John Knox, 2008.

Jewett, Robert. *Paul's Anthropological Terms: A Study of their Use in Conflict Settings.* Leiden: Brill, 1971.

–. *Romans: A Commentary.* Hermeneia. Minneapolis: Fortress Press, 2007.

Johnson, Luke T. *Reading Romans: A Literary and Theological Commentary.* Reading the New Testament. Macon, GA.: Smyth & Helwys, 2001.

–. "Romans 3:21–26 and the Faith of Jesus." *Catholic Biblical Quarterly* 44 (1982): 77–90.

Kallas, James. "Romans 13:1–7: An Interpolation." *New Testament Studies* 11 (1964): 365–374.

Karris, Robert J. "Romans 14:1–15:13 and the Occasion of Romans." Pages 65–84 in *The Romans Debate.* Edited by Karl P. Donfried. Rev. and enl. ed. Peabody, Mass.: Hendrickson, 1991.

Käsemann, Ernst. *Commentary on Romans.* Translated by George W. Bromiley. Grand Rapids, Mich.: Eerdmans, 1980.

Keck, Leander E. "The Function of Rom 3:10–18: Observations and Suggestions." Pages 141–157 in *God's Christ and his People: Studies in Honour of Nils Alstrup Dahl.* Edited by Jacob J. Jervell and Wayne A. Meeks. Oslo: Universitetsforlaget, 1977.

Kruger, M. A. "Τινὰ καρπὸν, 'Some Fruit,' in Rom 1:13." *Westminster Theological Journal* 49 (1987): 168–170.

Kümmel, Werner G. *Römer 7 und das Bild des Menschen im Neuen Testament.* Munich: Kaiser, 1974.

Lampe, Peter. "Prisca/Priscilla." Pages 467–468 in vol. 5 of *Anchor Bible Dictionary.* Edited by David Noel Freedman. 6 vols. New York: Doubleday, 1992.

Larmour, David H. J., Paul Allen Miller and Charles Platter, eds. *Rethinking Sexuality: Foucault and Classical Antiquity.* Princeton: Princeton University Press, 1998.

Levenson, John D. *Resurrection and the Restoration of Israel: The Ultimate Victory of the God of Life.* New Haven, Conn.: Yale University Press, 2006.

Longenecker, Bruce W., ed. *Narrative Dynamics in Paul: A Critical Assessment.* Louisville, Ky.: Westminster John Knox, 2002.

–. "Narrative Interest in the Study of Paul: Retrospective and Prospective." Pages 3–16 in *Narrative Dynamics in Paul: A Critical Assessment.* Edited by Bruce W. Longenecker. Louisville, Ky.: Westminster John Knox, 2002.

Lopez, Davina C. *Apostle to the Conquered: Reimagining Paul's Mission.* Paul in Critical Contexts. Minneapolis: Fortress Press, 2008.

Luther, Martin. *Lectures on Romans: Glosses and Scholia*. Vol. 25 of *Luther's Work*. Edited by Jaroslav Pelikan. Translated by Jacob A. O. Preus. Saint Louis, Mo.: Concordia, 1972.

Macquarrie, John. *An Existentialist Theology: A Comparison of Heidegger and Bultmann*. New York: The MacMillan Company, 1955.

Malherbe, Abraham. *Paul and the Popular Philosophers*. Minneapolis: Fortress Press, 1989.

–. *Paul and the Thessalonians: The Philosophic Tradition of Pastoral Care*. Philadelphia: Fortress Press, 1987.

Malina, Bruce J. *The New Testament World: Insights from Cultural Anthropology*. Rev. and enl. ed. Louisville, Ky.: Westminster John Knox, 1993.

Marchal, Joseph A. *The Politics of Heaven: Women, Gender, and Empire in the Study of Paul*. Paul in Critical Contexts. Minneapolis: Fortress Press, 2008.

Marguerat, Daniel and Yvan Bourquin. *La Bible se raconte: initiation à l'analyse narrative*. Paris – Genève – Montréal: Cerf – Labor et Fides – Novalis, 1998.

Martin, Dale B. *Slavery as Salvation: The Metaphor of Slavery in Pauline Christianity*. New Haven, Conn.: Yale University Press, 1990.

Martin, Luther H. "The Anti-Individualistic Ideology of Hellenistic Culture." *Numen* 41 (1994): 117–140.

Martínez-Vázquez, Hjamil A. "Breaking the Established Scaffold: Imagination as a Resource in the Development of Biblical Interpretation." Pages 71–91 in *Her Master's Tools? Feminist and Postcolonial Engagements of Historical-Critical Discourse*. Edited by Caroline Vander Stichele and Todd Penner. Atlanta: Society of Biblical Literature, 2005.

–. "The Postcolonizing Project: Constructing a Decolonial Imaginary from the Borderlands." *The Journal of World Christianity* 1 (2009): 1–28.

Matlock, R. Barry. "Detheologizing the ΠΙΣΤΙΣ ΧΡΙΣΤΟΥ Debate: Cautionary Remarks from a Lexical Semantic Perspective." *Novum Testamentum* 42 (2000): 1–23.

–. "The Arrow and the Web: Critical Reflections on a Narrative Approach to Paul." Pages 44–57 in *Narrative Dynamics in Paul: A Critical Assessment*. Edited by Bruce W. Longenecker. Louisville, Ky.: Westminster John Knox, 2002.

Meech, John L. *Paul in Israel's Story: Self and Community at the Cross*. Oxford: Oxford University Press, 2006.

Meeks, Wayne A. "Judgment and the Brother." Pages 290–300 in *Tradition and Interpretation in the New Testament: Essays in Honor of E. Earle Ellis for his 60th Birthday*. Edited by Gerald F. Hawthorne and Otto Betz. Grand Rapids, Mich. – Tübingen: Eerdmans – Mohr Siebeck, 1987.

Melanchthon, Philipp. *Loci Communes 1521. Werke in Auswahl 2.1*. Edited by Reinhard Stupperich. Gütersloh: Bertelsmann, 1952.

Minear, Paul S. *The Obedience of Faith: The Purposes of Paul in the Epistle to the Romans*. Naperville, Ill.: Allenson, 1971.

Moo, Douglas J. *The Epistle to the Romans*. New International Commentary on the New Testament. Grand Rapids, Mich.: Eerdmans, 1996.

Moore, Stephen D. *God's Beauty Parlor and Other Queer Spaces in and around the Bible*. Stanford: Stanford University Press, 2001.

–. *Poststructuralism and the New Testament: Derrida and Foucault at the Foot of the Cross*. Minneapolis: Fortress Press, 1994.

Morris, Leon. *The Epistle to the Romans*. Grand Rapids, Mich.: Eerdmans, 1988.

Moxnes, Halvor. "Asceticism and Christian Identity in Antiquity: A Dialogue with Foucault and Paul." *Journal for the Study of the New Testament* 26 (2003): 3–29.

Murray, John. *The Epistle to the Romans: The English Text with Introduction, Exposition and Notes. 2 vols.* New International Biblical Commentary on the New Testament. Grand Rapids, Mich.: Eerdmans, 1959. Repr., Grand Rapids, Mich.: Eerdmans, 1984.

Nicolet-Anderson, Valérie. "Tools for a Kierkegaardian Reading of Paul: Can Kierkegaard Help Us Understand the Role of the Law in Romans 7:7–12?" Pages 247–273 in *Reading Romans With Contemporary Philosophers and Theologians.* Edited by David Odell-Scott. New York: T&T Clark, 2007.

Nygren, Anders. *Commentary on Romans.* Translated by Carl C. Rasmussen. Philadelphia: Muhlenberg, 1949.

O'Neill, John C. *Paul's Letter to the Romans.* Pelican New Testament Commentaries. Harmondsworth: Penguin, 1975.

Poster, Mark. "Foucault and the Tyranny of Greece." Pages 205–220 in *Foucault: A Critical Reader.* Edited by David Couzens Hoy. London: Basil Blackwell, 1986.

Rabinow, Paul. Introduction to *Ethics: Subjectivity and Truth: Essential Works of Foucault.* Vol. 1 of *Essential Works of Foucault, 1954–1984.* Edited by Paul Rabinow. New York: The New Press, 1997.

–. Introduction to *The Foucault Reader.* Edited by Paul Rabinow. New York: Pantheon Books, 1984.

Räisänen, Heikki. *Paul and the Law.* Wissenschaftliche Untersuchungen zum Neuen Testament 29. Tübingen: Mohr, 1983.

–. "Römer 9–11: Analyse eines geistigen Ringens." *ANRW* 25.4: 2891–2939. Part 2, *Principat,* 25.4. Edited by Hildegard Temporini and Wolfgang Haase. New York: de Gruyter, 1989.

Rauer, Max. *Die "Schwachen" in Korinth und Rom nach den Paulusbriefen.* Freiburg im Breisgau: Herder, 1923.

Richlin, Amy. "Foucault's History of Sexuality: A Useful Theory for Women?" Pages 138–170 in *Rethinking Sexuality: Foucault and Classical Antiquity.* Edited by David H. J. Larmour, Paul Allen Miller and Charles Platter. Princeton: Princeton University Press, 1998.

Sanday, William and Arthur C. Headlam. *A Critical and Exegetical Commentary on the Epistle to the Romans.* International Critical Commentary 32. 3d ed. New York: Scribners, 1897.

Sanders, E. P. *Paul and Palestinian Judaism: A Comparison of Patterns of Religion.* Philadelphia: Fortress Press, 1977.

–. *Paul, the Law and the Jewish People.* Philadelphia: Fortress Press, 1983.

Schmid, Muriel. "Illusion et passion dans l'expérience humaine: essai anthropologique en regard de Rm 7." Mémoire de diplôme de spécialisation en Nouveau Testament. University of Neuchâtel, 1992.

Schmithals, Walter. *Der Römerbrief: ein Kommentar.* Gütersloh: Gütersloher Verlaghaus Gerd Mohn, 1988.

Segovia, Fernando F, and R. S. Sugirtharajah, eds. *A Postcolonial Commentary on the New Testament Writings.* Bible and Postcolonialism. London: T&T Clark, 2007.

Stacey, David. *The Pauline View of Man in Relation to its Judaic and Hellenistic Background.* London – New York: Macmillan – St. Martin's Press, 1956.

Stendhal, Krister. *Final Account: Paul's Letter to the Romans.* Minneapolis: Fortress Press, 1995.

–. "Paul and the Introspective Conscience of the West." *Harvard Theological Review* 56 (1963): 199–215. Repr. pages 78–96 in *Paul Among Jews and Gentiles and Other Essays.* Philadelphia: Fortress Press, 1976.

Stowers, Stanley K. *A Rereading of Romans: Justice, Jews, and Gentiles.* New Haven, Conn.: Yale University Press, 1994.

–. "Romans 7. 7–25 as a Speech-in-Character (prosōpopoiia)." Pages 180–202 in *Paul in his Hellenistic Context.* Edited by Troels Engberg-Pedersen. Minneapolis: Fortress Press, 1995.

–. *The Diatribe and Paul's Letter to the Romans.* Chico, Calif.: Scholars Press, 1981.

Taylor, Charles. *Sources of the Self: The Making of Modern Identity.* Cambridge, Mass.: Harvard University Press, 1989.

Thurèn, Lauri. *Derhetorizing Paul: A Dynamic Perspective on Pauline Theology and the Law.* Harrisburg, Pa.: Trinity Press International, 2002.

Vander Stichele, Caroline and Todd Penner, *Contextualizing Gender in Early Christian Discourse: Thinking Beyond Thecla.* London: T&T Clark, 2009.

– eds., *Her Master's Tools? Feminist and Postcolonial Engagements of Historical-Critical Discourse.* Atlanta: Society of Biblical Literature, 2005.

–. "Mastering the Tools or Retooling the Masters? The Legacy of Historical-Critical Discourse." Pages 1–29 in *Her Master's Tools? Feminist and Postcolonial Engagements of Historical-Critical Discourse.* Edited by Caroline Vander Stichele and Todd Penner. Atlanta: Society of Biblical Literature, 2005.

–. "Paul and the Rhetoric of Gender." Pages 287–310 in *Her Master's Tools? Feminist and Postcolonial Engagements of Historical-Critical Discourse.* Edited by Caroline Vander Stichele and Todd Penner. Atlanta: Society of Biblical Literature, 2005.

Vernant, Jean-Pierre. "The Individual within the City State." Pages 318–333 in *Mortals and Immortals: Collected Essays.* Edited by Froma I. Zeitlin. Princeton: Princeton University Press, 1991.

Veyne, Paul. *Foucault: sa pensée, sa personne.* Paris: Albin Michel, 2008.

Watson, Francis. *Paul, Judaism and the Gentiles: A Sociological Approach.* Cambridge: Cambridge University Press, 1986.

–. "The Two Roman Congregations: Romans 14:1–15:13." Pages 203–215 in *The Romans Debate.* Edited by Karl P. Donfried. Rev. and enl. ed. Peabody, Mass.: Hendrickson, 1991.

Wedderburn, A. J. M. "The Purpose and Occasion of Romans Again." Pages 195–202 in *The Romans Debate.* Edited by Karl P. Donfried. Rev. and enl. ed. Peabody, Mass.: Hendrickson, 1991.

Weiss, Johannes. "Beiträge zur paulinischen Rhetorik." Pages 165–247 in *Theologischen Studien: Herrn Wirkl. Oberkonsistorialrath Professor D. Bernhard Weiss zu seinem 70. Geburtstage dargebracht.* Edited by Caspar René Gregory et al. Göttingen: Vandenhoeck & Ruprecht, 1897.

Westerholm, Stephen. *Perspectives Old and New on Paul: the 'Lutheran' Paul and his Critics.* Grand Rapids, Mich.: Eerdmans, 2004.

Wiefel, Wolfgang. "The Jewish Community in Ancient Rome and the Origins of Roman Christianity." Pages 85–101 in *The Romans Debate.* Edited by Karl P. Donfried. Rev. and enl. ed. Peabody, Mass.: Hendrickson, 1991.

Wikenhauser, Alfred. *New Testament Introduction.* New York: Herder and Herder, 1958.

Wilckens, Ulrich. *Der Brief an die Römer. 3 vols.* Evangelisch-katholischer Kommentar zum Neuen Testament 6. Zurich – Neukirchen: Benziger Verlag – Neukirchener Verlag, 1978–1982.

Wilson, Walter T. *Love without Pretense: Romans 12:9–21 and Hellenistic-Jewish Wisdom Literature.* Wissenschaftliche Untersuchungen zum Neuen Testament 46. Tübingen: Mohr, 1991.

Witherington III, Ben. *Paul's Narrative Thought World: The Tapestry of Tragedy and Triumph*. Louisville, Ky.: Westminster John Knox, 1994.

Wright, N. T. *Paul for Everyone: Romans: Part One: Chapters 1–8*. Louisville, Ky.: Westminster John Knox, 2004.

–. *The New Testament and the People of God*. Minneapolis: Fortress Press, 1992.

Yoder, John Howard. *The Politics of Jesus: Vicit Agnus Noster*. Grand Rapids, Mich.: Eerdmans, 1994.

Zahn, Theodor. *Der Brief des Paulus an die Römer*. Leipzig: Deichert, 1910.

Index of Ancient Sources

A. Hebrew Scriptures and Septuagint

B. Other Ancient Sources

C. New Testament

Index of Authors

Index of Subjects

Wissenschaftliche Untersuchungen zum Neuen Testament

Alphabetical Index of the First and Second Series

Becker, Eve-Marie: Das Markus-Evangelium im Rahmen antiker Historiographie. 2006. *Vol. 194.*

Becker, Eve-Marie and *Peter Pilhofer* (Ed.): Biographie und Persönlichkeit des Paulus. 2005. *Vol. 187.*

– and *Anders Runesson* (Ed.): Mark and Matthew I. 2011. *Vol. 271.*

Becker, Michael: Wunder und Wundertäter im frührabbinischen Judentum. 2002. *Vol. II/144.*

Becker, Michael and *Markus Öhler* (Ed.): Apokalyptik als Herausforderung neutestamentlicher Theologie. 2006. *Vol. II/214.*

Bell, Richard H.: Deliver Us from Evil. 2007. *Vol. 216.*

– The Irrevocable Call of God. 2005. *Vol. 184.*

– No One Seeks for God. 1998. *Vol. 106.*

– Provoked to Jealousy. 1994. *Vol. II/63.*

Bennema, Cornelis: The Power of Saving Wisdom. 2002. *Vol. II/148.*

Bergman, Jan: see *Kieffer, René*

Bergmeier, Roland: Das Gesetz im Römerbrief und andere Studien zum Neuen Testament. 2000. *Vol. 121.*

Bernett, Monika: Der Kaiserkult in Judäa unter den Herodiern und Römern. 2007. *Vol. 203.*

Betho, Benjamin: see *Clivaz, Claire.*

Betz, Otto: Jesus, der Messias Israels. 1987. *Vol. 42.*

– Jesus, der Herr der Kirche. 1990. *Vol. 52.*

Beyschlag, Karlmann: Simon Magus und die christliche Gnosis. 1974. *Vol. 16.*

Bieringer, Reimund: see *Koester, Craig.*

Bird, Michael F. and *Jason Maston* (Ed.): Earliest Christian History. 2012. *Vol. II/320.*

Bittner, Wolfgang J.: Jesu Zeichen im Johannesevangelium. 1987. *Vol. II/26.*

Bjerkelund, Carl J.: Tauta Egeneto. 1987. *Vol. 40.*

Blackburn, Barry Lee: Theios Aner and the Markan Miracle Traditions. 1991. *Vol. II/40.*

Blackwell, Ben C.: Christosis. 2011. *Vol. II/314.*

Blanton IV, Thomas R.: Constructing a New Covenant. 2007. *Vol. II/233.*

Bock, Darrell L.: Blasphemy and Exaltation in Judaism and the Final Examination of Jesus. 1998. *Vol. II/106.*

– and *Robert L. Webb* (Ed.): Key Events in the Life of the Historical Jesus. 2009. *Vol. 247.*

Bockmuehl, Markus: The Remembered Peter. 2010. *Vol. 262.*

– Revelation and Mystery in Ancient Judaism and Pauline Christianity. 1990. *Vol. II/36.*

Bøe, Sverre: Cross-Bearing in Luke. 2010. *Vol. II/278.*

– Gog and Magog. 2001. *Vol. II/135.*

Böhlig, Alexander: Gnosis und Synkretismus. Vol. 1 1989. *Vol. 47* – Vol. 2 1989. *Vol. 48.*

Böhm, Martina: Samarien und die Samaritai bei Lukas. 1999. *Vol. II/111.*

Börstinghaus, Jens: Sturmfahrt und Schiffbruch. 2010. *Vol. II/274.*

Böttrich, Christfried: Weltweisheit – Menschheitsethik – Urkult. 1992. *Vol. II/50.*

– and *Herzer, Jens* (Ed.): Josephus und das Neue Testament. 2007. *Vol. 209.*

Bolyki, János: Jesu Tischgemeinschaften. 1997. *Vol. II/96.*

Bosman, Philip: Conscience in Philo and Paul. 2003. *Vol. II/166.*

Bovon, François: New Testament and Christian Apocrypha. 2009. *Vol. 237.*

– Studies in Early Christianity. 2003. *Vol. 161.*

Brändl, Martin: Der Agon bei Paulus. 2006. *Vol. II/222.*

Braun, Heike: Geschichte des Gottesvolkes und christliche Identität. 2010. *Vol. II/279.*

Breytenbach, Cilliers: see *Frey, Jörg.*

Broadhead, Edwin K.: Jewish Ways of Following Jesus Redrawing the Religious Map of Antiquity. 2010. *Vol. 266.*

Brocke, Christoph vom: Thessaloniki – Stadt des Kassander und Gemeinde des Paulus. 2001. *Vol. II/125.*

Brunson, Andrew: Psalm 118 in the Gospel of John. 2003. *Vol. II/158.*

Büchli, Jörg: Der Poimandres – ein paganisiertes Evangelium. 1987. *Vol. II/27.*

Bühner, Jan A.: Der Gesandte und sein Weg im 4. Evangelium. 1977. *Vol. II/2.*

Burchard, Christoph: Untersuchungen zu Joseph und Aseneth. 1965. *Vol. 8.*

– Studien zur Theologie, Sprache und Umwelt des Neuen Testaments. Ed. by D. Sänger. 1998. *Vol. 107.*

Burnett, Richard: Karl Barth's Theological Exegesis. 2001. *Vol. II/145.*

Byron, John: Slavery Metaphors in Early Judaism and Pauline Christianity. 2003. *Vol. II/162.*

Byrskog, Samuel: Story as History – History as Story. 2000. *Vol. 123.*

Calhoun, Robert M.: Paul's Definitions of the Gospel in Romans 1. 2011. *Vol. II/316.*

Cancik, Hubert (Ed.): Markus-Philologie. 1984. *Vol. 33.*

Capes, David B.: Old Testament Yaweh Texts in Paul's Christology. 1992. *Vol. II/47.*

Caragounis, Chrys C.: The Development of Greek and the New Testament. 2004. *Vol. 167.*
– The Son of Man. 1986. *Vol. 38.*
– see *Fridrichsen, Anton.*
Carleton Paget, James: The Epistle of Barnabas. 1994. *Vol. II/64.*
– Jews, Christians and Jewish Christians in Antiquity. 2010. *Vol. 251.*
Carson, D.A., O'Brien, Peter T. and *Mark Seifrid* (Ed.): Justification and Variegated Nomism.
Vol. 1: The Complexities of Second Temple Judaism. 2001. *Vol. II/140.*
Vol. 2: The Paradoxes of Paul. 2004. *Vol. II/181.*
Caulley, Thomas Scott and *Hermann Lichtenberger* (Ed.): Die Septuaginta und das frühe Christentum – The Septuagint and Christian Origins. 2011. *Vol. 277.*
– see *Lichtenberger, Hermann.*
Chae, Young Sam: Jesus as the Eschatological Davidic Shepherd. 2006. *Vol. II/216.*
Chapman, David W.: Ancient Jewish and Christian Perceptions of Crucifixion. 2008. *Vol. II/244.*
Chester, Andrew: Messiah and Exaltation. 2007. *Vol. 207.*
Chibici-Revneanu, Nicole: Die Herrlichkeit des Verherrlichten. 2007. *Vol. II/231.*
Ciampa, Roy E.: The Presence and Function of Scripture in Galatians 1 and 2. 1998. *Vol. II/102.*
Classen, Carl Joachim: Rhetorical Criticsm of the New Testament. 2000. *Vol. 128.*
Claußen, Carsten (Ed.): see *Frey, Jörg.*
Clivaz, Claire, Andreas Dettwiler, Luc Devillers, Enrico Norelli with *Benjamin Bertho* (Ed.): Infancy Gospels. 2011. *Vol. 281.*
Colpe, Carsten: Griechen – Byzantiner – Semiten – Muslime. 2008. *Vol. 221.*
– Iranier – Aramäer – Hebräer – Hellenen. 2003. *Vol. 154.*
Cook, John G.: Roman Attitudes Towards the Christians. 2010. *Vol. 261.*
Coote, Robert B. (Ed.): see *Weissenrieder, Annette.*
Coppins, Wayne: The Interpretation of Freedom in the Letters of Paul. 2009. *Vol. II/261.*
Crump, David: Jesus the Intercessor. 1992. *Vol. II/49.*
Dahl, Nils Alstrup: Studies in Ephesians. 2000. *Vol. 131.*
Daise, Michael A.: Feasts in John. 2007. *Vol. II/229.*

Deines, Roland: Die Gerechtigkeit der Tora im Reich des Messias. 2004. *Vol. 177.*
– Jüdische Steingefäße und pharisäische Frömmigkeit. 1993. *Vol. II/52.*
– Die Pharisäer. 1997. *Vol. 101.*
Deines, Roland, Jens Herzer and *Karl-Wilhelm Niebuhr* (Ed.): Neues Testament und hellenistisch-jüdische Alltagskultur. III. Internationales Symposium zum Corpus Judaeo-Hellenisticum Novi Testamenti. 21.–24. Mai 2009 in Leipzig. 2011. *Vol. 274.*
– and *Karl-Wilhelm Niebuhr* (Ed.): Philo und das Neue Testament. 2004. *Vol. 172.*
Dennis, John A.: Jesus' Death and the Gathering of True Israel. 2006. *Vol. 217.*
Dettwiler, Andreas and *Jean Zumstein* (Ed.): Kreuzestheologie im Neuen Testament. 2002. *Vol. 151.*
– see *Clivaz, Claire.*
Devillers, Luc: see *Clivaz, Claire.*
Dickson, John P.: Mission-Commitment in Ancient Judaism and in the Pauline Communities. 2003. *Vol. II/159.*
Dietzfelbinger, Christian: Der Abschied des Kommenden. 1997. *Vol. 95.*
Dimitrov, Ivan Z., James D.G. Dunn, Ulrich Luz and *Karl-Wilhelm Niebuhr* (Ed.): Das Alte Testament als christliche Bibel in orthodoxer und westlicher Sicht. 2004. *Vol. 174.*
Dobbeler, Axel von: Glaube als Teilhabe. 1987. *Vol. II/22.*
Docherty, Susan E.: The Use of the Old Testament in Hebrews. 2009. *Vol. II/260.*
Dochhorn, Jan: Schriftgelehrte Prophetie. 2010. *Vol. 268.*
Downs, David J.: The Offering of the Gentiles. 2008. *Vol. II/248.*
Dryden, J. de Waal: Theology and Ethics in 1 Peter. 2006. *Vol. II/209.*
Dübbers, Michael: Christologie und Existenz im Kolosserbrief. 2005. *Vol. II/191.*
Dunn, James D.G.: The New Perspective on Paul. 2005. *Vol. 185.*
Dunn, James D.G. (Ed.): Jews and Christians. 1992. *Vol. 66.*
– Paul and the Mosaic Law. 1996. *Vol. 89.*
– see *Dimitrov, Ivan Z.*
–, *Hans Klein, Ulrich Luz,* and *Vasile Mihoc* (Ed.): Auslegung der Bibel in orthodoxer und westlicher Perspektive. 2000. *Vol. 130.*
Ebel, Eva: Die Attraktivität früher christlicher Gemeinden. 2004. *Vol. II/178.*
Ebertz, Michael N.: Das Charisma des Gekreuzigten. 1987. *Vol. 45.*

Eckstein, Hans-Joachim: Der Begriff Syn-
eidesis bei Paulus. 1983. *Vol. II/10.*
– Verheißung und Gesetz. 1996. *Vol. 86.*
–, *Christoph Landmesser* and *Hermann Lich-
tenberger* (Ed.): Eschatologie – Eschato-
logy. The Sixth Durham-Tübingen Research
Symposium. 2011. *Vol. 272.*
Ego, Beate: Im Himmel wie auf Erden. 1989.
Vol. II/34.
Ego, Beate, Armin Lange and *Peter Pilhofer*
(Ed.): Gemeinde ohne Tempel – Community
without Temple. 1999. *Vol. 118.*
– and *Helmut Merkel* (Ed.): Religiöses Lernen
in der biblischen, frühjüdischen und früh-
christlichen Überlieferung. 2005. *Vol. 180.*
Eisele, Wilfried: Welcher Thomas? 2010.
Vol. 259.
Eisen, Ute E.: see *Paulsen, Henning.*
Elledge, C.D.: Life after Death in Early Juda-
ism. 2006. *Vol. II/208.*
Ellis, E. Earle: Prophecy and Hermeneutic in
Early Christianity. 1978. *Vol. 18.*
– The Old Testament in Early Christianity.
1991. *Vol. 54.*
Elmer, Ian J.: Paul, Jerusalem and the Judaisers.
2009. *Vol. II/258.*
Endo, Masanobu: Creation and Christology.
2002. *Vol. 149.*
Ennulat, Andreas: Die 'Minor Agreements'.
1994. *Vol. II/62.*
Ensor, Peter W.: Jesus and His 'Works'. 1996.
Vol. II/85.
Eskola, Timo: Messiah and the Throne. 2001.
Vol. II/142.
– Theodicy and Predestination in Pauline
Soteriology. 1998. *Vol. II/100.*
Farelly, Nicolas: The Disciples in the Fourth
Gospel. 2010. *Vol. II/290.*
Fatehi, Mehrdad: The Spirit's Relation to the
Risen Lord in Paul. 2000. *Vol. II/128.*
Feldmeier, Reinhard: Die Krisis des Gottes-
sohnes. 1987. *Vol. II/21.*
– Die Christen als Fremde. 1992. *Vol. 64.*
Feldmeier, Reinhard and *Ulrich Heckel* (Ed.):
Die Heiden. 1994. *Vol. 70.*
Felsch, Dorit: Die Feste im Johannesevange-
lium. 2011. *Vol. II/308.*
Finnern, Sönke: Narratologie und biblische Ex-
egese. 2010. *Vol. II/285.*
Fletcher-Louis, Crispin H.T.: Luke-Acts:
Angels, Christology and Soteriology. 1997.
Vol. II/94.
Förster, Niclas: Marcus Magus. 1999. *Vol. 114.*

Forbes, Christopher Brian: Prophecy and In-
spired Speech in Early Christianity and its
Hellenistic Environment. 1995. *Vol. II/75.*
Fornberg, Tord: see *Fridrichsen, Anton.*
Fossum, Jarl E.: The Name of God and the
Angel of the Lord. 1985. *Vol. 36.*
Foster, Paul: Community, Law and Mission in
Matthew's Gospel. *Vol. II/177.*
Fotopoulos, John: Food Offered to Idols in
Roman Corinth. 2003. *Vol. II/151.*
Frank, Nicole: Der Kolosserbrief im Kontext
des paulinischen Erbes. 2009. *Vol. II/271.*
Frenschkowski, Marco: Offenbarung und
Epiphanie. Vol. 1 1995. *Vol. II/79* – Vol. 2
1997. *Vol. II/80.*
Frey, Jörg: Eugen Drewermann und die bibli-
sche Exegese. 1995. *Vol. II/71.*
– Die johanneische Eschatologie. Vol. I. 1997.
Vol. 96. – Vol. II. 1998. *Vol. 110.* – Vol. III.
2000. *Vol. 117.*
Frey, Jörg, Carsten Claußen and *Nadine Kessler*
(Ed.): Qumran und die Archäologie. 2011.
Vol. 278.
– and *Cilliers Breytenbach* (Ed.): Aufgabe und
Durchführung einer Theologie des Neuen
Testaments. 2007. *Vol. 205.*
– *Jens Herzer, Martina Janßen* and *Clare K.
Rothschild* (Ed.): Pseudepigraphie und Ver-
fasserfiktion in frühchristlichen Briefen.
2009. *Vol. 246.*
– *James A. Kelhoffer* and *Franz Tóth* (Ed.): Die
Johannesapokalypse. 2012. *Vol. 287.*
– *Stefan Krauter* and *Hermann Lichtenberger*
(Ed.): Heil und Geschichte. 2009. *Vol. 248.*
– and *Udo Schnelle (Ed.):* Kontexte des Jo-
hannesevangeliums. 2004. *Vol. 175.*
– and *Jens Schröter* (Ed.): Deutungen des
Todes Jesu im Neuen Testament. 2005.
Vol. 181.
– Jesus in apokryphen Evangelienüberliefe-
rungen. 2010. *Vol. 254.*
–, *Jan G. van der Watt,* and *Ruben Zimmer-
mann* (Ed.): Imagery in the Gospel of John.
2006. *Vol. 200.*
Freyne, Sean: Galilee and Gospel. 2000.
Vol. 125.
Fridrichsen, Anton: Exegetical Writings. Edited
by C.C. Caragounis and T. Fornberg. 1994.
Vol. 76.
Gadenz, Pablo T.: Called from the Jews and
from the Gentiles. 2009. *Vol. II/267.*
Gäbel, Georg: Die Kulttheologie des Hebräer-
briefes. 2006. *Vol. II/212.*
Gäckle, Volker: Die Starken und die Schwachen
in Korinth und in Rom. 2005. *Vol. 200.*

Garlington, Don B.: 'The Obedience of Faith'. 1991. *Vol. II/38.*
– Faith, Obedience, and Perseverance. 1994. *Vol. 79.*
Garnet, Paul: Salvation and Atonement in the Qumran Scrolls. 1977. *Vol. II/3.*
Gemünden, Petra von (Ed.): see *Weissenrieder, Annette.*
Gese, Michael: Das Vermächtnis des Apostels. 1997. *Vol. II/99.*
Gheorghita, Radu: The Role of the Septuagint in Hebrews. 2003. *Vol. II/160.*
Gordley, Matthew E.: The Colossian Hymn in Context. 2007. *Vol. II/228.*
– Teaching through Song in Antiquity. 2011. *Vol. II/302.*
Gräbe, Petrus J.: The Power of God in Paul's Letters. 2000, ²2008. *Vol. II/123.*
Gräßer, Erich: Der Alte Bund im Neuen. 1985. *Vol. 35.*
– Forschungen zur Apostelgeschichte. 2001. *Vol. 137.*
Grappe, Christian (Ed.): Le Repas de Dieu / Das Mahl Gottes. 2004. *Vol. 169.*
Gray, Timothy C.: The Temple in the Gospel of Mark. 2008. *Vol. II/242.*
Green, Joel B.: The Death of Jesus. 1988. *Vol. II/33.*
Gregg, Brian Han: The Historical Jesus and the Final Judgment Sayings in Q. 2005. *Vol. II/207.*
Gregory, Andrew: The Reception of Luke and Acts in the Period before Irenaeus. 2003. *Vol. II/169.*
Grindheim, Sigurd: The Crux of Election. 2005. *Vol. II/202.*
Gundry, Robert H.: The Old is Better. 2005. *Vol. 178.*
Gundry Volf, Judith M.: Paul and Perseverance. 1990. *Vol. II/37.*
Häußer, Detlef: Christusbekenntnis und Jesusüberlieferung bei Paulus. 2006. *Vol. 210.*
Hafemann, Scott J.: Suffering and the Spirit. 1986. *Vol. II/19.*
– Paul, Moses, and the History of Israel. 1995. *Vol. 81.*
Hahn, Ferdinand: Studien zum Neuen Testament.
Vol. I: Grundsatzfragen, Jesusforschung, Evangelien. 2006. *Vol. 191.*
Vol. II: Bekenntnisbildung und Theologie in urchristlicher Zeit. 2006. *Vol. 192.*
Hahn, Johannes (Ed.): Zerstörungen des Jerusalemer Tempels. 2002. *Vol. 147.*

Hamid-Khani, Saeed: Relevation and Concealment of Christ. 2000. *Vol. II/120.*
Hannah, Darrel D.: Michael and Christ. 1999. *Vol. II/109.*
Hardin, Justin K.: Galatians and the Imperial Cult? 2007. *Vol. II /237.*
Harrison, James R.: Paul and the Imperial Authorities at Thessalonica and Rome. 2011. *Vol. 273.*
– Paul's Language of Grace in Its Graeco-Roman Context. 2003. *Vol. II/172.*
Hartman, Lars: Text-Centered New Testament Studies. Ed. von D. Hellholm. 1997. *Vol. 102.*
Hartog, Paul: Polycarp and the New Testament. 2001. *Vol. II/134.*
Hasselbrook, David S.: Studies in New Testament Lexicography. 2011. *Vol. II/303.*
Hays, Christopher M.: Luke's Wealth Ethics. 2010. *Vol. 275.*
Heckel, Theo K.: Der Innere Mensch. 1993. *Vol. II/53.*
– Vom Evangelium des Markus zum viergestaltigen Evangelium. 1999. *Vol. 120.*
Heckel, Ulrich: Kraft in Schwachheit. 1993. *Vol. II/56.*
– Der Segen im Neuen Testament. 2002. *Vol. 150.*
– see *Feldmeier, Reinhard.*
– see *Hengel, Martin.*
Heemstra, Marius: The Fiscus Judaicus and the Parting of the Ways. 2010. *Vol. II/277.*
Heiligenthal, Roman: Werke als Zeichen. 1983. *Vol. II/9.*
Heininger, Bernhard: Die Inkulturation des Christentums. 2010. *Vol. 255.*
Heliso, Desta: Pistis and the Righteous One. 2007. *Vol. II/235.*
Hellholm, D.: see *Hartman, Lars.*
Hemer, Colin J.: The Book of Acts in the Setting of Hellenistic History. 1989. *Vol. 49.*
Henderson, Timothy P.: The Gospel of Peter and Early Christian Apologetics. 2011. *Vol. II/301.*
Hengel, Martin: Jesus und die Evangelien. Kleine Schriften V. 2007. *Vol. 211.*
– Die johanneische Frage. 1993. *Vol. 67.*
– Judaica et Hellenistica. Kleine Schriften I. 1996. *Vol. 90.*
– Judaica, Hellenistica et Christiana. Kleine Schriften II. 1999. *Vol. 109.*
– Judentum und Hellenismus. 1969, ³1988. *Vol. 10.*
– Paulus und Jakobus. Kleine Schriften III. 2002. *Vol. 141.*

– Studien zur Christologie. Kleine Schriften IV. 2006. *Vol. 201.*
– Studien zum Urchristentum. Kleine Schriften VI. 2008. *Vol. 234.*
– Theologische, historische und biographische Skizzen. Kleine Schriften VII. 2010. *Vol. 253.*
– and *Anna Maria Schwemer:* Paulus zwischen Damaskus und Antiochien. 1998. *Vol. 108.*
– Der messianische Anspruch Jesu und die Anfänge der Christologie. 2001. *Vol. 138.*
– Die vier Evangelien und das eine Evangelium von Jesus Christus. 2008. *Vol. 224.*
– Die Zeloten. ³2011. *Vol. 283.*
Hengel, Martin and *Ulrich Heckel* (Ed.): Paulus und das antike Judentum. 1991. *Vol. 58.*
– and *Hermut Löhr* (Ed.): Schriftauslegung im antiken Judentum und im Urchristentum. 1994. *Vol. 73.*
– and *Anna Maria Schwemer* (Ed.): Königsherrschaft Gottes und himmlischer Kult. 1991. *Vol. 55.*
– Die Septuaginta. 1994. *Vol. 72.*
–, *Siegfried Mittmann* and *Anna Maria Schwemer* (Ed.): La Cité de Dieu / Die Stadt Gottes. 2000. *Vol. 129.*
Hentschel, Anni: Diakonia im Neuen Testament. 2007. *Vol. 226.*
Hernández Jr., Juan: Scribal Habits and Theological Influence in the Apocalypse. 2006. *Vol. II/218.*
Herrenbrück, Fritz: Jesus und die Zöllner. 1990. *Vol. II/41.*
Herzer, Jens: Paulus oder Petrus? 1998. *Vol. 103.*
– see *Böttrich, Christfried.*
– see *Deines, Roland.*
– see *Frey, Jörg.*
Hill, Charles E.: From the Lost Teaching of Polycarp. 2005. *Vol. 186.*
Hoegen-Rohls, Christina: Der nachösterliche Johannes. 1996. *Vol. II/84.*
Hoffmann, Matthias Reinhard: The Destroyer and the Lamb. 2005. *Vol. II/203.*
Hofius, Otfried: Katapausis. 1970. *Vol. 11.*
– Der Vorhang vor dem Thron Gottes. 1972. *Vol. 14.*
– Der Christushymnus Philipper 2,6–11. 1976, ²1991. *Vol. 17.*
– Paulusstudien. 1989, ²1994. *Vol. 51.*
– Neutestamentliche Studien. 2000. *Vol. 132.*
– Paulusstudien II. 2002. *Vol. 143.*
– Exegetische Studien. 2008. *Vol. 223.*

– and *Hans-Christian Kammler:* Johannesstudien. 1996. *Vol. 88.*
Holloway, Paul A.: Coping with Prejudice. 2009. *Vol. 244.*
– see *Ahearne-Kroll, Stephen P.*
Holmberg, Bengt (Ed.): Exploring Early Christian Identity. 2008. *Vol. 226.*
– and *Mikael Winninge* (Ed.): Identity Formation in the New Testament. 2008. *Vol. 227.*
Holtz, Traugott: Geschichte und Theologie des Urchristentums. 1991. *Vol. 57.*
Hommel, Hildebrecht: Sebasmata. Vol. 1 1983. *Vol. 31.* Vol. 2 1984. *Vol. 32.*
Horbury, William: Herodian Judaism and New Testament Study. 2006. *Vol. 193.*
Horn, Friedrich Wilhelm and *Ruben Zimmermann* (Ed.): Jenseits von Indikativ und Imperativ. Vol. 1. 2009. *Vol. 238.*
Horst, Pieter W. van der: Jews and Christians in Their Graeco-Roman Context. 2006. *Vol. 196.*
Hultgård, Anders and *Stig Norin* (Ed): Le Jour de Dieu / Der Tag Gottes. 2009. *Vol. 245.*
Hume, Douglas A.: The Early Christian Community. 2011. *Vol. II/298.*
Hvalvik, Reidar: The Struggle for Scripture and Covenant. 1996. *Vol. II/82.*
Inselmann, Anke: Die Freude im Lukasevangelium. 2012. *Vol. II/322.*
Jackson, Ryan: New Creation in Paul's Letters. 2010. *Vol. II/272.*
Janßen, Martina: see *Frey, Jörg.*
Jauhiainen, Marko: The Use of Zechariah in Revelation. 2005. *Vol. II/199.*
Jensen, Morten H.: Herod Antipas in Galilee. 2006; ²2010. *Vol. II/215.*
Johns, Loren L.: The Lamb Christology of the Apocalypse of John. 2003. *Vol. II/167.*
Jossa, Giorgio: Jews or Christians? 2006. *Vol. 202.*
Joubert, Stephan: Paul as Benefactor. 2000. *Vol. II/124.*
Judge, E. A.: The First Christians in the Roman World. 2008. *Vol. 229.*
– Jerusalem and Athens. 2010. *Vol. 265.*
Jungbauer, Harry: „Ehre Vater und Mutter". 2002. *Vol. II/146.*
Kähler, Christoph: Jesu Gleichnisse als Poesie und Therapie. 1995. *Vol. 78.*
Kamlah, Ehrhard: Die Form der katalogischen Paränese im Neuen Testament. 1964. *Vol. 7.*
Kammler, Hans-Christian: Christologie und Eschatologie. 2000. *Vol. 126.*
– Kreuz und Weisheit. 2003. *Vol. 159.*

Lambers-Petry, Doris: see *Tomson, Peter J.*
Lampe, Peter: Die stadtrömischen Christen in den ersten beiden Jahrhunderten. 1987, ²1989. *Vol. II/18.*
Landmesser, Christof: Wahrheit als Grundbegriff neutestamentlicher Wissenschaft. 1999. *Vol. 113.*
– Jüngerberufung und Zuwendung zu Gott. 2000. *Vol. 133.*
– see *Eckstein, Hans-Joachim.*
Lange, Armin: see *Ego, Beate.*
Lau, Andrew: Manifest in Flesh. 1996. *Vol. II/86.*
Lawrence, Louise: An Ethnography of the Gospel of Matthew. 2003. *Vol. II/165.*
Lee, Aquila H.I.: From Messiah to Preexistent Son. 2005. *Vol. II/192.*
Lee, Pilchan: The New Jerusalem in the Book of Revelation. 2000. *Vol. II/129.*
Lee, Sang M.: The Cosmic Drama of Salvation. 2010. *Vol. II/276.*
Lee, Simon S.: Jesus' Transfiguration and the Believers' Transformation. 2009. *Vol. II/265.*
Lichtenberger, Hermann: Das Ich Adams und das Ich der Menschheit. 2004. *Vol. 164.*
– see *Avemarie, Friedrich.*
– see *Caulley, Thomas Scott.*
– see *Eckstein, Hans-Joachim.*
– see *Frey, Jörg.*
Lierman, John: The New Testament Moses. 2004. *Vol. II/173.*
– (Ed.): Challenging Perspectives on the Gospel of John. 2006. *Vol. II/219.*
Lieu, Samuel N.C.: Manichaeism in the Later Roman Empire and Medieval China. ²1992. *Vol. 63.*
Lindemann, Andreas: Die Evangelien und die Apostelgeschichte. 2009. *Vol. 241.*
– Glauben, Handeln, Verstehen. Studien zur Auslegung des Neuen Testaments. 2011. *Vol. II/282.*
Lincicum, David: Paul and the Early Jewish Encounter with Deuteronomy. 2010. *Vol. II/284.*
Lindgård, Fredrik: Paul's Line of Thought in 2 Corinthians 4:16–5:10. 2004. *Vol. II/189.*
Livesey, Nina E.: Circumcision as a Malleable Symbol. 2010. *Vol. II/295.*
Loader, William R.G.: Jesus' Attitude Towards the Law. 1997. *Vol. II/97.*
Löhr, Gebhard: Verherrlichung Gottes durch Philosophie. 1997. *Vol. 97.*
Löhr, Hermut: Studien zum frühchristlichen und frühjüdischen Gebet. 2003. *Vol. 160.*
– see *Hengel, Martin.*

Löhr, Winrich Alfried: Basilides und seine Schule. 1995. *Vol. 83.*
Lorenzen, Stefanie: Das paulinische Eikon-Konzept. 2008. *Vol. II/250.*
Luomanen, Petri: Entering the Kingdom of Heaven. 1998. *Vol. II/101.*
Luz, Ulrich: see *Alexeev, Anatoly A.*
– see *Dunn, James D.G.*
Lykke, Anne und *Friedrich T. Schipper* (Ed.): Kult und Macht. 2011. *Vol. II/319.*
Lyu, Eun-Geol: Sünde und Rechtfertigung bei Paulus. 2012. *Vol. II/318.*
Mackay, Ian D.: John's Relationship with Mark. 2004. *Vol. II/182.*
Mackie, Scott D.: Eschatology and Exhortation in the Epistle to the Hebrews. 2006. *Vol. II/223.*
Magda, Ksenija: Paul's Territoriality and Mission Strategy. 2009. *Vol. II/266.*
Maier, Gerhard: Mensch und freier Wille. 1971. *Vol. 12.*
– Die Johannesoffenbarung und die Kirche. 1981. *Vol. 25.*
Markschies, Christoph: Valentinus Gnosticus? 1992. *Vol. 65.*
Marshall, Jonathan: Jesus, Patrons, and Benefactors. 2009. *Vol. II/259.*
Marshall, Peter: Enmity in Corinth: Social Conventions in Paul's Relations with the Corinthians. 1987. *Vol. II/23.*
Martin, Dale B.: see *Zangenberg, Jürgen.*
Maston, Jason: Divine and Human Agency in Second Temple Judaism and Paul. 2010. *Vol. II/297.*
– see *Bird, Michael F.*
Mayer, Annemarie: Sprache der Einheit im Epheserbrief und in der Ökumene. 2002. *Vol. II/150.*
Mayordomo, Moisés: Argumentiert Paulus logisch? 2005. *Vol. 188.*
McDonough, Sean M.: YHWH at Patmos: Rev. 1:4 in its Hellenistic and Early Jewish Setting. 1999. *Vol. II/107.*
McDowell, Markus: Prayers of Jewish Women. 2006. *Vol. II/211.*
McGlynn, Moyna: Divine Judgement and Divine Benevolence in the Book of Wisdom. 2001. *Vol. II/139.*
McNamara, Martin: Targum and New Testament. 2011. *Vol. 279.*
Meade, David G.: Pseudonymity and Canon. 1986. *Vol. 39.*
Meadors, Edward P.: Jesus the Messianic Herald of Salvation. 1995. *Vol. II/72.*
Meiser, Martin: see *Kreuzer, Siegfried.*

Meißner, Stefan: Die Heimholung des Ketzers. 1996. *Vol. II/87.*

Mell, Ulrich: Die „anderen" Winzer. 1994. *Vol. 77.*

– see *Sänger, Dieter.*

Mengel, Berthold: Studien zum Philipperbrief. 1982. *Vol. II/8.*

Merkel, Helmut: Die Widersprüche zwischen den Evangelien. 1971. *Vol. 13.*

– see *Ego, Beate.*

Merklein, Helmut: Studien zu Jesus und Paulus. Vol. 1 1987. *Vol. 43.* – Vol. 2 1998. *Vol. 105.*

Merkt, Andreas: see *Nicklas, Tobias*

Metzdorf, Christina: Die Tempelaktion Jesu. 2003. *Vol. II/168.*

Metzler, Karin: Der griechische Begriff des Verzeihens. 1991. *Vol. II/44.*

Metzner, Rainer: Die Rezeption des Matthäusevangeliums im 1. Petrusbrief. 1995. *Vol. II/74.*

– Das Verständnis der Sünde im Johannesevangelium. 2000. *Vol. 122.*

Mihoc, Vasile: see *Dunn, James D.G.*

– see *Klein, Hans.*

Mineshige, Kiyoshi: Besitzverzicht und Almosen bei Lukas. 2003. *Vol. II/163.*

Mittmann, Siegfried: see *Hengel, Martin.*

Mittmann-Richert, Ulrike: Magnifikat und Benediktus. *1996. Vol. II/90.*

– Der Sühnetod des Gottesknechts. 2008. *Vol. 220.*

Miura, Yuzuru: David in Luke-Acts. 2007. *Vol. II/232.*

Moll, Sebastian: The Arch-Heretic Marcion. 2010. *Vol. 250.*

Morales, Rodrigo J.: The Spirit and the Restorat. 2010. *Vol. 282.*

Mournet, Terence C.: Oral Tradition and Literary Dependency. 2005. *Vol. II/195.*

Mußner, Franz: Jesus von Nazareth im Umfeld Israels und der Urkirche. Ed. von M. Theobald. 1998. *Vol. 111.*

Mutschler, Bernhard: Das Corpus Johanneum bei Irenäus von Lyon. 2005. *Vol. 189.*

– Glaube in den Pastoralbriefen. 2010. *Vol. 256.*

Myers, Susan E.: Spirit Epicleses in the Acts of Thomas. 2010. *Vol. 281.*

Myers, Susan E. (Ed.): Portraits of Jesus. 2012. *Vol. II/321.*

Nguyen, V. Henry T.: Christian Identity in Corinth. 2008. *Vol. II/243.*

Nicklas, Tobias, Andreas Merkt und Joseph Verheyden (Ed.): Gelitten – Gestorben – Auferstanden. 2010. *Vol. II/273.*

– see *Verheyden, Joseph*

Nicolet-Anderson, Valérie: Constructing the Self. 2012. *Vol. II/324.*

Niebuhr, Karl-Wilhelm: Gesetz and Paränese. 1987. *Vol. II/28.*

– Heidenapostel aus Israel. 1992. *Vol. 62.*

– see *Deines, Roland.*

– see *Dimitrov, Ivan Z.*

– see *Karakolis, Christos.*

– see *Klein, Hans.*

– see *Kraus, Wolfgang.*

Nielsen, Anders E.: "Until it is Fullfilled". 2000. *Vol. II/126.*

Nielsen, Jesper Tang: Die kognitive Dimension des Kreuzes. 2009. *Vol. II/263.*

Nissen, Andreas: Gott und der Nächste im antiken Judentum. 1974. *Vol. 15.*

Noack, Christian: Gottesbewußtsein. 2000. *Vol. II/116.*

Noormann, Rolf: Irenäus als Paulusinterpret. 1994. *Vol. II/66.*

Norelli, Enrico: see *Clivaz, Claire.*

Norin, Stig: see *Hultgård, Anders.*

Novakovic, Lidija: Messiah, the Healer of the Sick. 2003. *Vol. II/170.*

Obermann, Andreas: Die christologische Erfüllung der Schrift im Johannesevangelium. 1996. *Vol. II/83.*

Öhler, Markus: Barnabas. 2003. *Vol. 156.*

– see *Becker, Michael.*

– (Ed.): Aposteldekret und antikes Vereinswesen. 2011. *Vol. 280.*

Okure, Teresa: The Johannine Approach to Mission. 1988. *Vol. II/31.*

Onuki, Takashi: Heil und Erlösung. 2004. *Vol. 165.*

Oropeza, B. J.: Paul and Apostasy. 2000. *Vol. II/115.*

Ostmeyer, Karl-Heinrich: Kommunikation mit Gott und Christus. 2006. *Vol. 197.*

– Taufe und Typos. 2000. *Vol. II/118.*

Pao, David W.: Acts and the Isaianic New Exodus. 2000. *Vol. II/130.*

Park, Eung Chun: The Mission Discourse in Matthew's Interpretation. 1995. *Vol. II/81.*

Park, Joseph S.: Conceptions of Afterlife in Jewish Insriptions. 2000. *Vol. II/121.*

Parsenios, George L.: Rhetoric and Drama in the Johannine Lawsuit Motif. 2010. *Vol. 258.*

Pate, C. Marvin: The Reverse of the Curse. 2000. *Vol. II/114.*

Paulsen, Henning: Studien zur Literatur und Geschichte des frühen Christentums. Ed. von Ute E. Eisen. 1997. *Vol. 99.*

Pearce, Sarah J.K.: The Land of the Body. 2007. *Vol. 208.*

Peres, Imre: Griechische Grabinschriften und neutestamentliche Eschatologie. 2003. *Vol. 157.*

Perry, Peter S.: The Rhetoric of Digressions. 2009. *Vol. II/268.*

Pierce, Chad T.: Spirits and the Proclamation of Christ. 2011. *Vol. II/305.*

Philip, Finny: The Origins of Pauline Pneumatology. 2005. *Vol. II/194.*

Philonenko, Marc (Ed.): Le Trône de Dieu. 1993. *Vol. 69.*

Pilhofer, Peter: Presbyteron Kreitton. 1990. *Vol. II/39.*

- Philippi. Vol. 1 1995. *Vol. 87.* – Vol. 2 ²2009. *Vol. 119.*

- Die frühen Christen und ihre Welt. 2002. *Vol. 145.*

- see *Becker, Eve-Marie.*

- see *Ego, Beate.*

Pitre, Brant: Jesus, the Tribulation, and the End of the Exile. 2005. *Vol. II/204.*

Plümacher, Eckhard: Geschichte und Geschichten. 2004. *Vol. 170.*

Pöhlmann, Wolfgang: Der Verlorene Sohn und das Haus. 1993. *Vol. 68.*

Poirier, John C.: The Tongues of Angels. 2010. *Vol. II/287.*

Pokorný, Petr and *Josef B. Souček:* Bibelauslegung als Theologie. 1997. *Vol. 100.*

- and *Jan Roskovec* (Ed.): Philosophical Hermeneutics and Biblical Exegesis. 2002. *Vol. 153.*

Popkes, Enno Edzard: Das Menschenbild des Thomasevangeliums. 2007. *Vol. 206.*

- Die Theologie der Liebe Gottes in den johanneischen Schriften. 2005. *Vol. II/197.*

Porter, Stanley E.: The Paul of Acts. 1999. *Vol. 115.*

Prieur, Alexander: Die Verkündigung der Gottesherrschaft. 1996. *Vol. II/89.*

Probst, Hermann: Paulus und der Brief. 1991. *Vol. II/45.*

Puig i Tàrrech, Armand: Jesus: An Uncommon Journey. 2010. *Vol. II/288.*

Rabens, Volker: The Holy Spirit and Ethics in Paul. 2010. *Vol. II/283.*

Räisänen, Heikki: Paul and the Law. 1983, ²1987. *Vol. 29.*

Rehkopf, Friedrich: Die lukanische Sonderquelle. 1959. *Vol. 5.*

Rein, Matthias: Die Heilung des Blindgeborenen (Joh 9). 1995. *Vol. II/73.*

Reinmuth, Eckart: Pseudo-Philo und Lukas. 1994. *Vol. 74.*

Reiser, Marius: Bibelkritik und Auslegung der Heiligen Schrift. 2007. *Vol. 217.*

- Syntax und Stil des Markusevangeliums. 1984. *Vol. II/11.*

Reynolds, Benjamin E.: The Apocalyptic Son of Man in the Gospel of John. 2008. *Vol. II/249.*

Rhodes, James N.: The Epistle of Barnabas and the Deuteronomic Tradition. 2004. *Vol. II/188.*

Richards, E. Randolph: The Secretary in the Letters of Paul. 1991. *Vol. II/42.*

Riesner, Rainer: Jesus als Lehrer. 1981, ³1988. *Vol. II/7.*

- Die Frühzeit des Apostels Paulus. 1994. *Vol. 71.*

Rissi, Mathias: Die Theologie des Hebräerbriefs. 1987. *Vol. 41.*

Röcker, Fritz W.: Belial und Katechon. 2009. *Vol. II/262.*

Röhser, Günter: Metaphorik und Personifikation der Sünde. 1987. *Vol. II/25.*

Rogalsky, Sviatoslav: see *Karakolis, Christos.*

Rose, Christian: Theologie als Erzählung im Markusevangelium. 2007. *Vol. II/236.*

- Die Wolke der Zeugen. 1994. *Vol. II/60.*

Roskovec, Jan: see *Pokorný, Petr.*

Rothschild, Clare K.: Baptist Traditions and Q. 2005. *Vol. 190.*

- Hebrews as Pseudepigraphon. 2009. *Vol. 235.*

- Luke Acts and the Rhetoric of History. 2004. *Vol. II/175.*

- see *Frey, Jörg.*

- and *Trevor W. Thompson* (Ed.): Christian Body, Christian Self. 2011. *Vol. 284.*

Rudolph, David J.: A Jew to the Jews. 2011. *Vol. II/304.*

Rüegger, Hans-Ulrich: Verstehen, was Markus erzählt. 2002. *Vol. II/155.*

Rüger, Hans Peter: Die Weisheitsschrift aus der Kairoer Geniza. 1991. *Vol. 53.*

Ruf, Martin G.: Die heiligen Propheten, eure Apostel und ich. 2011. *Vol. II/300.*

Runesson, Anders: see *Becker, Eve-Marie.*

Sänger, Dieter: Antikes Judentum und die Mysterien. 1980. *Vol. II/5.*

- Die Verkündigung des Gekreuzigten und Israel. 1994. *Vol. 75.*

- see *Burchard, Christoph*

- and *Ulrich Mell* (Ed.): Paulus und Johannes. 2006. *Vol. 198.*

Salier, Willis Hedley: The Rhetorical Impact of the Semeia in the Gospel of John. 2004. *Vol. II/186.*

Salzmann, Jörg Christian: Lehren und Ermahnen. 1994. *Vol. II/59.*

Samuelsson, Gunnar: Crucifixion in Antiquity. 2011. *Vol. II/310.*

Sandnes, Karl Olav: Paul – One of the Prophets? 1991. *Vol. II/43.*

Sato, Migaku: Q und Prophetie. 1988. *Vol. II/29.*

Schäfer, Ruth: Paulus bis zum Apostelkonzil. 2004. *Vol. II/179.*

Schaper, Joachim: Eschatology in the Greek Psalter. 1995. *Vol. II/76.*

Schimanowski, Gottfried: Die himmlische Liturgie in der Apokalypse des Johannes. 2002. *Vol. II/154.*

– Weisheit und Messias. 1985. *Vol. II/17.*

Schipper, Friedrich T.: see *Lykke, Anne.*

Schlichting, Günter: Ein jüdisches Leben Jesu. 1982. *Vol. 24.*

Schließer, Benjamin: Abraham's Faith in Romans 4. 2007. *Vol. II/224.*

Schnabel, Eckhard J.: Law and Wisdom from Ben Sira to Paul. 1985. *Vol. II/16.*

Schnelle, Udo: see *Frey, Jörg.*

Schröter, Jens: Von Jesus zum Neuen Testament. 2007. *Vol. 204.*

– see *Frey, Jörg.*

Schutter, William L.: Hermeneutic and Composition in I Peter. 1989. *Vol. II/30.*

Schwartz, Daniel R.: Studies in the Jewish Background of Christianity. 1992. *Vol. 60.*

Schwemer, Anna Maria: see *Hengel, Martin*

Scott, Ian W.: Implicit Epistemology in the Letters of Paul. 2005. *Vol. II/205.*

Scott, James M.: Adoption as Sons of God. 1992. *Vol. II/48.*

– Paul and the Nations. 1995. *Vol. 84.*

Shi, Wenhua: Paul's Message of the Cross as Body Language. 2008. *Vol. II/254.*

Shum, Shiu-Lun: Paul's Use of Isaiah in Romans. 2002. *Vol. II/156.*

Siegert, Folker: Drei hellenistisch-jüdische Predigten. Teil I 1980. *Vol. 20* – Teil II 1992. *Vol. 61.*

– Nag-Hammadi-Register. 1982. *Vol. 26.*

– Argumentation bei Paulus. 1985. *Vol. 34.*

– Philon von Alexandrien. 1988. *Vol. 46.*

Siggelkow-Berner, Birke: Die jüdischen Feste im Bellum Judaicum des Flavius Josephus. 2011. *Vol. II/306.*

Sigismund, Marcus: see *Kreuzer, Siegfried.*

Simon, Marcel: Le christianisme antique et son contexte religieux I/II. 1981. *Vol. 23.*

Smit, Peter-Ben: Fellowship and Food in the Kingdom. 2008. *Vol. II/234.*

Smith, Julien: Christ the Ideal King. 2011. *Vol. II/313.*

Snodgrass, Klyne: The Parable of the Wicked Tenants. 1983. *Vol. 27.*

Söding, Thomas: Das Wort vom Kreuz. 1997. *Vol. 93.*

– see *Thüsing, Wilhelm.*

Sommer, Urs: Die Passionsgeschichte des Markusevangeliums. 1993. *Vol. II/58.*

Sorensen, Eric: Possession and Exorcism in the New Testament and Early Christianity. 2002. *Vol. II/157.*

Souček, Josef B.: see *Pokorný, Petr.*

Southall, David J.: Rediscovering Righteousness in Romans. 2008. *Vol. 240.*

Spangenberg, Volker: Herrlichkeit des Neuen Bundes. 1993. *Vol. II/55.*

Spanje, T.E. van: Inconsistency in Paul? 1999. *Vol. II/110.*

Speyer, Wolfgang: Frühes Christentum im antiken Strahlungsfeld. Vol. I: 1989. *Vol. 50.*

– Vol. II: 1999. *Vol. 116.*

– Vol. III: 2007. *Vol. 213.*

Spittler, Janet E.: Animals in the Apocryphal Acts of the Apostles. 2008. *Vol. II/247.*

Sprinkle, Preston: Law and Life. 2008. *Vol. II/241.*

Stadelmann, Helge: Ben Sira als Schriftgelehrter. 1980. *Vol. II/6.*

Stein, Hans Joachim: Frühchristliche Mahlfeiern. 2008. *Vol. II/255.*

Stenschke, Christoph W.: Luke's Portrait of Gentiles Prior to Their Coming to Faith. *Vol. II/108.*

Stephens, Mark B.: Annihilation or Renewal? 2011. *Vol. II/307.*

Sterck-Degueldre, Jean-Pierre: Eine Frau namens Lydia. 2004. *Vol. II/176.*

Stettler, Christian: Der Kolosserhymnus. 2000. *Vol. II/131.*

– Das letzte Gericht. 2011. *Vol. II/299.*

Stettler, Hanna: Die Christologie der Pastoralbriefe. 1998. *Vol. II/105.*

Stökl Ben Ezra, Daniel: The Impact of Yom Kippur on Early Christianity. 2003. *Vol. 163.*

Strobel, August: Die Stunde der Wahrheit. 1980. *Vol. 21.*

Stroumsa, Guy G.: Barbarian Philosophy. 1999. *Vol. 112.*

Stuckenbruck, Loren T.: Angel Veneration and Christology. 1995. *Vol. II/70.*

–, *Stephen C. Barton* and *Benjamin G. Wold* (Ed.): Memory in the Bible and Antiquity. 2007. *Vol. 212.*

Stuhlmacher, Peter (Ed.): Das Evangelium und die Evangelien. 1983. *Vol. 28.*

– Biblische Theologie und Evangelium. 2002. *Vol. 146.*

Sung, Chong-Hyon: Vergebung der Sünden. 1993. *Vol. II/57.*

Svendsen, Stefan N.: Allegory Transformed. 2009. *Vol. II/269.*

Tajra, Harry W.: The Trial of St. Paul. 1989. *Vol. II/35.*

– The Martyrdom of St.Paul. 1994. *Vol. II/67.*

Tellbe, Mikael: Christ-Believers in Ephesus. 2009. *Vol. 242.*

Theißen, Gerd: Studien zur Soziologie des Urchristentums. 1979, ³1989. *Vol. 19.*

Theobald, Michael: Studien zum Corpus Iohanneum. 2010. *Vol. 267.*

– Studien zum Römerbrief. 2001. *Vol. 136.*

– see *Mußner, Franz.*

Thompson, Trevor W.: see *Rothschild, Clare K.*

Thornton, Claus-Jürgen: Der Zeuge des Zeugen. 1991. *Vol. 56.*

Thüsing, Wilhelm: Studien zur neutestamentlichen Theologie. Ed. von Thomas Söding. 1995. *Vol. 82.*

Thurén, Lauri: Derhethorizing Paul. 2000. *Vol. 124.*

Thyen, Hartwig: Studien zum Corpus Iohanneum. 2007. *Vol. 214.*

Tibbs, Clint: Religious Experience of the Pneuma. 2007. *Vol. II/230.*

Tilling, Chris: Paul's Divine Christology. 2012. *Vol. II/323.*

Toit, David S. du: Theios Anthropos. 1997. *Vol. II/91.*

Tolmie, D. Francois: Persuading the Galatians. 2005. *Vol. II/190.*

Tomson, Peter J. and *Doris Lambers-Petry* (Ed.): The Image of the Judaeo-Christians in Ancient Jewish and Christian Literature. 2003. *Vol. 158.*

Toney, Carl N.: Paul's Inclusive Ethic. 2008. *Vol. II/252.*

– siehe *Frey, Jörg.*

Tóth, Franz: see *Frey, Jörg.*

Trebilco, Paul: The Early Christians in Ephesus from Paul to Ignatius. 2004. *Vol. 166.*

Treloar, Geoffrey R.: Lightfoot the Historian. 1998. *Vol. II/103.*

Troftgruben, Troy M.: A Conclusion Unhindered. 2010. Vol. II/280.

Tso, Marcus K.M.: Ethics in the Qumran Community. 2010. *Vol. II/292.*

Tsuji, Manabu: Glaube zwischen Vollkommenheit und Verweltlichung. 1997. *Vol. II/93.*

Twelftree, Graham H.: Jesus the Exorcist. 1993. *Vol. II/54.*

Ulrichs, Karl Friedrich: Christusglaube. 2007. *Vol. II/227.*

Urban, Christina: Das Menschenbild nach dem Johannesevangelium. 2001. *Vol. II/137.*

Vahrenhorst, Martin: Kultische Sprache in den Paulusbriefen. 2008. *Vol. 230.*

Vegge, Ivar: 2 Corinthians – a Letter about Reconciliation. 2008. *Vol. II/239.*

Verheyden, Joseph, Korinna Zamfir and *Tobias Nicklas* (Ed.): Prophets and Prophecy in Jewish and Early Christian Literature. 2010. *Vol. II/286.*

– see *Nicklas, Tobias*

Visotzky, Burton L.: Fathers of the World. 1995. *Vol. 80.*

Vollenweider, Samuel: Horizonte neutestamentlicher Christologie. 2002. *Vol. 144.*

Vos, Johan S.: Die Kunst der Argumentation bei Paulus. 2002. *Vol. 149.*

Waaler, Erik: The *Shema* and The First Commandment in First Corinthians. 2008. *Vol. II/253.*

Wagener, Ulrike: Die Ordnung des „Hauses Gottes". 1994. *Vol. II/65.*

Wagner, J. Ross: see *Wilk, Florian.*

Wahlen, Clinton: Jesus and the Impurity of Spirits in the Synoptic Gospels. 2004. *Vol. II/185.*

Walker, Donald D.: Paul's Offer of Leniency (2 Cor 10:1). 2002. *Vol. II/152.*

Walter, Nikolaus: Praeparatio Evangelica. Ed. von Wolfgang Kraus und Florian Wilk. 1997. *Vol. 98.*

Wander, Bernd: Gottesfürchtige und Sympathisanten. 1998. *Vol. 104.*

Wardle, Timothy: The Jerusalem Temple and Early Christian Identity. 2010. *Vol. II/291.*

Wasserman, Emma: The Death of the Soul in Romans 7. 2008. *Vol. 256.*

Waters, Guy: The End of Deuteronomy in the Epistles of Paul. 2006. *Vol. 221.*

Watt, Jan G. van der (Ed.): Eschatology of the New Testament and Some Related Documents. 2011. *Vol. II/315.*

– see *Frey, Jörg*

– see *Zimmermann, Ruben*

Watts, Rikki: Isaiah's New Exodus and Mark. 1997. *Vol. II/88.*

Webb, Robert L.: see *Bock, Darrell L.*

Wedderburn, Alexander J.M.: Baptism and Resurrection. 1987. *Vol. 44.*
– Jesus and the Historians. 2010. *Vol. 269.*
Wegner, Uwe: Der Hauptmann von Kafarnaum. 1985. *Vol. II/14.*
Weiß, Hans-Friedrich: Frühes Christentum und Gnosis. 2008. *Vol. 225.*
Weissenrieder, Annette: Images of Illness in the Gospel of Luke. 2003. Vol. II/164.
–, and *David L. Balch* (Ed.): Contested Spaces. 2012. *Vol. 285.*
–, and *Robert B. Coote* (Ed.): The Interface of Orality and Writing. 2010. *Vol. 260.*
–, *Friederike Wendt* and *Petra von Gemünden* (Ed.): Picturing the New Testament. 2005. *Vol. II/193.*
Welck, Christian: Erzählte ,Zeichen'. 1994. *Vol. II/69.*
Wendt, Friederike (Ed.): see *Weissenrieder, Annette.*
Wiarda, Timothy: Peter in the Gospels. 2000. *Vol. II/127.*
Wifstrand, Albert: Epochs and Styles. 2005. *Vol. 179.*
Wilk, Florian and *J. Ross Wagner* (Ed.): Between Gospel and Election. 2010. *Vol. 257.*
– see *Walter, Nikolaus.*
Williams, Catrin H.: I am He. 2000. *Vol. II/113.*
Wilson, Todd A.: The Curse of the Law and the Crisis in Galatia. 2007. *Vol. II/225.*
Wilson, Walter T.: Love without Pretense. 1991. *Vol. II/46.*
Winn, Adam: The Purpose of Mark's Gospel. 2008. *Vol. II/245.*
Winninge, Mikael: see *Holmberg, Bengt.*
Wischmeyer, Oda: Von Ben Sira zu Paulus. 2004. *Vol. 173.*
Wisdom, Jeffrey: Blessing for the Nations and the Curse of the Law. 2001. *Vol. II/133.*
Witmer, Stephen E.: Divine Instruction in Early Christianity. 2008. *Vol. II/246.*
Wold, Benjamin G.: Women, Men, and Angels. 2005. *Vol. II/2001.*

Wolter, Michael: Theologie und Ethos im frühen Christentum. 2009. *Vol. 236.*
– see *Stuckenbruck, Loren T.*
Worthington, Jonathan: Creation in Paul and Philo. 2011. *Vol. II/317.*
Wright, Archie T.: The Origin of Evil Spirits. 2005. *Vol. II/198.*
Wucherpfennig, Ansgar: Heracleon Philologus. 2002. *Vol. 142.*
Yates, John W.: The Spirit and Creation in Paul. 2008. *Vol. II/251.*
Yeung, Maureen: Faith in Jesus and Paul. 2002. *Vol. II/147.*
Young, Stephen E.: Jesus Tradition in the Apostolic Fathers. 2011. *Vol. II/311.*
Zamfir, Corinna: see *Verheyden, Joseph*
Zangenberg, Jürgen, Harold W. Attridge and *Dale B. Martin* (Ed.): Religion, Ethnicity and Identity in Ancient Galilee. 2007. *Vol. 210.*
Zimmermann, Alfred E.: Die urchristlichen Lehrer. 1984, ²1988. *Vol. II/12.*
Zimmermann, Johannes: Messianische Texte aus Qumran. 1998. *Vol. II/104.*
Zimmermann, Ruben: Christologie der Bilder im Johannesevangelium. 2004. *Vol. 171.*
– Geschlechtermetaphorik und Gottesverhältnis. 2001. *Vol. II/122.*
– (Ed.): Hermeneutik der Gleichnisse Jesu. 2008. *Vol. 231.*
– and *Jan G. van der Watt* (Ed.): Moral Language in the New Testament. Vol. II. 2010. *Vol. II/296.*
– see *Frey, Jörg.*
– see *Horn, Friedrich Wilhelm.*
Zugmann, Michael: „Hellenisten" in der Apostelgeschichte. 2009. *Vol. II/264.*
Zumstein, Jean: see *Dettwiler, Andreas*
Zwiep, Arie W.: Christ, the Spirit and the Community of God. 2010. *Vol. II/293.*
– Judas and the Choice of Matthias. 2004. *Vol. II/187.*

For a complete catalogue please write to the publisher
Mohr Siebeck • P.O. Box 2030 • D–72010 Tübingen/Germany
Up-to-date information on the internet at www.mohr.de